Queering Language, Gender and Sexuality

Queering Language, Gender and Sexuality

Edited by
Tommaso M. Milani

SHEFFIELD UK BRISTOL CT

Published by Equinox Publishing Ltd.

UK: Office 415, The Workstation, 15 Paternoster Row, Sheffield, South Yorkshire S1 2BX

USA: ISD, 70 Enterprise Drive, Bristol, CT 06010

www.equinoxpub.com

First published 2018

British Library Cataloguing-in-Publication Data

A catalogue record for this book is available from the British Library.

ISBN 978 1 78179 493 7 (hardback)
978 1 78179 494 4 (paperback)

Library of Congress Cataloging-in-Publication Data

Names: Milani, Tommaso M., editor.
Title: Queering language, gender and sexuality / edited by Tommaso M. Milani.
Description: Sheffield, UK ; Bristol, CT : Equinox Publishing Ltd, 2018. Includes bibliographical references and index. | Description based on print version record and CIP data provided by publisher.
Identifiers: LCCN 2017022681 (print) | LCCN 2017046149 (ebook) | ISBN 9781781796085 (ePDF) | ISBN 9781781794937 (hardcover) | ISBN 9781781794944 (softcover)
Subjects: LCSH: Gays--Language. | Sexual minorities--Language. | Language and languages--Sex differences. | Gender identity. | Discrimination in language.
Classification: LCC P120.G39 (ebook) | LCC P120.S48 Q435 2017 (print) | DDC 410.86/64--dc23
LC record available at https://lccn.loc.gov/2017022681

Typeset by JS Typesetting Ltd, Porthcawl, Mid Glamorgan.
Printed and bound in Great Britain by Lightning Source UK Ltd., Milton Keynes and in the USA by Lightning Source Inc., La Vergne, TN

Contents

Acknowledgements

Chapters 2–13 are drawn from previously published material, as follows:

- Rusty Barrett, Models of gay male identity and the marketing of 'gay language' in foreign-language phrasebooks for gay men, *Sociolinguistic Studies / Estudios De Sociolingüística* 4(2), © Equinox Publishing Ltd 2003.
- Costas Canakis, The desire for identity and the identity of desire: language, gender and sexuality in the Greek context, *Gender and Language* 9(1), © Equinox Publishing Ltd 2015.
- Tommaso M. Milani and Rickard Jonsson, Incomprehensible language? Language, ethnicity and heterosexual masculinity in a Swedish school, *Gender and Language* 5(2), © Equinox Publishing Ltd 2011.
- Rodrigo Borba and Ana Cristina Ostermann, Do bodies matter? Travestis' embodiment of (trans)gender identity through the manipulation of the Brazilian Portuguese grammatical gender system, *Gender and Language* 1(1), © Equinox Publishing Ltd 2007.
- Veronika Koller, Butch camp: on the discursive construction of a queer identity position, *Gender and Language* 3(2), © Equinox Publishing Ltd 2009.
- Lal Zimman, 'The other kind of coming out': transgender people and the coming out narrative genre, *Gender and Language* 3(1), © Equinox Publishing Ltd 2009.
- Russell Luyt, Constructing hegemonic masculinities in South Africa: the discourse and rhetoric of heteronormativity, *Gender and Language* 6(1), © Equinox Publishing Ltd 2012.
- Matthew Hall, Brendan Gough, Sarah Seymour-Smith and Susan Hansen, On-line constructions of metrosexuality and masculinities: a membership categorization analysis, *Gender and Language* 6(2), © Equinox Publishing Ltd 2012.

- Kristine Kohler Mortensen, A bit too skinny for me: women's homosocial constructions of heterosexual desire in online dating, *Gender and Language* 9(3), © Equinox Publishing Ltd 2015.
- Ksenija Bogetić, *Normal straight gays*: lexical collocations and ideologies of masculinity in personal ads of Serbian gay teenagers, *Gender and Language* 7(3), © Equinox Publishing Ltd 2013.
- Brian W King, Language, sexuality and place: the view from cyberspace, *Gender and Language* 5(1), © Equinox Publishing Ltd 2011.
- William L. Leap, Homophobia as moral geography, *Gender and Language* 4(2), © Equinox Publishing Ltd 2010.

We thank the copyright holders for permission to reproduce this material.

In addition, some of the arguments made in Chapter 1 have appeared in two other publications:

- Tommaso M. Milani (2012) Queering the matrix: language and identity troubles in HIV/AIDS contexts, *Stellenbosch Papers in Linguistics Plus* 41: 59–75.
- Tommaso M. Milani (2017) Language and sexuality, in Ofelia Garcia, Nelson Flores and Max Spotti (eds) *The Oxford Handbook of Language and Society* 403–422, Oxford: Oxford University Press.

1

Queering language, gender and sexuality: theory and practice

Tommaso M. Milani

UNIVERSITY OF GOTHENBURG, SWEDEN; UNIVERSITY OF THE WITWATERSRAND, JOHANNESBURG, SOUTH AFRICA

Introduction

Unlike most edited collections, which consist of previously unpublished work, the aim of this volume is to showcase research on language, gender and sexuality published in the journal *Gender and Language* over the last ten years. I want to state upfront that these scholarly contributions are in no way representative of the field of language, gender and sexuality in its entirety. Rather they have been chosen because they all share – to different degrees – a critical engagement with queer theory, a heuristic lens that has gained considerable momentum in the social sciences and humanities over the last three decades. As such they put to work queer theoretical ideas through detailed linguistic analysis.

The chapters that open the book engage with theoretical debates about identity and desire, and the relationships between these concepts. The following contributions offer linguistic precision to two key areas of queer theoretical interest, namely the critique of heteronormativity and the deconstruction of the gender binary. The final chapters pick up on some of the thematic threads of the book, but locate them within recent developments in the study of language and space. With examples from a variety of sociopolitical contexts – Denmark, Greece, Serbia, Sweden, South Africa and the USA – and discursive sites – phrasebooks, school interactions, literary texts, as well as online dating sites and chats – the chapters collectively illustrate how gender, sexuality and power can be queered through different approaches to linguistic analysis. And it is precisely what the act of *queering* entails that will be discussed in the next section.

Queer as political hermeneutics

Writing about a completely different subject – second language acquisition – Lourdes Ortega beautifully captures the complexities and pitfalls of any attempt to provide a coherent narrative about the development of a field of inquiry. 'Good stories always demand rhetorical sacrifices', Ortega writes, and this often entails that 'a big story rather than a collection of "small stories" ... must be produced' (Ortega 2008:xiii). Moreover, there's always a very personal element to any act of storytelling, and 'good stories tell as much about the narrator as they do about an event or discipline' (Ortega 2008:xiii). The history of the emergence and development of queer theory given in this introductory chapter is no exception (for complementary summaries, see Jagose 1996; Livia and Hall 1997; Cameron and Kulick 2003; Bucholtz and Hall 2004; Baker 2008; Motschenbacher and Stegu 2013; McCormick 2015). The summary presented in the remainder of this section is a simplification of a much more complex set of ideas, and might give the false impression of a temporal linearity that is badly attuned to the overlapping and recursive nature of academic discussions. Like Ortega, being 'painfully aware of these dangers ... I cannot honestly say that this awareness helped me to avoid the pitfalls' (Ortega 2008:xiii).

Historically employed as a slur in English-speaking contexts, the word *queer* underwent a process of resignification in the late 1980s when it began to be used as a positively laden in-group marker, one that sought to overcome the gendered splits created by the categories gay and lesbian, and create instead a broader constituency including anyone who goes against normality, irrespective of gender and sexual (self-)identification. Powerfully encapsulated in the slogan '*not gay as in happy but queer as in fuck you*', queer also marked a break with a specific type of politics geared to achieving the recognition of sexual minorities on the grounds of their identities, inaugurating instead a more radical activism that is less concerned with acceptance, inclusion and fitting in than with overt challenges to what is considered 'normal'.

In the academic world, the originally infamous slur queer was wed to the significantly more respectable word *theory* (Kulick 2005) as a type of hermeneutics that ultimately resists any definition, and hence negates its very essence as theory. Such reticence against precise categorisation emerges repeatedly in the foundational texts of what would later become the field of queer studies. There, queer is presented as 'whatever is at odds with the normal, the legitimate, the dominant. There is nothing in particular to which it necessarily refers. It is an identity without essence' (Halperin 1995:61–2). But, if this is the case, how can queer be productively operationalised as an analytical lens?

Jagose offers a more useful definition of queer theory as a critical enterprise that questions 'normative consolidations of sex, gender and sexuality – and that, consequently, is critical of all those versions of identity, community and politics that are believed to evolve 'naturally' from such consolidations' (Jagose 1996:99). This quote captures two key elements, which, in my view, lie at the heart of what counts as queer inquiry, and inform the contributions to this volume.

First, despite acknowledging that sex, gender and sexuality are separate categories, queer theory posits that these are constructs that have been socially entwined in such a way that they have developed a 'unique relationship' (Sauntson 2008:274) with each other. Hence, what a queer stance tries to highlight is how biological sex –the dichotomy between males and females on the basis of their reproductive organs – is mapped onto gender – the opposition between men and women in terms of masculinity and femininity – and how these pairs are in turn the foundations on which heterosexuality rests (see Butler [1990]1999:194). Put simply, queer theory scrutinises the ways in which feminine female bodies and masculine male bodies are consistently reproduced as ideal opposites attracting each other.

Not only that! Butler ([1990]1999) forcefully reminds us that the sex binary – male/female – is not a scientific axiom, but is itself a cultural construction. When a healthcare practitioner says in the context of a pregnancy scan or delivery: 'It's a girl!' or 'It's a boy!' these exclamations are not innocuous descriptions of the corporeality in front of their eyes. Put differently, they are not Austinian constatives, but performatives in that that they hail a small body into the linguistic pigeonhole of the pronouns he or she in Anglophone contexts. And, in doing so, bring into being very distinct set of rules and expectations about how that corporeality should look, think, and behave throughout the course of its life. Interestingly, doctors and midwifes don't happily say 'It's an intersex', but the allegedly 'natural' dimorphic character of sex is upheld culturally through the common practice of surgical intervention in any genital configuration that does not fit the penis/vagina binary (see also King 2015).

Second, the focus on 'normative consolidations' in Jagose's (1996) definition has led to increased focus on the more or less subtle ways in which *heteronormativity* operates, thus showing 'those structures, institutions, relations and actions that promote and produce heterosexuality as natural, self-evident, desirable, privileged and necessary' (Cameron and Kulick 2003:55).

The normalisation of heterosexuality and its concomitant normativity, however, are not the only targets of queer critique. Operating like the contrarian, unruly child of academia, one that 'rejects a minoritising logic of toleration or simple political interest-representation in favour of a more thorough resistance to regimes of the normal' (Warner 1993:xxvi), queer scholarship has also teased out the processes through which some forms of same-sex identities, desires and practices can be included in the domain of the 'normal' (see, in particular, McCormick 2015).

As the contributors to this volume skilfully demonstrate through detailed linguistic analysis, the gender binary and heteronormativity are alive and well. While Luyt's study (Chapter 8) offers a lucid analysis of the role played by the disavowal of male same-sex desire in defining who counts as a real man in South Africa, Mortensen's investigation of online dating activities of two Danish women (Chapter 10) illustrates how heterosexual desire is jointly constructed in a context of homosocial bonding among female friends. Heteronormativity does not remain uncontested, and binary conceptions of gender and sexuality can be manipulated and challenged. In the South African data analysed by Luyt, however, moments of acceptance of same-sex practices are indications of fleeting forms of resistance against dominant discourses of heterosexual masculinity. Reproduction and contestation is also present in Brazilian travestis' linguistic practices. Here, the grammatical gender binary of Brazilian Portuguese is certainly not overcome, but is deployed for specific identity purposes. The co-existence of femininity and maleness enables travestis to use both masculine and feminine grammatical features, and masculine forms are employed as discursive strategies through which to distance oneself from other travestis with whom they do not to identify (Borba and Ostermann, Chapter 5, this volume). In a similar vein, textual analysis of Lorna Gulston's essay on 'butch' illustrates the co-existence of traits of female masculinity and a camp sensibility typically associated with gay men in the construction of a particular lesbian identity position (Koller, Chapter 6, this volume).

That being said, all that glitters is not queer! What may at first sight appear as an anti-normative form of resistance to hegemonic masculinity –metrosexuality – is ultimately an old referent clad in a new stylish outfit (Hall et al., Chapter 9, this volume). Lal Zimman's careful analysis of transgender people's 'coming out' narratives (Chapter 7, this volume) questions the homonormative assumptions underpinning previous analyses of this genre, which made unwarranted universalising arguments about the whole LGBT community on the basis of data collected among a part of it, namely lesbian and gay participants. As Zimman convincingly demonstrates, coming out as a transgender person is in many ways different from coming out as a gay and lesbian person, and this has mainly to do with temporal relationships to the moment in time a transgender person changes gender role. While *declaration* is a type of coming out that 'refers to the initial claiming of a transgender identity', *disclosure* indicates the sharing of 'one's transgender history after transition' (Zimman, Chapter 7, this volume).

I have employed here the term 'homonormativity' to indicate the ways in which gay and lesbian norms and experiences are taken metonymically as representative of, and speaking for, a breadth of gender and sexual diversity issues, and lead *inter alia* to misconstruing and misrepresenting transgender people's experiences (Stryker 2008). More recently, however, homonormativity has 'become a critically chic term elsewhere' (Stryker 2008:149), indicating

> A politics that does not contest dominant heteronormative assumptions and institutions, but upholds and sustains them, while promising the possibility of a demobilized gay constituency and a privatized, depoliticized gay culture anchored in domesticity and consumption. (Duggan 2002:179)

This definition foregrounds less the downplaying and even erasure of transgender, genderqueer and non-binary experiences vis-à-vis cisgender gay and lesbian issues than the problems ensuing from the mainstreaming of non-normative sexualities through the circuit of consumer culture. A word of caution, however, is needed at this juncture to clarify the relationship between the different levels of normativity related to heterosexuality and same-sex desire, respectively. As Motschenbacher and Stegu point out,

> Heteronormative structures are ubiquitous and dominant, in the sense that they are firmly located on the social macro-level. Homonormativity, on the other hand, is invariably a phenomenon that is valid at the local level, namely in contexts where heterosexuality is not the unquestioned norm. (Motschenbacher and Stegu 2013:525)

This distinction is important not to lose sight of the different *scales* of sexual normativities. However, we should be careful not to draw too hasty conclusions about homormativity being necessarily located at the 'micro-level'. While normative heterosexuality and the gender binary have indeed underpinned many macro-projects of nationalism (see Yuval-Davis 1997), Puar (2007) has recently drawn our attention to *homonationalism*, 'an understanding and enactment of homosexual acts, identities, and relationships that incorporates them as not only compatible with but even exemplary of neoliberal democratic ethics and citizenships' (Kulick 2009:28). Simply judging from the degree of rights enshrined in national legislations, one might be tempted to unreservedly applaud the 'lesbian and gay friendliness' of, say, Israel or the Netherlands. Many years of lesbian and gay rights activism, it could be said, have finally succeeded in the recognition of non-normative sexualities on the part of certain nation- states. Such unconditional praise, however, would fail to account for the more pernicious side of homonationalism,

> which secures particular racial and class privileges for only a minority of homosexual subjects, ... and simultaneously produces whole populations of sexual and racial others whose rhetorical function is to provide a backdrop against which countries like the Netherlands or the United States can appear as progressive, democratic, desirable, and humanitarian. Through these kinds of processes, homophobia 'at home' can be downplayed and disavowed because it is projected onto other spaces and other bodies, which emerge as both uncivilized and threatening. (Kulick 2009:28; emphasis added)

To sum up, whether investigating hetero- or homonormativity, a key axiom in queer thinking is that we should be wary of making too easy conflations between sexual desires and practices (a man desiring and/or having sex with another man) on the one hand, and sexual identities (homosexual, gay) on the other (see Hall 2013, however, for a critical position on the separation of practices and identity). Through labels, desires and practices are congealed into identities, which, as Butler (1991:13–14) argues, can then be used for opposite purposes as either 'the normalizing categories of oppressive structures or as the rallying points for a liberatory contestation of that very oppression'. In other words, identities are inevitably caught up in power relations. And even when they are mobilised for emancipatory purposes, such as in the case of sexual minority movements, identity can in the best of cases only produce a temporary recalibration of power inequalities, but does not lead to a more radical transformation of the status quo (Fraser 1995; see also Stroud 2001 for a similar point in the context of linguistic minorities). If identity is so problematic, shall we completely abandon it?

Identity ... desire ... and the importance of 'beside'

Since the beginning of the twenty-first century, some scholars have called for the need for a 'moratorium' on identity in language and sexuality research (Kulick 2000:272). Championing this position, Deborah Cameron and Don Kulick (2003) pointed out that sexuality *is not* and *cannot* be reducible to sexual identity only. Drawing upon an eclectic group of what some scholars might consider rather incompatible thinkers – Freud, Lacan, Deleuze and Guattari – Cameron and Kulick argued that a deeper understanding of sexuality cannot leave out an engagement with the desire. It is important to highlight that an approach that foregrounds desire does *not* entail a complete rejection of identity as analytical construct. In fact, it is hard to dispute that 'people do self-identify and are labelled by others as male, female, gay, lesbian or heterosexual, etc. These identities "exist" within discourse, shaping the minds, bodies and lives of many people' (Baker 2008:194). Yet the point that Cameron and Kulick tried to make is that, whereas identity does matter, it is not enough to capture the complexity of sexuality as perceived, embodied and lived by people in their social contexts.

In line with Lacan (1998), Cameron and Kulick (2003) assert that desire is always *transitive*, that is, it is always for another person or object. Therefore, taking desire as an analytical object compels us 'to problematize both the subject and the object of desire, and investigate how the relationships between the two are materialized through language' (Cameron and Kulick 2003:107). Related to this, a focus on desire helps to capture the Gordian knot of gender, sexuality and other forms of social difference. After all, as Cameron and Kulick (2003:142) remind us, 'desiring subjects and desired objects are never genderless'. Thus, the domain of the erotic is *inherently* structured along gender lines, which, in turn, are likely to be laminated over by other axes of social categorisation such as age, social class and race.

These arguments generated a flurry of reactions critiquing the proposal of bringing desire and the unconscious into the study of language, gender and sexuality. Bucholtz and Hall were perhaps the strongest opponents, raising important theoretical and methodological concerns. The main problem, they argued, lies in the fact that the psychoanalytic theories on which Cameron and Kulick's arguments rest do not offer adequate analytical tools for the empirical study of the ways in which desire is materialised through language, for they would 'require sociolinguists, linguistic anthropologists, and discourse analysts to reinvent themselves as field psychoanalysts, ascribing repressed desires to those they study' (Bucholtz and Hall 2004:480). Moreover, in stating that 'desire is always mediated in some way by identity; that is, longing is always articulated through and against standpoints of belonging' (Bucholtz and Hall 2004:507), they also levelled a more fundamental objection to the notion of desire itself, as a by-product of identity.

Fifteen years later, one might wonder whether it is at all relevant to summarise the identity/desire debate – even in a cursory form. While some of the arguments advanced in this academic discussion might sound slightly trite now, it is important to remember the force of the debate and the level of passionate engagement that many prominent academics took in relation to identity versus desire in those years. As a PhD student at the beginning of my doctoral studies, it was not uncommon to be asked which position I was going to align myself to, and the expectation was always to take *one* side in the debate.

The chapters in this volume that deal with identity/desire emerge precisely out of an engagement with this debate. However, there seems to be consensus among the contributors that viewing identity and desire as excluding alternatives is misguided and analytically problematic. Rusty Barrett's incisive analysis of foreign-language phrasebooks for gay men sold in the USA (Chapter 2, this volume) is an early, empirically driven intervention that clearly illustrates how models of identity and desire should not be viewed as mutually exclusive, but as complementary alternatives through which to make sense of the ways in which same-sex experience is represented in phrasebooks. As Barrett puts it, 'although the phrasebooks are centred around gay male desire, the nature of that desire differs according to the ways in which an author imagines gay identity' (Barrett, Chapter 2, this volume). A more recent investigation of Greek written and spoken data similarly demonstrates 'the inextricable interplay of sexual desire with aspects of subjectivity in discourse produced in a variety of contexts' (Canakis, Chapter 3, this volume). At a time when affect is becoming increasingly more relevant in critical scholarship of language and discourse, it is unclear whether desire – as well as other emotions – will come back more prominently in language, gender and sexuality research. Perhaps, as Milani and Jonsson point out in a study of linguistic interactions in a Swedish school, desire and other emotions are important to capture the 'irreducible entanglement of thinking and feeling, knowing *that* and knowing *how*, propositional and nonpropositional knowledge' (Zerilli 2015:266; emphasis added). So the issue is not so much to go *beyond* identity as they say but to look at what lies *beside* it. As Eve Kosofky Sedwick suggests, beside 'seems to offer some useful resistance to the ease with which *beneath* and *beyond* turn from spatial descriptors into implicit narratives of, respectively, origin and telos' (Sedgwick 2003:8). Beside is then perhaps the best spatial descriptor of the current academic position on identity and desire. And its spatial connotations also allow me to transition to the notion of space/place in scholarship on gender and sexuality informed by queer theory.

How does space come into the picture?

Space/place is an important 'epistemological site' (Sunderland 2004) to conduct such an anti-normative enterprise not least because '[s]pace can be filled with all kinds of social, cultural, epistemic, and affective attributes. It then becomes "place", a particular space on which senses of belonging, property rights, and authority can be projected' (Blommaert 2005:222). It is a truism among social and cultural geographers that 'public space ... reflects social processes of articulation of power' (Lefebvre 1970). To this one could add the feminist insight that the private is no less political. Needless to say, the very dichotomy between public and private is itself problematic because, as Gal has pointed out, '"public" and "private" are not particular places, domains, spheres of activity, or even types of interaction. ... Public and private are co-constitutive cultural categories ... and equally importantly, indexical signs that are always relative' (Gal 2002:80). Public and private are furthermore signifiers that have historically carried gendered and sexual connotations that are not innocuous. In many Western and non-Western contexts, the domain of the home has been associated with women whereas public life has been viewed as an exclusively male precinct (for recent examples see Caldas-Coulthard 1995; Johnson and Ensslin 2007). Moreover, Foucault (1990) has argued that, since Victorian times, sexuality has been relegated to the domain of the home, which is what ultimately made sex in public not only illegal but also a form of moral 'deviance', which would breach 'public decency', whatever this may mean. Hence, a focus on sexuality when analysing space not only allows a questioning of the very constructedness of the private/public divide, but also offers us a deeper understanding of the ways in which modern power works, among other things, by hiding its own operations from the domain of the visible.

Once again, empirical case studies in this volume demonstrate the complexity of the intersections of gender and sexuality in relation to the public/private divide. Ksenija Bogetić's quantitative analysis of personal profiles in a Serbian online community of men looking for other men convincingly illustrates how expressions of non-normative sexualities may be very normative in the ways in which they valorise – fetishise even – certain gendered traits in public fora. This leads to forms of *recursive marginalisation,* through which gay men who are viewed as not sufficiently masculine 'are stigmatized both in the heterosexist society and in the intragroup context' (Bogetić, Chapter 11, this volume). While one might wonder to what extent fora such as the one analysed by Bogetić might be 'queer' because of the gendered normativities that they reproduce and circulate, Brian W. King illustrates how other online spaces may offer important sites for queer resistance, making publicly visible what heteronormative assumptions would rather have hidden. Here participants 'become sexual while slipping to "queer space"' (King, Chapter 12, this volume). Queer visibility in public spaces, however, comes at a price. As the chapter that closes this volume powerfully demonstrates, homophobia is still very much a reality in late modernity, despite legislation to protect the rights of gender and sexual non-normative citizenry. And through narratives of self-identified gay men about sexual violence it is possibly to unveil relationships between subjectivity and sense of place, showing how 'they position themselves, as sexual subjects and urban residents, in relation to the changing dynamics of race, class and privilege ... in the DC area' (Leap, Chapter 13, this volume).

Queer(ing) and its limits

Queer theory has come under fire from a variety of positions since its inception. To begin with, while queer was indeed born out of an anti-establishment spirit, in thirty years of life it has become institutionalised – through conferences, journals, and even academic jobs specifically dedicated to it. One might begin to wonder whether such institutional entrenchment is not at odds with the very spirit of queer as a form of insubordination against normative and normalising forces.

Moreover, critical voices from the global South question the Western/Northern bias of queer scholarship, and the concomitant erasure of radical work on sexuality in other parts of the world; they also interrogate the very relevance of the English word 'queer' in contexts like Brazil and South Africa, where this term not only has little traction, but also carries connotations of 'foreignness', 'whiteness' and 'middle-classness'. For example, in a study about identity labels among non-heterosexual women in Soweto, it was found that queer was the least used term for self-identification in a list topped by lesbian and *isitabane* (Pakade 2013:121). The latter is an isiZulu word employed to refer to both gender non-conformance and same-sex desire. Obviously, there is a qualitative difference between (1) queer as *noun*, a category invoked (or not) by individuals in their daily lives, and (2) queering as a *verb*, a process of hermeneutic deconstruction. Gunkel strongly argues that 'we cannot afford *not* to apply queer theory as a tool of analysis despite recent efforts to exclude it from sexualities research in the African context' (Gunkel 2010:15; original emphasis). This is because queer theory offers inter alia a useful conceptual apparatus through which to understand the historical production of normality versus deviance in the colonial project, as well as opening up the 'possibility of understanding gender differently, as already racialized, sexualized and localized' (Gunkel 2010:15, see also Barnard 1999 for an earlier similar position on what he calls 'queer race'). But, if we want to be sensitive to unequal power relationships in the production of knowledge across the globe, we might wish to avoid the unreflective application of Northern labels in Southern contexts.

As a provocative alternative, the Brazilian scholar Larissa Pelúcio draws upon the work of the Spanish thinker Paul B. Preciado in order to suggest a *teoria cu* – a theory of the *asshole* – which 'is more than an attempt to translate "queer" ... to highlight our anthropophagy by placing a certain structural emphasis on assholes and mouths; assholes and marginal production' (Pelúcio 2014:47). While this is a standpoint from which Pelúcio seeks to (re)launch Brazilian scholarship as a worthy margin in the global geopolitics of knowledge on sexuality, a return to the anus might also be germane to injecting some much needed anti-normative force into the queer academic project.

Whether through queer or asshole, the fetishisation of anti-normativity has also been recently criticised insofar as it is said to violate queer theory's anti-essentialist principles and its distrust of any form of identity consolidation. As Robyn Wiegman puts it,

> Through its own self-animating antinormative intentions, then, Queer Studies gets to have its cake and eat it too: it can function as an organizing referent for queer theory while simultaneously forging an interdisciplinary critique of it; it can promise to fulfill queer theory's anti-identitarian commitments while proliferating identity commitments of its own; it can refuse institutionality while participating in and generating its own institutionalized forms. (Wiegman 2012:332)

In other words, queer theory operates by reifying an anti-identitarian, anti-foundationalist and anti-normative enterprise, and this goes against the very basic tenet of anti-essentialism. And this anti-normative positioning of queer theory has itself become a norm, against which both scholarly and political projects are evaluated and judged.

These critical points notwithstanding, if queer has something that distinguishes itself from other approaches to the study of gender and sexuality, then its distinctiveness lies in its ability to

> create anxiety and discomfort, and a feeling that theorists and researchers are going where they shouldn't go, lighting lights that ought to stay dark, examining what many would prefer be ignored, and waking up bears that should have been left sleeping. (Kulick 2012:31; my translation)

Of course, we might wish to ask ourselves whether the verb form *queering* might have become worn out and lost much of its edginess. A quick Google search might confirm that 'queering' has indeed been overused by academics and activists, and I have contributed to the inflation of this verb, but I am reticent to let it go and not deploy it. In a time of Trump, Nazi revival, and overt racist, sexist, homophobic and transphobic utterances in public discussions, there is in my view still a lot of queering to be pursued. Many, including some colleagues, will roll their eyes thinking 'those queers again'. So be it! The eye rolling should reassure us that we have hit the mark!

References

Baker, Paul (2008) *Sexed Texts: Language, Gender and Sexuality*. London: Equinox.

Barnard, Ian (1999) Queer race. *Social Semiotics* 9: 199–212. https://doi.org/10.1080/10350339909360432

Blommaert, Jan (2005) *Discourse*. Cambridge: Cambridge University Press. https://doi.org/10.1017/CBO9780511610295

Bucholtz, Mary and Hall, Kira (2004) Theorizing identity in language and sexuality research. *Language in Society* 33: 469–515. https://doi.org/10.1017/S0047404504334020

Butler, Judith ([1990]1999) *Gender Trouble: Feminism and the Subversion of Identity*. New York: Routledge.

Butler, Judith (1991) Imitation and gender insubordination. In Diana Fuss (ed.) *Inside/Out: Lesbian Theories, Gay Theories* 13–31. New York: Routledge.

Caldas-Coulthard, Carmen (1995) Man in the news: the misrepresentation of women speaking as news-in-narrative-discourse. In Sara Mills (ed.) *Language and Gender: Interdisciplinary Perspectives* 226–39. London: Longman.

Cameron, Deborah and Kulick, Don (2003) *Language and Sexuality*. Cambridge: Cambridge University Press.

Duggan, Lisa (2002) The new homonormativity: the sexual politics of neoliberalism. In Russ Castronovo and Dana Nelson (eds) *Materializing Democracy: Toward a Revitalized Cultural Politics* 175–94. Durham, NC: Duke University Press. https://doi.org/10.1215/9780822383901-007

Foucault, M. (1990) *The Will to Knowledge: The History of Sexuality*, vol. 1. London: Penguin.

Fraser, N. (1995) From redistribution to recognition? Dilemmas of justice in a 'post-socialist' age. *New Left Review* I/212: 68–93.

Gal, Susan (2002) A semiotics of the public/private distinction. *Differences* 13: 77–95. https://doi.org/10.1215/10407391-13-1-77

Gunkel, Henriette (2010) *The Cultural Politics of Female Sexuality in South Africa*. London: Routledge.

Hall, Kira (2013) 'It's a hijra': queer linguistics revisited. *Discourse and Society* 24: 634–42. https://doi.org/10.1177/0957926513490321

Halperin, David (1995) *Saint Foucault: Towards a Gay Hagiography*. New York: Oxford University Press.

Jagose, Annamarie (1996) *Queer Theory: An Introduction*. New York: NYU Press.

Johnson, Sally and Ensslin, Astrid (2007) 'But her language skills shifted the family dynamics dramatically': language, gender and the construction of publics in two British newspapers. *Gender and Language* 1: 229–54. https://doi.org/10.1558/genl.v1i2.229

King, Brian W. (2015) Reclaiming masculinity in an account of lived intersex experience: language, desire, and embodied knowledge. In Tommaso M. Milani (ed.) *Language and Masculinities: Performances, Intersections, Dislocations* 220–42. London. Routledge.

Kulick, Don (2000) Gay and lesbian language. *Annual Review of Anthropology* 29: 243–85.

Kulick, Don (2005) Four hundred thousand Swedish perverts. *GLQ: A Journal of Gay and Lesbian Studies* 11: 205–35. https://doi.org/10.1215/10642684-11-2-205

Kulick, Don (2009) Can there be an anthropology of homophobia? In David A. B. Murray (ed.) *Homophobias: Lust and Loathing across Time and Space* 19–33. Durham, NC: Duke University Press.

Kulick, Don (2012) En unken och beklaglig människosyn: män, sex och fuktionshinder. In Lucas Gottzén and Rickard Jonsson (eds) *Andra män – maskulinitet, normskapande och jämställdhet* 25–44. Lund: Gleerups.

Lacan, Jean-Jacques (1998) *The Four Foundational Concepts of Psychoanalysis*. New York: W. W. Norton.

Lefebvre, Henri (1970) *The Urban Revolution*. Minneapolis, MN: University of Minnesota Press.

Livia, Anna and Hall, Kira (1997) 'It's a girl!' Bringing performativity back to linguistics. In Anna Livia and Kira Hall (eds) *Queerly Phrased: Language, Gender and Sexuality* 3–18. Oxford: Oxford University Press.

McCormick, Tracey Lee (2015) A critical engagement? Analysing same-sex marriage discourses in *To Have and to Hold: The Making of Same-Sex Marriage in South Africa* (2008) – a queer perspective. *Stellenbosch Papers in Linguistics Plus* 46: 105–26. https://doi.org/10.5842/46-0-656

Motschenbacher, Heiko and Stegu, Martin (2013) Queer linguistic approaches to discourse. *Discourse and Society* 24: 519–35. https://doi.org/10.1177/0957926513486069

Ortega, Lourdes (2008) *Understanding Second Language Acquisition*. Abingdon: Routledge.

Pakade, Nomancotsho (2013) What's in a name? Exploring the sexual identity of black women-loving-women in Soweto. *Agenda* 27: 117–27.

Pelúcio, Larissa (2014) Possible appropriations and necessary provocations for a *Teoria Cu*. In Sarah E. Lewis, Rodrigo Borba, Branca Falabella Fabricio and Diana de Souza Pinto (eds) *Queering Paradigms IV: South-North Dialogues on Queer Epistemologies, Embodiments and Activisms* 53–66. Frankfurt: Peter Lang.

Puar, Jasbir (2007) *Terrorist Assemblages: Homonationalism in Queer Times*. Durham, NC: Duke University Press. https://doi.org/10.1215/9780822390442

Sauntson, Helen (2008) The contributions of queer theory to gender and language research. In Kate Harrington, Lia Litosseliti, Helen Sauntson and Jane Sunderland (eds) *Gender and Language Research Methodologies* 271–82. Basingstoke: Palgrave Macmillan.

Sedgwick, Eve K. (2003) *Touching Feeling: Affect, Pedagogy, Performativity*. Durham, NC: Duke University Press.

Stroud, Christopher (2001) African mother-tongue programmes and the politics of language: Linguistic citizenship versus Linguistic Human Rights. *Journal of Multilingual and Multicultural Development* 22: 339–55. https://doi.org/10.1080/01434630108666440

Stryker, Susan (2008) Transgender history, homonormativity, and disciplinarity. *Radical History Review* 100: 145–57. https://doi.org/10.1215/01636545-2007-026

Sunderland, Jane (2004) *Gendered Discourses*. Basingstoke: Palgrave Macmillan. https://doi.org/10.1057/9780230505582

Warner, Michael (1993) Introduction. In Michael Warner (ed.) *Fear of a Queer Planet* vii–xliv. Minneapolis, MN: University of Minnesota Press.

Wiegman, Robyn (2012) *Object Lessons*. Durham, NC: Duke University Press.

Yuval-Davis, Nira (1997) *Gender and Nation*. Thousand Oaks, CA: Sage. https://doi.org/10.1215/9780822394945

Zerilli, Linda M. G. (2015) The turn to affect and the problem of judgment. *New Literary History* 46: 261–86.

Part I
Identity and desire

2

Models of gay male identity and the marketing of 'gay language' in foreign-language phrasebooks for gay men

Rusty Barrett
UNIVERSITY OF KENTUCKY, USA

Introduction

GABRIEL: It's not that I hate them [gay men], it's just that I feel I don't fit in with them, you know, culturally.
MARK: You suck dick, don't you? (Schafer 1999)

The above interaction from the film *Trick* reflects two very different ways of understanding what it means to be a gay man. Gabriel's sense of 'gay culture' reflects a model of the gay community based on shared cultural identity, while Mark sees gay identity solely in terms of sexual practice. Although the two men both categorise themselves as 'gay' and see themselves as part of a 'gay community', the ways in which they imagine that community are contradictory. For Gabriel, gay culture is central to his personal identity, while for Mark gay culture doesn't even exist. These two views have been a persistent part of the development of modern understandings of homosexuality in Western countries, particularly in the United States. The first view (what I will call the *culture-based model*) holds that gay identity is about much more than sexual behaviour or desire. In the culture-based model, there is a distinct gay culture founded on shared experiences and personal tastes, common social sensibilities and social practices. In this view, the main point of difference between gays and heterosexuals is one of cultural affiliation. Differences in sexual desire are often minimised, while alternative gender performance is recognised as a unique and important form of gay cultural expression. The culture-based view usually analyses sexuality in terms of gender. Within this view, it is accepted that alternative gender display may be a central part of gay identity for some individuals.

The opposing view (what I will call the *desire-based model*) sees the only difference between gay men and heterosexual men as a difference in sexual desire and sexual practice. In this view, there is no gay culture. The gay community and its shared social practices are meaningless epiphenomena resulting from interactions founded on sexual desire. Within the desire-based model, transgender persons may be objects of sexual desire, but they are not a more general part of 'gay sensibility' Advocates of the desire-based model tend to minimise differences between gay men and heterosexual men. In contrast, those supporting the culture-based model tend to emphasise these differences, while minimising the role of sexual desire and sexual practice in the construction of gay communities. In this chapter, I will consider the impact of these seemingly contradictory views on understanding the relationship between language and sexuality. These competing models of culture and desire are similar to the competing models of difference and dominance in language and gender studies (Uchida 1992). The 'difference' model held that men and women are socialised in different cultures and that miscommunication in cross-gender communication resulted from cultural differences. In contrast, the 'dominance' approach assumed that miscommunication in cross-gender communication was primarily the result of male attempts to assert power over their female interlocutors. As with difference and dominance, these models of gay male identity may lead to opposing analyses of identical data. The assumptions inherent in these models not only limit the possible conclusions reached in sociolinguistic research, but also limit the range of questions that research can even ask. After examining the role of these models in the recent history of gay political movements, I will discuss their implications for understanding the relationship between language and sexuality both in academic research and the ways in which these models are used to market foreign-language phrasebooks specifically designed for gay men. I conclude by arguing that meaningful understanding of the relationship between sexuality and language requires moving beyond the binary opposition offered by these two competing models.

Competing models of gay community

Within queer theory, individual personal identity (and the desires associated with that identity) arises from performative repetitions of pre-existing historicised citations. It is assumed that a statement like 'I am gay' is a performative speech act because repetition of this statement creates gay identity and marks an individual as a member of an imagined gay community. The history of any given culture contains a finite set of possible citations carrying indexical force, so that the range of possible expressions of gender or sexual identity is limited by the restricted set of previous citations. Thus, the set of citations that performatively construct gay identity simultaneously limit the range of possible manifestations of that identity.

Because gender identity and sexual desire are both manifest through individual psychology, their social construction may be masked by the immediacy of personal experience. In terms of language (and other social practices), the markers of gay identity may be extended to gay individuals in other cultures through fractal recursion (Gal and Irvine 2000). The differences in social manifestations of homosexuality that occur across cultures may also undergo erasure (Gal and Irvine 2000) to form a monolithic uniform and universal view of sexual identity.

Self-categorisation as *gay* comes relatively late in life compared with most other aspects of social identity (such as gender or ethnicity) which are typically assigned at birth. Although debates concerning a biological basis for sexual orientation are yet to be settled, the decision to publicly acknowledge one's homosexuality (i.e. to 'come out') is a personal choice. The decision to openly take on the label of 'gay' is always a negotiation carried out through social interaction. This is one of the reasons why the very existence of a 'gay community' is highly contested (Barrett 1997). Given the lack of unambiguous social guidelines for delineating a 'gay community', individuals may imagine gay identity in different ways. The ways in which an individual imagines a gay community, however, are dependent on social context and shared personal experiences. Views of what homosexuality means and how it should be interpreted vary across history as particular ideas and social practices move in and out of fashion (Halperin 2000). The early history of gay movements in the United States reflected a dialectal relationship between the culture-based model and the desire-based model. The view that gay men and lesbians form a distinct minority community has remained constant since the early days of the gay rights movement. Shifts in political understandings of that community have been historically and have often (but certainly not always) been associated with shifts back and forth between viewing that community in terms of culture or in terms of desire.

The idea of a shared gay identity became solidified in the United States in the years following World War II and became politically manifest with the homophile movement of the 1950s and 1960s (Marcus 1992; Duberman 1993). The homophile movement fought against the prevailing idea that homosexuality revolved solely around 'effeminate men'. Instead, the homophile movement argued that homosexuality was based solely on a difference in sexual desire, independent of gender (Marcus 1992; Chauncey 1994). While the homophile movement saw gay men as forming a distinct minority, they did not promote the idea of 'an autonomous homosexual culture' and intended 'social assimilation' of gays and lesbians (Seidman 1993:111). Some leaders of the homophile movement went so far as to impose a dress code for protest demonstrations, with gay men having to wear suits and ties and lesbians having to wear dresses (Duberman 1993). This assimilationist stance was deemed necessary given the ideological position that sexuality was purely a matter of the object of sexual desire and that nothing else distinguished gay men from heterosexual men.

The gay liberation movement that emerged following the Stonewall riots of 1969 (Duberman 1993) marked a major turn in the focus for the gay rights movement. The Stonewall riots occurred when patrons (particularly drag queens) fought back during a police raid at a gay bar ('The Stonewall') in Greenwich Village. After the riots, the gay liberation movement began to take shape, aligning itself with other social movements of the late 1960s and early 1970s, including feminism and the civil rights movement. The Gay Liberation Front (GLF), the predominant political group following Stonewall, 'saw gay oppression as simply one face of a comprehensive oppression that affected working people, racial minorities, and women' (Valocchi 1999:214). The gay liberation movement assumed that all individuals were inherently androgynous and saw their main political goal as 'freeing individuals from the constraints of a sex/gender system that locked them into mutually exclusive homo/hetero and feminine/masculine roles' (Seidman

1993:110). The goals of the GLF went well beyond civil rights for gay men and lesbians and membership was open to anyone, regardless of their sexual identity. The GLF envisioned a gender-free society in which ideas such as 'homosexual' and 'heterosexual' would become irrelevant and saw the role of gay culture as providing a foundation for this androgynous gay-centred utopian society.

The social theory behind the culture-based model as articulated by the GLF assumes that gay men and lesbians form particular identity groups that deserve legal protection from discrimination. Following trends in feminism at the time, the culture-based model was also fairly essentialist in its assumptions about identity and community, entrenching the 'minority' model set forward by the homophile movement (albeit with very different assumptions concerning the nature of that community). Although there was conflict between various social groups, the GLF viewed lesbians, gays, and transgender people as a crucial part of their movement. Homosexuality was theorised 'overwhelmingly in terms of gender' (Jagose 1996:39) during this period. As such, it is not surprising that the culture-based model typically considers alternative gender display as central to the understanding of gay male communities and gay communication.

The 'beginning of the end' for the gay liberation movement was the establishment of the National Gay Task Force (NGTF) in 1973. Rather than view gay rights as part of a larger social oppression, the NGTF focused on the view of gay men and lesbians as a minority group and limited their political goals solely to the struggle for civil rights for gay men and lesbians (Marcus 1992; Valocchi 1999). The NGTF was run by white middle-class men who rejected alternative gender performance as important to gay culture (Duberman 1993:62). As the NGTF gained momentum, the homophile view that gay men have nothing more in common than shared desires for particular sexual practices came back into vogue (Signorile 1997) and gay identity became more grounded in sexual desire. This reemergence of the desire-based model downplayed the relationship between gender and sexuality, often rejecting alternative gender identity altogether (Jagose 1996) and placing a new emphasis on masculinity (Signorile 1997). This period also saw the emergence of gay subcultures based on stereotypes of masculinity, such as the 'gay clones' who generally wore moustaches and dressed in denim jeans and flannel lumberjack shirts, or the leathermen who typically wore leather 'biker' gear and tended to practice S/M (sadomasochism).

The desire-based model assumes that outside of sexual practice, gay men are no different from straight men. Following from this assumption, ideas about 'gay culture' are rejected altogether. Although the homophile movement had shifted the focus from gender to desire, they had not been outspoken about sexual matters. Later incarnations of the desire-based model have placed an increased importance on sexual desire and sexual practice within gay culture. As sexual practice became the focal point of gay identity, other identities based on particular sexual practices began to demand recognition as minority groups within the gay community, leading to debates about the potential rights of other groups such as bisexuals, sadomasochists and even paedophiles (Jagose 1996:68–71).

In his study of social stigma, Goffman (1963) notes that a common reaction to stigmatisation is to embrace and flaunt the source of stigmatisation. If one assumes that gay men are stigmatised solely on the basis of their sexual behaviour, the flaunting of that stigma would entail making sexual desire and practice central to one's individual identity. The emphasis on physical attractiveness, youthfulness, physique and (above all) masculinity in the gay community can be viewed as partially resulting from placing sexual desire at the centre of gay identity. Signorile (1997), for example, sees the desire-based model as more of a religious cult of masculinity that leads gay men down a path of self-destruction. Signorile holds this 'cult of masculinity' responsible for the emergence of particular identity categories associated with unsafe sexual practices, such as 'circuit boys' or 'barebackers'. 'Circuit boy' is a stereotyped category of gay men who travel from city to city following a 'circuit' of parties vaguely centred around new-age spirituality and fund-raising for gay political and health organisations. These parties have been highly criticised for the prevalence of drug use and unsafe sex associated with them (Signorile 1997). Taking sexual desire as a most basic identity are 'barebackers', men whose identity rests primarily upon their refusal to use condoms.

Signorile sees the cumulative effect of the desire-based model as detrimental to the political interests of the gay community because the resulting 'cult of masculinity' reproduces negative stereotypes about gay sexual practice, presents physical danger to individuals (through drug use and unsafe sex) and causes gay men undue psychological stress related to an over-emphasis on body image.

The period from the emergence of the NGTF (1973) to the onset of AIDS (1981) saw a growth in the divisiveness between various groups involved in the gay rights movement. As the concept of a 'gay community' became more widely accepted, gay identities began to diversify, so that describing movements purely in terms of the culture-based vs. the desired-based model would be a gross simplification. One attraction of the desire-based model of gay identity is that it reduces the differences between gay and straight men, downplaying difference in order to claim the right to the power held by heterosexual men. Although some women supported the celebration of sexual diversity offered by the desire-based model (e.g. Rubin 1982), many lesbians felt that the goals of the desire-based approach primarily served the interest of gay men at the expense of lesbians, who would still be oppressed as women regardless of straight ideas about homosexuality (e.g. Frye 1983). The desire-based model of gay male identity thus contributed to the rift between gay rights activists and lesbian feminists. In addition, many ethnic minorities began to criticise the racism of the gay rights movement and ethnic divisions began to arise in gay politics (Seidman 1993). The move from essentialism to social constructionism in feminism also contributed to the predominance of the desire-based model, as aspects of gay identity other than sexual desire were recognised to be socially constructed behaviours independent of one's sexual orientation.

The AIDS crisis and the homophobic political climate of the 1980s made it clear that discrimination was based on more than sexual desire alone. In the early

1990s the culture-based model returned in the 'queer' movement. The activist group Queer Nation along with academics working in queer theory, advocated a new image of identity and community, based on an idealised community of 'queers' who were not defined by their common sexual desires or social practices, but rather by their oppositional stance towards mainstream heterosexual hegemonic culture. While queer theory rejected identity categories and identity politics, it did envision a view of community based on the reclaiming of the term 'queer' as an identity label. The imagined 'queer' community harked back to the GLF's utopian view of community and was seen as including anyone with non-normative sexuality or gender. As the focus turned towards performativity and identity, transgender persons and alternative gender norms returned to the centre of discussions about sexuality (Butler 1990, 1993). The tension between the desire-based model of the early 1980s and the new queer version of the culture model emerged in debates over what to call the 1993 March on Washington for Lesbian, Gay, and Bisexual Rights and Liberation. In the final decision, bisexuals were included, but officials decided to exclude transsexuals or transgender persons. It was during this period that work in queer theory began to see both desire and gender identity as components in a larger system of performative citations, attempting to overcome the division between the two views of gay identity. Although the culture-based model and the desire-based model are both grounded in particular historical contexts, both continue to serve as contemporary models for imagining gay communities. Although queer theory assumes that there is no *a priori* reason to assume that sexuality is closer to gender than to any other aspect of identity such as ethnicity or age (Sedgwick 1990), alternative gender norms have returned to a central place in theories of homosexuality (Butler 1990, 1993). Rather than assume that gender expression is somehow naturally associated with sexuality, Butler suggests that sexuality comes to be expressed through gender identity because the social prohibitions on homosexuality are so deeply rooted that there are no mechanisms for the direct expression of sexuality:

> Indeed, it may well be that what constitutes the sexually unperformable is performed instead as gender identification. To the extent that homosexual attachments remain unacknowledged within normative heterosexuality, they are not merely constituted as desires that emerge and subsequently become prohibited. Rather, these are desires that are proscribed from the start. (Butler 1993:293)

Thus, sexuality may come to be indirectly expressed through gender simply because the normative constraints against homosexuality are so strong that they make direct expression of sexuality virtually impossible.

The historical shifts between the culture-based model and the desire-based model cannot be separated from the social and economic forces that lead to a particular consensus (Seidman 1993; Valocchi 1999). The culture-based model has arisen during times of more liberal and egalitarian politics (such as the late 1960s and the beginning of the Clinton administration). The desire-based model tends to play a larger role during more conservative political eras (such as the homophile movement in the 1950s or the solidification of the desire-based model during the 1980s). The assimilationism often found with the desire-based model could be a reaction to homophobic social and political trends. Just as the ways in which the gay community is imagined seem to be tied to particular historical, political and economic moments, the shaping of individual identity cannot be separated from historical or social context. One's personal identity is inherently tied to the particular habitus (Bourdieu 1991) surrounding one's recognition, acknowledgement and eventual acceptance of 'gay' identity. As such, a given individual might come to maintain an understanding of homosexuality as primarily culture or desire throughout his life, even if political trends continue to shift between the models. Clearly an attempt to define all gay political movements purely along lines of these two models would oversimplify the complexity of gay political history. In the following section, I will examine the influence of these two models of gay community in the formation of researcher's attitudes towards language and sexuality, arguing that an over-reliance on divisions defined by culture or desire have greatly oversimplified the complexity of gay male linguistic behaviour.

Competing models of language and sexuality

In a review article titled 'Gay and lesbian language', Kulick (2000:247) concludes that 'there is no such thing as gay or lesbian language'. Kulick's paradox – that it is possible to write a 25-page review article on a subject that does not exist – emerges from his adherence to the desire-based model of gay community while reviewing a literature that often assumes the culture-based model. The culture-based model is perhaps best exemplified in the work of Leap (1995, 1996, 1997). Leap discusses gay male language in terms of Sapir's (1949) concept of 'authenticity', making the existence of gay culture an *a priori* assumption in his research. Leap sees 'gay men's English' primarily at the level of pragmatics, emerging in particular social interactions. For Leap, one becomes socialised in the use of gay language when one becomes part of the gay community. As with much work in the culture-based model, Leap's view of the gay community is somewhat limited. Models assuming a shared gay cultural identity will, however, always be problematic in that they can never fully capture the fluidity and diversity of actual gay men (Barrett 1997). Leap thus ends up reproducing the exclusive view of gay identity that motivated arguments for the use of 'queer' (Butler 1993). As is often found in the culture-based model, Leap feels that sexual matters are typically over-emphasised. Although he does not think sexual topics must be avoided altogether, Leap does feel that emphasising sexual matters has a negative effect on gay political interests. Leap argues that by 'minimizing the non-sexual dimensions of gay men's language, linguistic analysis validates some of the stereotypes of gay experience', such as the idea that gay men are always looking for sex and attempting to seduce heterosexual men (Leap 1995:xiv). Leap feels that acceptance of these stereotypes is detrimental to progress in the gay rights movement because it 'plays directly into efforts to curtail opportunities that would otherwise be accessible to gay men' (Leap 1995:xiv).

While Leap reflects a culture-based model, Kulick whole-heartedly embraces the desire-based model. Kulick criticises approaches like that of Leap and calls for a 'moratorium' (Kulick 2000:272) on studies founded on identity and suggests that research on language and sexuality should focus on the study of 'language and desire', including 'fantasy... repression, pleasure, fear, and the unconscious' (Kulick 2000:270). According to Kulick, one of the primary effects of such a change would be to shift inquiry 'from identity categories to culturally grounded semiotic practices' (Kulick 2000:273). As Eckert (2001:99) notes in her discussion of Kulick's proposal, identity categories are themselves 'culturally grounded semiotic processes' As with gender, the social normativity of sexuality constrains the possible psychological manifestations of desire. While there is nothing wrong with advocating research focusing on the psychology of desire, it would be detrimental to do so at the expense of research focusing on the social aspects of language.

Studies looking at sexuality and language all typically examine individuals who self-identify as straight, gay or lesbian. Kulick argues that research based on self-identification is flawed in that it cannot pass what Kulick calls 'Darsey's theorem': 'The fact that gays do X, does not make X gay' (Kulick 2000:259). Kulick (rightly) argues that there is not a one-to-one relationship between language variables and gay identity, because all of those variables felt to index 'gayness' are shared with other speakers who are not gay themselves. As Queen notes, this assumption not only removes the social from the psychological, but also seriously constrains any understanding of the social aspects of sexuality (Queen 2001:73). Any 'gay', 'lesbian' or 'queer' uses of language are not acquired from one's parents, but are acquired later in life as an individual takes on a particular identity and adopts language associated with that identity. It would be surprising to find any aspect of language that was uniquely 'gay' because 'gay language' emerges from the formation of shared identity across native speakers of different dialects and social backgrounds. In this sense, Kulick's proposal is analogous to the erroneous claim that Creole languages are not legitimate languages simply because their grammar and vocabulary overlap with various source languages. What is particularly 'gay' about 'gay language' is not the elements of language themselves, but the ways in which those elements are joined together to convey a particular identity.

In his historical study of the formation of gay identity in New York, Chauncey notes that gay men used the language of dominant culture in a particular way that enabled them 'to see themselves in the interstices of that culture' (Chauncey 1994:287). Chauncey argues that 'gay codes' served simultaneously as a way for gay men to see themselves in the dominant culture and 'to read the culture against the grain in a way that made them more visible than they were supposed to be, and to turn 'straight' spaces into gay spaces' (Chauncey 1994:288). The performative nature of identity relies on a pre-existing set of historicised cultural citations that are recognised as indexing a particular identity. When gay identities began to emerge, the citations within dominant heterosexual culture were the only source for citations available to heterosexuals and homosexuals alike. Social normativity operates through the restrictions on the possible range of citations and hegemonic forces that restrict the use of a particular citation to index a particular identity. The citations themselves are not 'gay' and anyone can use them. What 'makes X gay' (or 'queer' or whatever) is the unique way in which those citations are turned, reworked and used in new ways in order to force old (heterosexual) citations to index a new ('gay') identity. Darsey's theorem (1981) misses the entire point of 'queer linguistics': the question is not simply 'defining a gay dialect', but rather understanding how language resources are allocated, appropriated and redirected away from their original hegemonic meaning and 'queered' into a variety of new meanings.

If one wishes to examine the relationship between language and desire, one must first understand the ways in which desires are constructed and constrained by social normativity. Sexual acts between members of the same sex have radically different meanings in different cultures. The normative forces that simultaneously constrain and construct possible social identities also constrain and construct expressions of sexual desire.

As Eckert (2001) argues, a focus on desire mystifies sexuality, increasing the risk that desire might be seen as something natural to an individual and devoid of social meaning. Often, the differences between the ways in which cultures perceive and react to homosexual acts cannot be understood through a concept like 'desire' For example, the belief held by some Melanesian cultures that males cannot successfully grow to adulthood without ingesting the semen from older males (e.g. Herdt 1984) cannot be seen as simply the expression of same-sex desire. In such cases homosexuality is not seen as aberrant or forbidden, but is an accepted and *expected* part of one's experience. It is not clear that 'desire' even has a role here, since the practice of homosexual acts between men is culturally required and the actual will of any individual is of minor relevance to whether or not he participates in homosexual practices.

The role of culture in directing individual desire is quite clear in the distinction between 'gay' culture in the United States and Canada compared with traditional views of homosexuality in Mexico and Central America. In contemporary Western cultures, the concept of homosexuality is based on sexual desire for members of the same sex. A man with such desires may take on a 'gay' identity which, although grounded on same-sex desires, includes additional social and cultural features that move well beyond the original desire. The actual sexual acts a man performs is irrelevant to his being 'gay', although he may further identify as a 'top' or 'bottom' depending on his preferences for sexual acts. A 'top' generally prefers to be the active participant (penetrator) in anal intercourse and the receiver (fellated) in oral intercourse. A 'bottom' typically prefers the passive role in anal intercourse (penetrated) and the active role in oral intercourse (fellator). Generally, it is assumed that these roles or identities are fluid and that the vast majority of gay men sometimes perform acts not associated with their usual identity. Also, many gay men have no preference and will not identity as either 'top' or 'bottom', either choosing no label or identifying as 'versatile'. The actual distinction between 'top' and 'bottom' is primarily about sexual acts and has little to do with gender display. One may be 'butch' or 'femme' (roughly equivalent to masculine or feminine) regardless of one's role in sexual activities.

In the traditional system of Mexico and Central America (Carrier 1995; Murray 1995), only the passive participant (*pasivo*) in anal intercourse is considered homosexual (and is not expected to have sexual relations with women). The active participant in anal intercourse (*activo*) does not take on a particular 'gay' identity (despite performing sexual acts with other men) and is expected to marry and have children (though he may still maintain sexual relationships with men). More recently, with the globalisation of Western 'gay' culture and under political and economic pressure associated with an increase in gay tourism in Mexico, the additional terms *gai* and *internacional* have come into common usage (Cantú 2002). The term *internacional* refers to men who have no preference for particular sexual acts, while *gai* basically corresponds to the use of *gay* in the United States and Canada.

In contrast to the Anglo-American system, however, the traditional Latin American system reserves the stigmatised label of 'homosexual' for the *pasivo*. In Nicaragua, for example, the category *cochon* refers to *pasivos* while no specific social identity exists for the *activo* (other than that of a normal 'heterosexual' male). Thus, the *cochon* is viewed as desiring (and does desire) to be the passive partner in anal intercourse. Unlike in the Western system, oral sex is viewed as 'dirty' and its practice is not acknowledged, even by *cochones*. In the Nicaraguan system of sexuality, it is assumed that the 'normal' sexuality of a man is the desire for sexual penetration, regardless of whether it is with a man or a woman. The *cochon* on the other hand, is defined by his desire to be penetrated. In his study of sexuality and masculinity in Nicaragua, Lancaster (1992:250) compares the two systems as follows:

> Thus, the dominant Anglo-American rule would read as follows. A man gains sexual status and honor among other men through and only through his sexual transactions with women. Homosexuals appear as the active refuseniks of that system. In Nicaragua, the rule is built around different principles. A man gains sexual status and honor among other men through his active role in sexual intercourse (either with women or with other men). Cochones are (passive) participants in that system.

Because sexual desire is manifest as a psychological reality experienced on a personal level, it is easy to assume that sexuality is somehow less social than other aspects of one's identity. If same-sex desires are manifest in radically different ways across cultures, however, we must recognise that those desires are socially constructed. As Lancaster (1992:270) notes in his study of the *cochones*:

> However it is defined, desire – like gender, color, or class – exists not within us, but between us ... That [desire] is often felt as an 'inner', 'subjective' experience by no means diminishes its 'outer', 'social' character, for desire is always a relation between two relata; as such it is constitutive of as well as constituted by the subject of desire. And in this constitution of subjectivity, the desiring subject is traversed, even in his innermost experience of desire, by social forces: not simply at the most superficial level by the prohibitions, rules, and recommendations of sanctioned desire, but more significantly, by values, erotics, and evaluations that

> are part of and made possible by social language and by conflicts over them that are no less social in nature ... Desire is thus always part of the cultural, economic, and ideological world of social relations and social conflicts. It is not simply that these relations and conflicts act on some interior and preexisting sexuality 'from the outside' but that they constitute it 'from the inside' as well.

Sexuality and gender are similar in that they both seem to have a foundation in biology, but that this biological input is not directly manifested in individual psychology. An individual's gender and sexual identities are bound by normative social forces that control the direction, expression, and limitations of actual psychological states of desire. Thus, identity and desire cannot be truly separated as each is inextricably joined to the other and expressions of both are dependent on larger social and cultural norms and political and economic contexts. As such, Kulick's call to include desire, need not imply the need to abandon identity altogether as he seems to propose.

In the remainder of this chapter, I will examine the role of these two models of homosexuality in shaping the ways in which gay identity and desire are constructed and marketed in foreign-language phrasebooks intended for gay male travellers. While the phrasebooks claim to meet the linguistic needs of gay men, the language associated with gay men and the desires and social practices of gay men are all constrained by a particular view of what it means to be gay. As the phrasebooks present these competing models of gay community in extreme forms, they present a fairly 'pure' image of what 'gay language' would look like in the competing models of desire and culture.

Competing models of gay men's language

The first gay-oriented foreign-language phrasebook, *The Gay Girl's Guide to the US and the Western World*, is reported to have been published as early as 1949 (Kulick 2000). Despite this early precedent, such phrasebooks are not particularly common. In 1995 and 1996, however, at least three distinct phrasebooks were published specifically for gay travellers. These are *How to Say Faaabulous! in 8 Different Languages* (Mryglot and Marks 1995; hereafter HTSF), *Gay Phrasebook* (McKay 1995; hereafter GPB), and *Hot! International Gay* (Appel and Balido 1996; hereafter HIG). The books were all published by relatively small companies and were sold at gay-oriented bookstores. The books are organised like compact phrasebooks intended for travellers (such as the Berlitz series). They include various headings based on particular social settings such as dining out, shopping or going to the doctor. Under each heading a set of potentially useful phrases typically given in a frame such as 'I'd like a ...' followed by a short list of words that may be used to fill the frame.

The languages covered in the books vary. All of the books include French, German, Spanish, Italian and either Iberian or Brazilian Portuguese. HTSF also includes Russian and Japanese. HIG also includes Czech, while GPB includes Dutch. With the exception of Japan in HTSF, all three phrasebooks tend to be focused on travel to Europe or Latin America. All occasionally include some terms unique to either Castilian or Latin American Spanish and all mark these terms as specific to a particular country or region. While GPB is aimed primarily at a British audience, the other books are aimed primarily at an American and Canadian audience. As such, the languages chosen represent stereotypical vacation locations for gay men (particularly in the US), such as Mexico and Western Europe. Each of the phrasebooks claims to provide the necessary vocabulary for gay men to use when travelling outside of English-speaking countries, yet each has a different perspective on what gay men 'do' with language. HIG deals primarily with sexual matters. Although the book is meant to facilitate 'love and sex' in six different languages, it includes other aspects of life (such as emergencies and shopping). In representing gay identity, HIG adheres closely to the desire-based model. As one might expect from the title, HTSF follows the culture-based model, viewing gay identity as something quite distinct from (but including) sexual desire. The view of gay identity in HTSF is constructed around particular social practices (especially unique uses of language) and is closely related to displays of gender. In GPB, gay identity is somewhere in between the other books: not entirely about sex, but not as closely linked to gender as in HTSF.

Although some gay men might purchase one of the books solely for amusement or curiosity, the books represent themselves as providing a legitimate and much-needed service for the gay community. All three books state that they are intended to help gay travellers by providing the linguistic tools for social situations unique to gay men. Yet even in describing their intended goals, the different views of gay culture become clear. The primary social good the authors of HTSF claim to provide is knowledge of gay 'codes' and innuendo, which allows a speaker to present himself as a gay man. The author chose the book's title 'from a theory ... that heterosexual men never use the word 'fabulous' –and if a man does, it's a tip-off he's acquainted with Dorothy' (Mryglot and Marks 1995:foreword). The authors claim that their book reveals 'equivalent telltale words' in various languages. Thus, the book claims to make it possible for one to use language to construct a gay identity by passing on the covert forms of communication in another language, a goal based on the assumption of a unique and distinct gay culture that crosses national and linguistic borders. In contrast, the authors of HIG emphasise that their work serves to protect the health and safety of gay men by making them aware of potentially violent situations and teaching them to communicate about 'safe sex' in another language. This goal is not unique to HIG. Each of the books provides pejorative terms for gay men so that one might recognise a dangerous situation and avoid being the victim of a hate crime. Each of the books also emphasises 'safe sex' and HIV awareness. *Gay phrasebook* even includes sample 'safe sex' erotic dialogues for language practice translated from texts produced by a group called *Gay men fighting AIDS*. As the authors of HIG state:

> awareness of AIDS and other sexually-transmitted diseases can vary quite a bit from country to country and from person to person. Your new friend might be willing to jump into bed unprotected, but you shouldn't be –and now you can say so clearly, in his own language. (Appel and Balido 1996:5)

All three books see language as a crucial tool for avoiding dangerous situations. HIG even goes so far as to include expressions for convincing someone not to drive while intoxicated. Thus, 'gay language' is not simply something that might enhance one's vacation, but is a basic need to ensure one's personal safety. The assumption that gay men have unique linguistic needs serves as a marketing tool to justify the need for such phrasebooks in the first place.

Although the intent of the books may be to convey practical information, the information is framed within the context of gay male desire. The aim of that desire varies according to the image of gay identity presented in the text. For example, HTSF maintains a gender-based view of gay identity and is focused toward a desire for cross-dressing, while in both HIG and GPB gay male sexual desire is central in marketing the book towards a gay audience. These desires correspond to particular views of gay identity as either tied to gender norms in gay culture or based (primarily or entirely) in sexual desire. The particular desires and behaviours associated with individuals who claim a 'gay' identity are dependent on what one imagines 'gay' identity to mean.

The different phrasebooks market these assumed desires both in their presentation and in their choice of language included in the work. HTSF is presented in a scarlet cover with gold typeface and contains no illustrations. In contrast, both HIG and GPB (which are more aimed at sexual desires) have pictures of bare-chested men on their covers. Both HIG and GPB also have occasional photographs of men in their underwear dispersed through the text. In addition, HIG includes a blank page for noting 'contacts', or phone numbers and addresses of the men one meets on vacation. In a similar vein, the inside covers of GPB contain advertisements for erotic male magazines and videos with titles like *Euroboy* and *Just Eighteen*.

The choice of language included in the text reflects a marketing strategy that exploits particular desires. The choice of language included in each phrasebook is inherently tied to the assumed identity of the reader. These identities are associated with a distinct set of desires, particularly desires for participation in an unique set of social practices that (like the desires themselves) are bound to a particular imagined identity. The vocabulary items and phrases included in each book correspond to these social practices and the things men with a particular 'gay' identity might do on an imagined vacation. The ways in which desires are tied to identity can be illustrated with the different items included under the heading 'Shopping' in HIG and HTSF (Table 2.1).

Here, the same social practice (shopping) is imagined to occur in radically different ways. The act of shopping and the items one desires to shop for are dependent on a particular view of gay identity. While the HTSF shopper is searching the flea market for old records, dolls and jewellery, the HIG shopper is looking for pornography, tit clamps, whips and chains. The choice of included locations and objects to shop for add to the set of social practices associated with a particular view of identity. The constraints on the actions and desires of the imagined traveller follow expectations about gay male desires and social practices that are largely dependent on viewing social identity in terms of culture or desire.

Table 2.1 List of lexical items related to 'shopping'.

HIG	HTSF
lubricated/unlubricated condoms	thrift store
large condoms	antique store
(water-soluble) lubricant	flea market
I need a dildo/butt plug	department store
A cockring/pair of chaps, please	shopping mall
I'd like some tit clamps	second-hand
Where are your porn magazines/videos	This flea market is pretty cruisy!
Do you sell gay guides?	I'm interested in ...
I'll take a whip	old records, old books, old photos
Some chains, please	movie memorabilia, jewelry, dolls, dishes
I'd like a massage	This piece of crap? Have you flipped?
How much will it cost?	Those shoes! I must have those shoes!
I don't pay (for sex)	Wrap it up, honey, cause I'm taking it home
	I would like to find a gorgeous, original Art Deco lamp in mint condition for $10

The two phrasebooks also assume different uses of language during the act of shopping. The sentences in HIG are short, straight-forward, and direct (e.g. 'How much will it cost?') while maintaining the most basic level of politeness (e.g. 'Some chains, please'). As such, they are structural similar to phrasebooks for travellers aimed at a more general audience (such as 'Could we please have a table further away from the band?' or 'Could you tell me how to get to the nearest metro station?'). The primary difference between the 'gay' phrasebook and any other similar book (for a presumed heterosexual audience) is the semantic content of the phrases themselves. The content differs not only in terms of what items one shops for (e.g. 'I need a butt plug'), but also by including sexual topics in a traveller's phrasebook at all. The general similarity with 'straight' travel books is not surprising, given the assumption in HIG that 'gay' identity differs from 'straight' identity solely with regard to sexual desire and sexual practice. If one assumes no difference in social behaviour beyond the sexual, one would expect there to be no 'gay' language and that the phrases needed by homosexual men would be, for the most part, structurally identical to those used by heterosexuals.

The shopping phrases in HTSF, however, differ from those found in other phrasebooks in several ways. They contain 'gay' vocabulary (e.g. 'This flea market is pretty cruisy!') and 'gay' uses of language, particularly the use of 'camp' expressions (e.g. 'Wrap it up honey, cause I'm taking it home!') and highly exaggerated gender display (e.g. 'Those shoes! I must have those shoes!'). As the desire for jewellery, shoes and dolls is inherently tied to other aspects of social identity related to gender display, the language used to express those desires reflects the assumed 'gay' identity by itself being an example of a 'gay' gender performance.

Language and the marketing of sexual desire

All of the books contain vocabulary referring to sexual acts between men. Although HTSF does include sections on 'Safe sex' and 'At the bathhouse', these sections are a relatively small part of the overall vocabulary included in the book. There are roughly the same number of terms for 'Safe sex', as there are for 'What do you do for a living?' and 'Hair, make-up and glamour'. Thus, from the culture-based perspective, sexual behaviour is no more important than other aspects of one's identity. Both HIG and GPB include much more sexual language, including details of language specific to sexual contexts. Of the terms included in HIG, for example, 93 per cent (384 out of 410) fall under headings directly related to sex or relationships. In HIG and GPB, the phrases and terms given for non-sexual situations (such as shopping or health) tend to actually be about sex in some way. If 'gayness' is reduced to sexual desire and sexual practice, then the only 'gay' language is language directly related to sex. Thus, under 'Health' in GPB, the only illnesses listed are sexually transmitted diseases and the only parts of the anatomy given as sources of physical pain are the throat, the anus, and the penis. In fact, almost all of the words listed under 'Health' have to do with sex in some way. The complete list is as follows:

- I need to see a doctor/a pharmacy
- I have ... /Do you have something for ...
  - gonorrhea
  - syphilis
  - crabs
  - lice
  - herpes
  - scabies
- I hurt here. I'm bleeding. I'm itching
- My throat/penis/anus hurts

In both GPB and HIG, 'health' is actually 'sexual health', reinforcing the idea that the only 'special' language gay men need is language related to sexual desire and practice since sexuality is the only source of difference between 'gay' and 'straight' identity.

The preoccupation with sex and the extensive lists of language for use in sexual encounters suggest that these phrasebooks have more to do with the exploitation of gay male sexual desire than with practical language skills for use on vacation. Despite studies that suggest gay men use more erotic talk during sexual activity compared with other social groups (Woods 1990), it is doubtful that one would frequently consult a phrasebook during sexual intercourse. Yet HIG even goes so far as to include a special listing for 'Moans'. Some of the phrases seem like they would only arise at inconvenient or inappropriate times for consulting a dictionary (e.g. 'Don't give me a hickey/lovebite' or 'Did you come?' from HIG). Others seem virtually impossible to look up at the intended moment (e.g. 'I'm getting close!' or 'Take the handcuffs off!' also from HIG). As this vocabulary would have to be memorised in advance to be very useful in a real-world situation, its inclusion probably has more to do with fuelling gay sexual desire as a means of marketing than with actually serving as a practical tool for communication during sexual activity. Learning the terms fuels sexual fantasies related to one's planned vacation. The same is true of the 'erotic' dialogues included in GPB, which present sexual fantasies written in each of the six languages included in the book. Of these dialogues, only one (German) does not involve a sexual encounter. These fantasy sexual encounters involve specific vacation situations, such as having sex with the porter and a passenger on a train in French or taking a shower with an unknown tourist at the youth hostel.

The dialogues also exploit Anglo-American stereotypes about the sexual practices associated with particular national or ethnic identities. For example, the Dutch conversation takes place in a leather bar, the Italian encounter occurs in the sand dunes on a public beach, and the Portuguese encounter involves sex with a young man who has just been disowned and thrown out onto the street by his parents. The attitudes towards safe sex in the dialogues reflects Anglo-American stereotypes about 'hot-blooded' and dangerous sexuality of Italians and Iberians. The French speaker travels 'with a bag of condoms' (McKay 1995) and the Dutch speaker carries 'plenty – and strong ones!' (McKay 1995). In sharp contrast, both the Italian speaker and the Spanish speaker attempt to have unprotected sex while the English-speaking traveller must coerce them to do otherwise.

Despite the stereotypes involved in depictions of particular sexual situations, the actual sexual practices and social stances towards sex depict a uniform 'gayness' that transcends national or ethnic boundaries. Although particular nationalities may be associated with certain tendencies (such as the stereotype of the Dutch as leathermen), the sexual acts and vocabulary to describe sexual acts are treated as basically equivalent across different languages in all of the phrasebooks. There is an implicit assumption that gay men in any given country will be more or less identical in terms of sexual behaviour and the sexual vocabularies of various languages are presented as if they all contain the same set of words all of which have equivalent meanings. In HIG, for example, the English terms *top* and *bottom* are given the Spanish translations *pasivo* and *activo*. The terms are clearly not equivalent (at least as used in Latin American Spanish). While *top* and *bottom* refer to particular preferences for both anal and oral intercourse, *pasivo* and *activo* refer only to anal intercourse.

Also, in some Latin American cultures, an *activo* is not even considered gay, so that the unified 'gay' identity of a *top* or a *bottom* cannot be directly mapped onto the *pasivo/activo* distinction. Finally, the *activo/pasivo* distinction has been traditionally viewed as absolute so it is not generally possible to reject both labels (i.e. it is assumed that all men have a preference). Gay men in Anglo-American culture, on the other hand, often reject the *top/bottom* distinction and choose a label like 'flexible' or 'versatile'. Although the sexual practices of men in Latin America may not have ever strictly conformed to the social norms requiring strict adherence to *activo/pasivo* identity, the shift in identity categories is fairly recent (Cantú 2002). However, the terms in HIG do not include *internacional* and the English term 'flexible' is translated into Spanish as *¡Hago de todo!* ('I do it all!'), an expression with very different connotations compared with English terms such as 'versatile' or 'flexible'. There are no 'gaps' in the sexual vocabulary of any of the languages included in the three books. The translation of the name for a particular sex act implies that at least some of the people speaking a given language perform the act in question. Thus, it is assumed that the sexual acts listed are practised anywhere a person might travel.

The possibility that attitudes towards particular sex acts might vary across languages and cultures is never raised. Thus, for example, all three books give terms for both oral and anal sex for each language with no mention of the possibility that there are distinct cultural preferences for particular types of sex. Yet studies show that sexual behaviour correlates directly with particular aspects of one's identity. A study of heterosexual women in the United States, for example, found direct correlations between ethnic identity and the frequency for engaging in particular sexual acts (Quadagno et al. 1998). Thus, while oral sex is more prevalent than anal sex in Anglo-American white gay culture, the reverse would be true in a cultural setting such as Nicaragua (Lancaster 1992). Although the desire to engage in particular sexual acts is culturally situated, the phrasebook authors (like most individuals) are blind to the relationship between sexual acts and cultural difference. For example, both HIG and GPB include 'fisting' in their list of terms for particular sexual acts. The custom of 'fisting' (inserting one's hand into another's anus) is not a universal (or even widespread) practice. Hence, it is not part of the sexual vocabulary in most languages. The translators deal with this either by borrowing the English term or by giving a description of the act (as opposed to a given name). While both books give equivalent translations for German (*der Faustfick*, the literal equivalent of the English term), they also give the English word as a borrowing (*das Fisten* or *Fistfucking*). Both books give loan words for French and Italian (*le/il fistfucking*), though both also give the English term in Spanish (*el fistfucking*), HIG supplements the term with an explanation (*la follada con el puño*). For Portuguese, both books give explanations rather than translations (*a penetração com o punho* [HIG], *de enfiar a mão no cú* [GPB]). The only exception to this is the term for another marginal sex act, 'water sports' or 'golden showers' (urinating on one's sexual partner), which HIG notes as 'NE' or 'no exact equivalent' (although definitions are given) in Portuguese (*mijar em alguém*) or Czech (*čuáni při sexu*). Thus, even when there is no term for a particular act, the author usually ensures that one is listed, producing one-to-one equivalents for sexual terminology across languages. When this is not possible, a definition is given so that one can still attempt to 'translate' their desire onto another situation. This has the effect of 'naturalising' sexual desire and masking the role of cultural difference in the social construction of sexual practice.

The choice of entries in GPB and HIG not only limit the sexual expression within other cultures, but even constrain expressions of sexuality within Anglo-American culture. The image of 'gay' culture in HIG and GPB is based on a stereotype of white middle-class urban gay men who probably live in gay neighbourhoods and have extensive social networks centred around shared sexual identity. This stereotyped view of gay culture includes an obsession with physical appearance, masculinity and youthfulness (Signorile 1997). In this stereotyped view of gay culture, men who aren't particularly attractive or physically fit are not likely to gain acceptance from other gay men. This follows fairly naturally from the view of gay identity as founded only on sexual desire. If gay identity were founded in sexual desire, then the most important personal trait one could possess would be sexual desirability. In addition to socially constructing and constraining the types of sexual activities one might engage in, the books also construct an image of what is sexually desirable. The GPB includes vocabulary for reading or writing personals advertisements with a long list of adjectives in small print, under a larger heading 'I am looking for ... '. After the list of adjectives, the text returns to large print and gives additional terms, including vocabulary for 'no effeminates' and 'no fats'. The phrase 'no fats/no femmes' is common to the language of gay personals ads and reflects the stereotype that heavy and effeminate men are dispreferred as sexual partners. Similarly, in HIG the question 'How old are you?' is followed by the two possible responses 'How old do you think I am?' and 'I'm twenty/thirty-two years old'. The first option gives an indirect way to opt out of the question while the second allows one to respond, but constricts the possible ages for the reply. The two together suggest that if one isn't between 22 and 32 years of age, one would naturally avoid answering questions about age.

In HIG and GPB, 'gay' language and the social contexts for its use centre primarily around sex and sexual desirability. The gay community in these books is imagined primarily through the desire-based model. The sexual practices of gays in other cultures are simultaneously imagined as identical to and different from those found in Anglo-American culture. Cantú (2002) finds the same pairing of similarity and difference in the publications aimed at drawing gay tourists to Mexico. As Cantú argues, the view of 'sameness' reassures the potential traveller that a 'gay' vacation can have all of the 'comforts of home' such as gay bars and neighbourhoods where one need not worry about homophobia or violence. In contrast, the 'differences' across cultures target the fantasy of an exotic gay 'other' with a 'raw' or primitive sexuality unavailable 'in suburban American home life' (Cantú 2002:148).

Language and sexual identity

Although GPB definitely tends towards the desire-based model in HIG, there are 'gay' expressions in GPB that do not focus solely on sexual desires. For example, the sections of GPB called 'Expressions' and 'Other useful vocabulary' contain 'gay' vocabulary and expressions that could covertly convey a gay identity. These expressions are generally items that don't fall easily into the other sections of the book such as 'Cruising' or 'At his place/your place ... '. These 'useful' expressions fall into four basic categories: basic communicative needs ('I'm sorry', 'Excuse me', numbers), obscene interjections and off-colour terms ('Shit!', 'Fuck off!', 'A bitch', 'A slut'), gender-marked responses ('Darling!', 'How wonderful', 'Oh dear!'), and 'gay' expressions and vocabulary ('He's a friend of Dorothy', 'As camp as knickers', 'A butch dyke', 'To come out', 'A fag hag'). The inclusion of obscenities and interjections adds to the 'taboo' nature of the phrasebook and its goal of filling in voids left by other traditional phrasebooks, serving as a marketing tool framing the phrasebooks as guides to language that is normally 'off-limits' By including the gender-marked responses, GPB allows for alternative gender expression (although without including so many examples as to make this the prevalent form of gay communication). The 'gay' terms reference identity that moves beyond sexual preference to a larger set of shared social practices. Unlike HTSF, however, GPB does not emphasise alternative gender expression as the main form of gay language. For GPB, 'gay' identity is somewhere between that found in HIG and that found in HTSF; alternative gender expression and 'gay' language exist and are part of being gay but the main focus of gay language (at least for the gay traveller) is the fulfilment of sexual desire.

Following the culture-based model, the focus of HTSF is on gay culture that is distinct from sexual orientation and is built upon common experiences, desires and social practices. In this view, sexual behaviour is only a small part of what makes the gay community unique. The potential members imagined for this community are delineated in HTSF in the section called 'What do you do for a living?'. The response to this question is given as 'I'm a(n) ... ' followed by a list of potential professions. The full list is as follows:

> actor, antique dealer, artist, bartender, businessman, chef, choreographer, government employee, computer specialist, dancer, doctor, fashion model, figure skater, fitness trainer, flight attendant, florist, hairdresser, heiress, interior decorator, lawyer, makeup artist, nurse, paid escort, priest, psychotherapist, physical therapist, retail store manager, sales clerk, social worker, teacher, tourist guide, translator, travel agent, waiter, word processor, writer.

Although the list does contain some professions that are not stereotypically gay (doctor, computer specialist, lawyer), the bulk of the list is made up of jobs that reflect stereotypes of gay men (actor, figure skater, choreographer, etc.). There is also a conspicuous absence of working class jobs, linking gender and class and reinforcing the general absence of masculinity throughout the phrasebook. The list also includes humorous responses (heiress, priest) that are very unlikely to be true, but could be used as a 'camp' response in a gay setting. Responding with 'priest', for example, could be used to deflect unwanted advances while mitigating the rejection with humour. The inclusion of these humorous responses suggests that the prevalence of such jobs on the list is likely intended to also be humorous, rather than to adequately provide a list of actual professions. This type of self-directed mocking is itself a form of 'camp' expression that serves as a type of stereotype 'reclaiming' in which stereotypes often used against gay individuals are turned in order to mark in-group identity. This use of camp (both in the structure of the phrasebook and the terms included in it) marks the potential reader as someone who will understand in-group humour by recognising a highly restricted and selective set of citations (Harvey 2000). As such, it constructs an imagined gay community that is entirely independent from sexual desire.

The use of 'camp' is prevalent in the organisation and content choices throughout HTSF. While HIG and GPB include sections on 'Cruising', HTSF has a corresponding section on 'Boy watching' The vocabulary sections include a special list for 'Hair, make-up, and glamour' with terms for cosmetics, women's shoe styles and fabrics. For each language, there is a special section on 'Gay icons' with terms for talking about one's favourite celebrities. The section begins with a list of opening expressions such as 'Don't you just hate ...' and 'I worship at the altar of ...'. In addition to 'fabulous', one is also taught how to say 'I miss Judy!' in '8 different languages'. Each language has a list of gay icons that include Anglo-American 'gay icons' and 'icons' associated with speakers of the language in question.

The inclusion of a section on 'Gay icons' constrains the imagined gay community in terms of attitudes towards gender. As many gay men might reject 'gay icons' as inherently effeminate, their inclusion constructs the prototypical gay man as someone for whom 'icons' hold extreme importance. The basic list of English-speaking icons is fairly constant across languages: Judy Garland, Liza Minelli, Barbra Streisand, Marilyn Monroe, Bette Davis, Joan Crawford, Doris Day. This list further constrains the imagined gay community across various axes of social difference as this is primarily a set of icons intended for older middle-class white men in the United States. With the possible exception of Barbra Streisand (who happens to be Jewish), the authors have created a list with no ethnic diversity.

The list also restricts 'gayness' along the lines of age. Most of these 'icons' are dead and their potential appeal is restricted to a very specific (older) age group. The foreign 'icon' lists vary from language to language and sometimes include parenthetic information on what the particular celebrity actually does (singer, actress, etc.). If Paloma San Basilio or Iris Chacón happen to come up in conversation you can check your phrasebook and see that they are singers. The direct equivalence of the 'icon' concept assumes a shared gay cultural trait that transcends languages and cultures. The opposing lists however, create boundaries within that shared culture. The parenthetic information on foreign icons constructs a binary opposition between 'our' icons and 'their' icons; those that require no explanation and those that the reader is assumed to know nothing about. Thus, the imagined gay traveller knows all about Doris Day, but has to be told that Luis Miguel is a singer. This opposition is especially clear in this subset from the list for Brazilian Portuguese:

- Marilia Pêra (actress)
- Glória Menezes (actress)
- Dalva de Oliveira (singer)
- Carmen Miranda (you know!)
- Angela Maria (singer)
- Beth Carvalho (samba singer)

Carmen Miranda merits the parenthetical expression marking her as the icon of the other, but rather than fill the parenthesis with her actual profession the authors write 'you know!'. In other words, she's one of 'their' icons, but 'we' love her too. In the culture-based view of gay signs, a hat made entirely of fruit speaks to a universal audience.

The gay identity imagined in HTSF is not limited solely to alternative gender display. HTSF includes a vocabulary section on 'Politics' that allows for discussions about gay rights issues. The Politics list assumes that gay men in other countries will have shared political views and experiences of homophobia. Questions like 'Is there any gay bashing here?' and 'Is your country plagued by religious fundamentalists?' assume that the American gay experience is universal. Yet, as with the 'Gay icons' section, there are differences in the details of imagined gay experience and specific political slogans are presented from political rallies in Mexico (e.g. '*¡Lucha, lucha, todas a la lucha, no somos machas pero somos muchas!*' or 'Fight, fight, everyone to the fight, we aren't butch but there are a lot of us!') and France (e.g. '*Pédés, gousdous, réveillez-vous!*' or 'Queers, dykes, wake up!').

As with the presentation of sexual terminology in HIG, the expression of gay identity in HTSF simultaneously marks 'foreign' gay men as simultaneously the same as and different from gay men in the United States. The belief that gay men in one's destination also have 'gay icons' and 'religious fundamentalists' offers the familiarity of home, while the chance to learn new political slogans or gay icons feeds the desire for the exotic 'other' Although HIG and HTSF both present radically different views of a gay community, gay men in other countries are presented as 'just like us but more exotic' in both phrasebooks.

The vocabulary in HTSF produces a stereotyped image of a member of the gay community, particular when it comes to alternative gender performance. The social contexts in the book constrain the imagined social practices of gay men. In addition to shopping for dolls and movie memorabilia, there are terms for ordering low fat or fat free food at a restaurant and using the Nautilus machine at the gym. The actual language included in HTSF extends this set of social practices to language use while simultaneously relying on an iconic (Gal and Irvine 2000) relationship in which a particular use of language can index the entire set of social practices associated with gay identity. HTSF contains much more 'core' gay vocabulary than the other books, but also includes strategies for using camp in various situations.

HTSF assumes that the production of in-group 'camp' humour is a basic need for the gay traveller and 'camp' expressions are included throughout the work. When 'Dining out', one might tell a friend 'You've had worse things in your mouth!' or tell the waiter 'Hurry up! My clothes are going out of style!'. When at the gym one might want to jest that 'The only exercise I get is combing out my wig!'. One might decide to celebrate his arrival in Europe by shouting 'Toto! I don't think we're in Kansas anymore!' in French. Like the list of professions or the inclusion of a section on gay icons, these camp phrases serve as a form of in-group self-mockery and an assumed gay appreciation for displays of camp wit.

HTSF provides the gay traveller with the tools for being flamboyant and marking gay identity in every aspect of one's life. The imagined behaviour of the gay traveller in each of these phrasebooks reflects a highly stereotyped image of gay men. It is almost as if the traveller in HTSF goes abroad to find women's shoes in larger sizes, while the traveller in HIG goes abroad because he has already slept with everyone in his own country. The community in GPB is somewhere in between the other two extremes, negotiating between opposing views of what it means to be gay. Although all three books present a very limited view of potential members of the gay community, they also imagine that community to transcend linguistic, cultural and geographic areas. This assumption of the universality of gay experience occurs regardless of the fact that gay experience is imagined in very different and even competing ways.

Conclusion

In these phrasebooks, 'gay language' is a commodity to be marketed to gay consumers. The books differ in their views of what a 'gay consumer' might be, presenting opposing images of how gay individuals are expected to behave. While the gay community in HTSF is founded on the culture-based model, the community in HIG is based on the desire-based model. The mixed representation in GPB represents a negotiation between these two extremes. In the desire-based model, differences between gay and straight uses of language are minimised, while in the culture-based model they are exaggerated. The differences in the phrasebooks demonstrate that the 'gay community' may be imagined in very different ways, even by individuals who share a common self-categorisation as members of that community. The social and sexual practices associated with 'gayness' and the desire to participate in those practices are entirely dependent on the way in which one imagines the gay community. Thus, while gay men may claim to share identity, they may still have radically different ideas about how that identity should be understood. The culture-based model typically reduces the diversity among homosexual men into a particular view of a 'gay' community that cannot adequately capture the capricious nature of gay identity. In contrast, the desire-based model tends to reduce the breadth of gay social practices to a single concept of sexual desire.

Although the phrasebooks are centred around gay male desire, the nature of that desire differs according to the ways in which an author imagines gay identity. Because desire is dependent on views concerning identity, a desire-based approach to the study of language and sexuality like that proposed by Kulick (2000) is also insufficient for understanding the complex relationships between desire, personal identity and social normativity. The reality of 'gay language' is certainly not the picture presented in any of the three phrasebooks. Of the three, however, GPB probably comes the closest by negotiating between competing views of gay community rather than adhering strictly to either model of gay identity.

Just as neither HIG nor HTSF adequately represents 'gay language', the theoretical frameworks proposed by Leap (1996) and Kulick (2000) are both unable to represent the full breadth of the relationship between language and sexuality. By remaining entrenched in one of the two competing models of gay identity, both frameworks simply reproduce popular ideas already found in the gay community. This is why the culture/desire distinction between Leap and Kulick is basically identical to debates about gay language between Hayes (1981) and Darsey (1981) twenty years before. Hayes (1981), like Leap (e.g. Leap 1996), felt that gay language was part of a larger gay culture based on shared assumptions about community membership. Kulick, however, follows Darsey (1981) in holding that there can be no such thing as 'gay language' because the core features are borrowed from other varieties. Rather than simply reproduce or restate commonly held stereotypes, research into language and sexuality should bring insight into the ways in which language serves to create and maintain the stereotypes themselves.

Once research in language and gender moved beyond the binary opposition of difference and dominance (Uchida 1992; Coates 1993), research in language and gender experienced a 'boom' of exciting and interesting research. Researchers in language and gender are now addressing a much wider range of issues related to the construction of communities, the fluidity of identity, the political economy of gender, and the variety of social meanings that can be associated with gendered language. By abandoning a strict adherence to either the culture-based or the desire-based model of gay identity, researchers studying language and sexuality may also begin to ask new questions that cannot be asked in models focused solely on culture or desire.

Most research on language and sexuality has focused on searching for and describing gay language. The subtle nature of 'gay language' requires the development of new methods for considering how sexuality is perceived and conveyed. For example, Palmer (2002) used computer-manipulated speech samples to demonstrate that increasing the duration of [s] was sufficient for changing a listener's perception of the speaker from 'straight' to 'gay'. This suggests that the possibility that the perception of sexuality depends primarily on minute alterations in suprasegmental phonology (such as intonation, pitch, duration, pausing, etc.). A 'shopping list' of features of 'gay language' fails to capture the subtlety and gradient nature of such variation.

In addition to more subtle descriptions, we need to begin to consider the function of various linguistic forms in relation to the expression of sexuality. The question should not be whether or not gay language exists, but when and how language itself becomes an important resource for indexing one's sexual identities and desires. Language varieties will always be fuzzy prototype categories that overlap with one another. Debates over how to draw clear boundaries between these categories and 'what makes X gay' obscure the actual overlapping nature of the categories and make it more difficult to ask important and interesting questions that might have broad implications.

There is an assumption implicit in most sociolinguistic research that particular linguistic variables are tied to particular identities. As such, most research focuses on the distribution and frequency of a small number of variables across speakers. The challenge of 'gay language' is that it forces a recognition that linguistic variables are part of an open marketplace and may be unexpectedly adopted by speakers for purposes that may be quite different from the original indexical meaning. In his description of 'camp' talk, Harvey (2000) demonstrates the importance of particular juxtapositions in producing 'camp' language. These types of juxtapositions may also occur with sociolinguistic variables, producing 'camp' through the juxtaposition of linguistic varieties and styles. Studies examining the contact between varieties inherent in gay and lesbian language (e.g. Barrett 1997, 1998; Queen 1997) demonstrate that the association between signs and indexical meanings may be mercurial and context-dependent. A sign typically associated with a particular identity category may be turned so that it indexes a different meaning. In my research on the language of African American drag queens, for example, I found that Lakoff 's original concept of 'women's language' (Lakoff 1975) may be used to index meanings associated with ethnicity and class in addition to meanings associated with gender (Barrett 1998, 1999). The study of 'gay language' opens the possibility that identity (and desire) might be found not in the use of a particular linguistic variety, but rather in the particular choices and combinations of linguistic forms drawn from several distinct linguistic varieties.

Abandoning the binary models would allow us to ask questions about how individuals may use the indexical power of language to highlight particular aspects of their identity in particular contexts (Podesva, Roberts and Campbell-Kibler 2001) and how individuals may manipulate assumptions concerning the indexical meaning of sociolinguistic variables (Barrett 1998, 1999; Queen 1997) and how indexical meanings acquire value in the linguistic marketplace (Barrett 1995; McElhinny 2001).

In addition to questioning the relationship between identity and language, we must also question identity categories themselves. Because identity labels change across time and context, they are a form of language that reflects shifts in social structure. As they are often assumed in sociolinguistic research, the ways in which identity categories operate as a sociolinguistic system have not received adequate attention. Cantú (2002), for example, shows how political and economic forces associated with gay tourism in Mexico has pushed a shift towards adopting the Anglo- American model of gay identity. Research such as that of Wong (Wong and Zhang 2000; Wong 2001) considers the way in which the Chinese category of *Tongzhi* has developed and changed meaning over time. In addition to study of different categories based on sexuality, we also need more research comparing categories related to gender (e.g. Hall 1997; Gaudio 1997). By examining the full range of categories associated with both gender and sexuality across cultures we should be able to begin to understand if, when, and how gender and sexuality are related to one another. If we abandon simplistic and monolithic models of sexuality as entirely formed through culture or desire, we can begin to consider the variety of ways in which indexical meanings may be used and re-used as citations with the performative force to construct and manipulate identities across various social settings and interactional contexts (Barrett 2001). Then perhaps, we can move beyond arguments about how to define inherently vague concepts such as 'sexuality' and 'gayness' and move on to questions that will have important implications beyond the study of language and sexuality.

References

Appel, D. and Balido, P. (eds) (1996) *Hot! International Gay: Love and Sex in Seven Languages.* New York: Babelcom.

Barrett, R. (1995) 'Supermodels of the world, unite!' Political economy and the language of performance among African American drag queens. In W. Leap (ed.) *Beyond the Lavender Lexicon: Authenticity, Imagination, and Appropriation in Lesbian and Gay Languages* 203–23. Newark, NJ: Gordon & Breach.

Barrett, R. (1997) The 'homo-genius' speech community. In Livia and Hall (1997): 181–201.

Barrett, R. (1998) Markedness and style switching in performances by African American drag queens. In C. Myers-Scotton (ed.) *Codes and Consequences: Choosing Linguistic Varieties* 139–61. New York, NY: Oxford University Press.

Barrett, R. (1999) Indexing polyphonous identity in the speech of African American drag queens. In M. Bucholtz, A. Liang and L. Sutton (eds) *Reinventing Identities: The Gendered Self in discourse* 313–31. New York, NY: Oxford University Press.

Barrett, R. (2001) Is queer theory important for sociolingusitic theory? In Campbell-Kibler et al. (2001): 25–44.

Bourdieu, P. (1991) *Language and Symbolic Power*. Cambridge, MA: Harvard University Press.

Butler, J. (1990) *Gender Trouble: Feminism and the Subversion of Identity*. New York: Routledge.

Butler, J. (1993) *Bodies that Matter: One the Discursive Limits of 'Sex'.* New York: Routledge.

Campbell-Kibler, K., Podesva, R. J., Roberts, S. and Wong, A. (eds) (2001) *Language and Sexuality: Contesting Meaning in Theory and Practice*. Stanford, CA: Stanford University Center for the Study of Language and Information.

Cantú, L. (2002) *De ambiente*: Queer tourism and the shifting boundaries of Mexican male sexualities. *GLQ* 8(1–2): 139–66. https://doi.org/10.1215/10642684-8-1-2-139

Carrier, J. (1995) *De los otros: Intimacy and Homosexuality among Mexican Men.* New York: Columbia University Press.

Chauncey, G. (1994) *Gay New York: Gender, Urban Culture, and the Makings of the Gay Male World, 1890–1940.* New York: Basic Books.

Coates, J. (1993) *Women, Men and Language: A Sociolinguistic Account of Sex Differences in Language.* London: Longman.

Darsey, J. (1981) 'Gayspeak': A response. In J. Chesbro (ed.) *Gayspeak: Gay Male and Lesbian Communication* 58–67. New York: Pilgrim Press.

Duberman, M. (1993) *Stonewall.* New York: Dutton.

Eckert, P. (2001) Demystifying sexuality and desire. In Campbell-Kibler et al. (2001): 99–110.

Frye, M. (1983) *The Politics of Reality: Essays in Feminist Theory*. New York: The Crossing Press.

Gal, S. and Irvine, J. (2000) Language ideology and linguistic differentiation. In P. Kroskrity (ed.) *Regimes of Language: Ideologies, Polities, and Identities* 35–83. Santa Fe, NM: School of American Research Press.

Gaudio, R. (1997) Not talking straight in Hausa. In Livia and Hall (1997): 416–29.

Goffman, E. (1963) *Stigma: Notes on the Management of Spoiled Identity*. Englewood Cliffs, NJ: Prentice-Hall.

Hall, K. (1997) Go suck your husband's sugarcane!: Hijras and the use of sexual insult. In Livia and Hall (1997): 430–60.

Halperin, D. (2000) How to do the history of male homosexuality. *GLQ* 6(1): 87–124. https://doi.org/10.1215/10642684-6-1-87

Harvey, K. (2000) Describing camp talk: Language/pragmatics/politics. *Language and Literature* 9: 240–60. https://doi.org/10.1177/096394700000900303

Hayes, J. (1981) Gayspeak. In J. Chesbro (ed.) *Gayspeak: Gay Male and Lesbian Communication* 45–57. New York: Pilgrim Press.

Herdt, G. (1984) *Ritualized Homosexuality in Melanesia.* Berkeley, CA: University of California Press.

Jagose, A. (1996) *Queer Theory: An Introduction.* New York: New York University Press.

Kulick, D. (2000) Gay and lesbian language. *Annual Review of Anthropology* 29: 243–85. https://doi.org/10.1146/annurev.anthro.29.1.243

Lakoff, R. (1975) *Language and Woman's Place.* New York: Harper & Row.

Lancaster, R. (1992) *Life is Hard: Machismo, Danger, and Intimacy of Power in Nicaragua.* Berkeley, CA: University of California Press.

Leap, W. (1995) Introduction. In W. Leap (ed.) *Beyond the Lavender Lexicon: Authenticity, Imagination, and Appropriation in Lesbian and Gay Languages* vii–xx. Newark, NJ: Gordon & Breach.

Leap, W. (1996) *Word's Out: Gay Men's English.* Minneapolis, MN: University of Minnesota Press.

Leap, W. (1997) Performative effect in three gay English texts. In Livia and Hall (1997): 310–25.

Livia, A. and Hall, K. (eds) (1997) *Queerly Phrased: Language, Gender and Sexuality.* New York: Oxford University Press.

Marcus, E. (1992) *Making History: The Struggle for Gay and Lesbian Equal Rights, 1954–1990.* New York: HarperCollins.

McElhinny, B. (2001) Language, sexuality and political economy. In Campbell-Kibler et al. (2001): 111–34.

McKay, B. (1995) *Gay Phrasebook.* London: Cassell.

Mryglot, G. and Marks, T. (1995) *How to Say Faaabulous! in 8 Different Languages: A Foreign Phrasebook for Gay Men.* New York: The Translator Network.

Murray, S. (1995) *Latin American Male Homosexualities.* Albuquerque, NM: University of New Mexico Press.

Palmer, J. (2002) The role of /s/ duration in the perception of gay-sounding speech. MA thesis, Department of Linguistics, University of North Carolina, Chapel Hill, NC.

Podesva, R. J., Roberts, S. and Campbell-Kibler, K. (2001) Sharing resources and indexing meanings in the production of gay styles. In Campbell-Kibler et al. (2001): 175–90.

Quadagno, D., Sly, D., Harrison, D., Eberstein, I. and Soler, H. (1998) Ethnic differences in sexual decisions and sexual behavior. *Archives of Sexual Behavior* 27(1): 57–75. https://doi.org/10.1023/A:1018657825068

Queen, R. (1997) 'I don't speak spritch!' Locating lesbian language. In Livia and Hall (1997): 233–56.

Queen, R. (2001) A matter of interpretation: the 'future' of 'Queer Linguistics'. In Campbell-Kibler et al. (2001): 69–87.

Rubin, G. (1982) The leather menace. In SAMOIS (eds) *Coming to Power: Writings and Graphics on Lesbian S/M* 194–229. Boston, MA: Alyson Publications.

Sapir, E. (1949) *Culture, Language, and Personality: Selected Essays* (ed. D. Mandelbaum). Berkeley, CA: University of California Press.

Schafer, J. (writer) (1999) *Trick* (dir. J. Fall; prod. E. d'Arbeloff, J. Fall and R. Katz; co-prod. R. Hawk). Beverly Hills, CA: Roadside Attractions (dist. FineLine Features).

Sedgwick, E. (1990) *Epistemology of the Closet.* Berkeley, CA: University of California Press.

Seidman, S. (1993) Identity and politics in a 'postmodern' gay culture: some historical and conceptual notes. In M. Warner (ed.) *Fear of a Queer Planet: Queer Politics and Social Theory* 105–42. Minneapolis, MN: University of Minnesota Press.

Signorile, M. (1997) *Life Outside: The Signorile Report on Gay Men: Sex, Drugs and the Passages of Life.* New York: HarperCollins.

Uchida, A. (1992) When 'difference' is 'dominance': a critique of the 'antipower-based' cultural approach to sex differences. *Language in Society* 21(4): 457–568. https://doi.org/10.1017/S0047404500015724

Valocchi, S. (1999) The class-inflected nature of gay identity. *Social Problems* 46(2): 207–24. https://doi.org/10.2307/3097253

Wong, A. and Zhang, Q. (2000) The linguistic construction of the *Tongzhi* community. *Journal of Linguistic Anthropology* 10(2): 248–78. https://doi.org/10.1525/jlin.2000.10.2.248

Wong, A. (2001) The semantic derogation of *Tongzhi*. In Campbell-Kibler et al. (2001): 161–74.

Woods, J. (1990) The sexual vocabularies of heterosexual and homosexual males and females for communicating erotically with a sexual partner. *Archives of Sexual Research* 19(2): 139–47. https://doi.org/10.1007/BF01542228

3

The desire for identity and the identity of desire: language, gender and sexuality in the Greek context

Costas Canakis
UNIVERSITY OF THE AEGEAN, GREECE

Introduction

The emergence of two main trends, one based on 'identity' and the other on 'desire', in research into language and sexuality may be viewed as the outcome of getting to grips with 'one of the inherent problems of trying to study language', namely 'that it is at once a property of individuals and a property of groups of individuals' (Queen 2007:326).

Advocating sexuality as desire (Kulick 2000, 2003; Cameron 2005; Cameron and Kulick 2003, 2005, 2006) has worked as a catalyst for the field. It has been operative in polarising research between 'desire' and 'identity' as if they were sharply distinguishable, provoking an 'identity backlash' (Bucholtz and Hall 2004, 2005) at a time when identity was already questioned (Brubaker and Cooper 2000; Valentine 2006). Yet recent research (Sauntson and Kyratzis 2007; Morrish and Leap 2007; Canakis 2010, 2013) has shown both concepts to be manifestly relevant to the study of language and sexuality, and intricately implicated in gendered self- and other-representation, given heteronormativity. Moreover, both concepts have been used in intersectional critical approaches to heteronormativity, the mainstay of queer linguistics from its earlier articulations (Livia and Hall 1997) to date (Motschenbacher 2010, 2011; Leap and Motschenbacher 2012; Motschenbacher and Stegu 2013; Coates 2013; Leap 2013), despite differences of opinion on specifics (Leap 2002; Hall 2005, 2013). As language and sexuality research is coming of age, the very concepts are resignified, challenging exclusivist theorising.

The first part of this chapter argues that viable analyses of sexually relevant language cannot afford to disregard either desire or identity, especially as the relation of language, gender and sexuality is rarely presented as polarised between the two in actual language production across genres (e.g. Bucholtz and Hall 2004, 2005; Hall 2005; Canakis 2010; Motschenbacher 2010). Moreover, the critical approach to normative discourses, which has characteristically informed most relevant research, will have to be taken into account, whether one explicitly subscribes to a queer linguistics or not.

The second part focuses on data derived from recently published studies on Modern Greek (Canakis 2010; Daleziou 2011; Kefala 2011), showing the inextricable interplay of sexual desire with aspects of subjectivity in the linguistic production of gendered and sexed subjects projecting a variety of identities, given heteronormativity. These studies, diverse as they are, focus on the indexical relation between language, gender and sexuality (Ochs 1992; Pavlidou 2006b, 2011; Canakis 2010, 2013) as experienced by socially positioned agents whose subjectivity is constructed with reference to their desires and whose desires allude to intelligible (and eroticisable) subjectivities. The claim that any theorising based on an exclusivist platform, inspired by either identity or desire alone, fails to capture crucial aspects of sexually relevant language may not be new (cf. the contributions in Campbell-Kibler, Podesva, Roberts and Wong 2002; Barrett 2003; Morrish and Leap 2007; Leap 2008; Morrish and Sauntson 2007; Motschenbacher 2010; Coates 2013). On the other hand, the 'critical approach to heteronormativity' emphatically advocated by queer linguistics can hardly be dissociated from issues of identity and desire in language, as heteronormativity specifically aims at policing their correlation vis-à-vis gender norms (Coates 2013:536). This chapter aims at focusing on the interconnection of desire and identity through the lens of the 'critical approach to normative discourse' (and the thorny issue of categorisation in queer approaches).[1]

Theorising language and sexuality: identity, desire and queer linguistics

Over the last two decades studies on language and sexuality have begun complementing the far more extensive and established research on language and gender, inviting us to reconsider their relation. Issues of sexual identity became initially associated with political movements and advocacy groups constituting the platform *par excellence* for the study of language and sexuality, as they did for language and gender research (Pavlidou 2006b, 2011; Makri-Tsilipakou 2010). Identity, as a widely circulating concept, was an obvious candidate for an analytic tool. The lay use of identity, often indistinct from – and unfit for – academic uses (Brubaker and Cooper 2000), became associated with enhanced social visibility and recognition and prevailed in the study of sexually relevant language (Kulick 2000), despite charges of essentialism. Moreover, since earlier research focused on the sexuality of non-heterosexuals, language and sexuality became synonymous with gay and lesbian language, and heterosexuality remained unexamined, strengthening its regulatory potential (Cameron and Kulick 2003).

Yet it is possible to distinguish between sexual identity – as commensurate with sexual orientation and the relevant categories – and the notion of identity as subjectivity and/or inter-subjectivity, sense of self, sense of belonging, and so on. Identity has its own intellectual history, although one which often merges with conceptualisations of essence in the Western world, making the two notions hard to distinguish. This is a recurrent point in work scrutinising its usefulness (e.g. Brubaker and Cooper 2000; Kulick 2000; Valentine 2006). Brubaker and Cooper (2000:1) in fact argue that identity is called to do so much work that it ends up being inoperable as an analytical tool, especially as even constructivist uses of identity tend to 'objectify "identity", to treat it as a "thing", albeit a malleable one, that people "have", "forge", and "construct"'(Brubaker and Cooper 2000:28). It is in this intellectual climate that identity came to be considered as artificially limiting the study of language and sexuality to sexual orientation (Kulick 2002; Cameron and Kulick 2003).

Kulick (2000), reviewing the literature on gay and lesbian language, claims that such work, predominantly informed by the concept of identity and aligned with identity politics, does not constitute research on language and sexuality but on sexual orientation. Instead, he urges for engagement with the investigation of 'everything that arguably makes sexuality sexuality – namely, fantasy, desire, repression, fear, and the unconscious' (Kulick 2000:270) – and, viewing sexuality as part of the wider study of desire in language, proposes a psychoanalytic (Lacanian) approach.[2] This point, which is further developed in Kulick (2003) and Cameron and Kulick (2003, 2005), and has caused a heated debate, has developed out of the queer critique of identity (and LBGT identity politics) since the 1990s (cf. Bersani 1995). It is inspired by the perceived conservatism of identity politics in the post-Stonewall era and an alleged reluctance to talk openly about sexual practices at a time when LBGT visibility was significantly enhanced. Moreover, identity was felt to be a more advantageous platform for claiming partnership and/or marriage and adoption rights (cf. Canakis and Chalkidou 2014).

Although Kulick's psychoanalytic approach has not been widely utilised yet, desire has given new momentum to the study of language and sexuality over the last decade (not always excluding identity). At the same time, theorists such as Bucholtz and Hall have expressed serious reservations regarding desire-centred research, claiming that '[s]uch an approach artificially restricts the scope of the field by overlooking the close relationship between identity and desire' (Bucholtz and Hall 2004:469) and suggesting that 'this connection emerges clearly in queer linguistics, an approach to language and sexuality that incorporates insights from feminist, queer, and sociolinguistic theories to analyse sexuality as a broad sociocultural phenomenon' (Bucholtz and Hall 2004:469). Referring to queer theory and linguistics in the context of identity-centred research may come as a surprise, since identity has constituted the historical target of queer theorising (cf. Bersani 1995). However, recent approaches to queer linguistics (Motschenbacher 2010, 2011) are attempting to unify research. In Bucholtz and Hall's (2004) outline of an analytic framework for identity as 'social intersubjectivity', where identity 'is understood as the outcome of intersubjectively negotiated practices and ideologies' (Bucholtz and Hall 2004:469), desire is considered an aspect of identity. This is a manifestly different understanding of identity from that implied in Cameron and Kulick: whereas in their work, identity is largely limited to overt (and essentialised) identity claims, Bucholtz and Hall propose a model of diverse indexical processes not limited to consciously or overtly articulated identity claims. Cameron and Kulick's response acknowledges that the disagreement between them concerns the distinctiveness of desire from identity and psychoanalysis as a perspective (Cameron and Kulick 2005:119). Still, both teams acknowledge identity and desire as aspects of language and sexuality research. Nevertheless, it is clear that Bucholtz and Hall consider desire in the context of the negotiation of identity, whereas Cameron and Kulick treat desire as pivotal to identity formation. These approaches differ in perspective while arguing for the prevalence of one concept over the other rather than for reductive theorising (Canakis in press).

Overall, however, the identity versus desire debate brought desire to the forefront and promoted intersectional studies. At the same time, it became more apparent that the two concepts are often used *metonymically* (to the extent that desires and identities are intelligible): desires may be pivotal in the formation of identities, while identities often become the object of desire (Canakis 2010, 2013). Crucially, studies that have been inspired predominantly by one of these concepts do not necessarily constitute evidence against the other's relevance (even vis-à-vis the very same data). Indeed, recent proposals for the purview of a queer linguistics incorporating studies dealing with both identity and desire in a wider context of approaching heteronormativity testify to this.

Queer theory reached linguistics later than other disciplines, although explorations of a queer linguistics, questioning identity categories and the normative discourses sustaining them (cf. the contributions in Livia and Hall 1997), predated the identity versus desire debate. The 'desire turn' may therefore be seen as a contribution in this direction. It would be, nevertheless, inaccurate to equate desire-centred research with queer linguistics. Over the last few years, proponents of a queer linguistics, describing it as 'critical heteronormativity research from a linguistic point of view' (Motschenbacher and Stegu 2013:522), have attempted to redefine it as arguably encompassing the whole gamut of language and sexuality research. In this sense, studies that engage in challenging the heteronormative status quo and the gender binarism on which it is founded can be described as queer. Queer linguistics dismisses a perceived alignment with LGBT studies (Motschenbacher and Stegu 2013:521), explicitly stating that its goal is to deal with both homosexualities and heterosexualities.[3] This new version of queer linguistics, emerging in the aftermath of the identity versus desire debate, 'does not resemble the queer linguistics of an earlier time, when the focus of research addressed the linguistic practices of sexually marginalised subjects, and then, freed of the constraints of predetermined identities, began to explore linguistic representations of desire' (Leap 2013:643). Instead, it affirms its origins in queer theory by emphasising the critical approach of heteronormativity, which becomes its overall defining characteristic. Research which does not explicitly self-identify as queer, but has taken this course, can be thought of as encompassed in this new queer linguistics. Even granting that this is a matter of onomasiology rather than content, one cannot fail to notice that recent work has attempted a more systematic integration of queer theory into linguistics.

Motschenbacher (2010, 2011) has undertaken to show how poststructuralist, queer linguistics can be applied in sociolinguistic research. To this effect, he addresses three common points of criticism: (i) its alleged limited relevance, (ii) its implication in issues of political agency and (iii) its applicability. The author successfully responds to questions of relevance (dissociating queer linguistics from 'queer' subjects) and applicability (by outlining potential applications in discourse). However, although few would question the political aspect of language, gender and sexuality research, criticisms regarding queer politics remain, crucially, unresolved. It is demonstrably possible to question heteronormativity without sharing a queer political agenda or subscribing to all tenets of queer linguistics. A detailed critique of queer linguistics is beyond the scope of this chapter, but a couple of points should be made, and Hall (2013:640) does that eloquently:

> From a political perspective, I am concerned that queer theory, by maintaining its analytic distinction between practice and identity, ignores the subjectivity of those it was initiated to defend. From a sociocultural linguistic perspective, I am concerned that this distinction leads to a static account of the indexical processes that give rise to social meaning.

Hall's second point relates to (linguistic and social) categorisation at large. This may be fuzzy (rather than Aristotelian; cf. Lakoff 1982, 1987; Taylor 2010) and dynamic (rather than static), but it is *inescapable*; and so are the indexical relations between categories themselves (which Bucholtz and Hall 2004, 2005 have attempted to capture). Motschenbacher's (2010:170ff.) otherwise original discussion of how gendering people relates to linguistic wounding and to potentially (im)polite behaviour misses this point; for gendering has to do with categorisation, which is not a matter of manners as it is not entirely intentional. This problematic view of categorisation is part and parcel of the queer political agenda (cf. Butler 1990) and it is typically inherited in queer linguistics. Therefore, criticisms regarding its politics and applicability are not necessarily separable.

Queer politics emphasises the subversion of 'dominant discourses of sex and gender' (Hall 2005:140–41)[4] by 'resisting' entrenched categories, generally choosing to ignore what we know about the mechanisms of categorisation. Yet these mechanisms are indispensable for understanding the indexical processes informing language, gender and sexuality research (cf. Ochs 1992; Bucholtz and Hall 2004; Canakis 2010). In seeking to critique normative categories, queer linguistics needs to focus on well-documented facts regarding category membership, category networks, prototypical effects, and so on – for categorisation cannot be glibly 'resisted'. On the other hand, we are not at the mercy of preexisting categories: indeed, we can even construct *ad hoc categories* (Barsalou 1983) in order to achieve specific goals (Canakis in press).

Leap considers the subject matter of queer linguistics to be 'one of many ways in which queer linguistics models the fluid and fractured properties of the sociolinguistic experiences that it purports to theorise' (Leap 2013:643). Reservations for this iconicity notwithstanding, the explicit recognition of queer linguistics as a major influence in the editorial for the inaugural issue of the *Journal of Language and Sexuality* (Leap and Motschenbacher 2012) clearly bespeaks a renewed interest (and investment) in it as a theoretical platform.

Identity, desire and the critique of heteronormativity: evidence from Modern Greek

Focusing on data derived from recently published studies on Modern Greek, I attempt to document the inextricable interplay of sexual desire with aspects of subjectivity in the linguistic production of gendered and sexed subjects, while showing that their relation can be fruitfully employed towards a critical approach to the heteronormative order.

Same-sex online personals

The study of online personals by men who seek sexual encounters with other men in the virtual community of practice (Eckert and McConnell-Ginet 1992, 2007) of www.gay.gr, an online dating site for 'gay, lesbian, bi, and trans' people, shows that same-sex desire is a pivotal issue in user profiles. Nevertheless, aspects of identity are routinely reified and eroticised in users' accounts of who they are and what they are looking for in a partner. The focus is on the discourse of men who pursue same-sex encounters and relations over the internet, often describing themselves using terms like *γκέι* [géi] 'gay', *ομοφυλόφιλος* [omofilófilos] 'homosexual', *πούστης* [pústis] 'fag', *αδερφή* [aδerfí] 'sissy', among others.[5]

The data are drawn from the fields 'I am' and 'I want you to be' of profiles posted by males seeking same-sex sexual contacts and relations, out of a total of 200 profiles randomly chosen from within a sub-category occurring by a conjunction of the parameters 'men, homosexual, versatile' (precisely because these parameters turned out most profiles). I chose to focus on these fields because answers do not have predetermined values (as do age, height, weight, education, etc.). Although in written form, these texts exhibit strong elements of orality. On the other hand, as is usually the case with written texts, discourse here is an already finished product and traces of intersubjective negotiation are not as obvious as in *viva voce* talk.

Since I have not communicated with any of the specific users, my only source is their own linguistic production at a given point in time. However, www.gay.gr already constitutes a context: a *virtual community of practice* in which the discourse of any user indirectly answers to the discourse of all other users as well as to dominant discourses at large.

Consider the 'I want you to be' field of the profile in Example 1 below.[6]

Example 1

Adapted fragment from Canakis (2010:148).

Δεν με ενδιαφέρουν οι Bisexuals οι εχέμυθοι και όλοι όσοι δεν μπορούν να αποδεχτούν το γεγονός ότι είναι gay

I do not care for bisexuals, discreet [guys] and all of those who cannot accept the fact that they are gay

In Example 1, the user's object of desire is the very sexual identification with the category GAY, indiscriminately attributed to all males pursuing same-sex practices. The category BISEXUAL is questioned and conceptualised as the negation of the gay version of homoeroticism, which is spatiotemporally conditioned (Weeks 1985) and cannot account for male same-sex experience at large, especially outside Angloamerican and western European contexts (cf. Yannakopoulos 2001; Kahlina 2011; Canakis 2013; Viteri 2014). Thus, the user simultaneously expresses his desire for all the predicates (and semiotic paraphernalia) of the category GAY – not only homoeroticism but also its acceptance as a constitutive element of identity, through the process of *coming out*, which entails enhanced social visibility, becoming a major vehicle of political pressure. This detail nicely explains the repudiation of discreetness, which indexes a traditional model of discreet homosexuality in Greece (Yannakopoulos 2001). Desire, here, is inextricable from a political position and commensurate with inclusion in a group and its political aspirations. This is the kind of discourse often adopted by gay activism, at least until the 1990s, in which bisexuality has often been attacked. It is also a discourse typically targeted by the queer critique on normativity.

The user in Example 1 adopts a *homonormative* stance extrapolating from the heteronormative order. If heteronormativity accords certain versions of heterosexuality the status of norm, homonormativity aims at regulating and valorising certain forms of homosexuality as the norm.[7] Nevertheless, Motschenbacher and Stegu (2013:525) point out that, contrary to ubiquitous heteronormativity, ubiquitous homonormativity 'is invariably a phenomenon that is valid at the local level, namely in contexts where heterosexuality is not the unquestioned norm'. Making normativity (whether hetero- or homo-) the focus of queer critique is understandable. However, the very discussion of homonormativity along with heteronormativity, nowadays, shows the inexorable strength of normative discourses, which typically thrive on social intelligibility – and the current intelligibility of 'gay' cannot be dissociated from homonormative discourses which, in turn, relegate some subjects to a double state of precarity (cf. Butler 2009).

Another point that emerges in same-sex online personals is the frequent eroticisation of masculinity *qua* gender; indeed, a macho masculinity predominantly associated with heterosexual people and heteronormative discourses, as in Example 2.

Example 2

Adapted fragment from Canakis (2010:151).

arrenopos-drastirios-goustaro ta sport kai ton erota! auto pou psaxno einai kapoion pou na goustaro na kikloforo mazi tou xoris na ntrepomai kai na nai magkaki! [...] (thiliprepeis kai gematoi please min mpainete se kopo)

Manly-active; dig sports and love! What I look for is someone to enjoy going out with without shaming myself and who is a dude [too]! [...] (effeminates and full-bodied guys please don't bother)

Homoerotic desire in Example 2 is described primarily in terms of male homosociality. Moreover, the term *μαγκάκι*[8] [magáki] (a diminutive of *μάγκας* 'cool guy, dude, (Br.) lad') situates desire within a traditional, hegemonic and heteronormative masculinity which it claims transgressively, since in that context the desire for another man (in contrast to outdoorsy activities) is hardly articulated without subterfuge. A man's desire for a *μαγκάκι* is a desire for a version of traditional Greek masculinity – for a subjectivity which is eroticised. Indeed, since a *μαγκάκι*, in contrast to an effeminate man, goes virtually unnoticed, a potential relationship with him may save his partner the pains of shame, stigmatisation or persecution; it is considered the safest way out of the state of precarity associated with unintelligible sexualities (Butler 2009). Thus, the transgression which is at the core of homoerotic practices is counterbalanced by an alignment with dominant laddish masculinity along with an open and curt denunciation of effeminacy (cf. Baker 2003; Milani 2013). 'Shame' enhances alignment with heteronormative values and cancels out the search for a μαγκάκι as a factor that 'queers up' this profile. Moreover, the aggressive appropriation of aspects of mainstream hegemonic masculinity, arguably aimed at undermining the time-honoured stereotype of the effeminate homosexual, is instrumental in forging another stereotype: that of the fit macho gay man.

This negotiation of the boundaries of masculinity and homosexuality can be seen as yet another aspect of desire. For desire, sexual or other, is often about categories *qua* categories (Canakis and Chalkidou 2014). It is through identity predicates that the users in Examples 1 and 2 talk of their (strikingly different) desired others. In a few lines, they condense contemporary conceptualisations of male homosexuality in Greece drawing on the interplay of desire, identity and (homo-/hetero-)normativity. Failing to address any of these aspects artificially restricts our analyses.

Doing heterosexuality in conversation

The co-optation of desire and identity in the context of heteronormativity is central in Daleziou's (2011) examination of conversational data from a mixed-sex interaction among friends. The author focuses on how participants in a community of practice (Eckert and McConnell-Ginet 1992), the unit of sociability known as παρέα [paréa] ('party of people'), on an island of the Cyclades, reproduce and maintain or challenge the heteronormative order. Daleziou addresses participant contributions in terms of both gender identity and sexual desire emphasising the discursive construction (Kitzinger 2006; Morrish and Leap 2007) and performance (Butler 1990) of heterosexuality as 'natural' and unremarkable.

Participants feature three women (Flora, Marina, Rita) and five men (Vlasis, Rafos, Markos, Charilaos, Yorgos) all them over 45 years old, except for Rita, the researcher, who is 33. Flora and Marina are sisters, and, like Rita, unmarried. With the exception of Vlasis, who is divorced, all other men are also married. On this occasion they are eating and drinking on Easter Monday (a holiday). This group of people has often sat around a table for coffee, drinks or a meal (occasionally including others), although they could not be described as very close friends. Nevertheless, as the atmosphere is convivial and light-hearted, jokes and banter are the order of the day.[9]

Example 3

Adapted fragment from Daleziou (2011:242–3).

26	Markos:	άντε πάμε μαζί (.) >Οι φακλάνες **let's go together (.) >The fat-assed hags** δε θα σηκώσουνε τον κώλο τους (.) Δεν τις **will not lift their ass (.) Don't you** βλέπεις;<((joking)) **see them?<**
27	Flora:	[<u>βρε ουστ</u>] **<u>[Get out of here]</u>**
28	Marina:	[ρε άει] κατούρα. Δεν κοιτάς **[Go] take a piss. You don't look at** τη σούρα σου ((laughter)) **your besotted drunk face**
29	Yorgos:	τη Φλώρα μόνο να μη μου πάρετε (.) **just don't take Flora away from me (.)**
30	Flora:	[ε]; **[huh?]**
31	Charilaos:	[τι] τηνε θες ρε μαλάκα; **[what] do you want her for you jerk?**
32	Yorgos:	((laughing and coughing)) ( ) τον κώλο **( ) the ass**
33	Vlasis:	τι λέει; (2) Να σου [πιάσει **What is he saying? (2) To [grab your** Τον κώλο]; **ass]?**
34	Flora:	[τι λες μωρέ πάλι;] **[say, what are you blabbering about again?]**
35	Vlasis:	((laughs loudly))
36	Yorgos:	((turns towards where Flora's voice is coming from)) έλα να μου κάτσεις **come sit for me**

```
                    λίγο (2) έλα
                    a little (2) come on

// ((omitted line))

38   Vlasis:        μην τα μάθει αυτά η Μπατζαγκλαρίνα
                    should Batzaglarína find out about this
                    (2) στο χαλάκι θα κοιμηθείς πάλι μαλάκα
                    (2) you will sleep on the doormat again you jerk

39   Flora:         ((laughs)) ε αμέ
                    uhuh that's right

// ((omitted lines))

44   Flora:         [δεν κοιτάς το χάλι σου (2)
                    [why, you don't look at your sorry self(2)
                    θες να] γαμήσεις κιόλας
                    you wanna] fuck too

45   Yorgos:        όχι (.) προς θεού κυρία μου
                    no (.) for God's sake my lady
                    (2) εγώ μόνο το κωλαράκι να σου πιάσω θέλω
                    (2) grab your little ass is all I want
                    ((laughter))

46   Everyone:      ((loud laughter))

47   Flora:         άντε (.) μετά μπορεί να σ' αφήσω
                    go now (.) maybe later I'll let you
                    να μου το πιάσεις (.) άμα είσαι καλό παιδί.
                    grab it (.) if you are a good boy.

48   Yorgos:        μάλιστα κυρία μου ((laughter))
                    yes my lady
```

I will limit my discussion of Example 3 to aspects of this mixed-sex conversation that position some participants as heterosexuals. The reference to Yorgos's wife as Μπατζαγκλαρίνα (turn 38) inadvertently portrays him as a married heterosexual male (cf. Kitzinger 2006), crowning the heteronormative hierarchy (Rubin 1999; Cameron and Kulick 2006; Coates 2013). Moreover, using the feminine form of her husband's nickname – Μπατζάγκλαρος – to refer to her, Vlasis discursively constructs Yorgos as an old-fashioned Greek male. Nevertheless, Yorgos's heterosexuality is also the product of his own, quite intentional contributions, iterating his desire to fondle Flora's ass (turns 29, 32, 36, 45).

Since they have been drinking for several hours (cf. turn 28: 'you don't look at your besotted drunk face') the atmosphere is quite relaxed and defences are down. Yet the heteronormative order is only partly disturbed. Markos (turn 26) uses the risqué epithet φακλάνες 'fat-assed hags', addressing the women with the same ease that Charilaos (turn 31) and Vlasis (turn 38) use the ubiquitous colloquial address form μαλάκα 'jerk-off, wanker' to Yorgos. Moreover, Flora's (turns 27, 44) and Marina's (turn 28) contributions are also not exactly ladylike (cf. Makri-Tsilipakou 2010). This is one of several indexes of the admittedly high solidarity among participants. However, the women's contributions also construct them as gatekeepers when it comes to male advances (even when made in jest), in line with local heteronormative expectations.[10] In turns 27–8, Flora and Marina rebuke Markos's insulting address form (φακλάνες in turn 26): 'get out of here; go take a piss'. Moreover, Flora repeatedly tells Yorgos off (turn 34: 'say, what are you blabbering about again?'; turn 39: 'uhuh, that's right') and in turn 44 does so curtly: 'why, you don't look at your sorry self, you wanna fuck too' (as Daleziou notes, probably tired of being the centre of attention). In fact, Flora's indirect reference to Yorgos's serious eyesight problem (cf. χάλι 'plight' in turn 44) and her condescending promise to let him have his way if he is 'a good boy' (turn 47) brings his masculinity in question in the same way that Vlasis's (turn 38) reference to a wife to be reckoned with is a textbook attempt to compromise it – especially in the presence of women and while Yorgos engages in sexual banter towards Flora. Yorgos's own sheepish response (turn 48) to Flora ('Yes my lady') momentarily affirms this state of affairs.

Drawing on Coates (2003), Kiesling (2006), and Archakis and Lampropoulou (2011), Daleziou (2011:250–51) argues that Yorgos's masculinity is doubly hurt when Flora agrees (turn 39) with Vlasis's comment (turn 38): 'should Batzaglarina find out about this you will sleep on the doormat again you jerk'. Vlasis seizes the opportunity to construct his own hegemonic version of masculinity at Yorgos's expense (reinforcing the impression of Yorgos's wounded manhood brought up by Charilaos's earlier reference to him as *gavós* 'blind-as-a-bat'). Hegemonic masculinity is constructed by antagonistic dominance of a man over a woman (Makri-Tsilipakou 2006:102, 115–16) as much as through dominance over another man (Kiesling 2006:130), even in the context of light-hearted fun.

All of the above testify to the discursive construction (as opposed to prediscursive assumptions; cf. Morrish and Leap 2007:36) and performance of gendered and sexed subjectivities and to the untenable separation of sexuality from gender (Coates 2013:538) or of practice from identity (Hall 2013:634), *pace* queer theoretic tenets. Indeed, as Hall cautions, '[t]he indexical processes that work to produce social meaning are multi-layered and always shifting across time and space, even within systems of heteronormativity. It is this semiotic evolution that should become the cornerstone of a (new) queer linguistics' (Hall 2013:634). In this excerpt, participants coconstruct identity and desire through conversational practice. The gender and sexual categories ascribed to them are pivotal in the complex network of indexical relations selectively mentioned above as well as in 'queering' them (cf. Coates 2013). They relate to a specific community of practice and to presuppositions holding therein. As Coates mentions:

> speakers in everyday conversation do a great deal of discursive work to position themselves in heteronormative space. Heteronormativity constrains our agency by asserting the naturalness of heterosexuality, and by concealing the cultural work that has to be done to maintain it. (Coates 2013:550)

The cultural work done in Example 3 features both a struggle for the maintenance of the heteronormative order and a number of subversions – notably, the freedom (indeed, permissiveness) all participants allow themselves in this mixed-sex conversation. These unladylike women and ungentlemanly men play the heterosexual game, but in a refreshingly 'disturbed' manner directly linked to the local norms of a *paréa*.

Coming out narratives

If heterosexuality is naturalised and thereby constructed as an unmarked, invisible category (Kitzinger 2006:187; Coates 2013:187), the opposite is true of homosexuality, often associated with *coming out* (Butler 1990; Cameron and Kulick 2003; Canakis 2010) as a ritualised declaration of identity. Kefala's (2011:272) 'second-hand narratives' of original coming-out declarations are based on a rich corpus of coming out stories of Greek women and men collected through semi-structured interviews. I will argue that desire is pivotal in this emblematic narrative of self-identification (and identification with a social group), albeit not in itself sufficient for such identification.

Kefala (2011), drawing on Chirrey (2003:27), notes that orientation to same-sex desire is a psychological process which constructs lesbianism/gayness as an aspect of one's sense of self. Coming out, as the potential outcome of this process, is a declarative speech act, not simply describing but constituting – *performing* – the non-heterosexual self (cf. Austin 1962; Butler 1990). In Example 4, Irene talks of the *fear of inevitability* (turns 2, 3, 7, 14) and discursively constructs same-sex orientation as the basis of her identity: something she had to *accept* (turn 3) against various odds.

Example 4

Adapted fragment from Kefala (2011:274–5).[11]

Irene, 35 years old

```
1    Κοίταξε, στο λύκειο, στην πρώτη, Δευτέρα
     λυκείου με ρωτούσανε φίλοι οι
2    οποίοι ήταν ομοφυλόφιλοι, ξέρω 'γω «παίζει
     κάτι;» αλλά εγώ φοβόμουνα
3    // φοβόμουνα να το παραδεχτώ.

// ((omitted lines))

6    το αρνιόμουνα, απλά δεν μπορούσα να το
     παραδεχτώ ρε παιδί μου, δεν
```

7 μπορούσα να εκδηλώσω αυτό που ένιωθα (.)
για μια γυναίκα. Φοβόμουν,
8 ντρεπόμουνα και όλα αυτά. Και ήρθε κάποια
στιγμή//

// ((omitted lines))

11 [...]και εκεί γνώρισα
12 ένα άτομο τελοσπάντων, ε και υπήρχε αυτό
το καταλαβαίνω ότι κάτι, ξέρεις,
13 υπάρχει αλλά δεν εκδηλώνεται ούτε από
μένα ούτε από σένα. Ε και κάποια
14 στιγμή έγινε το μοιραίο. Και ήμασταν μ'
αυτό το άτομο 4 χρόνια
15 περίπου μαζί [...] αυτή η σχέση από τη
μία με απελευθέρωσε, μου 'βγαλε
16 πράγματα, από την άλλη μου δημιούργησε
πρόβλημα γιατί το άλλο άτομο
17 δεν αποδεχόταν αυτό που συνέβαινε. Ναι
μεν ήμασταν μαζί, παράλληλα
18 έκανε σχέσεις και με άτομα του άλλου φύλου.

1 Look, in senior high, at first, second
grade, friends who were gay
2 asked me, you know 'is something going
on?' but I was afraid
3 // afraid to admit it.

// ((omitted lines))

6 I denied it, I just couldn't admit it,
you know, couldn't
7 express what I felt (.) for a woman.
I was afraid,
8 ashamed and all that. And there came a
moment //

// ((omitted lines))

11 [...]and there I met
12 a person anyway, eh and there was this
I understand that something, you know,
13 is there but is not expressed neither from
me nor from you. And so at some point
14 the inevitable happened. And we were
almost 4 years together
15 with this person [...] this relationship
on the one hand liberated me,

16 brought things out of me, one the other
it created a problem because the other person
17 didn't accept what was happening. While
we were together, at the same time
18 [she] had relationships with persons of the opposite sex.

In narrating her coming out experience, Irene recalls *fear* (turns 2, 3,7), *denial* (turn 6) and *shame* (turn 8) springing from an *awareness* of her desire (turns 7, 12, 13), the *inevitability* of this desire (turn 14), which led to a *relationship* (turns 14, 15) with *liberating effect* (turn 15) and offered her renewed *awareness* (turn 16) – despite *problems* due to *lack of acceptance* of the other 'person' (turn 17) who was *not exclusively* homosexual (turn 18). Her desire for another woman (habitually referred to as 'person') is discursively constructed as an element informing her sexual orientation and identity, despite the deafening absence of the term λεσβία [lesvía] 'lesbian' in the fragment, which should come as no surprise, as it is often avoided given its special weight and wounding potential (Kantsa 2011).

Although Irene suspected her same-sex desire, she had to confirm it through a relationship first (Kefala 2011:275). Therefore, her sexual identity crucially develops out of sexual desire and practice, a state of affairs which her narrative shares with others.[12] Her open references to desire are meant to *index* lesbian identity (which she does not contest), despite the absence of the term. Again we see that desire and identity are in a metonymic relation. Whereas in Example 1 the gay man talks in terms of identity in the context of sexual desire, here Irene does the reverse: by mentioning desires and practices she intelligibly indexes a lesbian identity (cf. Ochs 1992).

Intelligibility is crucial in coming out narratives and an apple of contention in queer critique (cf. Motschenbacher and Stegu 2013; Hall 2013). On the one hand, coming out goes *de facto* against the heteronormative order; it 'queers up' the world, enhancing the visibility and intelligibility of the stigmatised. On the other hand, it may be seen as insidiously supporting and reproducing heteronormativity, in that, by disclosing one's sexuality as noteworthy, one sustains the perceived normalcy of heterosexuality and affirms the *heterosexual matrix* (Butler 1990), while arguably contributing to one's own *precarity* (Butler 2009). The enhanced visibility and intelligibility of homosexuality has been instrumental in homonormativity, which casts some homosexual people to a double state of precarity.

Irene's emphasis on a 'relationship' is likely to be perceived as homonormative. However, normativity is closely related with enhanced intelligibility and, by making it the target of its critique, queer linguistics, like queer theory, may risk ignoring 'the subjectivity of those it was initiated to defend' (Hall 2013:640). If homonormativity is indeed 'a phenomenon that is valid at the local level, namely in contexts where heterosexuality is not the unquestioned norm' (Motschenbacher and Stegu 2013:525), then this is, arguably, because the LBGT movement fought for different norms. Yet, norms, being regulatory, end up being invariably oppressive for some of us. By the same token, the norms governing gendered and sexual categorisation, which queer linguistics seeks to resist and eventually subvert (Motschenbacher 2010, 2011), will infallibly result to yet another set of norms in the future. This is why queer linguistics needs to engage thoroughly with the *principles of categorisation* and not only with resisting the by-products of this process (categories) (Canakis in press). Such an engagement should become the pivotal point of divergence between queer theory and queer linguistics – a point which goes hand in hand with their different understanding of 'localized communities of practice' (Hall 2005:140). After all, the very evolutionary history of *queer* (and QUEER) is telling.

Conclusions

In supporting that identity, desire, and gender and sexual norms are hardly separable aspects of the discursive construction of sexuality, I have drawn on three recent Greek studies focusing on the indexical relation between language, gender and sexuality as experienced by socially positioned agents whose subjectivity is constructed with reference to their desires and whose desires allude to intelligible and eroticisable subjectivities. I have documented the inextricable interplay of sexual desire with aspects of subjectivity in discourse produced in a variety of contexts, while showing that their quasi metonymic relation is crucially involved in critical approaches of the heteronormative order.

Gender and sexuality cannot be disentangled (Coates 2013:538), and this closeness is a prerequisite for the maintenance of the heteronormative order (Coates 2013:536) targeted by queer linguistics. On this basis, critical approaches to heteronormativity can hardly be dissociated from issues of identity and desire in language, as heteronormativity specifically aims at policing their correlation vis-à-vis gender norms. In this light, I have argued for the emergence of new (and 'disturbed') normativities as resulting from the enhanced visibility and intelligibility of alternative alignments of gender and sexuality (which allows for new stereotypes and forms of stigmatisation).

In the aftermath of the identity versus desire debate which dominated language and sexuality research and the advent of a queer linguistics eager to encompass both, I have focused on non-exclusivist research that has utilised all three concepts in approaching sexual discourse, expressing reservations towards queer treatments of categorisation and the shifting indexical processes producing social meaning (Hall 2013).

Notes

1 I am grateful for this comment to one of the anonymous reviewers.

2 This is echoed in Eckert's (2002:104) suggestion that the study of desire is perhaps located within a broader study of affect.

3 The special issue of *Discourse and Society* on Queer Linguistic Approaches to Discourse (June 2013) is an attempt to show the purview of this new queer linguistics, including reinterpretations of research that deals with issues of identity (e.g. Coates 2013) in a queer linguistic framework.

4 Indeed, Hall (2005:141) mentions that 'Hijras have become particularly vulnerable to this kind of theorising, as scholars from varied poststructuralist traditions have focused on the disruptive nature of hijra identity.'

5 It should be noted that γκέι [géi] ≠ *gay*; the former is a non-native term in Greek and is distinguished from the latter not only by its phonetic shape (typically two syllables and thus no gliding, as for μπάι [bái] 'bi'), but also in its semantic content and potential, which is to be understood in contra-distinction to a time-honoured form of discreet homosexuality (cf. Yannakopoulos 2001). Plenty of terms are used for other-representation of men-desiring men; these cover the range from the *comme-il-faut* terms τοιούτος [tiútos] 'such' and απ' τους άλλους [ap' tus álus] lit. 'one of the others', to the older πισωλούρης [pisolúris] 'back-belt', the 2000s coinage πισωγλέντης [pisoγléndis] 'who-has-fun-from-behind', and plenty of others. Apostolidou (2010:44) mentions 'an interactive Greek slang dictionary [inventorising] 400 finds that relate to the male homosexual, varying from disgusting and highly phobic metaphors to hilarious, sarcastic, and even endearing synonyms'.

6 All examples appear on an as-is basis, keeping original orthography. There are missing characters, misspellings and all manner of idiosyncratic uses of writing conventions and combinations of the Greek and Latin alphabets.

7 I am consciously using *homonormative* as defined here. There is, however, another established usage of *homonormative* within queer theory which describes the practices of gay men and lesbians who act like heterosexuals, thereby reaping the benefits of heteronormativity. Motschenbacher and Stegu (2013:524) discuss these uses and (independently) propose a broadening of *homonormativity* so as to capture the fact that 'non-heteronormative contexts may show their own internal normativities'. Hall (2013:636) crucially notes that this 'need to redefine the concept of homonormativity' is 'the first hint of tension between queer theory and queer linguistics'.

8 Note that the diminutive form does not bear disparaging connotations in this context.

9 For reasons of space, I will only use fragments of her extensive transcribed data (adhering to the conventions and line numbering of the original). The following transcription conventions are used. **((xxx))**: metalinguistic comments and notes. **(.)**: pause of less than 1 second. **(1)**, **(2)**, **(3)**: timed pauses. **[xxx]**: overlap. **>xxx<**: faster speech. **xxx**: emphasis. **(   )**: unclear talk.

10 Cf. Kiesling (2013) on flirting vis-à-vis normative sexualities in this connection.

11 In this adapted fragment, I adhere to the conventions and line numbering of the original. **xxx//xxx**: interruption. **[...]**: omitted talk. **(.)**: pause of less than 1 second.

12 Thorne (2013) shows that the sexuality of women in a bisexual support group is questioned because they have not yet 'acted' on it. The identity and the desire are there but the *practice* is missing.

References

Apostolidou, A. (2010) Inscribing gendered and national anxieties on insulting language: linguistic depictions of Greek male homosexuality. In Canakis et al. (2010): 41–61.

Archakis, A. and Lampropoulou, S. (2011) Σεξουαλικότητα, αρσενικότητες και η αφηγηματική κατασκευή ταυτοτήτων. [Sexuality, masculinities, and the narrative construction of identities.] In Canakis (2011): 183–201.

Austin, J. L. (1962) *How to Do Things with Words*. Cambridge, MA: Harvard University Press.

Baker, P. (2003) No effeminates please: a corpus-based analysis of masculinity via personal adverts in *Gay News/Times* 1973–2000. In B. Benwell (ed.) *Masculinity and Men's Lifestyle Magazines* 243–60. Oxford: Blackwell.

Barrett, R. (2003) Models of gay male identity and the marketing of 'gay language' in foreign-phrasebooks for gay men. *Sociolinguistic Studies* 4: 533–652. https://doi.org/10.1558/sols.v4i2.533

Barsalou, L. (1983) Ad hoc categories. *Memory and Cognition* 11: 211–27. https://doi.org/10.3758/BF03196968

Bersani, L. (1995) *Homos*. Cambridge, MA: Harvard University Press.

Brubaker, R. and Cooper, F. (2000) Beyond 'identity'. *Theory and Society* 29: 1–47. https://doi.org/10.1023/A:1007068714468

Bucholtz, M. and Hall, K. (2004) Theorizing identity in language-and-sexuality research. *Language in Society* 33: 469–515. https://doi.org/10.1017/S0047404504334020

Bucholtz, M. and Hall, K. (2005) Identity and interaction: a sociocultural linguistic approach. *Discourse Studies* 7: 585–614. https://doi.org/10.1177/1461445605054407

Butler, J. (1990) *Gender Trouble: Feminism and the Subversion of Identity*. New York: Routledge.

Butler, J. (2009) Performativity, precarity and sexual politics. *Revista de Antropología Iberoamericana* 4: i–xiii.

Cameron, D. (2005) Language, gender, and sexuality: current issues and new directions. *Applied Linguistics* 26: 482–502.

Cameron, D. and Kulick, D. (2003) *Language and Sexuality*. Cambridge: Cambridge University Press.

Cameron, D. and Kulick, D. (2005) Identity crisis? *Language and Communication* 25: 107–25. https://doi.org/10.1093/applin/ami027

Cameron, D. and Kulick, D. (eds) (2006) *The Language and Sexuality Reader*. Abingdon: Routledge.

Campbell-Kibler, K., Podesva, R. J., Roberts, S. J. and Wong, A. (eds) (2002) *Language and Sexuality: Contesting Meaning in Theory and Practice*. Stanford, CA: CSLI.

Canakis, C. (2010) Eroticizing male homo-subjectivities in online personals. In Canakis et al. (2010): 143–70.

Canakis, C. (ed.) (2011) Γλώσσα και Σεξουαλικότητα: Γλωσσολογικές και Ανθρωπολογικές Προσεγγίσεις [*Language and Sexuality: Linguistic and Anthropological Perspectives*]. Athens: Eikostos Protos.

Canakis, C. (2013) The 'national body': language and sexuality in the Balkan national narrative. In F. Tsibiridou and N. Palantzas (eds) *Myths of the Other in the Balkans: Representations, Social Practices, Performances* 305–20. Thessaloniki: University of Macedonia.

Canakis, C. (in press) Categorization and indexicality in language and sexuality research. In Kira Hall and Rusty Barrett (eds) *The Oxford Handbook of Language and Sexuality*. Oxford: Oxford University Press.

Canakis, C. and Chalkidou, A. (2014) Discourses of same-sex parenthood in Greece: 'doing being ordinary' in extraordinary circumstances. Paper presented at *Kinship and Medical Technology: Assisted Reproduction in Greece*, Mytilene, 30–31 May.

Canakis, C., Kantsa, V. and Yannakopoulos, K. (eds) (2010a) *Language and Sexuality: (Through) and Beyond Gender*. Newcastle upon Tyne: Cambridge Scholars Publishing.

Chirrey, D. A. (2003). 'I hereby come out': what sort of speech act is coming out? *Journal of Sociolinguistics* 7: 24–37.

Coates, J. (2003) *Men Talk: Stories in the Making of Masculinities*. Malden, MA: Blackwell.

Coates, J. (2013) The discursive production of everyday heterosexualities. *Discourse and Society* 24: 536–52. https://doi.org/10.1177/0957926513486070

Daleziou, M. (2011) Η αναπαραγωγή του κανονιστικού ετεροσεξουαλικού κόσμου στην καθημερινή γλωσσική παραγωγή. [The reproduction of the normative heterosexual world in everyday linguistic production.] In Canakis (2011): 231–61.

Eckert, P. (2002) Demystifying sexuality and desire. In Campbell-Kibler et al. (2002): 99–110.

Eckert, P. and McConnell-Ginet, S. (1992) Think practically and look locally: language and gender as community-based practice. *Annual Review of Anthropology* 21: 461–90. https://doi.org/10.1146/annurev.an.21.100192.002333

Eckert, P. and McConnell-Ginet, S. (2007) Putting communities of practice in their place. *Gender and Language* 1: 27–37. https://doi.org/10.1558/genl.2007.1.1.27

Hall, K. (2005) Intertextual sexuality: parodies of class, identity, and desire in liminal Delhi. *Journal of Linguistic Anthropology* 15(1): 125–44. https://doi.org/10.1525/jlin.2005.15.1.125

Hall, K. (2013) Commentary I: 'It's a hijra!' Queer linguistics revisited. *Discourse and Society* 24: 634–42. https://doi.org/10.1177/0957926513490321

Kahlina, K. (2011) Nation, state and queers: ethnosexual identities in the interface between social and personal in contemporary Croatia. In A. G. Jónasdóttir, V. Bryson and K. B. Jones (eds) *Sexuality, Gender and Power: Intersectional and Transnational Perspectives* 30–44. New York: Routledge.

Kantsa, V. (2011) Λεσβία: η αβάσταχτη βαρύτητα μιας λέξης. [*Lesvía*: the unbearable gravity of a word.] In Canakis (2011): 111–34.

Kefala, M. (2011) *Φτου και βγαίνω!* Coming out και η γλωσσική επιτέλεση της σεξουαλικότητας. [*Ftu kai vgaino!* Coming out and the linguistic performance of sexuality.] In Canakis (2011): 265–303.

Kiesling, S. F. (2006) Playing the straight man. In Cameron and Kulick (2006): 118–31.

Kiesling, S. F. (2013) Flirting and 'normative' sexualities. *Journal of Language and Sexuality* 2: 101–21. https://doi.org/10.1075/jls.2.1.04kie

Kitzinger, C. (2006) Speaking as a heterosexual. In Cameron and Kulick (2006): 169–88.

Kulick, D. (2000) Gay and lesbian language. *Annual Review of Anthropology* 29: 243–85. https://doi.org/10.1146/annurev.anthro.29.1.243

Kulick, D. (2003) Language and desire. In J. Holmes and M. Meyerhoff (eds) *The Handbook of Language and Gender* 119–41. Oxford: Blackwell.

Lakoff, G. (1982) On categories: an essay in cognitive linguistics. In Linguistic Society of Korea (ed.) *Linguistics in the Morning Calm* 139–93. Seoul: Hanshin.

Lakoff, G. (1987) *Women, Fire, and Dangerous Things: What Categories Reveal about the Mind.* Chicago, IL: University of Chicago Press.

Leap, W. L. (2002) Not entirely in support of a queer linguistics. In Campbell-Kibler et al. (2002): 45–63.

Leap, W. L. (2008) Queering gay men's English. In K. Harrington, L. Litosseliti, H. Sauntson, and J. Sunderland (eds) *Gender and Language Research Methodologies* 283–96. Basingstoke: Palgrave Macmillan.

Leap, W. L. (2013) Commentary II: Queering language and normativity. *Discourse and Society* 24: 643–8. https://doi.org/10.1177/0957926513490320

Leap, W. L. and Motschenbacher, H. (2012) Launching a new phase in language and sexuality studies. *Journal of Language and Sexuality* 1: 1–14. https://doi.org/10.1075/jls.1.1.01lea

Livia, A. and Hall, K. (1997) 'It's a girl!' Bringing performativity back to linguistics. In A. Livia and K. Hall (eds) *Queerly Phrased: Language, Gender, and Sexuality* 21–34. Oxford: Oxford University Press.

Makri-Tsilipakou (2006). Συμφωνία/διαφωνία: αλληλεγγύη και αντιπαλότητα στις συνομιλίες γυναικών και ανδρών. [Agreement/ disagreement: solidarity and adversariness in conversations of men and women.] In Pavlidou (2006a): 81–117.

Makri-Tsilipakou, M. (2010) Η 'γυναικεία γλώσσα' και η γλώσσα των γυναικών. ['Women's language' and the language of women.] In V. Kantsa, V. Moutafi and E. Papataxiarchis (eds) Φύλο και Κοινωνικές Επιστήμες στη Σύγχρονη Ελλάδα [*Gender and the Social Sciences in Contemporary Greece*] 119–46. Athens: Alexandria.

Milani, T. (2013) Are 'queers' really 'queer'? Language, identity and same-sex desire in a South African online community. *Discourse and Society* 24: 615–33. https://doi.org/10.1177/0957926513486168

Morrish, L. and Leap, W. (2007) Sex talk: language, desire, identity, and beyond. In Sauntson and S. Kyratzis (2007a): 17–40. https://doi.org/10.1057/9780230625136_2

Morrish, L. and Sauntson, H. (2007) *New Perspectives on Language and Sexual Identity.* Basingstoke: Palgrave Macmillan.

Motschenbacher, H. (2010) *Language, Gender and Sexual Identity: Poststructuralist Perspectives.* Amsterdam: John Benjamins.

Motschenbacher, H. (2011) Taking Queer Linguistics further: sociolinguistics and critical heteronormativity research. *International Journal of the Sociology of Language* 212: 149–79. https://doi.org/10.1515/ijsl.2011.050

Motschenbacher, H. and Stegu, M. (2013) Queer linguistic approaches to discourse. *Discourse and Society* 24: 519–35. https://doi.org/10.1177/0957926513486069

Ochs, E. (1992) Indexing gender. In A. Duranti and C. Goodwin (eds) *Rethinking Context: Language as an Interactive Phenomenon* 335–58. Cambridge: Cambridge University Press.

Pavlidou, T.-S. (ed.) (2006a) Γλώσσα – Γένος - Φύλο [*Language - Grammatical Gender - Social Gender*], 2nd edition. Thessaloniki: Institute of Modern Greek Studies.

Pavlidou, T.-S. (2006b) Γλώσσα – γένος – φύλο: προβλήματα, αναζητήσεις και ελληνική γλώσσα. [Language – grammatical gender – social gender: problems, inquiries and the Greek language.] In Pavlidou (2006a): 15–64.

Pavlidou, T.-S. (2011) Gender and interaction. In R. Wodak, B. Johnstone and P. Kerswill (eds) *The Sage Handbook of Sociolinguistics* 412–27. London: Sage.

Queen, R. (2007) Sociolinguistic horizons: language and sexuality. *Language and Linguistics Compass* 1: 314–30. https://doi.org/10.1111/j.1749-818X.2007.00019.x

Rubin, G. (1999) Thinking sex: notes for a radical theory of the politics of sexuality. In R. Parker and P. Aggleton (eds) *Culture, Society, and Sexuality: A Reader* 143–78. London: University College London Press.

Sauntson, H. and Kyratzis, S. (eds) (2007a) *Language, Sexualities, and Desires: Cross-Cultural Perspectives*. Basingstoke: Palgrave Macmillan.

Sauntson, H. and Kyratzis, S. (2007b) Introduction: language, sexualities, and desires. In Sauntson and S. Kyratzis (2007a): 1–16.

Taylor, J. R. (2010). *Linguistic Categorization.* Oxford: Oxford University Press.

Thorne, L. (2013) 'But I'm attracted to women': sexuality and sexual identity performance in interactional discourse among bisexual students. *Journal of Language and Sexuality* 2: 70–100. https://doi.org/10.1075/jls.2.1.03tho

Valentine, D. (2006) 'I went to bed with my own kind once': the erasure of desire in the name of identity. In Cameron and Kulick (2006): 245–57.

Viteri, M. A. (2014) Citizenship(s), belonging and xenophobia: Ecuador and NYC. *Journal of Language and Sexuality* 3(1): 121–35.

Weeks, J. (1985) *Sexuality and Its Discontents: Meanings, Myths and Modern Sexualities*. London: Routledge.

Yannakopoulos, K. (2001) Ανδρική ταυτότητα, σώμα και ομόφυλες σχέσεις: μια προσέγγιση του φύλου και της σεξουαλικότητας. [Male identity, body and same sex relations: an approach of gender and sexuality.] In S. Dimitriou (ed.) Η Ανθρωπολογία των Φύλων [*The Anthropology of Genders*] 162–87. Athens: Savalas.

4

Incomprehensible language? Language, ethnicity and heterosexual masculinity in a Swedish school

Tommaso M. Milani

UNIVERSITY OF GOTHENBURG, SWEDEN;
UNIVERSITY OF THE WITWATERSRAND, JOHANNESBURG

Rickard Jonsson

STOCKHOLM UNIVERSITY, SWEDEN

Introduction

'Few things are as disabling as a poor language with bad accent or incorrect pronunciation.' That is how an announcer introduced a television debate under the title *Kanon TV - språk i förfall?* (*Canon TV - Language in Decay?*) – a programme which was broadcast on a Swedish private channel on 5 May 2006. In his preamble, the speaker went on to claim that:

> the Swedish language is undergoing a process of change. Swedish youth speak and write in bad Swedish, regardless of whether they are immigrants or native Swedes. A new variety of Swedish is emerging among young people in the suburbs of large urban areas, a language that is hardly comprehensible for those who speak usual Swedish. In the media, the so-called 'Million Swedish' is celebrated as something which must be acknowledged and respected. At the same time, literacy problems have increased among young people. What happens when our language, as we know it, dies? What happens to Swedes, the old and the new ones?[1]

At first glance, the introductory lines of this commentary may suggest that we are witnessing another instance of a generational anxiety expressed by adult media practitioners about youth language, preoccupations which are not dissimilar to those documented by Thurlow (2007) with regard to the so-called 'teenspeak' in the United States. In the extract above, however, the generational aspect is complicated further by the representation of an ethnic division among the adolescents in question – 'immigrants' versus 'native Swedes'. What should also be emphasised is that the 'new variety of Swedish' allegedly spoken by young people in the suburbs is measured against the benchmark of 'usual Swedish'. Therefore, it is described as 'hardly comprehensible' and therefore as potentially impacting on young people's literacy skills.

Most importantly, this example is not an isolated instance of pronouncements about standard Swedish being encroached on, or even endangered, by new linguistic varieties. But, as a growing body of sociolinguistic literature has shown, such pronouncements have been a common trope in the Swedish media landscape during the last two decades (see Jonsson and Milani 2009; Milani 2010; Stroud 2004). In particular, Stroud (2004) has convincingly illustrated how a linguistic variety – *rinkebysvenska* (lit. Rinkeby Swedish) – that is perceived as 'deviant' from 'Swedish norms' has over time become associated with ethnic Otherness and social problems. As Stroud (2004) explains, the signification of *rinkebysvenska* is neither random nor innocuous. Rather, it is the manifestation of discursive processes that take place in a moment of uncertainty when the ethnic composition of the Swedish population is shifting as a result of transnational migration flows. These are processes through which the Swedish *Self* seeks to re-assert its position of authority by devaluing the linguistic practices of the *ethnic Other*. More recently, however, there have been public attempts to redefine the name, meaning and value of the linguistic phenomenon previously labelled as *rinkebysvenska*. For example, in a print-mediated debate orchestrated by the Swedish newspaper *Dagens Nyheter* in 2006, the labels *blattesvenska*[2] (lit. immigrant Swedish) and *miljonsvenska*[3] (lit. million Swedish) were used and pitted against each other.

In a similar vein, we have analysed elsewhere (Jonsson and Milani 2009; Milani 2010) a recent media debate (April–May 2006) in which different social actors have engaged in a struggle for redefining the name, meaning and value of the linguistic practices previously labelled as *rinkebysvenska*. We have shown how the dispute about the names *blattesvenska* (lit. immigrant Swedish) versus *miljonsvenska* (lit. Million Swedish) is not a terminological triviality but ultimately reflects a deeper opposition between very different cultural images of the speakers to whom this linguistic phenomenon is said to refer. Analogous to the arguments in the extract above and the pronouncements investigated by Stroud (2004), this debate dealt with what was perceived as the incomprehensibility of the speech of the youth in the suburbs, together with its negative impact on their career success. Yet, one of the novelties of this debate lies in its overt *gendered* component. Put briefly, *miljonsvenska* is described by its proponents in positive terms as an example of linguistic creativity resulting from the interaction between young people, irrespective of their ethnicity and gender. This view, however, is opposed by those who, employing the label *blattesvenska*, portray it as a sexist and homophobic 'multiethnic lads' slang' (Witt-Brattström 2006). One of the points that we have raised in our analysis is that the claims about sexism and homophobia are not substantiated by examples of actual linguistic practices, but rest on a 'presupposed common representation' (Chilton 2004:181) of 'multiethnic' young males as *inherently* sexist and homophobic bigots. Moreover, we have argued that this 'double discourse' (Cameron 2003:448), which simultaneously defines linguistic *as well as* gender deviance, has subtle nationalistic undertones in the sense that standard Swedish and Swedish men are implicitly represented as less sexist, less homophobic, more gender equal, and ultimately more 'normal' than the linguistic and ethnic Other (cf. de los Reyes and Mulinari 2005).

Overall, these studies illustrate that, whether targeting *rinkebysvenska*, *blattesvenska* or *miljonsvenska*, metalinguistic pronouncements enabled by the Swedish media constitute a discursive terrain where complex negotiations of identities are played out. Viewed from a diachronic perspective, the intertextual and interdiscursive connections of these debates also testify to a process of sedimentation – naturalisation even – whereby linguistic practices among adolescents in the suburbs seem to have become *icons* (Irvine and Gal 2000), meaning essentialised traits, of ethnic Otherness, social and educational problems and, more recently, of an aggressive masculinity embodied in sexist and homophobic behaviour.

In the light of this contextual background, the aim of this chapter is to take a queer perspective (Cameron and Kulick 2003:149) that seeks to *denaturalise* those media discourses that promote images of certain linguistic practices as normal and intelligible while devaluing others as deviant and incomprehensible. By queer we mean a sceptical stance that problematises 'normative consolidations of sex, gender and sexuality – and that, consequently, is critical of all those versions of identity, community and politics that are believed to evolve "naturally" from such consolidations' (Jagose 1996:99). To this, we would add that queer can be expanded beyond the remit of gender and sexuality so as to encompass 'the ways that race, ethnicity, postcolonial nationality criss-cross with these [i.e. gender and sexuality] *and other* identity-constituting, identity-fracturing discourses' (Sedgwick 1993:9, original emphasis). These observations resonate well with Cameron and Kulick's standpoint that, notwithstanding the 'special relationship between sexuality and gender, it is also important to consider the ways in which sexuality ... will also be inflected by other kinds of socially salient differences, for instance those of race, ethnicity, generation, class and culture' (Cameron and Kulick 2003:144; for a similar standpoint, see also Johnson 1997; McElhinny 2003). To put it another way, we do not dispute that gender and sexuality have been 'casually entangled in knots that must be undone' (Butler 1998:225–6), but we also believe that such a deconstructionist enterprise would always be curtailed if it did not address how the boundaries between what counts as 'normal' versus 'deviant' are upheld through the complex intersections between gender, sexuality and other axes of social categorisation.

To this end, we investigate the ways in which a group of those 'multi-ethnic young lads' whose linguistic practices have been singled out as incomprehensible, sexist and homophobic in the Swedish media actually use language in a school in a suburb of Stockholm. Essentially, the argument is that the linguistic repertoire of the participants in our study indeed encompasses, though is not reducible to, ethnic, sexist and homophobic insults and jokes. However, such language use is by no means incomprehensible, but conveys specific social meanings and serves particular interactional purposes. Before delving into a detailed analysis of a few excerpts from these young men's talk, however, we offer some ethnographic insights into the educational environment in which these interactions have taken place.

School in context: Swedish school policy, the local setting and the peer group

The data used below come from an ethnographic study of a group of male pupils in a 'compulsory school' (*grundskola*)[4] located on the outskirts of Stockholm. The data were gathered by Rickard Jonsson (hereafter RJ) through participant observation – in classrooms and during breaks in the schoolyard and in the school's hallway – about three days a week during one year. The researcher openly wrote down his field notes while observing different interactions, and tape-recorded some speech activities. In addition, semi-structured interviews (both individually and in groups) were conducted with some of the pupils and teachers. However, in order to explain why this particular group of male adolescents was chosen for the study, we first want to position this school within the broader context of Swedish educational policies.

Although Swedish school policy in modern history has had a clear remit to offer all children an equivalent, democratic and compulsory education (Sveriges Riksdag 1985), different schools' *unequal* conditions and resources have been noted in recent educational and sociological research. In particular, this scholarship has pointed to the emergence of a neoliberal shift in Swedish educational policies which has opened up the opportunity for pupils to choose their educational career from the very first years of schooling. This enhanced freedom has created a situation where children from socioeconomically wealthy families choose schools with high status, and this has had a segregating effect on society (Bunar 2001; Bunar and Kallstenius 2007; Hartman 2005). Moreover, several researchers working in the field of intercultural education assert that the Swedish school system with its mission to foster pupils and to provide them with nationally defined knowledge objectives may contribute to the establishment of ethnic boundaries. Here, 'Swedishness' – whatever that might be – is constructed as normative whereas experiences of migration are considered as a deficiency which needs to be compensated for through education (Gruber 2007; Lahdenperä 1997; Runfors 2003). It appears clear then that understanding a school's locality and its relationship to other schools, as well as its role in (re)producing forms of ethnic categorisation, are critical prerequisites for making sense of the everyday interactions of the particular educational environment in which this study was conducted.

Like many similar neighbourhoods in the outer surroundings of the capital, the suburb in which the school is situated has a specific place in the city's socioeconomic and semiotic map: it is an urban space with a diverse population in terms of ethnic identification and income level. However, it is also quite an 'anonymous' neighbourhood in the sense that it has not been explicitly targeted by media narratives. Despite the fact that both the school and the neighbourhood have remained relatively unaffected by media attention, the link between ethnic Otherness and social problems is constantly tangible here. To mention just one example, the school principal seems to be in two minds with regard to the ethnic diversity of the school cohort. After proudly announcing that 'we have got 50 per cent Swedish and 50 per cent immigrant pupils', she quickly adds a note of reservation, arguing that high numbers of 'immigrant' children might nonetheless threaten the good reputation of the school (see also Jonsson 2007). Moreover, she emphasises that '*boys* with an immigrant background' constitute a special segment that requires further research.

It is partly as a result of these processes of ethnic and gender differentiation that RJ decided to focus in his fieldwork on a group of 10 pupils in grade 9[5] who are addressed by many of their peers and teachers as 'boys of immigrant background' (*killar med invandrarbakgrund*), despite the fact that several of them were actually born in Sweden and are Swedish citizens. Needless to say, it is not purely the ethnic identity attributed to them that makes these boys a group. What singles them out as a rather discrete social network are both institutional and informal practices: the boys attend the same Swedish and English classes, but they also cluster together more freely during the breaks, a leisure time that they spend mostly sitting around some of the tables in the hallway beside the main entrance of the school. The tables are in a sense located at the school's centre, which not only contributes to enhancing the visibility of the boys as a group, but might also have an effect on how they are perceived by other students. When the researcher asked about the young men in the hallway, the teachers as well as the other pupils seem to be aware of them, describing them in positive terms as good friends or as 'popular' or the 'cool and funny guys'. On a more negative note, they are also portrayed as 'cocky hip hoppers' who 'believe that they own the school' by some of those who identify themselves as 'Swedish guys'. On the whole, the ways in which they were categorised, coupled with their centrality in the school, made this group ethnographically salient for an analysis of the intersections between language, gender and ethnicity in this particular school environment.

Critical junctions: language practices, ethnicity, gender and sexuality

The following extracts are taken from a series of interactions that took place in the context of the Swedish classes taught by Åsa, a teacher who places importance on developing students' language skills as well as creating an educational environment where everyone should feel accepted and respected regardless of ethnicity, gender and sexual orientation. As will emerge below, Åsa is worried about the lack of respect on the grounds of ethnicity expressed through certain words that she has heard among her students. Therefore, at some point, she took the decision to initiate a discussion about ethnic insults through a teaching and learning activity in which everyone should tell the class where they come from and what language(s) they speak at home.[6]

Extract 1

```
1   Åsa:      mmm Nejib?
2   Nejib:    jag är från Marocko
```

3	*Åsa:*	*du är från Marocko. Du pratar?*
4	*Nejib:*	*svenska*
5	*Åsa:*	*nåt annat modersmål?*
		vad har du hemma?
6	*Nejib:*	*svenska*
		(killarna skrattar)
7	*Mengistu:*	*hörru din arabfitta säg sanningen!*
8	*Nejib:*	*jag pratar visst svenska hemma*
9	*Jamal:*	*ja det är sant*
10	*Åsa:*	*svenska, jag har för mig,*
		du säger att du är,
		vad sade du att du var?
11	*Nejib:*	*marockan*
12	*Åsa:*	*marockan, du kommer från?*
13	*Nejib:*	*Marocko*
14	*Åsa:*	*och pratar?*
15	*Nejib:*	*svenska!*
16	*Åsa:*	*ja, inget annat, inget annat språk?*
17	*Kille:*	*han är svensk, ser du inte det?*
18	*Mengistu:*	*(till Åsa) får jag bara fråga en fråga?*
		tror du att jag är bög bara om
		jag färgar mitt hår blont?
		(skratt från eleverna)
19	*Kille:*	*ja, om du gör det*
20	*Åsa:*	*va?*
21	*Mengistu:*	*tror du att jag är bög?*
		(Hakan kommer in sent)
22	*Åsa:*	*Hakan öh, kan jag få tänka på din fråga*
		lite grand Mengistu,
		men nu är det faktiskt Hakan
		Ja, Hakan?
23	*Hakan:*	*mmm*
24	*Åsa:*	*av med huvan*
		så att jag ser dig! Hakan
25	*Hakan:*	*(tyst) ja, jag kommer från Turkiet*
26	*Åsa:*	*mmm*

1	Åsa:	mmm Nejib?
2	Nejib:	I'm from Morocco!
3	Åsa:	you are from Morocco. And you speak …?
4	Nejib:	Swedish.
5	Åsa:	any other mother tongue?
		what do you speak at home?

6 Nejib: Swedish

(the boys laugh)

7 Mengistu: listen, you Arab cunt, tell the truth!
8 Nejib: I do speak Swedish at home!
9 Jamal: yes it's true.
10 Åsa: Swedish, I thought,
you said you were,
what [nationality] did you say you were?
11 Nejib: Moroccan.
12 Åsa: Moroccan, you come from?
13 Nejib: Morocco.
14 Åsa: and speak…?
15 Nejib: Swedish!
16 Åsa: ok, nothing else? any other language?
17 One of the boys: he's Swedish, can't you see?
18 Mengistu: (to Åsa) may I just ask a question?
do you think I'm gay
if I dye my hair blond?

(laugh from the students)

19 One of the boys: yes, if you do it.
20 Åsa: what?
21 Mengistu: do you think I'm gay?

(Hakan enters late)

22 Åsa: Hakan, uh, may I think about your question
a little, Mengistu?
but now it's actually Hakan's turn.
yes, Hakan.
23 Hakan: mmm.
24 Åsa: take off your hood
so I can see you, Hakan.
25 Hakan: (quietly)yes, I come from Turkey.
26 Åsa: mmm.

After everyone in the classroom had had their turn, Åsa provided a brief summary of what they had just discussed and spelled out the aim of this exercise.

Extract 2

1 Åsa: vi talar om vad man pratar,
om man pratar nåt mer modersmål än svenska,
nu ska jag inte saga att ni kallar varann,
men jag hör att ni, jag hör ord

som arab och kurd och så hör jag ibland
arab …
2 Emre: fitta
3 Åsa: jag tanker så här, ni är stolta över
var ni kommer ifrån och har andra nationaliteter och
det ska så vara,
sen är det en annan sak när vi är inne i ett klassrum,
och när vi är på skolan, i [namnet på förorten],
utanför oss så pågår mycket krig
och så mycket elände,
så mycket konflikter så mycket konflikter
så jag tänkte att här inne …
4 Jamal: ska vi ha fred
5 Åsa: så tar vi och är stolta over var vi kommer ifrån,
men vi försöker göra det lite neutral,
för att inte saga mycket, för vad jag är rädd för
är att det är någons nationalitet
som man till slut inte kan va stolt
over. Vi pratar svenska och har ett annat modersmål,
men här inne så försöker vi jobba over konflikter
och nationaliteter så långt det går

1 Åsa: we're talking about what [language] one speaks,
whether one speaks another mother tongue than Swedish,
now I'm not going to tell you what to call each other,
but I hear that you, I hear words
like Arab and Kurd and sometimes I hear
Arab …
2 Emre: cunt.
3 Åsa: I'm thinking this: you are proud of
where you come from and have other nationalities, and
that's how it should be,
but it's different when we're inside a classroom,
and when we're at school, in [name of suburb],
outside there're lots of wars going on
and so much misery,
so many conflicts, so many conflicts
that I was thinking that in here…
4 Jamal: we should have peace
5 Åsa: so let's be proud of where we come from,
but let's try to make it a little neutral,
not to say very [neutral], because I'm afraid
that someone's nationality
will ultimately become something one cannot be proud
of. We speak Swedish and have other mother tongues,
but in here we try to work across conflicts
and nationalities as much as possible.

For clarity of exposition, we want to begin by looking at the teacher's remarks in Extract 2 because they will allow us to understand the discursive conditions in which these interactions take place. And these are conditions that are not specific for this particular classroom, but impinge more broadly on Swedish public discourse. This is insofar as Åsa's last turn is perhaps the clearest textual manifestation in the data of a dominant ideology in Swedish society – one could call it an *ideology of equality* – according to which everyone should be treated as equal, irrespective of their social, ethnic and linguistic backgrounds. It lies outside the scope of this article to offer a comprehensive overview of the historical development of this ideology (see however Milani 2007, 2008 for a more detailed discussion). Suffice it to say, however, that dominant societal ideologies can be conceptualised *pace* Butler (1997) as forms of *implicit censorship*, in the sense that they subtly define the boundaries of what it is acceptable to say, or not, in public discourse (cf. Kulick 2005). These theoretical observations can be productively applied to the examples above because we believe that it is only in the light of this ideology that we can appreciate Åsa's concerns as well as the unfolding of these (meta) linguistic exchanges.

To begin with, it is interesting to note how the teacher constructs a spatial boundary between outside and inside the classroom. The former is portrayed as a place of dire conflict that little can be done to change. By contrast, the classroom and the school are represented as safe havens of equality where disagreement can be avoided, and the centrifugal forces of nationalism toned down. However, at the same time, Åsa's utterances reveal an essentialist view of ethnic and national belonging. This is perhaps most explicitly manifested when the teacher represents her pupils' origins and nationality as *other* from the default mode: Swedish (turn 3, line 2). As mentioned earlier, the image of some boys in the school as ethnically 'other' is not restricted to this particular instance, but has emerged frequently in the interviews with the teaching staff. The problematic aspect of the categories 'immigrant', 'other' or 'non-Swedish' lies in the fact that they more or less implicitly *erase* (Irvine and Gal 2000) the complexity of the ethnic background of these young men, most of whom were actually born in Sweden and are Swedish citizens. Finally, it should be observed how nationality/ethnicity, language, and conflict become controversially entangled in Åsa's closing remark (turn 5). The first deictic pronoun 'we' is ambiguous because it is unclear whether it only refers to the pupils in the classroom or encompasses more broadly the Swedish population in its entirety. Either way, what is relevant is that, through the deictic expression, the teacher is constructing an 'imagined community' (Anderson 1991) of speakers, in which Swedish coexists with other mother tongues. Thus, the multilingual repertoire of the pupils and/or the Swedish population is acknowledged. However, the conjunction 'but' does important ideological work in this context. This is because it creates a contrast between (1) 'we speak Swedish and have another mother tongue' and (2) 'we work across conflicts and nationalities as much as possible'. Accordingly, the conjunction functions as a logic connector implying that multilingualism might be closely tied to conflicts and divisions.

Overall, one could conclude that the teacher's speech is framed within an ideological matrix that dictates that equality should be acknowledged and promoted. This leads to an overt attempt on her part towards the recognition of multilingualism and ethnic diversity among the pupils. That said, the teacher's utterances are revealing of the belief that such diversity might be at the very heart of divisions and conflicts. Furthermore, these utterances testify to a process of 'othering' (Jaworski 2007) whereby Åsa more or less explicitly portrays her pupils as 'non-Swedes'. Crucially, it is this tension between an attempt to acknowledge diversity and essentialist forms of categorisation that also underpins the exchange in Extract 1, to which we will now turn.

This episode was generated by Åsa's request for information about her pupils' ethnic/national origin and their language choice at home. Whereas the teacher's questions might appear to be fairly innocuous, they galvanised a discursive struggle for truth which is manifested in the prolonged opposition between Nejib's statement that he speaks Swedish at home, on the one hand, and the teacher's questioning of this claim, on the other. Of course, Åsa's fill-in questions could be interpreted, in the light of the ideology of equality, as prompts through which she is trying to elicit answers that might help her to flag up the multilingual profile of the class. Conversely, her dismissal of Nejib's replies could also be interpreted as the materialisation of an essentialist language ideology which envisions a one-to-one relationship between language and ethnicity. According to this ideology, if you are not a Swede, you speak your 'mother tongue' at home, and this would certainly not be Swedish. But, as Foucault (1980) has cogently pointed out, struggles for truth are ultimately contestations of power and authority, and vice versa. Hence, Nejib's adamant replies cannot simply be treated as an obstinate opposition to the teacher's ideological standpoint, but should also be seen as a way of undermining her professional authority in the matter. Furthermore, this discursive struggle is not confined to Åsa and Nejib, but takes the form of a collaborative work that involves the other pupils as well. It is in this contest for power and truth that we can better understand Mengistu's usage of the disparaging expression 'Arab cunt' directed at Nejib.

Recent research on language and masculinity has urged us to move beyond a disapproval of verbal slurs, and instead try to grasp their social function in precise sites of interaction. In a groundbreaking study of a group of young people in Barcelona, Joan Pujolar i Cos (1997) has demonstrated how insults are linguistic resources through which the men in the group can bond together by 'asserting and defending a particular form of masculinity associated with heterosexuality, physical strength and size, and a certain aggressiveness manifested in verbal terms' (Pujolar i Cos 1997:90). Reasoning along similar lines, Ann-Carita Evaldsson's (2006) investigation on male pre-adolescents in a multiethnic school in Stockholm illustrates that 'insulting is not primarily an adversary act ... [that] accomplishes more than simply to exclude particular boys by associating them with non-acceptable masculine behaviours. The use of exclusion is, simultaneously, inclusion into a particular local discourse' (Evaldsson 2006:777). In the same way, the ethnographic observations of the participants in this study have led RJ to conclude elsewhere that verbal duelling and slurs are linguistic means, through which these male adolescents (re)negotiate their social relations with one another in informal settings outside the classroom (see Jonsson 2007 for detailed evidence). In sum, if we pull together all these considerations and apply them to the extract above, we believe that we are better equipped to understand the meaning and purpose of the insult 'Arab cunt' in this particular context.

There is little doubt that the compound word where a marker of ethnic identification is attached to a strongly derogatory label for female genitals allows Mengistu[7] to *subordinate* Nejib by investing him with an ethnic and gendered position. More specifically, the process of subordination works here through the metaphorical assignment of a feminine position to a man, a position which relies on a misogynist discourse in which women are reduced to a sexual organ and therefore nearly dehumanised (cf. Coates 2007:55; Kiesling 2002:251). Hence, by tying a pejorative form of gender categorisation to an ethnic marker, Mengistu devalues his classmate and weakens the truth value of Nejib's answers, securing for himself at the same time an authoritative stance in agreement with the teacher. However, one could also argue, from a pragmatic perspective, that the choice of a verbal slur is a move through which Mengistu can enter a 'particular local discourse' (Evaldsson 2006:777), in which derogatory expressions are an integral part of building rapport in informal conversations with his classmates. Thus, in using an insult in Åsa's presence, Mengistu breaks the more or less overt rules of the classroom (see Extract 2); he downplays his stance of collusion with the teacher while showing solidarity with his peers.

In contrast to Mengistu, another classmate supports Nejib (turn 17) and challenges the teacher by playing along the lines of the same essentialist language ideology according to which ethnicity univocally correlates to language practices. According to this young man, Nejib *is* a Swede, and the implicature of this statement is that he certainly speaks Swedish at home. Admittedly, claiming that Nejib is a Swede complicates Nejib's own act of identification as a Moroccan. However, this claim is jokey. And this is the result of the rhetorical strategy of *paradox*. If we agree with Harvey that, 'In verbal paradox, two apparently contradictory notions or views are held simultaneously' (Harvey 2000:244), the paradoxical element here is produced by the question 'don't you see it?' which plays on the opposition between (1) what is 'there' and patently visible – Nejib's bodily features (i.e. dark hair and skin) and (2) what is 'not there' but is performatively brought into being by the question itself – a conventional image of how a Swedish man looks. We argue that it is precisely this contrast that also triggers Mengistu's ensuing concern about homosexuality (turn 18).

Clearly, Mengistu's question is an example of how 'the dread spectre of homosexuality' (Cameron 1997:61) is persistently lurking behind male adolescents' self-perceptions in school environments (see Redman and Mac an Ghaill 1996). Yet what is particularly remarkable in this context is how Mengistu associates a conventional trait of Swedishness (i.e. blond hair) with homosexuality, which is something that is both troublesome *and* enticing. On the one hand, we know that he has actually wanted for quite some time to die his hair blond. On the other hand, he manifests his fear of how that bodily change might affect the general perception of his self. Like Nejib's unyielding answers about speaking Swedish at home, Mengistu's plan of modifying his hair colour can be interpreted as one of the subtle ways through which these young men play with crossing the boundaries of what is 'expected' behaviour and appearance for someone who is classified in the school as an 'immigrant pupil'. However, transgressing norms and expectations can be a risky business: for Nejib, it fuelled the intense questioning on the part of the teacher; for Mengistu, it is his credentials as a heterosexual man that might be at stake. Having said that, it would be an oversimplification to conclude that Mengistu's concerns with homosexuality directly follow from his ethnic and/or cultural background, which is an argument, however, that more or less explicitly recurs in media discourse (see Milani 2010). Rather, as we will illustrate in the next section, heteronormativity and a negative portrayal of homosexuality are deeply embedded in teaching and learning activities.

Enacting discipline and homosocial desire through homosexual innuendos

In order to contextualise the episodes below, we want to note how most teachers in the school reacted with visible astonishment when asked whether they had had homosexual pupils or colleagues. Some of them justified their surprise by pointing out that schools are not an easy environment in which to come out as a homosexual. Others claimed that their pupils are too young – admittedly most of them are in full blown puberty – and might not yet have 'discovered' their homosexuality. This picture is not dissimilar from what other researchers have described with regard to other Swedish educational environments. Lundgren (2008) has demonstrated how many heterosexual teachers in the school that she investigates claim never to have had a homosexual colleague. Even when they do, these teachers openly admit that homosexual peers should play down their sexual identity at school in order *not* to influence their pupils' conduct. Undoubtedly, according to such a view, homosexuality should be relegated to the domain of 'the unspeakable' (Butler 1997:133) – the realm of the invisible even. However, what needs highlighting from a queer perspective is that heterosexuality is implicitly treated as *unproblematic* by the participants in Lundgren's (2008) study, not least as a result of their lack of awareness that they *qua* heterosexuals might as well shape pupils' choices and self-perceptions.

This conclusion can be strengthened by the existing body of evidence that shows how heterosexuality might not be patently 'flaunted' in schools as well as elsewhere, yet is continuously (re)produced as a given through mundane semiotic practices, e.g. through pictures of heterosexual families on staff desks or the use of kinship categories husband and wife by female and male participants respectively (Ambjörnsson 2004; Jonsson 2007; see also Kitzinger 2005 for a compelling analysis of how heterosexuality is not necessarily the main topic of conversation but constitutes the unquestioned common ground on which talk in interaction unfolds). However, this more or less overt display of heterosexuality does not translate into a complete silencing of homosexuality. On the contrary, it is through subtle representations of homosexuality as bad and deviant that heterosexuality can uphold its normal and normative status (see e.g. Cameron 1997; Kehily and Nayak 1997). Therefore, it is perhaps not completely unexpected that same sex desire emerges in several interactions in our data, of which the examples below can be considered representative cases in point.

The brief episode reproduced in Extract 3 is taken from a Swedish language class conducted by a heterosexual male teacher, Roger. After writing a few irregular verb forms on the white board, the teacher asked the pupils to form sentences conjugating those verbs. According to the ethnographic field notes, the pupils quickly started to become impatient seemingly not understanding what they had been asked to do. This led Roger to decide to explain the exercise again from the beginning. However, he did not succeed in gathering the pupils' attention: Ibrahim freely talked to a classmate, and Ramiz burst out in a fit of anger.

Extract 3
(RJ, field notes)

Ramiz: *sug kuk*
Roger: *era hobbies får ni ta på lunchen.*
Ibrahim, jag vet att du också vill vara med på ett hörn där, men det får du ta med dom sen!

(Ramiz skrattar, ruskar på huvudet och vänd mot forskaren förklarar han att deras lärare har rolig humor.)

Ramiz: Suck [my] cock
Roger: You can do your hobbies during lunchtime.
Ibrahim, I know that you also want to participate in a corner there but that's something you can do with them later.

(Ramiz laughs, shakes his head and, turned toward the researcher, explains that their teacher has a good sense of humour.)

On another occasion, Roger has just asked the students to work independently on an exercise from the textbook when Johan and Mats started talking to each other and got involved into a lighthearted fight, possibly as a pretext to avoid doing the exercise. This led the teacher to make an explicit comment on the intimacy between two students.

Extract 4
(RJ, field notes)

Roger: *Johan och Mats ska alltid ta på varandra*
Ibrahim: *jag såg dem slicka på varandra!*
Roger: *Är du avundsjuk?*

```
(Alla ler)

Roger:     Johan and Mats always need to touch each other
Ibrahim:   I saw them lick each other!
Roger:     Are you jealous?

(Everyone smiles)
```

It is important to clarify that the derogatory expression uttered by Ramiz in Extract 3 is not directed at the teacher but epitomises dissatisfaction with his own inability to understand the topic of this teaching and learning activity. However, unlike in Extracts 1 and 2 where Åsa openly opposes verbal slurs, the swearword prompts a different strategy of classroom management from Roger. Instead of overtly reprimanding the student's language usage, Roger makes a comment alleging homosexual activities between Ramiz and the other boys, a comment that is immediately extended to Ibrahim, who has been talking during the recapping of the explanation. By the same token, in Extract 4, the undisciplined behaviour of Johan and Mats is met by the teacher's allegation that they are sexually attracted to each other. When Ibrahim seeks to support the teacher's standpoint by providing further evidence of such homosexual attraction, he is immediately silenced by a remark about his jealousy of the boys' intimacy.

Roger's comments can be described as innuendos to a purported same sex desire, Interestingly, their function is to serve as disciplinary tools in the service of classroom management. In other words, these innuendos are discursive strategies through which the teacher can expose a pupil to public humiliation, while allowing himself a position of control. This is realised by associating unruly behaviour to something else that is widely understood as 'bad' or 'unacceptable'. As a large body of scholarship on masculinity has reiterated many times, there is nothing worse for a boy than 'to have his attitudes and behaviors likened to those of girls or to be called gay' (Francis and Skelton 2001:15). This is insofar as anything that is culturally scripted as feminine represents the 'constitutive outside' (Butler 1997:180) which polices the borders of masculinity. Or, to put it another way, culturally shared traits of femininity stand vis-à-vis the 'symbolic universe' of masculinity as its 'defining limit or exteriority, one which, were it imported into that universe, would destroy its integrity and coherence' (Butler 1997:180).

In the examples above, it is rather patent that homosexual innuendos are employed by Roger as ways in which to reprimand and silence the pupils. Nonetheless, their potentially disruptive force is toned down by a shared agreement that these allegations of homosexuality are ironic: they are 'not meant literally' and seem 'to be intended to amuse' (Tannen 2005:164). That Roger's remarks should be interpreted as 'jokey' is warranted further by Ramiz's laugh, coupled with an appreciative comment on the teacher's sense of humour in Extract 3, as well as by their smiles in Extract 4. To this, one should add that the teacher himself discloses in an interview that he finds it acceptable to make fun of homosexuality because everyone is the class is heterosexual. In order to justify this position and possibly protect himself from potential homophobic allegations, he adds that the pupils are well aware of his own commitment to equal opportunities. Espousing the same principles of the ideology of equality expressed by Åsa in Extract 2, Roger is adamant pointing out how he often puts emphasis on the importance of acknowledging everyone's *equal* rights regardless of sexual orientation. As a corollary to this, he clarifies that sexual innuendos can be a fruitful teaching tool because they help him to keep order and discipline while creating a friendlier atmosphere in the class.

Roger's comments are not dissimilar from the remarks made by another male teacher explaining his flirtatious behaviour with a few female students in Francis and Skelton's (2001) canonical study on heterosexual masculinity in British schools. The striking similarity between these teachers' explanations lies in their explicit articulation of 'classroom management as one which relied on "sociability"' (Francis and Skelton 2001:16). Such a teaching approach entails among other things the use of humour as a teaching strategy through which to establish friendly relationships with their pupils. Despite these similarities, the main difference lies in the *homosocial* (Sedgwick 1990) nature of the rapport between Roger and the young men in the study.

It is at this juncture that we should remind ourselves that men's homosocial desire – the need to bond with other men – brings with it an inherent conundrum. Dominant discourses of masculinity dictate that heterosexual men should strive to build solidarity with one another. But the more they pursue this bonding enterprise, the more they run the risk of being perceived as entering the realm of same-sex desire, which would paradoxically undermine the performance of their heterosexual masculinity (Kiesling 2005:720). In the light of this, it is true that Roger is muscular and wears tight T-shirts that exalt his body-builder's figure, literally embodying a near hypermasculine identity. Nonetheless, because of his preoccupation with appearance, he is often perceived by the pupils as 'conceited' – a potentially demasculinising trait because of its conventional associations with femininity (see also Benwell 2002 for the challenge posed by body grooming to conventional forms of heterosexual masculinity in British men's lifestyle magazines). Therefore, it is our contention that the displacement of same-sex desire into the domain of ridicule is a necessary pre-requisite for this teacher to engage in 'safe' homosocial banter with his male students, thus eschewing the danger of falling into the disruptive terrain of homosexuality. Furthermore, if read against the backdrop of the conditions and constraints of this Swedish public discourse, one could argue that the innuendos are a discursive manoeuvre through which Roger can reject homosexuality into indignity (cf. Bourdieu 1998:46) *without* overtly contravening the rules set by the ideology of equality, namely, the unacceptability of public discriminatory discourse and harassment. This is because the ironic nature of the innuendos allows 'a disjunction, opposition or contradiction between the surface form of an utterance and its underlying meaning or context' (Benwell 2004:4). Notably, this semantic instability not only makes ironic utterances difficult if not impossible to counter, but also helps speakers to mitigate their responsibility vis-à-vis the propositional content of their own speech (Benwell 2002:163).

All in all, one could reach a similar conclusion to that drawn by Cameron (1997) with regard to the social significance of gossip in informal all-male peer groups: homosexual innuendos are 'not just one way, but the most appropriate way' (Cameron 1997:61) through which this particular teacher can keep discipline while staging homosocial desire and enacting heterosexual masculinity in relation to his male students in a Swedish class. This is not to say, however, that such complex social endeavour is by any means innocuous. Precisely because of their fleeting character – they are embedded in, and allegedly contribute to, a friendly and smooth flow of classroom activities – homosexual innuendos are but another example of those 'banal' (Billig 1997) linguistic foreclosures that, by associating homosexuality to troublesome classroom conduct, label it as 'bad' and 'deviant' and thereby implicitly legitimise its counterpart – heterosexuality – as 'good' and 'appropriate'. However, as Sedgwick (1990) notes, the disavowal of homosexuality is not the only strategy through which homosocial desire can be acceptably upheld within the confines of heterosexual masculinity; talk and rivalry about women represent other key ingredients of the homosocial project (cf. Kiesling 2002), a topic that we will now move on to present.

Negotiating a masculine order through desire

In a well-known study on a group of teenagers in an American school, Eckert has illustrated how the transition from childhood to adolescence is marked by a drive to 'demonstrating new "mature" behaviors. And, in pre-adolescence, those new behaviors involve engagement in the heterosexual market' (Eckert 1994:3). The notion of a heterosexual market aims to capture the importance of heterosexual relationships – whether real, purported or fictitious – as a form of capital (Bourdieu 1991) through which boys and girls can purchase a position of prestige in the symbolic economy of peer group exchanges. However, as Eckert (2002) points out, active participation in the heterosexual market has less to do with 'real' involvement in intimate relations with a partner of the opposite gender, than to *talk about* such relations. In a similar vein, it was rare to the see boys in this study overtly engage in acts of affection with girls at school, although women are a very common topic of their talk in informal situations (see Jonsson 2007). It was with a view to understand the role played by women in lives of these male adolescents that the first author of the present chapter initiated an informal discussion on this topic (see Extract 5).

Extract 5

```
1   Alem:   det där var Anne i somras!
2   Nejib:  ja, hon har jag hört,
            hon har jag hört, hon är nice.
3   Mark:   hon hos Danne?
4   Alem:   oh, det där var en omgång alltså!
            hon bara blow,
            jag bara (extatiskt röst) ahh!
```

5 Mark: Alem, du var den femte!
6 Alem: sug min mammas död, jag var den första!
horunge, jag var den första som fick blow!
hon bara kom såhär.
7 Mark: ja, men du baza [knulla] henne fem!
8 Alem: jag baza aldrig henne!
9 Mark: du sa ju det! du bara, vilket hål
ska jag stoppa in den i?
10 Alem: (skriker) jag är oskuld! (skratt)
11 Mark: du sa så här, vilket hål
ska jag stoppa den i? (skratt)
12 Alem: nej, alltså, jag drev men …
13 Mark: ljug inte! … du var femma!
14 Alem: (högt) jag var etta!
15 Mark: efter alla hade pippat henne,
han pippa henne!
16 Alem: jag hade aldrig fått nåt,
jag stod mot väggen så här bara,
åh nu kommer jag snart,
hon bara drog ner byxorna,
hon tog fram den då var den redan bånge!
(Alem visar med handen i luften).
den såhär det var svårt du vet,
ah! (skratt) sen jag,
jag vet inte vad som hände … vad var det?
(många skratt) det var mörkt också,
jag kunde inte se vart fittan var! (skratt)
jag bara vart ska jag stoppa in den?
hon stod där, hon mecka med den som en bilmotor
så här. (Alem visar med handen
i luften)

(killarna skrattar)

17 Forskare: vaddå Mark, att han var femma?
var ni flera som hade sex med henne?
18 Alem: ja (skratt) [---]

(En diskussion uppstår om olika namn på killar som var med
och Alem tillägger att de senare fortsatte ut till en badplats,
där sexet skulle ha fortsatt)

19 Emre: fick Salle baz då?
20 Mark: hur länge red hon, en timme?
21 Alem: alltså, mitt ute vid badplatsen,
sen, hon bara börja blowa honom, vi bara,
hon driver med mister president [penisen], så här.
22 Emre: ey, vad heter hon? [---]
23 Mark: vad heter hon?

24 Alem: Anne.
25 Calle: vem fan vill ha henne nu liksom,
hon är fan knullad överallt!

1 Alem: that was Anne last summer!
2 Nejib: yeah, I've heard about her,
I have heard about her, she's good.
3 Mark: at Danne's?
4 Alem: oh, that was really a round!
she like blew,
I just like (ecstatic voice) ahh!
5 Mark: Alem, you were the fifth!
6 Alem: suck my mother's death, I was the first one!
bastard, I was the first one who got sucked!
she just came like this.
7 Mark: yeah, but you fucked her fifth!
8 Alem: I never fucked her!
9 Mark: you said you did! you said, which hole
should I stick it in?
10 Alem: (yells) I'm a virgin! (laughs)
11 Mark: you said like this, which hole
should I stick it in? (laughs)
12 Alem: no, I mean, I did but …
13 Mark: don't lie! … you were fifth!
14 Alem: (loud) I was first!
15 Mark: after everybody screwed her,
he screwed her!
16 Alem: I had never gotten any,
I just stood against the wall like this
oh now I'm coming soon,
she like pulled down my pants,
she took it out and it was already hard!
(Alem shows with his hand in the air).
like this it was difficult you know,
ah (laugh) then I,
I don't know what happened … what was it?
(many laughs) it was dark outside too,
I couldn't see where the pussy was! (laughs)
I'm like, where should I stick it?
she stood there, she worked with it like a car
engine like this (Alem shows with his hand in
the air)

(the boys laugh)

17 Researcher: what do you mean Mark, about him being fifth?
were there several of you who had sex with her?
18 Alem: yes (laughs) [---]

(A discussion about different names of boys who participated ensues, and Alem adds that they went to a beach where the sex supposedly continued)

19 Emre: did Salle get some then?
20 Mark: how long did she ride, an hour?
21 Alem: well, right outside at the beach,
then she started blowing him, we like,
she's playing with mister president [the penis],
like this.
22 Emre: ey, what's her name? [---]
23 Mark: what's her name?
24 Alem: Anne.
25 Calle: who the hell wants her now, she's fucked all over!

If we cast a cursory glance at the *form* of this episode, it would not be particularly contentious to conclude that this interaction is a typical instance of male antagonism (between Mark and Alem), which is broadly in tune with the many examples provided by Coates (1997) in her analyses of all-male talk in the British context. As for *content*, we might well infer that this extract is a textual manifestation of misogynist discourse, in which the female character (Anne) is reduced to a sexual commodity, an object that, having been used, no one wants any more. However, as we will illustrate in the remainder of this section, such interpretations, albeit not unwarranted, are too simplistic, not least because they fail to do justice to the multilayered complexity of this interaction.

If we set aside for a moment the sexist undertones of the narrative, and concentrate instead on how the story builds up, this episode can be described as a 'small story' (Georgakopoulou 2007:598) in the sense that, unlike a lengthy monologue, it is an interactionally achieved, relatively short lived narrative that literally unfolds as it is being told. And this is the result of both *competition* and *cooperation* between the participants (cf. Cameron 1997:58–9). The competitive element is patent in Mark's dual challenge towards Alem as the *narrator* and *main character* of the narrative, the two being closely intertwined. In fact, Mark disputes the truth value of the content of Alem's account, viz. what specific type of sexual activity took place (i.e. oral versus vaginal intercourse). What is particularly relevant, however, is how Alem shifts his line of argument *after* Mark's threefold objection (turns 7, 9 and 11). Of course, the discrepancy between Mark's and Alem's viewpoints on the matter, coupled with Alem's sudden backtracking, could be interpreted as indices of the fictional nature of this story. As it would be pointed out several months later, it was only 'exaggerated talk'. Alternatively, Alem's backtrack could also be interpreted as a textual cue of his *cooperation* in constructing a shared narrative together with Mark. According to such a view, accommodating to Mark and admitting to having had vaginal sex are by no means signs of failure. Rather, they are strategic moves through which Alem takes advantage of a challenge emerging *within* the interactive situation, and appropriates it so as to display himself as a more sexually experienced young man. The accomplishment of this powerful heterosexual masculine identity, however, is undermined by Mark's textual attacks directed at Alem as a character in the story.

First, no sooner has Alem started to describe the pleasure resulting from the sexual act than he is immediately undermined in his role of protagonist. This is insofar as Mark questions his classmate's position in the hierarchy of the other participants in the group sex activity. Needless to say, being first (and not fifth) is a highly valuable position. It is obvious then that the questioning of such primacy generates the immediate reaction of Alem, who counter-attacks with the derogatory expression 'Suck my mother's death!' Here the creative combination of two formulaic insults – 'suck my dick' and 'I swear on my mother's death' – allows Alem to swear himself free from an accusation without sounding compliant; through the verb 'suck,' he can defend himself *and* be offensive at the same time.

Mark's second textual attack targets Alem's sexual skills. In this respect, it is interesting how Mark skilfully manages this potentially face-threatening accusation by attributing to Alem the question: 'Where should I put it in?' Whether Alem 'really' asked this question is ultimately beyond the point. But what is key for the purpose of this interaction is that, by displacing the authorship of the question on to Alem, Mark downplays his responsibility and thereby contributes to mitigating the negative force of his attack. That said, Alem reappropriates and recontextualises the utterance attributed to him. Through recontextualisation, the meaning of the question changes in such a way that it has rather less to do with his sexual (in)experience than with the darkness of the location in which the sexual act allegedly took place. Thus, in making fun of himself, Alem not only takes control of the accusation, but also employs humour as a strategy through which he can tone down his potential failure and save face.

Finally, one should observe Mark's and Alem's 'non-standard' usage of the adverb *bara* (lit. just/only) as a quotative, which reminds of one the functions of the discourse marker 'like' in American English (Cameron 1997). It is now well-established that the usage of *bara* as a quotative is age-dependent and characterises youth language, irrespective of gender and ethnic identification. These findings have recently been substantiated further by a study (Svensson 2009) that shows how *bara* and its shortened form *ba* are the most frequent quotative marker in the conversation of twelve female teenagers in the city of Malmö. Interestingly, Svensson argues that, from a pragmatic perspective, *bara* in itself does not indicate any form of cooperation between the participants in her study; its usage 'as a quotative marks nonetheless [a sense of] belonging to youth language. Therefore, a sense of community and proximity is enhanced among those who use this discourse particle' (Svensson 2009:225).

To sum up, the storytelling reproduced in Extract 5 is indeed competitive. This does not mean though that competition necessarily rules out cooperation. As Cameron puts it, 'Participants in a conversation or other speech event may compete with each other and at the same time be pursuing a shared common project or common agenda' (Cameron 1997:59). In our view, *interactional enjoyment* constitutes another vital component of the common project in this speech event. The notion of desire will help us to explain this point.

However controversial and fuzzy this concept might be, we concur with Cameron and Kulick (2003:138ff) that desire can help us to *move beyond* the description of palpable 'acts of identities' (Le Page and Tabouret-Keller 1985) in talk in interaction, so as to grasp what remains partly unsaid, but can be perceived (among other things) through ethnographic observation. This is *not* equal to saying that identity is irrelevant in the extract above. What Alem does (with the help of Mark) is to display himself as a heterosexual young man who vocalises – quite literally – his erotic attraction to women. In turn, the reinscription of heterosexuality is a warrant for homosociality not to fade into homosexuality. Yet, to the extent that sexuality is not only about sex, desire cannot be reducible to the domain of the erotic only (Bucholtz and Hall 2003; Cameron and Kulick 2003; Eckert 2002), but, together with fear, captures more broadly the role played by 'powerful feelings in shaping forms of action' (Lemke 2007:23). Therefore, desire allows us to highlight another important aspect of this episode, namely the fact that these male adolescents are engaged in the *joint* creation of enjoyment. Semiotically, this not only emerges as sexual *juissance* in Alem's 'response cry' (Goffmann 1981) (turn 4), but is also manifested more mundanely in the many giggles, laughs and friendly atmosphere. Moreover, if we agree with Kiesling (undated) that we cannot understand identity performances without taking into account audiences as well, the shared production of enjoyment in Extract 5 is only meaningful if related to the person for whom this interaction is 'staged', namely the male researcher who initiated the discussion. On the basis of the ethnographic perception of this particular interaction, coupled with more long-standing observations of similar speech events, we would argue that the driving force behind the enjoyment of the participants is a powerful desire of *transgressing* the boundaries of what is considered 'taboo' for a teenager when an adult is present in the school environment. This leads us to conclude along similar lines to Eckert (2002:108) that 'exaggerated talk' about real or purported sexual activities is not just about sex; nor is it only about performing heterosexual masculinity, but it is also about displaying oneself as 'tough', 'daring,' and 'mature.'

In conclusion, this small story can be taken as an example of how the boys in our study construct a joint narrative event in which competition and cooperation are important strategies through which positions of power, authority, and solidarity are negotiated in a same sex environment in which a male researcher is present (cf. Kiesling 1997, 2002). Crucially, this apparently ephemeral hierarchy is not unrelated to the more stable *structural positions of power* occupied by the boys in the peer-group (cf. Kiesling 1997). Fieldwork observations attest to Alem's leading role as skilled orator in the group, one who has mastered the art of telling enjoyable stories and delivering quick lines, and therefore he occupies a position of privilege and respect among the boys. What this particular conversation exemplifies, however, is how status and prestige are not irreversible givens in the peer group, but can be undermined by an act of resistance on the part of Mark, who is otherwise quieter and more withdrawn. His sharp and persistent comments put Alem in a less favourable position; he who is normally 'at the top' of the group is portrayed as number five, or last. Hence, Mark *challenges* – albeit momentarily – the hierarchy in the boys' structural arrangements.

Concluding remarks

Butler provocatively proposes that 'If the term "queer" is to be a site of collective contestation, the point of departure for a set of historical reflections and futural imaginings, it will have to remain that which is, in the present, never fully owned, but always and only redeployed, twisted, queered from a prior usage and in the direction of urgent and expanding political purposes' (Butler 1993:228). Put differently, inherent to queer is a destabilising force which never bends itself to any pressure emanating from political and academic conformism, and thus produces often uncomfortable stories which seek to debunk dominant discourses of gender and sexuality. It goes without saying that we have not employed the term queer as a shorthand for gay and lesbian. Rather, the queer dimension of this chapter lies in the attempt to uncover the heteronormative underpinnings of many interactions in the school, as well as to unravel a multifaceted picture of the social significance of ethnic insults, homosexual innuendos and misogynist talk among a group of boys in a school context.

This academic enterprise has not been met without reservations in Sweden, because it is said to lack a clear declaration of male pupils' oppression of girls. Whilst we agree that we could have framed our analysis in the light of a theory of patriarchy, as a few commentators have suggested, we want to emphasise that we were moved in the direction of more 'urgent and expanding political purposes' (Butler 1993:228), which find their priority in countering prevailing media discourses about 'multi-ethnic lads' slang' (Witt-Brattström 2006). Unlike the media representations which depict such linguistic practices as *unintelligible* as well as *inherently* sexist and homophobic, we have shown how ethnic insults, gay innuendos and misogynist talk are *meaningful* in the sense that they constitute a rich pool of interactional resources that allow the young men in our study actively to partake in the negotiation of a 'local masculine order' (Evaldsson 2006:764) in which positions of power, authority and solidarity are enacted and/or contested.

Notes

1 All translations from Swedish are our own.

2 It is important to mention that the translation of the word *blatte* as 'immigrant' fails to render the complexity of its referential and social meanings. According to Svenska Språknämnden (the Swedish Language Council), the word is attested in written form as a derogatory synonym of *invandrare* (immigrant) or *utlänning* (foreigner) from 1986 (cf. Jonsson 2007: 10). However, Lacatus (2008) explains that *blatte* does not simply index ethnicity in the sense of anyone who is (perceived as) non-Swedish, but is a fluid concept encoding the link between *particular* ethnicities, social class, and cultural background. Furthermore, Lacatus (2008) insists that the derogatory loading is not inherent in *blatte* but depends on who uses it, in what context and for what purpose.

3 *Miljon* (lit. 'million') alludes to a social and architectural project which took place in Sweden in the mid-1960s – the so-called Miljonprogrammet (lit. 'Million Programme'). The Social Democratic government of the time set out to construct one million dwellings within a period of ten years (1965–1974). Rising immigration rates, together

with particular housing allocation policies and practices, led to an increasingly high concentration of migrants living in the high-rise buildings of the Million Programme.

4 'Compulsory school' is the official translation of *grundskola* given by the Swedish National Agency for Education (Skolverket). It refers to municipally run mandatory education for children between the ages of 7 and 16.

5 It is the last year of mandatory education.

6 Text in parentheses ( ) explains acts, facial expressions and other nonverbal cues. By [---] we show that information has been left out, whereas information in square brackets [ ] has been added to make the translation more idiomatic. In order to indicate a pause, we use ellipses .... .

7 Mengistu was born in Sweden and is of Somali descent. When asked how he identifies himself, Mengistu quickly answers: 'I call myself black' (*jag kallar mig svart*). We reveal this information because, as one of the anonymous reviewers aptly pointed out, Mengistu's usage of the slur 'Arab cunt' would have a very different meaning if he identified himself as 'Arab'. In that case, it would be a semantic reappropriation from within the category 'Arab'.

References

Ambjörnsson, F. (2004) *I en klass för sig: Genus, klass och sexualitet bland gymnasietjejer*. Stockholm: Ordfront.

Anderson, B. (1991) *Imagined Communities: Reflections on the Origins and Spread of Nationalism*, 2nd edition. London: Verso.

Benwell, B. (2002) Is there anything 'new' about these lads? The textual and visual construction of masculinity in men's magazines. In L. Litosseliti and J. Sunderland (eds) *Gender Identity and Discourse Analysis* 149–74. Amsterdam: John Benjamins. https://doi.org/10.1075/dapsac.2.09ben

Benwell, B. (2004) Ironic discourse: evasive masculinity in men's lifestyle magazines. *Men and Masculinities* 7: 3–21. https://doi.org/10.1177/1097184X03257438

Billig, M. (1997) *Banal Nationalism*. London: Sage.

Bourdieu, P. (1991) *Language and Symbolic Capital*. Cambridge, MA: Harvard University Press.

Bourdieu, P. (1998) *Practical Reason*. London: Polity Press.

Bucholtz, M. and Hall, K. (2003) Theorizing identity in language and sexuality research. *Language in Society* 33: 469–515.

Bunar, N. (2001) *Skolan mitt i förorten : Fyra studier om skola, segregation, integration och multikulturalism*. Eslöv: Symposium.

Bunar, N. and Kallstenius, J. (2007) *Valfrihet, integration och segregation i Stockholms grundskolor*. Stockholm: Utbildningsförvaltningen.

Butler, J. (1993) *Bodies that Matter: On the Discursive Limits of 'Sex'*. New York: Routledge.

Butler, J. (1997) *Excitable Speech: The Politics of the Performative*. New York: Routledge.

Butler, J. (1998) Afterword. In S. Munt (ed.) *Butch/Femme: Inside Lesbian Gender* 225–30. London: Cassell. https://doi.org/10.1177/136346098001003009

Cameron, D. (1997) Performing gender identity: young men's talk and the construction of heterosexual masculinity. In S. Johnson and U. H. Meinhof (eds) *Language and Masculinity* 47–64. Oxford: Blackwell.

Cameron, D. (2003) Gender and language ideologies. In J. Holmes and M. Meyerhoff (eds) *The Handbook of Language and Gender* 447–67. Oxford: Blackwell. https://doi.org/10.1002/9780470756942.ch19

Cameron, D. and Kulick, D. (2003) *Language and Sexuality*. Cambridge: Cambridge University Press. https://doi.org/10.1017/CBO9780511791178

Chilton, P. (2004) *Analysing Political Discourse: Theory and Practice*. London: Routledge.

Coates, J. (1997) One-at-a-time: the organization of men's talk. In S. Johnson and U. H. Meinhof (eds) *Language and Masculinity* 107–29. Oxford: Blackwell.

Coates, J. (2007) 'Everyone was convinced that we were closet fags': the role of heterosexuality in the construction of hegemonic masculinity. In H. Sauntson and S. Kyratzis (eds) *Language, Sexualities and Desires: Cross-Cultural Perspectives* 41–67. Basingstoke: Palgrave Macmillan.

De los Reyes, P. and Mulinari, D. (eds) (2005) *Intersektionalitet: Kritiska reflektioner över (o)jämlikhetens landskap*. Malmö: Liber.

Eckert, P. (1994) *Entering the Heterosexual Marketplace: Subordination as Developmental Imperative*. Working Papers on Learning and Identity no. 2. Stanford, CA: Stanford University. Retrieved on 10 October 2017 from https://web.stanford.edu/~eckert/PDF/subordination.pdf.

Eckert, P. (2002) Demystifying sexuality and desire. In K. Campbell-Kibler, R. J. Podesva, S. J. Roberts and A. Wong (eds) *Language and Sexuality: Contesting Meaning in Theory and Practice* 99–110. Stanford, CA: CSLI Publications.

Evaldsson, A.-C. (2006) Staging insults and mobilizing categorizations in a multiethnic peer group. *Discourse and Society* 16: 763–86. https://doi.org/10.1177/0957926505056663

Foucault, M. (1980) *Power/Knowledge*. New York: Pantheon.

Francis, B. and Skelton, C. (2001) Men teachers and the construction of heterosexual masculinity in the classroom. *Sex Education* 1: 9–21. https://doi.org/10.1080/14681810120041689

Georgakopoulou, A. (2007) 'On MSN with buff boys': Self- and other-identity claims in the context of small stories. *Journal of Sociolinguistics* 12: 597–626. https://doi.org/10.1111/j.1467-9841.2008.00384.x

Goffman. E. (1981) Response cries. In E. Goffman (ed.) *Forms of Talk* 78–112. Philadelphia, PA: University of Philadelphia Press.

Gruber, S. (2007) Skolan gör skillnad: Etnicitet och institutionell praktik. PhD dissertation, Linköping University, Sweden.

Hartman, S. (2005) *Det pedagogiska kulturarvet: traditioner och idéer i svensk undervisningshistoria*. Stockholm: Natur och Kultur.

Harvey, K. (2000) Describing camp talk: Language/pragmatics/politics. *Language and Literature* 9: 240–60. https://doi.org/10.1177/096394700000900303

Irvine, J. T. and Gal, S. (2000) Language ideology and linguistic differentiation. In P. V. Kroskrity (ed.) *Regimes of Language: Ideologies, Polities, and Identities* 35–83. Santa Fe, NM: School of American Research Press.

Jagose, A. (1996) *Queer Theory: An Introduction*. New York: New York University Press.

Jaworski, A. (2007) Language in the media: Authenticity and othering. In S. Johnson and A. Ensslin (eds) *Language in the Media: Representations, Identities, Ideologies* 271–80. London: Continuum.

Johnson, S. (1997) Theorizing language and masculinity: A feminist perspective. In S. Johnson and U. H. Meinhof (eds) *Language and Masculinity* 8–26. Oxford: Blackwell.

Jonsson, R. (2007) *Blatte betyder kompis: Om maskulinitet och språk i en högstadieskola*. Stockholm: Ordfront.

Jonsson, R. and Milani, T.M. (2009) Här är alla lika! Jämlikhetsideologi och konstruktionen av den 'Andre' i media och skola. *Utbildning & Demokrati* 18: 67–86.

Kehily, M. J. and Nayak, A. (1997) 'Lads and laughter': humour and the production of heterosexual hierarchies. *Gender and Education* 9: 69–87. https://doi.org/10.1080/09540259721466

Kiesling, S. F. (1997) Power and the language of men. In S. Johnson and U. H. Meinhof (eds) *Language and Masculinity* 65–85. Oxford: Blackwell.

Kiesling, S. F. (2002) Playing the straight man: Displaying and maintaining male heterosexuality in discourse. In K. Campbell-Kibler, R. J. Podesva, S. J. Roberts, A. Wong (eds) *Language and Sexuality: Contesting Meaning in Theory and Practice* 249–66. Stanford: CSLI Publications.

Kiesling, S. F. (2005) Homosocial desire in men's talk: Balancing and recreating cultural discourses of masculinity. *Language in Society* 34: 695–727. https://doi.org/10.1017/S0047404505050268

Kiesling, S. F. (undated) Language, desire and new thinking on masculinities. Unpublished manuscript.

Kitzinger, C. (2005) 'Speaking as a heterosexual': (How) does sexuality matter for talk-in-interaction? *Research on Language and Social Interaction* 38: 221–65. https://doi.org/10.1207/s15327973rlsi3803_2

Kulick, D. (2005) The importance of what gets left out. *Discourse Studies* 7 (4–5): 615–24. https://doi.org/10.1177/1461445605054408

Lacatus, C. (2008) *The (In)visibility Complex: Negotiating* Otherness *in Contemporary Sweden.* Stockholm: CEIFO Publishing.

Lahdenperä, P. (1997) *Invandrarbakgrund eller skolsvårigheter? En textanalytisk studie av* åtgärdsprogram *för elever med invandrarbakgrund.* Stockholm: HLS förlag.

Lemke, J. L. (2007) Identity, development and desire: Critical questions. In C. Caldas-Coulthard and R. Iedema (eds) *Identity Trouble: Critical Discourse and Contested Identities* 17–42. Basingstoke: Palgrave Macmillan.

Le Page, R. and Tabouret-Keller, A. (1985) *Acts of Identity: Creole-Based Approaches to Language and Ethnicity.* Cambridge: Cambridge University Press.

Lundgren. A. S. (2008) Spela roll. In L. Martinsson and E. Reimers (eds) *Skola i normer* 53–95. Malmö: Gleerups.

McElhinny, B. (2003) Theorizing gender in sociolinguistics and linguistic anthropology. In J. Holmes and M. Meyerhoff (eds) *The Language and Gender Handbook* 21–42. Oxford: Blackwell. https://doi.org/10.1002/9780470756942.ch1

Milani, T. M. (2007) Voices of authority in conflict: the making of the expert in a language debate in Sweden. *Linguistics and Education* 18: 99–120. https://doi.org/10.1016/j.linged.2007.07.002

Milani, T. M. (2008) Language testing and citizenship: a language ideological debate in Sweden. *Language in Society* 37: 27–59. https://doi.org/10.1017/S0047404508080020

Milani, T. M. (2010) What's in a name: language ideology and social differentiation in a Swedish print-mediated debate. *Journal of Sociolinguistics* 10: 116–42. https://doi.org/10.1111/j.1467-9841.2009.00435.x

Pujolar i Cos, J. (1997) Masculinities in a multilingual setting. In S. Johnson and U. H. Meinhof (eds) *Language and Masculinity* 86–106. Oxford: Blackwell.

Redman, P. and Mac an Ghaill, M. (1996) Schooling sexualities: heterosexual masculinities, schooling and the unconscious. *Discourse* 17: 243–56. https://doi.org/10.1080/0159630960170208

Runfors, A. (2003) *Mångfald, motsägelser och marginaliseringar: En studie av hur invandrarskap formas i skolan.* Stockholm: Prisma.

Sedgwick, E. K. (1990) *The Epistemology of the Closet*. Berkeley, CA: University of California Press.

Sedgwick, E. K. (1993) *Tendencies*. Durham, NC: Duke University Press. https://doi.org/10.1215/9780822381860

Sveriges Riksdag (1985) Skollag (1985:1100): Svensk författningssamling 1985:1100. Retrieved on 10 October 2017 from www.riksdagen.se/sv/dokument-lagar/dokument/svensk-forfattningssamling/skollag-19851100_sfs-1985-1100.

Stroud, C. (2004) Rinkeby Swedish and semilingualism in language ideological debates: a Bourdieuean perspective. *Journal of Sociolinguistics* 8: 163–230. https://doi.org/10.1111/j.1467-9841.2004.00258.x

Svensson, G. (2009) Diskurspartiklar hos ungdomar i mångspråkiga miljöer i Malmö. PhD dissertation, Lund University, Sweden.

Tannen, D. (2005) *Conversational Style: Analyzing Talk among Friends*. Oxford: Oxford University Press.

Thurlow, C. (2007) Fabricating youth: New-media discourse and the technologization of young people. In S. Johnson and A. Ensslin (eds) *Language in the Media: Representations, Identities, Ideologies* 213–49. London: Continuum.

Witt-Brattström, E. 2006. Vem äger svenskan? *Dagens Nyheter* (19 April). Retrived on 10 October 2017 from www.dn.se/kultur-noje/vem-ager-svenskan.

Part II

Beyond binaries?

5

Do bodies matter? Travestis' embodiment of (trans) gender identity through the manipulation of the Brazilian Portuguese grammatical gender system

Rodrigo Borba
FEDERAL UNIVERSITY OF RIO DE JANEIRO, BRAZIL

Ana Cristina Ostermann
UNIVERSIDADE DO VALE DO RIO DO SINOS, BRAZIL

Introduction

Individuals who overlap and blur ideological semiotic practices available for the construction of social gender have culturally marked subject positions in any society. To some extent, this cultural markedness also regards their language use which is believed to transgress impositions of how speakers should use language to straightforwardly index their identities. In the last three decades, researchers have attempted to depict transgenders' social configurations and subject-positions. Ethnographic studies of such phenomena (see e.g. the Tahitian *mahu*, Levy 1971; the Omani *xanith*, Wikan 1978; the Paraguayan *panema*, Clastres 1990; the native American *berdache* or 'two-spirited people', Epple 1998; and other multiple occurrences of transgenderism in various societies, Bolin 1988; King 1993; McKenzie 1994; Shapiro 1991) have focused on how transgender individuals cross gender boundaries through sociocultural symbolic practices. The literature available seems to indicate that transgenders use language fluidly in order to mark affiliations with different positions available in their specific *milieux*, namely global versus local identities (Besnier 2003), masculinity versus femininity (Livia 1997), and power versus solidarity (Hall and O'Donovan 1996). The juxtaposition of gender indexes on a single body, we believe, enables these individuals to take advantage of their privileged access to gendered meanings which do not seem to be available to traditionally gendered people. In this paper, we try to address the unanswered questions of when, how, and why a community of transgender people (southern Brazilian travestis) use masculine forms in the discursive construction of their identities. This chapter proposes to advance the discussion about an approach to language and transgender based on embodiment (i.e. the stamping of sociopolitically loaded cultural signs of gender and sexuality on individuals' bodies), as it suggests some questions that scholars may want to investigate further. Embodiment, for the purposes of this discussion, refers to the appropriation of signs that index gender and sexuality made by transgender people. Upon moulding their bodies to acquire the desired gender shapes, some transgender individuals juxtapose systems of signs that produce them as culturally *trans* (i.e. *trans*forming the body to *trans*gress its biological limitations). Embodiment, thus, is what enables transgender people to construct performances of gender (Butler 1990) which contrast with their biological morphology, thus making their positions highly fluid. When it comes to travestis, it is the performance of a feminine gender produced on a male body that makes their identities socially and linguistically malleable.

It is important to note that the concept of embodiment we adopt here tries to articulate two understandings of the relationship between sex and gender. One is a 'coat-rack' view, which states sex as a fundamental template over which gender is shaped (for a discussion of this view see McElhinny 2003). The other is the Butlerian view in which the gender performance is of importance whereas biological sex determination is believed to be an irrelevant mark of individuals' bodies. The latter view has been traditionally privileged in studies on transgender. Although the two views might seem in opposition, we believe that in order to understand the relationship between language and transgender, it is necessary to subscribe to an intermediate position which takes the performance of gender *as important as* individuals' sex, due to the fact that is it the transgender people performance of gender in addition to their biological morphology that make them *trans*. This intermediate position might explain why travestis' discursive gender performance is unsettled by their biological links to masculinity and to the discourses related to it.

To undertake the analysis, we investigate discursive practices of a group of travestis who, besides being sex workers, participate in a non-governmental organisation (Liberdade) that fights for travestis' rights, in Cidade do Sul, southern Brazil. More specifically, we scrutinise the manipulation of the Brazilian Portuguese grammatical gender system. As it will be described, travestis' body transformations enable them to deploy feminine and masculine grammatical forms in the construction of a multitude of gendered meanings to their identity positions.

The study is based on a corpus of approximately 50 hours of recordings collected during a 12-month fieldwork. The discussion at hand presents analysis of 10 hours and 30 minutes of audio-recorded interactions between researchers and travestis that took place in Liberdade headquarters.

Travestility: the juxtaposition of gendered signs

Simply put, travestis are biologically male individuals who use a myriad of *techniques du corps* (Mauss 1996) to accomplish physical features culturally associated with women. In contrast with transsexuals, travestis despise the mention of undergoing sex reassignment surgery. What they struggle for is femininity, not femaleness. Or, as Kulick (1998) puts it, travestis wish to 'feel like women'.

In order to accomplish their desire to be sexually attractive to men in a strongly heteronormative society, travestis undergo an on-going, never completed process of body transformations. The 'embodiment' (Csordas 1990) of feminine values on a biologically male body seems to give travestis a plethora of polymorphous social positionings. The travesti body is thus 'a project' (Shilling 1997:69), a template upon which her social identity will be constantly moulded and reinvented. Travestis dye their hair, use make-up, wear women's clothes and high-heeled shoes, and ingest large amounts of female hormones to 'feminise' their bodies. Hormonal treatments seem to be 'a ritual of passage' (Benedetti 2000b:88) through which the embodying of travestility[1] is fully accomplished.

Another salient substance-based practice travestis deploy in their construction of a new identity is the use of industrial and/or surgical silicone – an intervention believed to be an irreversible move in these individuals' lives.[2] In contrast with the use of hormones, the use of silicone is not a diacritic index of travestility. Even though it is highly valued by travestis, it is an expensive procedure, and not every travesti does it. However, those who use it seem to earn more physical capital (Bourdieu 1986) in their lives as prostitutes, and have more social capital among their peers. The acquisition of culturally acceptable feminine body shapes is fastened by the injection of silicone. However, it is also a painful and dangerous process to go through.[3]

The body type which travestis aspire to is that of the young teenage actresses famous throughout the country via some popular *novelas* (soap operas). The wish of having more delicate (but still exuberantly rounded) body forms might be viewed as an attempt to approximate the *patricinhas* (young bourgeois straight girls who are stereotypically represented as rich, consumerist, and sexy). It's important to note, however, that a travestis' penis is what marks her as culturally, biologically, and socially distinctive. Kulick (1998) notes that every travesti values her penis for (1) being a source of money in the sex markets and (2) being what identifies them as travestis. The combination of ideologically feminine semiotic signs with a key diacritic symbol of masculinity is what gives travestis a particular gendered/sexual place in Brazilian society.

The feminising processes travestis undertake seem to be well portrayed by Giddens (1993), who claims that anatomy is not humankind's destiny anymore. The changes these individuals impinge on their bodies support the concept that identity (especially gender identity) is a matter of life style and choice, not essence. Travestis' femininising processes demonstrate that the body is taken not as a passive means on which social meanings are nailed but as an active participant in the constructions of those meanings. Upon manipulating their masculine body forms, travestis embody flexible gendered and sexual meanings which are socially and linguistically perpetuated.

When it comes to using language, travestis usually adopt female names and commonly address one another with feminine grammatical forms in an attempt to make their discursive gender consistent with their new appearance. It is interesting to note that because of this seemingly consistency, travestis' language use has been taken to be quite irrelevant to the construction of their identity. A number of studies have aimed at scrutinising travestis' identity position in Brazil. Nevertheless, the majority of these studies have been relatively nonchalant about the importance of language (and more specifically of the grammatical gender system) in the construction of a travesti's social positions (Benedetti 2000a, 2000b; Mott 1987; Oliveira 1994; Pelúcio 2005; Silva 1993, 1996; Silva and Florentino 1996).

Kulick's (1998) monograph on travestis in northeastern Brazil is an exception in this respect, as he discusses some of the complexities involved in the use of language among travestis. According to Kulick (1998:216), 'when travesti speakers use the word *travesti* to talk about travestis, they will normally use grammatically masculine articles, pronouns, and adjectival endings'. Kulick notes that travestis rarely use the word 'travesti' in their talk; they prefer to use words like *bicha* (roughly translated as fag in English) which, being grammatically feminine, allows travestis the possibility of using feminine terms in their speech. When talking about the time before the travestis' body transformations took place, the author notes that travestis tend to refer to themselves in the masculine grammatical gender. The author also argues that 'whenever travestis use [the word *travesti*] to speak generally about travestis as a group, they seem shepherded by grammar to use masculine forms ... that agree with *travesti*' (Kulick 1999:612).

The travestis investigated here from southern Brazil have a high degree of political awareness and involvement. They do not consistently deploy feminine forms in their speech. Masculine forms are used in specific discursive contexts and seem to be attached to certain ideological constructs concerning broader discourses of femininity and masculinity. Within the community studied by Kulick, the mixing of gendered forms in travestis' talk seems to happen as a result of the influence that grammatical gender exerts on referential gender, at least with respect to uses of *bicha* and *travesti*. Among the travestis investigated here, the phenomenon is explained as a reflection of the relationship between grammatical gender and societal discourses of masculinity. In an attempt to deepen understandings of the polysemy of the grammatical gender system, we undertake an analysis of its manipulation by travestis in southern Brazil. As it will be discussed, travestis use masculine grammatical forms as a linguistic device to create complex, multilayered identities.

Analysis

Brazilian Portuguese marks nouns, adjectives, pronouns, and articles with masculine or feminine grammatical gender. Nouns that refer to human beings normally equate their grammatical gender with the sex of the person. This becomes a more complex issue when the person involved is a travesti. In traditional grammars, the word travesti is described as a masculine noun. However, early in the fieldwork, we became aware of the emic value of the feminine choices among travestis, as Excerpt 1 demonstrates.[4]

Excerpt 1

ROD: *E tu Thalia(.) Como é que tu definiria* ***o travesti****?=*
And you Thalia. How would you define **the (masc.) travesti (masc.)**?=

SANDRA: *=OLHA AQUI Ó(.) Vamo entrá no nível- num nível assim(.) Pra tu se enquadrá com a gente não é* ***O tra[ves]ti****(.)* ***A travesti.***
=LOOK GUY. Let's speak the same language let's speak the same language for you to become part of the group. It's not **THE (masc.) tra[vesti] (masc.) It's THE (fem.) travesti (fem.)**

ROD: *[ok]*
[ok]

The exchange above involved one of us, Rodrigo, Sandra (who is the female lawyer for Liberdade and not a travesti), and two travestis, Fabíola and Thalia. As it can be seen in the exchange, in Rodrigo's question he uses the word travesti as a masculine noun. Before even attempting to provide the information requested, Sandra responds with the most dispreferred type of repair, the other-initiated other-repair (Schegloff, Jefferson and Sacks 1977), in which she corrects Rodrigo's referral to travestis in the masculine form. She does so by invoking the wish to make him a member of that community; that is, if he desires to be part of that group, he should speak the 'same language'.

As the excerpt conveys, the community studied is aware of the power of language to reproduce and/or recreate identities. The feminine, rather than the normative masculine form, is the default emic choice for referring to travestis in this group. Nonetheless, during the interviews travestis still occasionally used the masculine forms. Given that the travestis studied do make a point of referring to themselves in the feminine forms, why is it the case that they occasionally used the masculine? After analyzing all instances in which travestis used masculine forms to refer to themselves or to other travestis, we realised that they fall into four different discursive contexts:

1 narratives about the time the body transformations took place;
2 reports produced by others when talking about travestis;
3 description of themselves within their family relationships; and
4 establishment of contrast between the travesti speaker and other travestis with whom the speaker does not identify.

The travestis studied use the linguistic gender system in a sophisticated fashion to construct a plethora of social meanings, which is grounded on their ambiguity as social actors. Travestis can undermine the grammatical constraints of their category to build a linguistic persona that converges with their gender performances (Butler 1990). We will discuss each of these different discursive contexts in turn.

Narratives about the time the body transformations took place

The most common use of masculine forms happens when the travestis talk about themselves before the time the body transformations took place or, in other words, before they entered the process of embodying travestility. The grammatical gender system is thus used as a tense marker. When travestis describe moments from their childhood, they usually use masculine forms to depict themselves at that moment (see Excerpts 2 and 3). As mentioned earlier, such use has also been reported by Kulick (1998) among travestis in the Brazilian northeastern city of Salvador.

Excerpt 2
[LIB 953 – CLCR]

```
CYNTHYA: Isso tem até num livro que eu li na na minha infância.
Quando eu era reprovado meu pai me deixava de castigo eu ficava
numa biblioteca lendo que falava da infância e da fase adulta.
This is even in a book that I book that I read in in childhood.
When I failed (masc.) my father would punish me and I stayed in
a library reading books about childhood and adulthood.
```

In Excerpt 2, we see Cynthya talking about childhood, before travestility, when she would be punished by her father for failing in school. She refers to the failing self in the masculine form. Another example of this use of the masculine form is in Excerpt 3.

Excerpt 3
[LIB 1653 – FTCLSR]

```
FABÍOLA: =É um começo né. Mas eu era novinho. Tinha o quê? Vinte
quatro vinte cinco anos como eu te falei. Aí fui viajá. Caí fora.
Fui pra São Paulo nessa época.
=It's a start, no. But I was very young (masc). I was what? Twenty-
four twenty-five years old as I told you. Then I went traveling.
Got away. I went to São Paulo that time.
```

In this narrative, Fabíola does not talk about childhood, as Cynthya does above, but about the time she had already come out. More specifically, she is describing the beginning of her life as a travesti. However, at that time, Fabíola had not yet started the process of body transformation. She refers to herself as being very young (*novinho*) then and does so in the masculine form.

Both these examples, and comments from travestis in interviews, suggest that the use of masculine forms has two explanations. First, because at the time in her life she is talking about, the speaker's travesti identity had not been moulded by the body transformations described above, the grammatical gender system is deployed to mark the stages of travestis' identification processes: masculine forms foreground their male period, and feminine forms their travestility. Second, travestis switch to masculine forms when talking about their life before travestility as an indexical sign of an emotional attachment to their up-bringing in their family sphere. This attachment seems to be also reflected in Excerpts 5 and 6 below.

Reported speech produced by others when talking about travestis

Travestis also use masculine forms to report on other people's discourse about travestis, as Excerpt 4 shows.

Excerpt 4
[LIB 1653 – FTCLSR]

FABÍOLA: *Às vezes dizem assim 'é porque* ***as bichas, os travestis*** *não gostam de mulher'. Dizem tu não gosta de mulher. Mas como eu não vô gostá de mulher? Eu me identifico com ELAS né? As mulheres são minhas AMIGAS. Eu me identifico com elas.*
Sometimes they say 'the fags (fem.) **the travestis (masc.)** they don't like women'. They say you don't like women. But how come I don't like women? I identify myself with THEM right? Women are my FRIENDS. I identify myself with them.

Fabíola reports what other people have said about travestis, more specifically, that travestis do not like women. She refutes what she claims to be a 'false' accusation by providing reasons why she obviously likes women, reiterating that she identifies herself with them. Since these are claims that the travestis do not align themselves with, this usage in quoted speech is in implicit contrast with their own usage. It may seem to distance them both from this way of referring to travestis as well as the views that are attributed to them. Interestingly, in Excerpt 4, although the word travesti comes immediately after a feminine word used to describe homosexuals in general (i.e. *bichas*), it is still employed as a masculine word. It seems that, although travestis themselves readily correct those who refer to them in the masculine, social views of travestis are so strongly rooted that they are not able to modify this fact in their spontaneous speech.

Description of themselves within their family relationships

Travestis also use masculine forms when describing themselves within their biological families, as shown through in Excerpts 5 and 6 below.

Excerpt 5
[LIB 1653 – FTCLSR]

THALIA: *=Mãe é mãe. Ela sabe que a gente nunca não vai sê uma mulher pra elas. A gente vai sê* ***um filho home****. Como ela sofreu pra ganhá todas as gentes né? Ele- como* ***eu eu fui o eu sô o filho mais velho,*** *ela quase morreu quando ela foi me ganhá. Por eu sê*

assim. A minha família me aceita do jeito que eu sô [...]
=A mother is a mother. She knows that we won't ever be women for them. We'll always be their **male child.** As she suffered to give birth to us right? He- like me, as **I I was the (masc.)- I am the elder son,** she almost died to give birth to me. For I am this way. My family accepts the way I am [...]

As we can see above, Thalia is talking about her mother's conceptions of her gender identity – once a male, forever one. Thalia uncritically reports that a mother will never take a travesti child as a woman. Note, however, that this is also like Excerpt 2, in that the speaker is talking about how others see them.

It is also striking the self-correction Thalia makes in 'as I I was the (masc.)- I am the elder son'. She starts by stating that she 'was' the eldest son, but changes mid-course into the present tense. There seems to be some tension involved here between having been 'the eldest son' (in the past) and still being the eldest child (in the present), but no longer the 'eldest *son*'. We see Joana making similar use of the masculine in Excerpt 6 to refer to herself within her biological family.

Excerpt 6
[LIB 1653 – JCMSR]

JOANA:	*[...] por respeito a ela eu não uso roupa de mulher. TENHO TODAS AS MINHAS ROUPAS lá. Ela sabe que eu tenho INÚMERAS roupas ma::s de casa eu não saio* ***vestido*** *de mulher.* [...] to respect her ((the mother)) I don't wear women's clothes. I HAVE ALL MY CLOTHES there. She knows I have SEVERAL clothes but I don't leave home **dressed (masc.)** in women's clothes.
RODRIGO:	*Sim. Tu sai e te veste em outro [lugar]* I see. You get out and dress up [elsewhere]
JOANA:	*[É.] Me visto em outro lugar.* [Yeah.] I dress up elsewhere.

Despite talking about dressing as a woman, Joana reports that, out of respect towards her mother, she does not leave home dressed as such. In doing so, she refers to herself in the masculine form, i.e. *vestido* 'dressed' (masc.). This use of the masculine forms seems to convey the travesti's awareness of some type of unacceptable ideological image of the travestis within society. In using the masculine form within environments in which they reiterate their respect towards their families, mainly towards their mothers, travestis seem to frame their awareness of such ideological construction.

Notice that in both cases in which the travestis mention respect to their biological families, they specifically refer to their mothers. Within the travesti community studied, mothers, despite not necessarily accepting their children's travestility, do not deny the children as theirs, as often seems to happen with the travestis' fathers.

Establishing the contrast me/us versus them: a face-saving strategy

Finally, perhaps the most revealing usage of the masculine forms by travestis in this study happens in contexts in which the travesti interviewed makes a point of distinguishing herself from other travestis. Within this context, the travesti speaker refers to other travestis with masculine forms when describing events in which these others were involved that the speaker understands in a negative way. Here travestis use gender distinctions to build a positive public image by contrasting the 'I' with other travestis with whom the speaker does not to identify, as can be seen in the Excerpts 7 and 8 below.

***Excerpt** 7*
[LIB 953 – CLCR]

CYNTHYA: *[...] Eu acho que não há a a necessidade de você tá:: colocando o teu corpo à mostra, os teus atributos porque muitas vezes tu tem que avaliá assim ó. Assim como essas pessoas se sentem ofendidas agredidas por uma visão corporal, ela elas sabem que não- por mais que seja um aspecto feminino não é uma mulher e:: muitas vezes assim ó. No MEU caso eu tenho família eu tenho meu sobrinho meus eu tenho irmã e eu:: sempre manten- mantive um pa- um padrão de de educacional da minha- dos meus familiares. De forma que nunca os agredisse. Agora sempre eu acho que pra tudo existe um local pra se fazê isso. Eu não gostaria que a minha sobrinha ou meu sobrinho passasse numa avenida e tivesse uma prostituta ou* ***um travesti exposto****, expondo sua genitália ou algo mais. [...]*
I think there's no need for you to show your body features on the street because many times you have to think this way. As these people feel offended, shocked because they see naked bodies on the streets they know it's not- although it has a feminine aspect it's not a woman. In MY case I have a family, I have a nephew I have my- I have a sister and I always keep a pattern of politeness for my relatives not to shock them. But I think there a specific place for everything. I wouldn't like my niece or my nephew to see a prostitute or **a (masc.) travesti (masc.) exposed (masc.)** showing her genitalia or something else. [...]

Cynthya uses the masculine form to refer to travestis who do not deserve public respect – those who expose their genitalia in public spaces. We consider it a face-saving strategy because as the interviewed travesti constructs a negative identity of other travestis (using masculine forms), she claims a positive identity for herself (using the contrasting feminine forms). The masculine forms are used to refer to travestis described as boisterous and dangerous to their public image. In other words, what she describes as negative behavior about other travestis is what she declares herself not to do.

In Excerpt 8, we see another travesti, Fabíola, making use of the masculine form in a similar way.

Excerpt 8
[LIB 1653 – FTCLSR]

```
CASSIANA:   =É:: era aquela coisa que tinha muito glamour né? Hoje
            em dia [não.]
            =Yeah::: it was a very glamorous thing right? Not
            [nowadays].
FABÍOLA:    [Tinha] tinha- travesti era LUXO. Mas hoje em dia não
            hoje tá muito vulgarizado. Porque eles mesmo deturparam
            a classe.
            [There was] there was- being a travesti used to be a
            luxurious thing. But nowadays ((travesti)) is very
            vulgarised (masc.). Because they (masc.) themselves
            (masc.) spoil the image of the community.
```

In talking about travestis in the plural form while making a critique, Fabíola is not making a generalisation about *all* travestis. She is talking specifically about some, those who 'vulgarise themselves' and with whom she seems not to identify.

What seems most striking about the use of the masculine form in Excerpts 7 and 8 is that the speakers still refer to a community to which they belong, but they are specifically talking about a particular travesti type with which they do not identify. Here gender seems to be operating like a marker of exclusion of the speaker from a certain type of group of travestis. This pattern of use of masculine grammatical forms seems to be similar to what Hall and O'Donovan (1996) found among the Indian *hijras* (eunuchs). The *hijras* also make use of the masculine to differentiate themselves from a certain type of *hijras* – those whom the *hijra* speaker does not believe to deserve to be addressed in the feminine because they are believed either to have a lower status in the community or to be disloyal to their status as *hijras.*

Do bodies matter? Transgender, language, and embodiment

So far, we have outlined travestis' identity as the product of sociocultural processes of impinging feminine gendered symbols on their biologically male bodies. These processes seem to allow for the coexistence of several gendered meanings since a femininely shaped body with a penis places travestis at the intersection of discourses about gender. In this section we advance the discussion about language and transgender through the perspective of embodiment by reviewing some research on the topic that, fundamental as they are, overlook the importance of transgenders' bodies to their linguistic practices.

In his brilliant review essay 'Transgender and language: A review of literature and suggestions for the future' Kulick (1999:616) asserts that 'the relationship between transgender and language is one of mutual *differánce*, of mutual fluidity that exceeds fixed meanings, remains always plural, and continually disrupts the marking of boundaries'. This has been shown in the analysis above and is also the case in Hall and O'Donovan's (1996) investigation of how Hindi-speaking *hijras* manipulate the linguistic gender system in Hindi. *Hijras* employ the grammatical gender to evoke 'a wide range of societal discourses on power and solidarity, difference and dominance' – whereas feminine forms are used to convey solidarity, masculine forms are used to index respect or contempt to one's social status (Hall and O'Donovan 1996:258). *Hijras*, thus, use the linguistic gender system to produce relations of power and/or solidarity in which local identities and gender understandings are negotiated.

Livia (1997) also highlights transgenders' awareness of the power that linguistic gender bending carries. In her analysis of the autobiography of the French transsexual Georgine Nöel, Livia focuses on how the author switches between masculine and feminine forms throughout the text. Although Nöel affirms to have always been female, her use of the French grammatical system varies. Livia contends that the switches from masculine to feminine forms convey a sense of success and triumph in Nöel's female self. As the author notes, upon using the feminine, Nöel distances herself from traditional conceptions of gender and heteronormativity, thus emphasising her female self as the privileged identity. Interestingly, according to Livia, the switches from feminine to masculine forms deploy frustration and failure towards her male body. This kind of switch is also used to demonstrate her superiority and authority in society as a male. Transgender people, Livia (1997:365) asserts, 'act as a troubleshooter for gender, revealing resources available in the gender system to which more traditional identities have scant resource'.

In a similar vein, Besnier (1997, 2003, 2007) investigates the constructions of a trangender identity in diasporic Tonga which is widely referred to as *fakaleiti*. Culturally speaking, *fakaleiti* are like travestis, *hijras* and transsexuals in that their bodily practices juxtapose womanhood and manhood. Linguistically speaking, these individuals fluidly construct their identities by switching from Tongan (the local language) to English (the language of modernity and extra-locality). By doing so, 'leiti position themselves on the side of prestige and worldliness ... in opposition to the use of Tongan and its localized connotations' (Besnier 2003:291).

Note that the Indian *hijras*, the French transsexual, the Tongan *fakaleiti*, and the Brazilian travestis switch codes in an attempt to occupy specific places in their identity market. This, we think, might be enabled by their liminal bodies. Transgenders, in part via their body practices, participate in a multitude of gendered discourses that enable them to linguistically position themselves in many ways.

With regard to travestis, their patterns of grammatical gender use demonstrate that the embodiment (Csordas 1990) of feminine values on biologically male bodies gives them undeniable ambiguity which is perpetuated socially and linguistically. Upon reinterpreting their shapes, travestis embody social understandings of femininity and masculinity in their gender negotiations. Thus, travestis strengthen their social polymorphy, which is also present in their speech. As Csordas (1990:36) asserts, 'bodies are not just objects to us; they are an integral part of the perceiving subject'. Travestis' bodies transcend the status of passive supports for their social modifications; they become active participants in building sociolinguistic meanings. This fact reaffirms Goffman's (1959) ideas of the body as a mediator between people's self-identity and their social identity. In the case of travestis, it is evident through the discursive practices described in this paper.

We would like to suggest that in order to deepen understandings of the links between gender and language use (especially in the case of transgender but not at all restricted to it) researchers should bear in mind how language users embody local understandings of gender and sexuality onto their bodies and how this embodiment enables users to frame their language use accordingly to surrounding ideologies about gendered and sexual beings. Transgender language should be taken as a result of the gendered meanings (re)constructed through body practices. As the body is the main medium through which transgenders assert their identities in the intersection of socially available genders, it must be understood as a catalyst for discourses of masculinity and femininity. Thus, it is upon (re) signifying their bodies that transgender people have privileged access to a multitude of identity positions which is partly conveyed in the ways they use language to place themselves between the boundaries of the gender dichotomy. Needless to say, gendered bodily meanings are contextbased, varying greatly from one culture to another. What we suggest, then, is that research on trangender and language take into consideration the various gendered meanings impinged on bodies and how these meanings are juxtaposed by trangender individuals to shape their identity and, consequently, language use. We agree with Walters (1999:203) who argues 'that sociolinguists [should] acknowledge that each speaker's body, itself socially constructed, simultaneously permits and regulates the subject's patterns of language use in complex ways'. As we have shown, this fact can be seen in the sophisticated fashion travestis manipulate their bodies and language to construct themselves as (trans)gendered individuals.

Notes

1 The term *travestilidade* 'travestility' was used by the psychologist William Siqueira during the X ENTLAIDS (National Gathering of Travestis and Supporters Fighting against AIDS and Struggling for Human Rights and Health), Porto Alegre (Brazil), June 2003.

2 The term 'substance-based practice' is borrowed from Herdt's (1981, 1984a, 1984b) and Elliston's (1995) studies in Melanesia.

3 For detailed discussions of travestis' use of industrial silicone, see Kulick (1998) and Benedetti (2000a, 2000b).

4 The transcription conventions were adapted from Du Bois, Schuetze-Coburn, Paolino and Cumming (1992).

References

Benedetti, Marcos R. (2000a) Toda Feita: O corpo e o gênero das travestis. Master's thesis, Programa de Pós-graduação em Antropologia Social, Universidade Federal do Rio Grande do Sul, Porto Alegre, Brazil.

Benedetti, Marcos R. (2000b) Hormonizada: Reflexões sobre o uso de hormônios e tecnologia do gênero entre travetis em Porto Alegre. In Ana Isabel Fabregas-Martinez and Marcos Reneto Benedetti (eds) *Na batalha: Identidade, sexualidade e poder no universo da batalha* 47–62. Porto Alegre: Da Casa Editora/GAPA-RS.

Besnier, Niko (1997) Sluts and superwomen: the politics of gender liminality in urban Tonga. *Ethnos* 62(1–2): 5–31. https://doi.org/10.1080/00141844.1997.9981542

Besnier, Niko (2003) Crossing genders, mixing languages: the linguistic construction of transgenderism in Tonga. In Janet Holmes and Myriam Meyerhoff (eds) *The Handbook of Language and Gender* 279–301. Oxford: Blackwell. https://doi.org/10.1002/9780470756942.ch12

Besnier, Niko (2007) Language and gender research at the intersection of the global and local. *Gender and Language* 1(1): 67–78. https://doi.org/10.1558/genl.2007.1.1.67

Bolin, Ann (1988) *In Search of Eve: Transsexual Rites of Passage*. South Hadley, MA: Bergin and Garvey.

Bourdieu, Pierre (1986) The forms of capital. In John Richardson (ed.) *Handbook of Theory and Research for the Sociology of Education* 241–325. New York: Greenwood Press.

Butler, Judith (1990) *Gender Trouble: Feminism and the Subversion of Identity*. New York: Routledge.

Clastres, Pierre (1990) *A sociedade contra o estado*. Rio de Janeiro: Francisco Alves.

Csordas, Thomas (1990) Embodiment as a paradigm for anthropology. *Ethos* 18: 5–47. https://doi.org/10.1525/eth.1990.18.1.02a00010

Du Bois, John W., Schuetze-Coburn, Stephan, Paolino, Danae and Cumming, Susanna (eds) (1992) *Discourse Transcription*. Santa Barbara, CA: University of Santa Barbara.

Elliston, Deborah A. (1995) Erotic anthropology: 'ritualized homosexuality' in Melanesia and beyond. *American Ethnologist* 22: 848–67. https://doi.org/10.1525/ae.1995.22.4.02a00100

Epple, Carolyn (1998) Coming to terms with navajo nadleehi: a critique of berdache, 'gay', 'alternative gender', and 'two spirit'. *American Ethnologist* 25(2): 267–90. https://doi.org/10.1525/ae.1998.25.2.267

Giddens, Anthony (1993) *A transformação da intimidade: Sexualidade, amor e erotismo nas sociedades modernas*. São Paulo: Editora da Universidade Estadual Paulista.

Goffman, Erving (1959) *The Presentation of Self in Everyday Life*. New York: Doubleday.

Hall, Kira and O'Donovan, Veronica (1996) Shifting gender positions among Hindi-speaking hijras. In Victoria Bergvall, Janet Bing and Alice Freed (eds) *Rethinking Language and Gender Research: Theory and Practice* 228–66. London: Longman.

Herdt, Gilbert H. (1981) *Guardians of the Flutes: Idioms of Masculinity*. New York: McGraw-Hill.

Herdt, Gilbert (1984a) Ritualized homosexual behavior in the male cults in Melanesia, 1862–1983: an introduction. In Gilbert H. Herdt (ed.) *Ritualized Homosexuality in Melanesia* 1–82. Berkeley, CA: University of California Press.

Herdt, Gilbert (1984b) Semen transactions in Sambia culture. In (1984a): 167–210.

King, Dave (1993) *The Transvestite and the Transsexual: Public Categories and Private Identities*. Aldershot: Avebury.

Kulick, Don (1998) *Travesti: Sex, Gender, and Culture among Brazilian Transgendered Prostitutes*. Chicago, IL: University of Chicago Press.

Kulick, Don (1999) Transgender and language: a review of literature and suggestions for the future. *Journal of Lesbian and Gay Studies* 5: 601–22.

Levy, Robert (1971) The community function of Tahitian male transvestism: a hypothesis. *Anthropological Quarterly* 44(1): 12–21. https://doi.org/10.2307/3316812

Livia, Anna (1997) Disloyal to masculinity: linguistic gender and liminal identity in French. In Anna Livia and Kira Hall (eds) *Queerly Phrased: Language, Gender, and Sexuality* 349–68. New York: Oxford University Press.

Mauss, Marcel (1996) Les techniques du corps. In Marcel Mauss (ed.) *Sociologie et antropologie* 363–8. Paris: PUF.

McElhinny, Bonnie (2003) Theorizing gender in sociolinguistics and linguistic anthropology. In Janet Holmes and Miriam Meyerhoff (eds) *The Handbook of Language and Gender* 21–42. Oxford: Blackwell. https://doi.org/10.1002/9780470756942.ch1

McKenzie, Gordene O. (1994) *Transgender Nation*. Bowling Green, OH: Bowling Green State University Popular Press.

Mott, Luiz (1987) Gilete na carne: Etnografia das automutilações dos travestis da Bahia. *Revista do Instituto de Medicina Social de São Paulo* 4: 41–56.

Oliveira, Neuza Maria de (1994) *Damas de paus: O jogo aberto dos travestis no espelho da mulher*. Salvador: Universidade Federal da Bahia.

Pelúcio, Larissa (2005) Na noite nem todos os gatos são pardos: Notas sobre a prostituição travesti. *Cadernos Pagu* 25: 217–48. https://doi.org/10.1590/S0104-83332005000200009

Schegloff, Emmanuel A., Jefferson, Gail and Sacks, Harvey (1977) The preference for selfcorrection in the organization of repair in conversation. *Language* 53: 361–82. https://doi.org/10.1353/lan.1977.0041

Shapiro, Judith (1991) Transsexualism: reflections on the persistence of gender and the mutability of sex. In Julia Epstein and Kristina Straub (eds) *Body Guards: The Cultural Politics of Gender ambiguity* 248–79. London: Routledge.

Shilling, Chris (1997) The body and difference. In Kathryn Woodward (ed.) *Identity and Difference* 63–107. London: Sage Publications.

Silva, Hélio R. S. (1993) *Travesti: A invenção do feminino*. Rio de Janeiro: Iser.

Silva, Hélio R. S. (1996) *Certas cariocas: Travestis e a vida de rua no Rio de Janeiro*. Rio de Janeiro: Relume-Dumará.

Silva, Hélio R. S. and Florentino, Cristina de Oliveira (1996) A sociedade dos travestis: Espelhos, papéis e interpretações. In Richard Parker and Regina Maria Barbosa (eds) *Sexualidades Brasileiras* 105–18. Rio de Janeiro: Relume-Dumará.

Walters, Keith (1999) 'Opening the door of paradise a cubit': educated Tunisian women, embodied linguistic practice, and theories of language and gender. In Mary Bucholtz, A. C. Liang and Laurel Sutton (eds) *Reinventing Identities: The Gendered Self in Discourse* 200–217. New York: Oxford University Press.

Wikan, Unni (1978) The Omani xanith: a third gender role? *Man* 13(3): 473–5.

6

Butch camp: on the discursive construction of a queer identity position

Veronika Koller

LANCASTER UNIVERSITY, UK

Introduction

This chapter will examine how one author discursively constructs a historically contingent subject position of lesbian female masculinity by selectively drawing on linguistic features that have become associated with gay male femininity. The text in question, Lorna Gulston's essay titled 'Butch', is remarkable not only for its hybrid and paradoxical use of gendered language features, but also for its position in the history of lesbian discourse. Published in 1980, it can be regarded as representative of a debate on gender and sexual identity that would dominate lesbian discourses throughout the decade and beyond, at least in western Europe (e.g. Jeffreys 1989; Nestle 1981). Towards the end of the 1970s, dissenting voices made themselves heard, claiming that the dominant representations of lesbians that were advocated by lesbian feminist discourse (i.e. overwhelmingly white and middle-class) excluded particular groups. Such exclusion meant that the identities of butches and femmes were made largely invisible by not being talked about and silenced by being denied discourse access. The detailed analysis in this chapter of the socio-historical context, the discursive practices surrounding the sample text, and the text itself, will trace how older and/or working-class women, who felt that their pre-Stonewall[1] culture and identity was at risk of being forgotten, reclaimed their position in the lesbian community. The text that I will focus on in this essay, a 1980 essay titled 'Butch', was written from a position outside the elite (i.e. white, middle-class lesbian feminist) discourse. Rather than attacking the dominant elite, however, author Lorna Gulston provides an ironic account of butch/femme identities which reminisces about pre-Stonewall bar culture while anticipating ideas about fluid gender identities that were propounded by queer theory ten years later.

In this chapter I will first outline the main points of critical discourse analysis as a theoretical framework, and especially the discourse-historical approach within it. This approach will then be discussed with regards to how it can be applied to the study of queer identity. The next section will address how the framework translates into a tripartite analysis of socio-political background, discursive practice and concrete linguistic investigation into texts. Accordingly, the analysis section will be divided into those three parts, with the linguistic analysis focusing on social actors and intertextuality/-discursivity. The chapter will close with a discussion of the text as an example of the historically contextualised construction of queer identity in discourse. In this way, the chapter will meet its main aim to describe, interpret and explain how a particular queer identity was constructed through language and discursive interaction at a particular historical moment.

Theory

This section will provide an overview of the basic tenets of critical discourse analysis (CDA) and its threefold model of linguistic analysis which takes into account socio-political factors, as well as the practices of production, distribution and reception that shape texts. The focus will here be on the discourse-historical model (Wodak 2001; Reisigl and Wodak 2016), showing how it can be utilised to study linguistic expressions of queer identity.

Before outlining the model, it seems appropriate to briefly address some of the criticisms that CDA has attracted over the years (e.g. Stubbs 1997; Widdowson 2004). The most pervasive and not always unjustified criticism is of a perceived circularity of argument, where ideological models held by the analyst are simplistically read off the text. This is seen to be aided by a non-accountable approach to data, meaning that mere text fragments are selected, and only those that conveniently corroborate the researcher's worldview are used. The discourse-historical approach responds to this by placing particular emphasis on triangulation, linking the text under investigation with other texts instantiating the same, or closely related, discourses. Further supporting evidence is provided by background information gleaned from ethnographic fieldwork. Accordingly, the text analysis in this chapter draws on a variety of historical sources as well as on published interviews as a form of oral history. Moreover, it is part of a larger study that also included semi-structured interviews with women who identified as part of a lesbian community in the 1970s and 1980s (see Koller 2008:34–5).

One of the central tenets of CDA is the belief that despite triangulation and being accountable in one's data selection and analysis, a completely impartial stance is impossible for any participant-observer. My own position as a researcher is influenced by the fact that I have been a part of local lesbian communities since the early 1990s, be it as a member of grassroots political groups or lesbian and gay event organisations, as one node in a friendship network or as a researcher. In the latter role, I approach lesbian discourses from a perspective that seeks to unravel how discourse participants use language and texts to convey a collective identity. However, I recognise that I am bound to be influenced by my own experiences with and in the community under investigation.

With these provisos in mind, the following paragraphs will outline the theoretical framework used in this chapter. Starting at the micro-level, texts can be seen as semantically coherent and syntactically cohesive units of written or spoken language. Such textual entities are self-contained in that they can be processed as separate units, although understanding often requires background knowledge of the contexts of their production (e.g. the cultural or political background of the text producer), including other, previous texts that a text usually refers back to, or any future texts it anticipates. For instance, the text analysed later in this chapter alludes to the classic lesbian novel *The Well of Loneliness* by Radclyffe Hall ([1928]1990), and knowledge of at least the title of the book and its status in lesbian history is required to understand the ironic function that mentioning it serves at that particular point in the text.

Being produced, distributed and received by text producers and recipients, one of the main functions of a text is to reinforce, question or subvert the relationships between discourse participants. Following Fairclough (2010), such textually mediated social action is here defined as discourse. As an analytical construct, discourse refers to a totality of texts, both written and spoken, that are related by a common topic (e.g. discourse on sexual identity) or a common stance (e.g. feminist discourse), both of which are often combined (e.g. feminist discourse on sexual identity). The texts that instantiate a particular discourse tend to be circulated in a particular social domain (e.g. a lesbian community) of which their producers are usually a part. Discourse serves both an interpersonal and an experiential metafunction (Halliday and Matthiessen 2014), by building and negotiating realities through texts. In short, discourse constitutes society and culture and is in turn constituted by them. It is therefore ideologically invested in the sense that its producers attempt to gain influence and power in the social world. Discourse thereby becomes a site of ideological struggle. The interrelations between the linguistic and the social aspects of discourse are accounted for in a three-dimensional framework consisting of text, discourse practice and socio-political context (Fairclough 2010:133). Starting from a specific text as a form of social action, critical analysis of discourse allows for conclusions to be drawn regarding both the discursive and socio-cultural context determinant of, and reproduced in, the text.

As mentioned above, texts, while self-contained units, routinely integrate earlier texts and occasionally anticipate future texts. This metaphorical 'dialogicality' (Bakhtin 1986) means that texts are always located in an historical context, including future contexts of reception. The same goes for the more abstract notion of discourse, which is historical in the sense that it is always connected to context, and to other discourses (Wodak 1996:17). In this sense, 'discourse has a history that not only precedes but conditions its contemporary usages' (Butler 1993:227). The discourse-historical approach within CDA (de Cillia, Reisigl and Wodak 1999; Reisigl and Wodak 2001:31–85, 2016; Wodak 2007) is problem-oriented, starting from a specific social phenomenon that is brought into being, negotiated and reinforced through 'a complex bundle of simultaneous and sequential interrelated linguistic acts that manifest themselves as ... texts' (Reisigl and Wodak 2001:36) – that is, through discourse. As a problem-based approach, discourse-historical analysis is inherently interdisciplinary, drawing on an eclectic range of analytical methods, empirical data and background knowledge in an attempt to 'transcend the purely linguistic dimension and to include ... the historical, political, sociological and/or psychological dimension in the analysis and interpretation of a specific discursive occasion' (Reisigl and Wodak 2001:35). As a consequence, discourse-historical research includes fieldwork and ethnography to study the phenomenon from the inside (Reisigl and Wodak 2016:32) and links textual analysis back to the contexts of discourse production, distribution and reception as well as the wider socio-political formation.

Given that the text analysed in this chapter, having been published in 1980, is historical, it is particularly important to look at the discourse formation at the time. Placed on the boundary of two decades, the essay can be read as reacting to lesbian feminist discourse of the 1970s by harking back to lesbian gender identities as lived in the 1950s and 1960s. By doing so, it represents an early contribution to a debate that was to characterise lesbian discourse in the 1980s. At the same time, however, the text anticipates later developments that were, at the time of its publication, still ten years in the future.

The 1990s started with the publication of Judith Butler's *Gender Trouble* ([1990]1999), which heralded the advent of queer theory. Conceived and first disseminated in academia, queer theory sees gender and sexual identity as located on a continuum instead of forming binary oppositions. In this framework, gender becomes a series of reiterable performative acts, which are characterised by parody and ironic reversal. Queer theory sees gender and sexuality as self-fulfilling prophecies in that they quote previous gender performances – language use, body posture, leisure time and consumption practices etc. – and by the same token reproduce a model that has no original instance. According to this line of thinking, 'identity is performatively constituted by the very "expressions" that are said to be its results' and attributes of gender and sexuality 'effectively constitute the identity they are said to express or reveal' (Butler [1990]1999:33, 180). Such a discursive construction of gender and sexuality can be endlessly repeated, but recontextualisation or 'displacement' will change the meaning of the gendered signifiers, affording potential subversive readings.

Queer theory finds its most obvious expression in the practice of camp, as instantiated in the text analysed in this chapter. Starting with Susan Sontag's seminal essay ([1964]1994), camp has usually been regarded as an attitude and behaviour mostly found in gay men. Its typical characteristics are exaggeration, flamboyance, aestheticism and (self-)irony, which often combine into a parody of stereotypical femininity. As the notions of irony and parody are hallmarks of queer theory, it is worthwhile quoting an early word of caution: Taking Nazism as an (admittedly extreme) example, Hoagland (1982:159) rightly states that 'the parody still validates Nazism by perpetuating the language game, the conceptual framework, and thereby allows those who work with deadly earnest toward fascism ... to live in an ideological framework necessary for their growth and development'. Seen as such, parody and irony are similar to negation in that they are frame-preserving (Lakoff 2002); that is, they still activate the mental models they seek to subvert.

Since the 1990s, communities have increasingly been regarded as 'based on the ways in which individuals imagine them rather than [as] identifiable entities' (Queen 1997:235). If there are no longer any transhistorical, essential qualities and characteristics which constitute identity, identities are but imagined and discursively constructed. As a result, the concept of a pre-discursive, unified identity is abandoned in favour of multiple identities cutting across each other in their permanent alteration. In its view of gender and sexual identity as fluid concepts that are continuously (re-)constructed and performed in discourse and material practices, queer theory is radically anti-essentialist. According to queer theorists such as Butler ([1990]1999:19) and Halberstam (1998b:35), 1970s discourse naturalised lesbian identity as an inherent, fixed and ahistorical component in the individual and as a basis for the formation of a collective group identity.

Ironically, however, lesbian feminism and queer theory start out from the same anti-essentialist premise, in that they both regard gender as a social construct. Most lesbian feminists conceive of gender as a heteropatriarchal invention propagated to maintain the dominance-submission relations between men and women (e.g. Dworkin [1987]2006:156). This is not too far away from Butler's notion of 'the heterosexual axis along which gender subordination is secured' (Butler 1997:121). As a consequence, queer theory's thrust to de-essentialise the links between sex and gender does hold some appeal for lesbian feminism (Wilkinson and Kitzinger 1996:378–9; see also Garber 2001 on the links between lesbian feminism and queer theory). However, for lesbian feminists such as Jeffreys, gender, understood as patriarchal notions of masculinity and femininity, is an eroticised binary difference, which becomes conflated with harmful inequality (Jeffreys 2003:44). In effect, every erotic desire and/or sexual practice that centres on dominance and submission becomes defined as 'heterosexual', and it is this kind of sexuality that reproduces gender as defined by most lesbian feminists (Jeffreys 1996). Queer theory on the other hand allows for a range of genders to be performed across contexts (see e.g. Roof 1998:35).

The text I am focusing on in this chapter is located at the divergence between lesbian feminism and queer theory. Butch/femme identities cannot be justified in lesbian feminism, which would regard them as reinforcing patriarchal inequality. In view of her particular historical context, the author counters this criticism by seemingly reinforcing pre-Stonewall notions of 'natural' gender identity but in fact anticipating queer notions of fluid gendered subject positions. The next section will spell out how this paradox can be captured in discourse-historical analysis.

Methods

The interrelatedness of text, context of production, distribution and reception, and wider socio-political context is mirrored in the linguistic analysis itself, which also works on three levels. In a data-driven approach, analysis always returns to the observed linguistic features at the textual level, such as form and frequency of reference to social actors, or traces of interdiscursivity. The analysis further accounts for the level of discursive practice and social institutions, taking into consideration the factors of setting and participants, as well as text production, distribution and reception. Finally, the wider social formation determining these factors is also analysed. Thus it becomes clear that each instance of text production is ultimately linked to a socio-political practice which is represented in social acts like speaking or writing, in social institutions providing the frame for social action (in the present case, independent media) and in the social formations in which such institutions are located. Given that the three levels are embedded in each other, the analysis can be bottom-up, starting from the text, or, as in the present chapter, top-down (i.e. first investigating the wider socio-political context of the time that the text originates from, investigating how that social formation impacts on the context of discourse production, distribution and reception, and finally analysing the text itself in linguistic detail). In this framework, a minute text analysis provides the evidence, in terms of linguistic features, that underpins the interpretation and explanation of the discursive construction of identity at the levels of interaction and socio-political context, respectively. The text thus analysed, Lorna Gulston's essay titled 'Butch', can be found at the beginning of the next section below. The extracts reproduced there comprise comments on the then reputation of butch women, on their appearance, growing up and professional preferences, followed by non-obvious cases of butchness and a plea for recognition.

As one linguistic parameter,[2] social actor representation tells us what individuals and groups are represented in what role in a text. Formally, social actor representation can be effected through personal pronouns and other deictic devices, and work in tandem with evaluation and metaphor. In his 'sociosemantic inventory of the ways in which social actors can be represented', van Leeuwen (2008:23) points out that social actors do not necessarily map onto grammatical actors; for instance, actors can be non-human entities that are still represented as engaged in particular actions. An example from the present text is 'tiny children far too young to have been moulded by those "environmental influences"' (lines 15–16), where in functional terms, 'environmental influences' is the actor in the clause. The following analysis will concentrate on human social actors, both groups and individuals, and on instances where social actors are actually named, thus also disregarding backgrounded and suppressed actors (van Leeuwen 2008:28–32). In the discourse-historical approach, social actors are referred to by referential or nominational devices, which can be further broken down into parameters such as labelling, euphemisms or pronoun usage (Wodak 2006:114).

The second major parameter of analysis covers intertextuality and interdiscursivity, both of which are key for a discourse-historical account. Following Fairclough (2003:17), intertextuality refers to the integration of (parts of) concrete texts into a text, while interdiscursivity means the incorporation of typical genre and discourse features into a text that instantiates a different discourse and/or genre. An example of the latter from the essay at hand is the reference to 'The Great Outdoors' as 'the butch's natural habitat' (lines 38–39), which both invokes essentialist discourses by using a collocation from biology to refer to a social actor, and alludes to the cultural myth of the lone ranger. The two devices show what other texts and discourses the author draws on and thus what models she aligns herself with or distances herself from.

The next section will put the above theoretical and methodological considerations into practice by carrying out a tripartite analysis of Gulston's 1980 essay 'Butch'.

Analysis

Extracts from Gulston's 1980 essay titled 'Butch' are reproduced below (with kind permission from the author).

> Once upon a time before the Well of Loneliness became a Whirlpool of Propinquity we were a force to be reckoned with, we oldfashioned butches. Even as recently as 15 years ago there were reported sightings of us at the Gateways, hair short-back-and-sides, trousers impeccably pressed, shirts crying scorn at Brand X, blazers smartly draped over square and capable shoulders, ties knotted to a millimetre, wafting our distinctive scent of aftershave lotion to entice a shy yet eager mate. Now, from the current trend of lesbian literature it seems that our endangered species is wellnigh extinct as boundaries blur, unisex-unisex takes over, and 'role-playing' is strictly for thespians. So before we quite sink without a trace, for those who think the only butch in the world is the Sundance Kid's buddy, let me try to analyse the *other* kind. …
>
> We dress *like* men (not *as* men) and smoke pipes and cigars because it feels absolutely natural and right, though we would be at a loss to explain why, or why as tiny children far too young to have been moulded by those 'environmental influences' invented by psychiatrists we instinctively loathed dolls and their dreadful mini-teasets, prams and other nasty appurtenances, and avidly collected soldiers, dinky cars, guns and cricket bats; why in adolescence we shunned frocks, frills, makeup, jewellery, flimsy shoes and all the other standard symbols of femininity which our classmates couldn't wait to rip off their gymslips to get into; why many of us have a rapport with fuse-boxes and wood and nails and electric drills and the entrails of vehicles; why we recoil in horror from chintzy ornamental tweeness and knicky-knacky clutter. Somewhere along the butch's assembly line the kind of built-in domesticity which womanly women displayed as they lay gurgling in their infant cots mentally redecorating their nurseries has been omitted. The sight of a holey sock or a detached button is not to the butch a stirring challenge for invisible repair but an urgent signal that it's time she found a skilful needlewoman to share her life, especially if the lady can also cook. …
>
> When it comes to choice of a career a butch gravitates towards the Forces where her penchant for uniforms and qualities of decisiveness and leadership can have full rein for, like or lump it, the butch is the type of woman to whom less forceful women instinctively turn in crises. … She is, however, unlikely to swell the ranks of hairdressing, cosmetic or lingerie saleswomanship, modelling, domestic or culinary work, air hostessing,

dressmaking or nannying. She stoically endures the brick and concrete prisons wherein the majority of livings are earned, for the typical butch's natural habitat is The Great Outdoors, preferably accompanied by a bevy of pet animals towards whom she is besottedly adoring and who in consequence exploit her shamefully.

At this stage I must make it clear that I don't presume to speak for the entire spectrum of butchness since that, like every other manifestation of human behaviour, is in the mind of the individual. Indeed, there may be butches who can lounge happily in high-rise flats, display a propensity for sheer nylon and stunning frocks, whip up a souffle which would turn a cordon bleu into a cordon blanche, collect Dresden Shepherdesses (in porcelain!), read those astounding cryptograms whimsically called knitting patterns with one eye and watch 'Coronation Street' with the other or run a hairdressing-salon-cum-beauty parlour while clutching a brace of babies to their bosoms. True, I have never *met* such a butch – but perhaps I just didn't recognise her. At the opposite extreme was the hulking stomping beerswelling Superbutch in donkey jacket and cowboy boots whom I encountered at a meeting Somewhere in Ulster. Growling 'C'mere, baby, I wancha' she grabbed and mauled every femme in sight, only to spoil the effect a trifle by leaving early, announcing as she lumbered out that her husband and four kids were awful good at lettin' her go to the meetings but she gotta get their supper now. …

Well, there you have us for what we're worth. We are rare now, collector's items, perhaps indeed museum pieces. Treat us with due deference for we are the sad survivors of a once proud tribe and it would be a Dodo-like tragedy if the only record of us left for posterity was that monstrous celluloid libel 'The Killing of Sister George'. … [Gentlemanly Fundamental Butches] also make enchanting household novelties and desirable Christmas Gifts for the Lesbian who has Almost Everything. Ladies, *is* there a Conservationist in the house?

Socio-political background: issues and arguments

The present text was published at a time when the unified and homogeneous lesbian community which had been discursively constructed during the 1970s – starting with the Radicalesbians' 1970 manifesto (see Koller 2008:48–59) and Johnston's 1973 autobiography – began to be fragmented and diversified. To some extent, conflicts were due to the different identities of subsequent lesbian generations, particularly women who had identified as gay before Stonewall and those who came out in the context of feminism. While some accounts foreground how '"old gays" ... were delighted to change their identity to lesbian-feminist' and were welcomed by the 'new lesbians' (Faderman 1991:210), other oral accounts hint at the gap between lesbian feminists on the one hand and lesbians who were not out and/or not politically active on the other: 'I don't always understand the big words feminists use. ... I used to sit in the women's group ... and feel that they were out of touch' (quoted in National Lesbian and Gay Survey 1992:49; see also Stein 1997:104). Some lesbian feminists regarded non-feminist lesbians as lacking political consciousness and analysis. At best, their consciousness was seen as 'less developed' and there was a feeling that they should receive help from feminists. Yet as contact between those two groups was only scarce, the reality of the respective other was often not recognised (see Stein 1997:97–9 for quotes betraying mutual distrust and alienation). It was not before the beginnings of the 1980s that lesbians who diverged from the established lesbian-feminist ideal of the politically active woman gained access to discourse.

A focal point of generational conflicts is the issue of butch and femme identities. To elaborate on the topic of butch/femme, it is necessary to go back to the 1950s. Sexologists had conflated butches and lesbians in the figure of the 'invert', rendering lesbian femininity invisible (Halberstam 1998a:7), but working-class and/or young lesbians after the Second World War organised their identities around masculine ('butch') as well as feminine ('femme') roles. In a fiercely heterosexual world, these roles were unsurprisingly modelled on the habitus and behaviour of straight men and women. Although this arrangement granted the femme a more liberated sexuality than heterosexual women enjoyed at the time, butch/femme lifestyle in the 1950s entailed a stark dichotomy which newcomers could not opt out of (Faderman 1991:168; Hall Carpenter Archives 1989:113, 126; Neild and Pearson 1992:59–60).[3] Linguistically, terms for self- and other-reference would equally be borrowed from heterosexual discourses and their gender stereotypes: 'It was fairly stereotypical language about being a wife. ... It was about being dainty or chivalrous' (quoted in Hall Carpenter Archives 1989:126, 128).

On the other hand, the homophobia of the 1950s and the 1960s, which resulted in frequent police raids on bars, turned butch/femme culture into a virtual *ersatz* family for its members, a safe social space in which butches would help other butches to fill their role and older femmes would initiate their younger counterparts (Hall Carpenter Archives 1989:129; Faderman 1991:174; Bender and Due 1994:103–4; Halberstam 1998a:62). Also, it has to be kept in mind that only some lesbians would even wish to become part of the bar culture or display butch/femme appearance and behaviour, a difference that more or less correlated with class membership. Other women chose to have private parties because they perceived the bars, which were infamous for violence, sex workers, petty criminals and police raids, as too risky (Wolf 1979:44, n.4). Certainly, the issue of butch/femme was controversial among lesbians even in the heyday of bar culture in the 1960s (Neild and Pearson 1992:76; Healey 1996:49; Stein 1997:29). Nevertheless, butch/femme culture has, in retrospect, become the dominant narrative about the time between the Second World War and Stonewall, just as lesbian feminism is now seen as the central paradigm of the 1970s.

As a result of this paradigm shift, the idea of butch/femme was frowned upon by 1970s lesbian feminism as an emulation of oppressive heterosexuality. To quote one influential lesbian feminist writer, the idea of butch/femme was misguided because '[t]he woman in relation to herself is not a butch or femme but a woman' (Johnston 1973:176; see also Penelope 1983; Jeffreys 1989; Hart 1996 for writings in this tradition). According to this line of thinking, femmeness signified uncritical acceptance of patriarchal stereotypes of femininity, while butches were devalued as male-identified. Consequently, the onset of lesbian feminism in the early 1970s meant that the lesbian bar culture of the 1950s and 1960s was marginalised, and although it never ceased to exist, it was restricted to public silence, practically eliminated from the dominant representation of a lesbian community (see Brownworth 1975, quoted in Halberstam 1998b:131; Case 1998). However, oral accounts are unanimous in describing the parallel world of lesbian bars, with butch/femme culture evident until the late 1970s and even early 1980s in places like London, Belfast and Manchester (Hall Carpenter Archives 1989:142, 189, 205; see also Wolf 1979:7, 47, 123).

It was only with the advent of queer theory in the early 1990s that butch/femme experienced a renaissance. By decoupling sex from gender, different lesbian identities could 'return as a viable lesbian practice instead of as a sell-out' (Roof 1998:33). Despite early attempts to counter the essentialist gender notions of lesbian feminism (Laporte [1971]1992), however, this post-modern resurrection of butch/femme identities was still a long way in the future at the end of the 1970s. Political lesbianism, while probably not a majority lifestyle, was the dominant ideology of the day and anything that resembled role play was generally discarded as 'male-identified' and hence anti-feminist (see e.g. Nichols, Pagano and Rossoff 1982:140 for this evaluation: 'participants in the feminist and lesbian liberation movements analysed and made unnecessary the butch-femme roles which many lesbians found oppressive and personally limiting'). The abyss that often opened up between lesbian feminists and older women identifying as butch or femme was exacerbated by the fact that generally higher levels of education granted lesbian feminists preferred access to influential discourses within the lesbian community, a position that some used to limit the distribution of material that contradicted their beliefs and values. As one woman put it in retrospect: 'The politically correct dykes were controlling the lesbian media' (quoted in Cassidy 2004:28).

Discursive practice: production, distribution and reception of texts

As mentioned above, the ideal of the political lesbian was in fact a construct and far from being the reality of every lesbian in the 1970s. This fact is often and easily overlooked since discourse was dominated by lesbian feminists, and others were to a large extent deprived of discursive resources. Apart from discrediting butches and femmes by aligning them with the opposed social formation of heterosexuals, they were also excluded as a topic from discourse (Roof 1998:29). Occasionally, territorial conflicts would turn literal, for example in the practice, reported by Stein (1997:98), of groups of lesbian feminists disrupting butch-femme couples dancing in gay bars by engaging in circle dances. Other non-verbal cues such as gesture, body posture and gait became similarly influenced by lesbian feminist ideals (Case 1998:41). Consequently, accounts of other self-images and identities are mainly to be found and elicited in oral texts. Another source for alternative identities was the rediscovered lesbian pulp novels of the 1950s and 1960s; although publishers such as Beacon and Fawcett at the time restricted the authors in that stories must not end with a happy lesbian relationship, the books often included authentic descriptions of butch-femme bar culture and lesbian sex. A number of books were re-published in the early 1980s and, with no official censorship to be taken into account, given a positive ending and less biased titles (Forrest 2005:xiii–xiv).[4]

It follows that the conflict between different groups of lesbians was in many ways a struggle not only about material practices and political strategy but also over discursive practices: Who in the lesbian community had access to the means of semi-public discourse production such as workshop and meeting space? Who had access to means of distribution such as newsletters and magazines, and who could persuade bookstores to display and sell their texts? Who was given the chance to receive instances of controversial discourse? Ultimately, this struggle over discursive practices boils down the issues of censorship and free speech (see Anthonissen 2008 for a discussion).

Consequently, when women who lived butch/femme styles first struggled for discursive space in the late 1970s, they reacted to what they perceived as the increasing prescriptivism that had come to dominate lesbian feminist discourse and which they sought to replace or enrich with different models of identity. The text at hand dates back to 1980, about ten years before the queer revival of butch/femme and at a point when prestige for role-playing was at its lowest in the lesbian feminist community. It is for this reason that the text is rather isolated, with hardly any other texts of the same period related to it. Still, it can be seen as implicitly quoting earlier, fictional accounts of butch/femme communities (e.g. the above-mentioned 1950s and 1960s lesbian pulp novels) and as anticipating later texts that signal a revival of butch/femme as fluid lesbian gender identities (e.g. the anthologies edited by Nestle 1992; Burana, Roxxie and Due 1994; Kuhnen 1997). The text's location between these historical periods and against the background of a dominant lesbian feminist ideology makes the text particularly interesting. As the textual analysis will show, the author employs irony, paradox and parody to make for an entertaining text that also communicates her ultimately queer identity position.

The magazine *Sequel*, in which the above text was published, was in the definition of the editors' collective a 'non-profit, bi-monthly magazine for isolated lesbians' and was published between 1978 and 1983. The distribution of the text was restricted, since the magazine in which it was published was available through subscription only and relied almost exclusively on word-of-mouth in order to sell at all. This means that the authors had rather specific knowledge of who they were writing for, and also that reception of the text was intentional (i.e. readers would have deliberately sought it out and responded to it in the form of letters).[5] The *Sequel* collective encouraged and printed contributions (poems, stories, letters) by readers and tried to include as many aspects of lesbian life as possible. The publication lacked a general layout, so that the variety of topics was reflected in a rather haphazard appearance, making it a typical low-budget project in which everybody worked on an unpaid basis. In 1983, the last issue was published and the collective stated that they saw themselves unable to continue due to 'lack of womanpower and lack of funds' (Sacha-Savannah 1983:3).

Text analysis

Social actors

The text was triggered by lesbian feminists' privileged access to discourse resources. The author clearly fears that butchness as a model of lesbian gender identity is in danger of being degraded and subsequently forgotten, and her text defines what it means to be butch, so as to strengthen that particular identity position. Unsurprisingly then, the one actor group to feature most prominently is 'butches' (e.g. line 44); a prototypical representative of that social group is given salience by being headlined. The in-group is mostly referred to by the inclusive 'we' and this personal pronoun also features in 'we oldfashioned butches' (line 2), the metaphoric elaboration 'our endangered species' (line 8) and the quantifier 'many of us' (lines 21–2). A stylistic variation in social actor representation consists of referring to the prototypical singular butch (lines 27–8, 31, 33); by scaling down the complexity of a whole group to an imagined prototypical individual, the author further facilitates comprehension and identification on part of the reader.

The attribute 'oldfashioned' (line 2) not only sets the scene for a nostalgic look back on the past, but also ironically reclaims a negative evaluation by others, because here it carries positive connotations by being linked to valuable old things such as 'collector's items' and 'museum pieces' (lines 59–60). Linguistically, being old-fashioned is illustrated by instances of formal speech, which can be found throughout the text. For instance, the syntax is generally hypotactic, showing a high degree of complexity. (At the most extreme, we find a sentence that spreads over lines 13–24 and contains no fewer than ten clauses at six different syntactic levels.) Positive evaluation of the paradigmatic butch is coupled with ironic self-commodification when the author closes by advertising butches as 'enchanting household novelties and desirable Christmas Gifts' (lines 64–5). The attributes here also parody perceived feminine speech styles (see Queen 2004:292).

Butchness as an identity is contrasted with female femininity, whose representatives are referred to as 'womanly women' (line 25) and 'less forceful women' (line 34). In accordance with the title, references to butches far outnumber those to feminine women, at 33 to 6 in the actor role. There is also a slight tendency to present butches rather than feminine women as initiating actions (e.g. 'entice a shy yet eager mate', line 7); thus, feminine women are in the actor role in 75 per cent of all processes in which they are involved, with butches in that role accounting for 82.05 per cent of all processes that involve them. While this difference is not statistically significant ($p = 0.430988$), it further foregrounds butches in qualitative terms. Throughout the text the author constructs an environment for these two social actor groups which is characterised by behaviours, appearances and artefacts carrying culturally masculine and feminine connotations. The text opens with a descriptive listing of the characteristics of butch appearance (lines 4–7). This enumeration serves to construct a stereotypically masculine image and one half of the gender dyad is thus set up. Further lists can be found when reference is made to preferred toys (lines 17–19) and special skills (lines 21–3). Masculinity is also prevalent in a butch's professional life and her particular penchant for the army (line 31).[6]

Next to the soldier, another figure of hegemonic masculinity (Connell 1995; Connell and Messerschmidt 2005), the cowboy or ranger, is alluded to by describing 'The Great Outdoors' as 'the typical butch's natural habitat' (lines 38–9).[7] Irony is at work when, in contrast to her role model, she does not tame wild beasts but is seen in the company of 'pet animals' (line 40) for whom she has a soft spot. The author also draws on external, homophobic stereotypes of female masculinity which she satirises in the description of the 'Superbutch' (line 53). This figure displays all the negative features usually ascribed to working-class men in that she lacks good manners, especially towards women ('grabbed and mauled every femme in sight', line 55), behaves without grace or elegance ('hulking stomping' in line 52, 'lumbered out' in line 56), and is generally uncouth ('beerswilling', line 52). Her language use also marks her as stereotypically masculine and working-class (with that class marker carrying connotations of heterosexual masculinity itself; see Livia 2002:91), in that she is inarticulate ('[g]rowling', line 54) and uses non-standard speech features, like phonetic variants of the -ing suffix ('lettin'', line 57), contractions ('c'mere', 'wancha', 'gotta' in lines 54 and 57) and substitution of adjectives for adverbs in attributive position ('awful good', line 57) (see Queen 1997:240). The irony here of course resides in this homophobic caricature of a butch turning out to be a man's wife and a mother.

In the dichotomy of femmeness and butchness, the 'femme is flamboyant, spectacular, showy, highly ornamented in dress [and] mannerisms' (Livia 1995:252) while the butch betrays typically masculine interests and qualities (e.g. firmness). The two parts to the dyad are entangled in the text, which is syntactically realised through the conjunctions 'but' and 'however' as well as the adverbial '[a]t the opposite extreme' (lines 28, 35, 52). The author therefore not only constructs particular identity representations in opposition to each other but furthermore presents these identities as brought into being through interaction between them. Textually, such 'tactics of intersubjectivity' (Bucholtz and Hall 2004:493–4) are at work whenever one of the two social actors acts with reference to the other, as in 'the butch is the type of women to whom less forceful women instinctively turn in crises' (lines 33–4) and 'entice a shy yet eager mate' (line 7). Such examples show how actors with different gender identities mutually authenticate each other.

The ideal-type images of a lesbian that were advanced by lesbian feminists are hinted at when the author describes how 'boundaries blur [and] unisex-unisex takes over' (line 9). The complexity of butch-femme identities and relations was disparagingly referred to as 'role-play' in lesbian feminist writing (e.g. Jeffreys 2003:127) and the present author intertextually quotes this label by putting inverted commas around 'role-playing' (line 9) and referring to 'the current trend of lesbian literature' (lines 7–8) as its source. On the whole, however, lesbian feminists are not granted the status of social actor, neither as a genericised group nor as specific individuals.

The distribution of social actors is quite complex as a whole; although the text focuses on butch as an identity, it also makes the point that this position is only brought into being through its counterpart, feminine women. We are therefore dealing with a representation of identity that incorporates particular interactive scripts. The notion of interaction is also realised metaphorically by the author integrating an array of discourses for parodic effect.

Interdiscursivity

The central irony of the text relies on the author adapting an essentialist discourse on gender in order to defy ideas of 'natural' gender identity. The stereotypical notions of gender that are often found in such discourses are mocked by the seemingly endless lists of feminine vs. masculine toys, interests and skills. The gender binary thus established is naturalised through intensified attributes such as 'absolutely natural and right' (line 14). The fact that the processes in lines 15–24 have a temporal sequence – illustrating the stages from early childhood to adolescence to the present – implies persistence of an allegedly pre-discursive identity. The idea that the butch's gender identity is 'natural' is also supported by lexis from the domain of biology, as in 'there were reported sightings of us' (line 3), which constructs the in-group as some natural phenomenon or species. Parallels to the animal world are further drawn by the expression 'a shy yet eager mate' (line 7), while reference to the in-group as 'proud tribe' (line 61) invokes the Euro-centric image of the 'noble savage' and once more associates butchness with naturalness. Metaphor supports interdiscursivity in the text in that it reinforces the idea of a natural, innate gender identity. Thus, in the opening paragraph, butches are referred to as 'our endangered species' (line 8), which uses biological terminology to metaphorically conceptualise a group of social actors and represent them as moribund. The metaphoric expressions 'natural habitat' (line 39) and 'Conservationist' (line 66) further underscore the author's tendency to ironically speak about her own in-group as a natural kind, stressing the ostensible naturalness of a masculine identity. Masculinity itself is suggested by the MACHINE metaphor realised in 'the butch's assembly line' (lines 24–5) and 'built-in domesticity' (line 25).[8] Of course, the subject position of the writer alone makes this interdiscursive strategy a prime example of queer irony. After all, it is one of the hallmarks of essentialist discourses on gender that its proponents assume direct causal links between biological sex, gender identity and desire. Being written by a masculine woman, the text ironically appropriates this particular discourse in order to prove it wrong, while pretending to subscribe to it.

In doing so, the author delivers a rare example of what could be called 'butch camp'. Harvey (2000) links camp to gay male culture and provides the following list of camp strategies and their surface features in (fictional) language:

- Paradox: incongruent registers, explicitness and covertness, 'high' culture and 'low' experience;
- Inversion: gendered proper nouns and grammatical gender markers, flouting expected rhetorical routines and established value systems;
- Ludicrism: heightened language awareness through motivated naming practices and puns, pragmatic force through sexual double entendre;
- Parody: of aristocratic mannerisms through the use of French, of femininity through innuendo, hyperbole, exclamation and vocatives. (Harvey 2000:243)

Cameron and Kulick (2003:99–104) have adapted Harvey's framework, re-interpreting the above four strategies as effects of particular linguistic features. In terms of speech act theory (Austin 1962), this re-interpretation shifts the focus from the speaker's assumed intention and the illocutionary force of an utterance to its perlocutionary effect on the hearer. Seen as such, 'camp talk [consists] of a set of resources that are available to all speakers of a language' (Cameron and Kulick 2003:102), making it part of how language is used to perform non-hegemonic identities. Given this performative potential of camp talk as a resource, Cameron and Kulick (2003:103) stress that it is not limited to gay men and cite the examples of 'opera divas ... actors, comics, witty heterosexual men'. One group of potential users of camp talk they do not mention, however, is lesbians (but see Queen 1997).

In fact, elements of camp can occasionally also be found in the linguistic style of femmes. Consider the following passage from *The Femme's Guide to the Universe* (Rednour 2000:124), where a femme addresses other femmes:

> Remember, you are the Queen, and shoes are the throne upon which you are perched, so choose that throne wisely; you wouldn't want any trash in the palace. Or, if you prefer, you are the goddess, and your shoes are the altar and are therefore to be approached only on bended knee. If your gal doesn't do religion, she will, because honey, it's worship time.

In the above quote there is incongruity of registers in that religious lexis is combined with colloquial expressions ('gal'); it further flouts the established system that grants higher values to all things male and masculine, there is possible double entendre ('on bended knee'), parodic reference to the aristocracy as well as hyperbole, exclamation (as shown in the stress on '*you*') and a vocative ('honey').

While engaging in a camp parody of femininity as a female is a hard enough thing to do, the 'essence of Camp, [namely] artifice and exaggeration' (Sontag [1964]1994:275) seems to downright contradict the stereotype of the butch as stoic and taciturn. Indeed, it has been argued that butch performance cannot be camp, since masculinity as the unmarked and more powerful gender position is both less noticeable and, to a certain degree, more acceptable in women than femininity in men (Kennedy and Davis 1993:77).[9] Nevertheless, Gulston's text manages to do the impossible and perform butch camp. The text is paradoxical at the macro-level in that it destabilises essentialist discourses of gender by adapting them, thus illustrating that the 'whole point of Camp is to dethrone the serious' (Sontag [1964]1994:288). Linguistically, paradox is realised through the high-culture term 'thespians' (line 10) – a pun on 'lesbians' and another instance of old-fashioned terminology – being used in the context of 1960s lesbian bar culture, indexed by the mention of one particular bar, 'Gateways' (line 4). While there is no gender inversion in pronouns or grammatical gender markers, the text does invert established value systems: Not only are the power dynamics between butch and femme portrayed as more complex than the simple dominance-submission pattern that critics accused them of; far from being 'a fake or bad copy' of heterosexual men (Butler 1991:17), butches are implicitly seen as superior to them, in that they are considerate, chivalrous and good-natured.

To continue, ludicrism is perhaps the strategy least employed in the text, although there is some word play ('thespians', line 10) as well as motivated naming ('Gentlemanly Fundamental Butches' or GFB as a label in lines 63–4). In terms of parody, French is used less to hint at aristocratic mannerism but rather to characterise stereotypical femininity ('whip up a souffle which would turn a cordon bleu into a cordon blanche', lines 46–7); in the butch's language use, frivolous French is replaced by sterner Latinate lexis, which is associated with the historically male spheres of learning and scholarship (e.g. '[p]ropinquity', 'spectrum', 'posterity' in lines 2, 43, 62). This replacement ties in with the last point: Obviously, it is not femininity as much as masculinity that is being parodied. The author engages in parody when she assumes a macho pose ('especially if the lady can also cook', lines 29–30), while another form of masculinity is depicted in the caricature of the 'Superbutch' (line 53), who embodies every stereotype of working-class loutishness in her linguistic and other behaviour, but turns out to be the wife of a man and a mother.

There is a final twist to the argument in that the author, once she has claimed masculinity as the defining characteristic for the in-group, dismantles it again, rendering any gendered subject position shifting and preliminary. The traits of hegemonic masculinity that she claims for herself (e.g. the cowboy image) are contradicted by elements that do not fit ('a bevy of pet animals', lines 39–40). Linguistically, there are the classical camp markers of exaggerated femininity as well, from vocatives ('[l]adies', line 66) and exclamations (note the frequent indication of stress, as in lines 12, 13, 51, 66) to innuendo and hyperbole. While innuendo is present when the author merely hints at the dominant lesbian feminist discourse ('current trend of lesbian literature', lines 7–8), the most dominant feature is hyperbole, as in the absurd exaggeration 'they lay gurgling in their infant cots mentally redecorating their nurseries' (line 26) or the three-part attribution 'hulking stomping beerswilling' (line 52). The exaggeration in meaning is mirrored by an exaggerated syntactic complexity and overly long lists of gendered traits. At the macro-level, hyperbole is present in the exaggerated dichotomous gender stereotypes. However, the author is quick to deconstruct this binary opposition again, by admitting that butchness is in the eye of the beholder, by introducing examples that contradict the dichotomy, and by including femininity markers in her own linguistic style. The double irony that characterises the text resides in the female author using feminine language features to claim an essentialist masculine gender identity for herself.

The text as a whole is thus camp in its 'parodic repetition of the original [that] reveals the original to be nothing other than the parody of the *idea* of the natural and original' (Butler [1990]1999:41). As an example of camp, the text appropriates features associated with gay male language use and transforms them into linguistic devices used to represent reality from a specifically lesbian perspective. This shows that camp can be used to invert itself. The text is also highly interdiscursive, mixing discourses, genres and styles in what can be described as a piece of queer writing *avant la lettre*.

Discussion

The author's statement that 'butchness ... is in the mind of the individual' (lines 43–4) claims that gender roles are mental representations, being 'performed by the selection of particular semiotic items encoding gender information' (Livia 1995:253), such as clothing, accessories or language. Such semiotic markers are decoded by their recipients who, for the sake of processing the information and creating meaning, rely on a matching socio-cultural and cognitive background. By describing butch semiotics in great detail then, the author assumes that her readers will be able to draw on the same prototypes and other background knowledge.

The fact that the last phrase in the text is a question provides an open ending, requiring an answer or action on part of the reader. Here, reading the text as an instance of camp is again helpful; camp, in contrast to kitsch, relies on an identification of the reader with the author as well as on the reader realising that they are indeed the intended audience (Sedgwick 1990:156). So while in essence the author seems to address all lesbians, she may in particular aim to draw in those readers who will recognise the camp nature of the text, seeking their understanding and help in the face of lesbian feminist criticism of butch/femme lifestyles. Although this criticism is only hinted at, the final question could still be read as a plea for solidarity against the silence surrounding such lifestyles in the heyday of lesbian feminism. By making such criticism public, the author uses her text to create a counter-public which 'make[s] possible new forms of gendered or sexual citizenship' (Warner 2002:57), here helping older and/or working-class women to reclaim their position in the lesbian community.

In her queer construction of lesbian genders as fluid and negotiable, the author is not so much behind than ahead of her time. The advent of queer theory in the 1990s would ultimately lead to a revival of a playful version of butch/femme. In 1980, however, the largely lesbian feminist-defined community was only just beginning to be challenged. The text at hand was one of the earliest examples – to be followed by historical accounts such as Nestle (1981) and Kennedy and Davis (1993) – and it was unique in combining memories of the pre-Stonewall past with the vision of a queer future.

In this chapter, then, I have conducted a discourse historical analysis of a 1980 essay in which the lesbian author engages in what I call 'butch camp' (i.e. strategically uses language features typically associated with gay male femininity in order to destabilise essentialist discourses on gender). This overall finding was arrived at by a tripartite analysis accounting for the linguistic features used in the text, notably social actor representation and intertextuality/discursivity, as well as for the discursive context of text production, distribution and reception. Both levels of analysis were linked, by means of triangulation, to the wider socio-political context at the time. The analysis is intended as a model for the investigation of how sexual and gender identities are constructed in text and discourse. Since the theoretical and methodological approach is very much indebted to CDA, I further hope that the present chapter may motivate a stronger focus on sexual identity than has hitherto been the case in critical studies of discourse.

Finally, the chapter wishes to make the case that social historical research needs to more fully integrate detailed linguistic analysis: It is only through establishing what language features text producers employ in their historically contingent identity constructions that sociologists, anthropologists and cultural theorists can go beyond mapping the content of discourses (*what*) and give reasons for their emergence (*why*). Any full-fledged study of identity and discourse will rest its claims on the minutiae of language (*how*) as it is used in the discursive construction of identity positions.

Notes

1 On 28 June 1969, the police raided the gay bar Stonewall in New York City's Christopher Street. The ensuing street fighting continued for days and marks – under the name of Stonewall Riots – the beginning of the lesbian and gay movement. The annual Pride marches held in many cities around the world celebrate this event.

2 For a full list and comprehensive discussion of linguistic parameters, see Koller (2008:23–36).

3 But see Faderman (1991:171–2) and Healey (1996:44) for sexual flexibility in butch/femme communities.

4 Naiad Press re-published a number of lesbian pulp novels in the 1980s, while a second wave of ironic-nostalgic recovery began in 2002 with the re-publications by Cleis Press. Lesbian pulp novels have also been collected in several connoisseurs' anthologies (Forrest 2005; Stryker 2001; Zimet 1999).

5 One letter sent in response to the text analysed in this chapter was mailed by the author's later partner and marked the beginning of their, long-term relationship (Lorna Gulston MBE, personal communication, July 2007).

6 This choice of profession has been corroborated by a number of biographical accounts (e.g. Neild and Pearson 1992:52). Faderman (1991:150–55) provides a harrowing account of homophobia in the US military in the 1950s.

7 Jones's (2012) ethnographic study of a lesbian walking group corroborates love of the 'great outdoors' as a lesbian identity marker, although her informants replace the image of the lone ranger conquering nature with the feminist model of women as a group interacting with nature.

8 Metaphor is here combined with metonymy, in that a butch's typical skills ('many of us have a rapport with fuse-boxes ... and electric drills and the entrails of vehicles', lines 21–3) come to stand in for her.

9 But see Core ([1984]1999:84) on the campness of male impersonators.

References

Anthonissen, Christine (2008) The sounds of silence in the media: when violator and violated withhold information. In Ruth Wodak and Veronika Koller (eds) *Handbook of Communication in the Public Sphere* (Handbook of Applied Linguistics 4) 401–28. Berlin: Mouton de Gruyter.

Austin, John Langshaw (1962): *How to Do Things with Words*. Oxford: Oxford University Press.

Bakhtin, Mikhail (1986) *Speech Genres and Other Late Essays* (trans. Vern W. McGee). Austin, TX: University of Texas Press.

Bender, Debbie and Due, Linnea (1994) Coming up butch. In Burana et al. (1994): 96–112.

Brownworth, Victoria (1975) Butch/femme, myth/reality or more of the same? *Wicce* 4: 7–10.

Bucholtz, Mary and Hall, Kira (2004) Theorizing identity in language and sexuality research. *Language in Society* 33: 469–515. https://doi.org/10.1017/S0047404504334020

Burana, Lily, Roxxie and Due, Linnea (eds) (1994) *Dagger: On Butch Women*. Pittsburgh, PA: Cleis Press.

Butler, Judith ([1990]1999) *Gender Trouble*, 2nd edition. New York: Routledge.

Butler, Judith (1991) Imitation and gender insubordination. In Diana Fuss (ed.) *Inside/Out: Lesbian Theories, Gay Theories* 13–31. New York: Routledge.

Butler, Judith (1993) *Bodies that Matter: On the Discursive Limits of 'Sex'*. New York: Routledge.

Butler, Judith (1997) *Excitable Speech: A Politics of the Performative*. New York: Routledge.

Cameron, Deborah and Kulick, Don (2003) *Language and Sexuality*. Cambridge: Cambridge University Press.

Case, Sue-Ellen (1998) Making butch: an historical memoir of the 1970s. In Munt and Smyth (1998): 37–45.

Cassidy, Christie (2004) Opening Pandora's box. *on our backs* (June/July): 28–9.

Connell, R. W. (1995) *Masculinities*. Berkeley, CA: University of California Press.

Connell, R. W. and Messerschmidt, James (2005) Hegemonic masculinity: rethinking the concept. *Gender and Society* 19(6): 829–59. https://doi.org/10.1177/0891243205278639

Core, Philip ([1984]1999) Camp: the lie that tells the truth. In Fabio Cleto (ed.) *Camp: Queer Aesthetics and the Performing Subject* 80–6. Edinburgh: Edinburgh University Press.

De Cillia, Rudolf, Reisigl, Martin and Wodak, Ruth (1999) The discursive construction of national identities. *Discourse and Society* 10(2): 149–73. https://doi.org/10.1177/0957926599010002002

Dworkin, Andrea ([1987]2006) *Intercourse*. New York: Basic Books.

Faderman, Lillian (1991) *Odd Girls and Twilight Lovers: A History of Lesbian Life in Twentieth-century America*. New York: Penguin.

Fairclough, N. (2010) *Critical Discourse Analysis*, 2nd edition. London: Longman.

Fairclough, Norman (2003) *Analysing Discourse: Textual Analysis for Social Research*. London: Routledge.

Forrest, Katherine. (2005) *Lesbian Pulp Fiction: The Sexually Intrepid World of Lesbian Paperback Novels 1950-1965*. San Francisco, CA: Cleis Press.

Garber, Linda (2001) *Identity Poetics: Race, Class, and the Lesbian-feminist Roots of Queer Theory*. New York: Columbia University Press. https://doi.org/10.7312/garb11032

Gulston, Lorna (1980) Butch. *Sequel* 15: 8–10.

Halberstam, Judith (1998a) Between butches. In Munt and Smyth (1998): 57–65.

Halberstam, Judith (1998b) *Female Masculinity*. Durham, NC: Duke University Press.

Hall, Radclyffe (1928[1990]) *The Well of Loneliness*. New York: Anchor Books.

Hall Carpenter Archives (1989) *Inventing Ourselves: Lesbian Life Stories*. London: Routledge.

Halliday, Michael A. K. and Matthiessen, Christian M. I. M. (2014) *Halliday's Introduction to Functional Grammar*, 4th edition. Abingdon: Routledge.

Hart, Nett (1996) From an eroticism of difference to an intimacy of equals: a radical feminist lesbian separatist perspective on sexuality. In Lilian Mohin (ed.) *An Intimacy of Equals: Lesbian Feminist Ethics* 69–77. London: Onlywomen Press.

Harvey, Keith (2000) Describing camp talk: Language/pragmatics/politics. *Language and Literature* 9: 240–60. https://doi.org/10.1177/096394700000900303

Healey, Emma (1996) *Lesbian Sex Wars*. London: Virago.

Hoagland, Sarah (1982) Sadism, masochism, and lesbian-feminism. In Linden et al. (1982): 153–63. East Palo Alto, CA: Frog in the Well Press.

Jeffreys, Sheila (1989) Butch and femme: now and then. In Lesbian Herstory Group (eds) *Not a Passing Phase: Reclaiming Lesbians in History, 1840–1985* 158–87. London: Women's Press.

Jeffreys, Sheila (1996) Heterosexuality and the desire for gender. In Diane Richardson (ed.) *Theorising Heterosexuality* 75–90. Buckingham: Open University Press.

Jeffreys, Sheila (2003) *Unpacking Queer Politics: A Lesbian Feminist Perspective*. Cambridge: Polity.

Johnston, Jill (1973) *Lesbian Nation: The Feminist Solution*. New York: Simon & Schuster.

Jones, Lucy (2012) *Dyke/Girl: Language and Identities in a Lesbian Group*. Basingstoke: Palgrave Macmillan.

Kennedy, Elizabeth and Davis, Madeline (1993) *Boots of Leather, Slippers of Gold: The History of a Lesbian Community*. New York: Routledge.

Koller, Veronika (2008) *Lesbian Discourses: Images of a Community*. New York: Routledge.

Kuhnen, Stephanie (ed.) (1997) *Butch/Femme: Eine erotische Kultur*. Berlin: Querverlag.

Lakoff, George (2002) *Moral Politics: How Liberals and Conservatives Think*, 2nd edition. Chicago, IL: University of Chicago Press. https://doi.org/10.7208/chicago/9780226471006.001.0001

Laporte, Rita ([1971]1992) The butch-femme question. In Nestle (1992): 208–19.

Linden, Robin, Pagano, Darlene, Russell, Diana and Star, Susan (eds) (1982) *Against Sadomasochism: A Radical Feminist Analysis*. San Francisco, CA: Frog in the Well Press.

Livia, Anna (1995) 'I ought to throw a Buick at you': fictional representations of butch/femme speech. In Kira Hall and Mary Bucholtz (eds) *Gender Articulated: Language and the Socially Constructed Self* 246–77. New York: Routledge.

Livia, Anna (2002) The future of queer linguistics. In Kathryn Campbell-Kibler, Robert Podesva, Sarah Roberts and Andrew Wong (eds) *Language and Sexuality: Contesting Meaning in Theory and Practice* 87–97. Stanford, CA: CSLI.

Munt, Sally and Smyth, Cherry (eds) (1998) *Butch/Femme: Inside Lesbian Gender*. London: Cassell.

National Lesbian and Gay Survey (eds) (1992) *What a Lesbian Looks Like: Writings by Lesbians on Their Lives and Lifestyles*. London: Routledge.

Neild, Suzanne and Pearson, Rosalind (1992) *Women Like Us*. London: Women's Press.

Nestle, Joan (1981) Butch-fem relationships: sexual courage in the 1950's. *Heresies* 12: 21–4.

Nestle, Joan (ed.) (1992) *The Persistent Desire: A Femme-Butch Reader*. Boston, MA: Alyson.

Nichols, Jeannette, Pagano, Darlene and Rossoff, Margaret (1982) Is sadomasochism feminist? A critique of the Samois position. In Linden et al. (1982): 137–45.

Penelope, Julia (1983) Whose past are we reclaiming? *Common Lives, Lesbian Lives* 9: 18.

Queen, Robin (1997) 'I don't speak spritch': locating lesbian language. In Anna Livia and Kira Hall (eds) *Queerly Phrased: Language, Gender, and Sexuality*, 233–56. New York: Oxford University Press.

Queen, Robin (2004) 'I am a woman, hear me roar': the importance of linguistic stereotype for lesbian identity performance. In Robin Lakoff (ed. Mary Bucholtz) *Language and Woman's Place*, 2nd edition, 289–95. Oxford: Oxford University Press.

Radicalesbians (1970[1988]) The woman identified woman [paper presented at the Second Conference to Unite Women, New York, May]. In Sarah Hoagland and Julia Penelope (eds) *For Lesbians Only: A Separatist Anthology* 17—22. London: Onlywomen Press.

Rednour, Shar (2000) *The Femme's Guide to the Universe*. Los Angeles, CA: Alyson.

Reisigl, Martin and Wodak, Ruth (2001) *Discourse and Discrimination*. London: Routledge.

Reisigl, Martin and Wodak, Ruth (2016) The discourse-historical approach (DHA). In Ruth Wodak and Michael Meyer (eds) *Methods of Critical Discourse Studies*, 3rd edition, 23–61. London: Sage.

Roof, Judith (1998). 1970s lesbian feminism meets 1990s butch-femme. In Munt and Smyth (1998): 27–35.
Sacha-Savannah (1983) Message to readers. *Sequel* 33: 3.
Sedgwick, Eve (1990) *Epistemology of the Closet*. Berkeley, CA: University of California Press.
Sontag, Susan ([1964]1994) Notes on 'camp'. In her *Against Interpretation* 275–92. London: Vintage.
Stein, Arlene (1997) *Sex and Sensibility: Stories of a Lesbian Generation*. Berkeley, CA: University of California Press.
Stryker, Susan (2001) *Queer Pulp: Perverted Passions from the Golden Age of the Paperback*. Vancouver: Chronicle Books.
Stubbs, Michael (1997) Whorf's children: critical comments on critical discourse analysis. In Ann Ryan and Alison Wray (eds) *Evolving Models of Language* 100–16. Clevedon: Multilingual Matters.
Van Leeuwen, T. (2008) *Discourse and Practice: New Tools for Critical Discourse Analysis*. Oxford: Oxford University Press.
Warner, Michael (2002) *Publics and Counterpublics*. New York: Zone Books.
Widdowson, Henry (2004) *Text, Context, Pretext: Critical Issues in Discourse Analysis*. Oxford: Blackwell. https://doi.org/10.1002/9780470758427
Wilkinson, Sue and Kitzinger, Celia (1996) The queer backlash. In Diane Bell and Renate Klein (eds) *Radically Speaking: Feminism Reclaimed* 375–82. London: Zed Books.
Wodak, Ruth (1996) *Disorders of Discourse*. Harlow: Longman.
Wodak, Ruth (2006) Discourse-analytic and socio-linguistic approaches to the study of nation(alism). In Gerard Delanty and Krishan Kumar (eds) *The Sage Handbook of Nations and Nationalism* 104–17. London: Sage. https://doi.org/10.4135/9781848608061.n10
Wodak, Ruth (2007) Discourse studies: Important concepts and terms. In Ruth Wodak and Michał Krzyżanowski (eds) *Qualitative Discourse Analysis in the Social Sciences* 1–29. Basingstoke: Palgrave.
Wolf, Deborah (1979) *The Lesbian Community*. Berkeley, CA: University of California Press.
Zimet, Janet (1999) *Strange Sisters: The Art of Lesbian Pulp Fiction 1949–1969*. New York: Viking Studio.

7

'The other kind of coming out': transgender people and the coming out narrative genre

Lal Zimman

UNIVERSITY OF CALIFORNIA, SANTA BARBARA, USA

Introduction

Coming out is among the most widely discussed and theorised aspects of queer life in Western societies. The practice of revealing stigmatised sexual desire in a heteronormative cultural context has frequently been seen as a crucial site of gay and lesbian identity development, attracting the attention of scholars interested in sexuality for at least the past three decades. Of course, some researchers writing on this topic have pointed out the limitations of a continued emphasis on the closet as the locus of gay and lesbian life, given the increasing routinisation of homosexual identities (Seidman, Meeks and Traschen 1999), while others have criticised the way the closet serves to reinforce social binaries, not least of which is the dichotomy between homo- and heterosexualities (Sedgwick 1990). Nevertheless, issues of identity management and coming out continue to prove relevant for scholars writing about queer communities (relatively recent work from varied disciplinary perspectives includes Corrigan and Matthews 2003; Fields 2001; Hunter 2007; Morrow 2006; Munt, Bassett and O'Riordan 2002; Whitman, Cormier and Boyd 2000).

Despite the abundance of work on coming out as gay or lesbian, coming out as transgender remains highly understudied. In discussions of coming out that aim to be inclusive of transgender experiences, queer organisations and scholars alike often treat sexual orientation and gender identity as analogous. For example, the Human Rights Campaign, a major gay and lesbian rights organisation, uses a typical definition of coming out on its website (Human Rights Campaign 2009a): 'the process in which a person first acknowledges, accepts and appreciates his or her sexual orientation or gender identity and begins to share that with others'. Characterisations such as these, which can also be found in academic works like Chirrey (2003), Coon (2003), Hunter (2007), Morrow (2006) and Rasmussen (2004) suggest that transgender people, by definition, have a gender identity[1] that clashes with how they are perceived by others. That is, they may self-identify as women, but they are perceived by others to be men – or vice versa. This is a narrow view of transgenderism that ignores the many transgender individuals who complete a transition from one gender role to the other. For these people, whose gender identity may very well align with how they are perceived by others, coming out does not mean revealing a gender *identity*, but rather a particular kind of gender *history* characterised by the movement from one gender category to another. Given the paucity of research on coming out as transgender (or bisexual, for that matter), scholars should take care not to treat coming out as though it were practiced and regarded homogenously across queer communities. However, some scholars clearly conflate the coming out experience of gays, lesbians, bisexuals and transgender people. For example, in her discussion of coming out as a performative speech act, Chirrey (2003:34) disclaims that while her 'discussion focuses on coming out in relation to lesbians and gay men, ... it is the case that coming out is crucially important to the lives of other sexual minorities, such as bisexuals and trans persons, and much of what is written here will echo their realities'. However, in this chapter I argue that coming out must be reconceptualised if scholars wish to account for the entire range of coming out experiences of members of the LGBT (lesbian, gay, bisexual and transgender) population.

Like Chirrey's analysis, which focuses on the act of coming out itself, studies of the narratives people tell about their coming out experiences have focused on gay and lesbian speakers. Liang (1997), for instance, analyses the coming out stories told by young gay men in informal 'rap sessions' conducted in the San Francisco Bay Area and proposes a set of core elements to be found in narratives of this genre. Yet, as my analysis demonstrates, neither the findings of Liang's study, nor those presented by Wood (1994, 1997), account for the stories told by transgender speakers. This discrepancy is particularly clear when it comes to the frequently repeated claim that coming out is necessarily a lifelong process. Liang argues that reference to the 'processual' nature of coming out – in other words, the fact that coming out is not a single event but is rather re-enacted time and again throughout an individual's life time – is a crucial component of the coming out narrative.[2] Wood (1997) reaches similar conclusions based on her study of coming out stories told by hearing and Deaf lesbians through email. Like Liang, Wood emphasises the ongoing nature of coming out, but locates processuality not simply in the content of coming out stories, but also in the formal characteristics of the narratives themselves. However, I argue that processuality, as these authors describe it, is not characteristic of transgender coming out narratives. Although neither Liang nor Wood explicitly address the potential universality of their claims, the narratives they present from gay and lesbian speakers are treated as representative of the coming out narrative genre.

In this chapter, I argue that transgender people's coming out narratives present a challenge to the assumption that the linguistic practices of gays and lesbians are representative of the LGBT community. Instead, my analysis of the differences between coming out as gay or lesbian on the one hand, and coming out as transgender on the other, demonstrates the importance of considering transgender individuals and their linguistic practices on their own terms, rather than relying on their apparent commonalities with other queer groups. Practices that appear to unify LGBT speakers, like the coming out narrative genre, cannot be fully understood through the study of lesbians and gay men alone. Furthermore, because transgender people tend to orient more to issues of gender identity rather than sexual orientation when providing accounts of their own identities – at least in the narratives collected in the study I discuss here – the study of these communities is likely to be of particular interest for scholars of language and gender.

I begin this chapter by offering a view of coming out as transgender that highlights the dissimilar natures of coming out before an individual changes their gender role and after. I argue that this distinction, beyond providing a useful way to discuss the experiences of transgender people, is salient to the community and reflected in members' talk about coming out. Next, the work of Liang and Wood provides a point of comparison between the coming out narratives of gays and lesbians and those told by transgender people. I argue that these authors' conclusions, while apparently valid for the populations with which they worked, provide an incomplete picture of the coming out narrative genre. Rather than reflecting the genre as a whole, their observations reveal local practices used by members of the gay and lesbian communities they studied. Based on these findings, I argue that the coming out narrative genre is characterised best as a venue in which stigmatised identities are enacted and negotiated, thus functioning to forge solidarity between members, to socialise those who are new to the group, and to contest the powerful ideologies that marginalise queer identities. These divergent practices demonstrate not only the flexibility of the coming out narrative genre, but also the differences that cut across the LGBT community.

The data that support these arguments are drawn from interviews I conducted during the spring and summer of 2007 with nine transgender volunteers. I recruited these individuals through online transgender communities and electronic mailing lists, describing myself as a researcher and member of the transgender community who was seeking participants for a study of transgender coming out narratives. During the interviews, I asked participants in an open-ended format to share their coming out stories, which were followed by a more structured sequence of questions about their experiences with and attitudes toward coming out. The resulting data set is made up of approximately four hours of talk. Interviewees were all native speakers of English and were raised in various regions of the United States with the exceptions of John, who lived in both Israel and the US as a child and speaks English and Hebrew bilingually, and Elizabeth, who was born in Australia, grew up mainly in Israel and now lives in California and uses a native-sounding American English accent. Although many participants had similar backgrounds in some respects – the majority were European-Americans[3] from middle-class backgrounds – it would be misleading to characterise this group as either homogenous or somehow representative of the transgender population. Additionally, though all participants had completed, or at least begun, their transition from one gender role to another, they experienced their identities as transgender in quite different ways. For example, when I spoke to Michael, a 33-year-old graduate student and warehouse manager who identifies as genderqueer and has a generally more radical attitude toward gender than most other participants in this study,[4] it seemed that being transgender and having a history living as a woman were important parts of his identity. On the other hand, John was a 21-year-old undergraduate who began identifying as male in high school, transitioned in his late teens, and saw himself simply as a man, considering his transgender past in many ways irrelevant to his gender identity.

Despite these differences, all of these individuals had one very significant shared experience with regard to gender as a social phenomenon: they had each come to identify with and live as the gender 'opposite' the one assigned to them at birth. I recognise the potential danger in reducing individuals with complex identities to a single potentially homogenising category. However, the relatively small sample in my study turned up no evidence for patterns like those found by previous researchers who have examined the coming out experiences of lesbians as compared to gay men (e.g. Markowe 1996) or across different points in the life-span (e.g. de Monteflores and Schultz 1978).[5] Nevertheless, I want to stress that I make no claims to homogeneity among this group of speakers. Rather, my analysis illustrates how these different individuals draw on experiences and ideologies that are – or, as I will show, are thought to be – common among transgender people without necessarily aligning themselves with other transgender speakers.

While the context in which I collected these narratives matches neither Liang's rap group setting nor Wood's email stories, there is obviously no reason to suppose that any of these contexts necessarily provides a glimpse of some 'true' coming out narrative. Indeed, the situations in which participants in my study reported having told their coming out stories covered a wide range of settings, from lecture halls to intimate conversations and from educational seminars to support groups. Each of these contexts will influence the enactment of a narrative, and the interview setting is no exception (see Briggs 1986). However, it seems useful to think of the stories discussed here as products of both a sociolinguistic interview and a dialogue between two community members. Unlike in interviews performed by community outsiders, the particular combination of roles I filled as an interviewer forced participants to manage a tension between two audiences: the implicit academic readership of this paper, whose awareness of transgender issues cannot be assumed, and the researcher, whose community membership implies a shared body of knowledge. I found examples of speakers orienting to both of these audiences as they chose either to explain or omit explanations for certain issues. For example, at one point during our meeting I shared a laugh with John about his mother's assumption that, as a man, he would be attracted only to women. In this case there was no need for him to explain that transgender people – just like anyone else – may be attracted to any combination of genders, even though the uninitiated often assume that they will be heterosexual after their transition. I will discuss the dual role of these narratives at greater length in the discussion section below.

At this point, it is worth noting that my use of the term *transgender* is not intended in the 'umbrella label' sense often found in literature dealing with issues of gender and sexuality. Nor is it intended as a pancultural descriptor to be applied to any gender variant community. Rather, my usage mirrors the meaning this term has taken on in many English-speaking transgender communities in the United States, in which it can serve as a demedicalised substitute for the term *transsexual*.[6] While transsexuality is often seen a concept that arises from the pathologisation of cross-gender identification, which assigns the labels of *pre-op* or *post-op* according to whether an individual has been made medically 'complete' as female or male, my use of *transgender* emphasises the social nature of living as a woman or man. Likewise, *transgender*, as it is used here, refers to a culturally and historically specific identity rooted in modern, Western conceptualisations of gender and the self. Within this context, then, I treat the category of transgender as comprised of those individuals whose sense of themselves as men or women runs contrary to the gender they were assigned at birth, and who have therefore decided to make a social transition from one gender role to another (regardless of what medical interventions, if any, are pursued). While other definitions may be more productive in other contexts, and while this characterisation excludes a number of individuals who might identify as transgender,[7] my emphasis on the positioning of speakers as male or female social actors is crucial for understanding the distinction I propose between the various ways transgender people come out.

Generic conventions for coming out narratives

As I suggested, the primary goal of the linguistic literature on coming out narratives has been the identification of thematic and linguistic features shared across stories in this genre. At the most basic thematic level, the narratives I collected from transgender people each described how the speaker came to live in their current gender role; in fact, this was the clear overarching topic in the majority of these stories, some of which only peripherally mentioned actual acts of coming out to others as transgender. In this broad sense, transgender coming out narratives are similar to gay and lesbian narratives, which Wood describes as being about 'coming-*into*-lesbianism' (Wood 1994:777).

Beyond this very broad level, Liang (1997) in particular seeks to uncover the generic conventions for coming out narratives – in other words, the normative expectations community members share surrounding the telling of stories in this genre. She argues that there are three core elements to coming out, which are reflected in the organisation of coming out narratives: 'self-definition as lesbian or gay to the self; self-presentation as lesbian and [*sic*] gay to others; membership in a series of ongoing acts of self-definition, and/or self-presentation as lesbian or gay' (Liang 1997:291). Liang observes that some speakers had relatively unproblematic experiences with coming out to themselves; however, even these individuals would preface their stories of coming out to others with an account of why their initial self-identification process did not present the expected challenges. Liang suggests that moves such as this mark speakers 'as communicatively competent members of an American gay community' (Liang 1997:307).

I found similar evidence of transgender speakers orienting to norms specific to the coming out narrative genre. The clearest example in the present body of data of speakers' sensitivity to these kinds of expectations comes from my interview with Gerry, a 64-year-old lesbian-identified trans woman from the Midwest who began her transition in 1998 while working as a software developer at the large corporation where she is still employed. Toward the end of our talk, Gerry explicitly referenced the way her experiences diverged from what she described as a common claim in trans people's coming out stories: 'they'll say they knew [their gender identity] at four years old' (lines 421–2).[8]

Excerpt 1: Gerry

```
G:  Um, ((sigh)) um, that, y'know you- you'll talk to a
    lot of transgender people and they'll say they knew at
    four years old, and um, I'm not sure that I knew that
    early. ((clears throat)) It's just something was going
    on most of my life y'know, that was in the background
    and um the older I got the more it occupied my
    thoughts and dreams.
```

Although Gerry does not report an early awareness of her female identity ('I'm not sure I knew that early', lines 422–3), she acknowledges that such an experience might be considered typical – and therefore expected – in transgender coming out stories.

While both homosexual and transgender speakers show sensitivity to generic expectations, what those particular expectations are seems to vary across these groups. For example, while Liang (1997) identifies coming out to the self as a crucial element in coming out stories told by gay men, several of the narratives I collected lacked any reference whatsoever to how the speakers came to identify as transgender. Instead, these speakers began their stories at a point when they had already decided to move from one gender role to the other and were beginning that process. In other words, the speakers in my study did not seem to orient to the issue of 'self-definition ... to self' (Liang 1997) which Liang posited as a highly salient generic norm.

A more important difference, however, is the issue of what Liang and Wood refer to as the 'processuality' of coming out. Here, processuality refers to the notion that coming out is not a single event, nor even a finite series of acts after which the individual may be considered completely out, but rather a lifelong process of claiming a gay or lesbian identity. For Liang (1997), processuality is among the three core elements of any act of coming out ('membership in a series of ongoing acts of self-definition, and/or self-presentation as lesbian or gay'), and both she and Wood (1994, 1997) find evidence for this claim in the narratives they collected. However, the narratives in my study indicate that coming out as transgender is very often not processual in the lifelong sense that these authors argue for.

A key reason that coming out as transgender lacks the processuality discussed by Liang and Wood is that transgender people experience coming out from two significantly different perspectives: before and after transitioning to their preferred gender role. The differences between these subjectivities must be examined before a full understanding of coming out as transgender, and the narratives that result from this practice, can be achieved. On the one hand, when a person first comes out as transgender, that individual is asserting a self-experienced gender identity that is different from the gender they are perceived to be by others. In this case, an invisible gender identity is being claimed in much the same way that gays and lesbians come out by claiming a sexual orientation that is often not visible to others. On the other hand, when a transgender person has assumed a gender role matching their identity, coming out does not involve asserting a hidden gender identity, but rather revealing the fact that they formerly occupied a different gender role. Of course, for those trans people who are visibly transgender after their transition, coming out as transgender is not necessarily something that must be done verbally; instead, a transgender person's former gender role may be revealed by their stature, hairline, or voice, for example. However, many transgender people are unquestionably seen as male or female after transitioning, and for them coming out means telling others about a transgender history, not revealing their identity as a man or woman.

I distinguish these two types of coming out through the use of two terms: *declaration*, to refer to the initial claiming of a transgender identity, and *disclosure*, to refer to sharing one's transgender history after transition. This distinction will allow for greater clarity regarding how transgender coming out stories are structured and, crucially, why they lack the processuality thought to be so important to the coming out narrative genre. Importantly, it is also a distinction community members are making themselves, as Michael did when he referred to disclosure as 'the other kind of coming out'.[9]

Indeed, the notion that declaration and disclosure are discrete processes is reflected in linguistic practices found among transgender speakers. I will briefly discuss two such practices that appear in these data. First, many transgender people, including a few participants in this study, make use of a set of lexical items that offer an alternative to mainstream ways of talking about coming out and the closet. Yet these terms are only found in discussions of disclosure, indicating that at least some transgender speakers sense the need for a vocabulary specific to that process. Second, when participants in this study were asked for their 'coming out stories', without any specific prompting regarding which experiences to discuss, they focused almost exclusively on declaration, rather than disclosure. This indicates that these speakers conceptualised 'coming out as transgender' in terms of the initial declaration of a gender identity and not in terms of disclosing a transgender past.

While declaration is frequently discussed using the same lexicon employed by gays and lesbians, including phrases such as *come out (of the closet)*, and *in the closet* or *closeted* to refer to those who haven't come out, many transgender people use different terminology when talking about disclosure. A few participants in this study made use of the term *disclose* instead of *come out* (the source of my own use of this term) and *stealth* instead of *in the closet*. My previous observations of transgender communities – both as a participant and as a researcher – confirm that these terms are in wide circulation. Each of these words, *disclose* and *stealth*, serves to challenge the ideological weight attached to mainstream coming out discourse – an issue to be discussed at greater length below. In brief, we may recognise that within gay and lesbian communities, *coming out* is typically thought of as a highly valuable process in which a person reveals an aspect of their 'true self' to others. This conceptualisation is congruent with the dominant attitude in the transgender community toward declaration, which is often seen as coming to terms with one's 'true' gender identity. Disclosure, on the other hand, is seen quite differently. Because transgender people generally emphasise the authenticity of their self-identified gender, rather than the gender they were assigned at birth, disclosure does not involve revealing a fundamental truth about one's identity in the same way that declaration does. On the other hand, non-transgender people typically assign primacy to a person's assigned gender role, and upon discovering a person's transgender status will often conclude that the individual is 'really' a woman, for example, even if they may look like and identify as a man. As a result of this schism, disclosing a transgender past may have the effect of undermining what the speaker sees as their true identity rather than illuminating it. By distinguishing between declaration – usually simply referred to as *coming out* – and *disclosure*, speakers are able to create a clear distinction between two practices that are regarded quite differently within the community (more about this below), and to indicate that while one of these practices is like gays' and lesbians' coming out, the other is distinct. Similarly, *stealth* functions as an alternative to *closeted* that does not carry the negative connotations that the latter term invokes. While describing a person as *closeted* suggests that they are ashamed of and hiding some part of their identity, calling someone *stealth* only entails that they choose not to share certain aspects of their life history or embodiment with others. As a result, while *in the closet* or *closeted* may be used to talk about pre-transition transgender people who hide their gender identities, *stealth* refers specifically and exclusively to post-transition transgender people who opt not to disclose their transgender status. This more neutral meaning reflects the relatively neutral attitude held by many in the transgender community toward being stealth.

In fact, it seems that stance toward coming out may play a significant role in motivating the use of these terms. For example, the participant in this study that made the greatest use of these alternative lexical items was John, a speaker who did not strongly identify with his transgender history and preferred to limit his disclosure. John was one of the few participants in this study who lived a relatively stealth lifestyle, and he was critical toward the idea that trans people have an obligation to be openly transgender. The terms *disclose* and *stealth* may thus serve as indices for this stance, as well as allowing John and others like him to manage and make sense of their own lack of disclosure without using language that condemns such behaviour.

As I just mentioned, the speakers in this study framed their coming out stories almost exclusively in terms of their experiences with declaration. This is true despite the fact that, when asked for their 'coming out stories' – a request that I intentionally left open-ended so as to best capture speakers' own notions of this genre – participants told narratives that differed greatly in their scope. Some speakers focused narrowly on one aspect of their gender transition, such as coming out at work. Others told much longer stories, as when Angie, a 42-year-old Italian-American trans woman originally from Florida who started coming out as transgender in her mid-thirties, told me a narrative that spanned from her early childhood to the present. In fact, it was Angie who was the only speaker to discuss an experience of disclosure without my prompting. This may be related to the epic nature of her narrative, and to the fact that this act of disclosure figured into the way Angie met her current partner, which was a significant milestone in her life story.

While the great majority of speakers in this study limited the scope of their coming out stories to declaration, one participant made a more explicit comment indicating that she thinks of coming out as transgender as having ended when one has finished the process of declaration. This participant was Elizabeth, a pansexual-identified 24-year-old trans woman from Australia who spent much of her childhood in Israel and now lives in the United States with her non-transgender female partner. In the following excerpt, Elizabeth is finishing a story about her last experience with declaration, which took place after she had been living as a woman for several years. While declaration typically occurs before or immediately after a transgender person begins living in their new gender role, in this case Elizabeth had not yet declared her female identity to her half-sisters in part because they were living in another country and had not seen her since her transition.

Excerpt 2: Elizabeth

```
E:   And she said that she hadn't realised, y'know, s- but
     she asked me a few questions and, y'know, are you
     seeing a doctor about this:? and I told her yes:.
     Y'know and I'd been s- this had been me for the last
     three years. And I showed her a photo, and y'know she
     said basically I accept you as my sister. And y'know,
     very cool about it.
LZ:  Mhm.
E:   Not a problem. At all.
LZ:  Mhm.
E:   And uh she was the last person I came out to.
```

At the end of this subnarrative, Elizabeth refers to her sister as 'the last person [she] came out to' (line 217). She does this despite the fact that when I inquired later, she reported quite a few experiences with disclosure. This indicates that when Elizabeth talks about the 'last' time she 'came out', she is speaking only of that initial process of declaration, and placing disclosure in a separate sphere.

If declaration serves as the basis of transgender coming out narratives, we can begin to understand how these stories challenge the assertion that coming out must necessarily be ongoing throughout a person's lifetime. Declaration ends when an individual aligns gender role with gender identity, and for the majority of the participants in this study – all but two of whom had been living in their preferred gender role for at least a few years – this process was complete. As a result, these speakers narrated coming out as a process that took place over a discrete period of time in the past. In the section that follows, I analyse the narratives of three such speakers in greater depth in order to demonstrate the lack of processuality in the form, as well as content, of these narratives. I accomplish this by showing how the stories I collected depart from those structural trends that Wood (1997) describes as iconic representations of coming out's processuality.

Iconic representations of processuality

Both Liang and Wood agree that processuality is a significant part of coming out narratives. Wood, however, takes her analysis a step further in proposing that the on-going nature of coming out is reflected in the linguistic form these narratives take. Wood (1997) argues for two distinct linguistic features that do this work: the structure of the narratives' resolutions and codas, and the tense accorded to verbs in the narratives' evaluations. In this section I analyse transgender coming out narratives from my own study using Wood's criteria and argue that they fail to conform to the linguistic patterns she observed.

The bulk of Wood's analysis focuses on the structure of the coming out narratives she collected from four lesbians through email. Following a Labovian model of narrative analysis, she focuses on each story's resolution and coda, the latter of which functions to '[return] the listener to the present time' (Labov 1972:369, quoted in Wood 1997:258), as well as the telling-frame coda, which marks the end of the story-telling frame (Schiffrin 1993:249–50, cited in Wood 1997). Wood observed that the speakers in her study would often begin to resolve one narrative only to interrupt its resolution in order to relate another experience. She argued that, rather than progressing in a linear way through a series of events that can then be resolved and evaluated, these stories linked together disparate instances of coming out, sometimes in haphazard ways. A number of the experiences her speakers described lacked clear resolutions, and codas were sometimes absent or would occur in unconventional positions within the structure of the narrative. According to Wood, this diversion from typical narrative organisation is iconic of the fact that coming out as lesbian is never complete. Because this is the focus of Wood's argument, I begin my own analysis here.

In the previous section, I argued that the coming out narratives of transgender speakers generally describe experiences of declaration rather than disclosure, meaning that they do not exhibit the kind of processuality Wood describes. I found no evidence among these speakers of the 'stop-start-stop narrative sequence' (Wood 1997:261) Wood observes. Rather, the stories tended to be linear and exhibit the expected sequence of resolution, evaluation, and coda. For example,

Gerry, whom I introduced in an earlier section of this chapter, ended her narrative in a typical way. In her story, she described how multiple traumatic experiences that occurred within a short period of time brought a vague lifelong discomfort to an apex, prompting her to pursue therapy for depression which 'got [her] thinking about, okay, where do you wanna be in five years?' This introspection led Gerry's feelings that she 'should be female' to intensify, and eventually she sought out other transgender people on the internet. She found local contacts to begin her transition, and reports having felt validated by the similarity her experiences bore to those of other transgender people. The following selection is the end of this story.

Excerpt 3: Gerry

G: so once I got into the trans
community, and found that everybody's stories were
kind of matching mine, y'know with minor variations.
Uh, people were sayin' the same things I was sayin'
and so forth. So I knew that I wasn't makin' this
stuff up in my head because you can't have this
disjointed mass hypnosis or something going on. So
that was very reassuring, and that started me
seriously going toward transition. And through those
organisations I found a psychologist who had
experience and uh and started that whole road. And
once you start down that road, ((clears throat)) as
long as you're not doing it for some other reasons,
y'know, as long as it's a valid gender dysphoria,
y'know. You're gonna come out the other end well-
adjusted and hopefully happier and and I did. Y'know,
so.

After describing how she made the necessary connection with a psychologist who could give her a referral for medical transition, Gerry provides a highly general evaluation: as long as one is motivated by 'a valid gender dysphoria',[10] (lines 484–8) transition from one gender role to the other will ultimately be a positive experience. The coda, 'and I did' (line 488), confirms that the generalisation holds true for Gerry, and that at this point in her life she is a well-adjusted and happier person. Rather than starting up another narrative as this one winds down, Gerry provides a clear conclusion that sums up the lesson to be taken from her story.

Another story that clearly progresses in a linear fashion and then closes with an unambiguous conclusion was the one told by Angie. Angie's story was the longest I collected, consisting of many small narratives that covered the major events of her gendered life from childhood to the present. All of these subnarratives advanced a single theme, however, and did so without stopping and starting different stories as Wood describes. The central issue in her narrative, more so for Angie than any other participant in this study, is how she came to be the woman she is today, far more content with life than she had been living as a man. This focus is made even more clear by how she chose to end her story: after describing her transition, she talks about her relationship with her partner and the artistic projects on which they were collaborating. She concludes in the following way:

Excerpt 4: Angie

```
939  A:                                    Anyway,
940       so we might do that, we've got another comic book
941       idea, so anyway, but it's uh, life's pretty good.
942       ((laugh))
```

Angie ends her story with a simple statement that serves as both an evaluation and a coda, 'life's pretty good' (line 941). Thus, not only does she provide a narrative coda in the expected location, it is a coda that confirms the suggestion from Wood noted earlier that coming out narratives are less about revealing a new identity to others than the overall process of assuming that identity and the correlating social role – a process which, for Angie and the other speakers under discussion here, is clearly complete. This theme is supported by the fact that instead of ending her narrative with an assessment of her coming out experiences, the evaluation in Angie's story (like Gerry's) serves the additional purpose of establishing her more general happiness in her life as a woman. Because popular notions of transsexuality tend to present the process of transition as unnecessary, misguided, or even a sign of mental instability, asserting the power of her gender role change in producing happiness and satisfaction acts as a powerful authentication of Angie's gender identity. As Gerry says, only someone with 'a valid gender dysphoria' (i.e. a psychologically legitimate identification with a different gender than that conferred at birth) would be happy after changing their gender role.

The other linguistic feature Wood (1997) analyses in her narratives is the way verbs are inflected in narrative resolutions. She argues that the lesbian speakers in her study exploit the meaning of different syntactic forms in order to signal that their coming out experiences are not yet over. For example, one speaker, Tess, says 'I don't have much of a coming out story to tell, because it *hasn't been* that dramatic for me or anyone else. I guess it *would be* different if I had a long-term relationship' (Wood 1997:266; emphasis added). Rather than saying that coming out '*wasn't* that dramatic' and that it 'would *have been* different', the present tense forms *hasn't been* and *would be* indicate that coming out is not conceptualised by this speaker as an event that took place in the past, but rather an ongoing process. In contrast, past tense forms are more common in these sorts of contexts within the transgender coming out stories I collected. For instance, John's coming out story, like Angie's, was a series of narratives that spanned a number of years and various contexts. John began by talking about how he came to identify as male while still in high school, came out and began his gender role change while serving in the Israeli armed forces, and finally told his family of his plans to transition as he began his higher education. At the end of his story, he evaluates his overall experience, much as Gerry and Angie did, as generally positive (line 482). It is worth noting that John includes 'getting access to hormones' (line 505) and 'going through ... bureaucratic bullshit' (line 506) as part of the coming out experience, demonstrating that his narrative too is as much about the general process of assuming a male gender role as it is about telling others about the corresponding gender identity.

Excerpt 5: John

```
482  J:   I just had a really a really positive experience
483       in general with coming out [to folks, to my=
484  LZ:                              [Mhm.
485  J:   =relatives, to folks in the army, to: ah my
486       friends. Ah I mean I had some friends back
487       from junior high that I was sort of still in touch
488       with, [but then, everybody being in the military in=
489  LZ:        [Mhm.
490  J:   =different places, like, didn't really have much time,
491       to hang out, but also like, I would s- try to like
492       still like be in touch with them?=
493  LZ:  Mhm.
494  J:   =And a lot of folks just sort of um dissipated,
495       [uh in a sense, even though=
496  LZ:  [Mhm.
497  J:   =I (xxx) sort of try to make the effort to: uh
498       not make that happen. But=
499  LZ:  Right.
500  J:   =I still have some friends from back then who are
501       still pretty cool and who still hang out with and it
502       wasn't a big deal at all. But yeah, but all in all,
503       like, a very positive experience, just coming out
504       and y'know bein' able to get ac- I mean,
505       getting access to hormones was: sort of a
506       nightmare within itself [just going through=
507  LZ:                          [Mhm.
508  J:   =different bureaucratic bullshit, [but eventually it=
509  LZ:                                    [Mhm.
510  J:   =did happen, so that that was that was good too. But
511       um yeah.
```

As this segment of talk shows, John tends to use past tense verbs when evaluating his coming out experiences. For example, he says that he 'just *had* a really positive experience in general with coming out' (lines 482–3) and that while 'getting access to hormones *was* sort of a nightmare within itself' he concludes that 'eventually it *did happen*, so that *was* good too' (lines 508–10). This gives an impression quite different from that achieved by the use of present tense forms in Wood's stories, indicating that the experiences John describes are complete. John's story is not atypical in this regard; for example, Gerry makes a similar move when she notes that '[she] *did*' end up happier and better-adjusted as a result of her transition (Excerpt 3, line 488).

Local ideologies

I have argued that there are significant differences between coming out as transgender and coming out as gay or lesbian, and that these differences are important when considering the linguistic form of coming out narratives. Yet perhaps the most striking dissimilarity between these groups – so much so that it served as the impetus for this project – is in the ideologies speakers draw on when discussing coming out. The most significant and pervasive of these ideological differences concerns what Rasmussen (2004) calls 'the coming out imperative'. This imperative, which has been one of the key tools of gay and lesbian activists, frames coming out as 'a valuable – if sometimes difficult – task, and [claims] that the act of coming out is likely to benefit the individual and their peers' (Rasmussen 2004:145). Rasmussen argues that the valorisation of coming out relegates those who are not out to 'a zone of shame and exclusion' (Rasmussen 2004:144). While the focus of her paper is the role and obligations of queer educators, her critique can be extended to the force with which the imperative is applied across more general contexts. She also mentions the way the imperative acts to further marginalise those whose identities include multiple levels of oppression, such as people of colour who are also sexual minorities, by privileging membership in the gay and lesbian community regardless of the consequences in other areas of an individual's life.

Rasmussen argues for the pervasiveness of the coming out imperative, and indeed it appears to be influential in the construction of coming out narratives. For example, Liang (1997) observed a tendency for speakers to present their former, closeted selves as deceptive and morally lacking protagonists. Similarly, Munt, Bassett and O'Riordan's (2002) investigation of coming out in an online lesbian community found that the majority of members' view of coming out was that it marked an individual as mature, brave, and possessing self-respect, suggesting that those who choose not to come out are lacking in these qualities. On the other hand, this was far from the case in the narratives of the transgender people with whom I spoke. While one participant did mention denial as a factor that kept him from coming out until his late thirties, the barrier that was mentioned most often was lack of access to transgender identities as culturally intelligible options. Furthermore, while declaration was certainly presented as a first step on a path toward a more honest and overall happier life, there was no invocation of the coming out imperative with regard to disclosure.

Because this research was prompted by an interest in this ideological issue, I asked each participant, after eliciting their narratives, where they stood on an issue that is frequently debated in many transgender communities: are trans people morally or politically obliged to be openly transgender after transition, or is it equally valid to remain mostly stealth? Despite (or perhaps partly because of) the controversial nature of this topic, every participant in this study expressed a 'live and let live' attitude toward disclosure. Only two participants said that they thought it better for those who feel safe and comfortable disclosing to do so, and even these individuals said they don't begrudge anyone the choice to be stealth, particularly in unfriendly climates. Several participants – including but not limited to those who themselves prefer to limit disclosure – explicitly mentioned that not every transgender person wants to be openly transgender, or sees their transgender status as relevant to their identity, regardless of how accepting or understanding the communities in which they live. Additionally, nearly every person I spoke with mentioned the ubiquitous danger of disclosing transgender status, even in relatively queer-friendly contexts – such as when Elizabeth made reference to the 2002 murder of San Francisco Bay Area transgender teenager Gwen Araujo, which shocked many residents of the area who had assumed it to be a safe place for all members of the LGBT community.

This study illustrates that transgender people cannot be uncritically grouped with gays, lesbians, and/or bisexuals in social scientific research, but the conflation of these communities happens at least as frequently in non-academic contexts. In fact, researchers who have treated 'LGBT' as a cohesive and even homogenous community for study have likely been influenced by gay and lesbian activism that has sought – for what are arguably valid historical and political reasons – to be inclusive of others oppressed as sexual and gender minorities. Yet if organisations truly wish to be inclusive of and serve transgender communities, they must recognise the ways in which both the experiences and the ideologies of these communities differ, or else risk reproducing the marginalisation and silencing of transgender people within those few spaces that actively claim to oppose transphobia. For example, as Rasmussen points out, the Human Rights Campaign (HRC) in the United States is probably the most influential institutional promoter of the coming out imperative through the organisation's National Coming Out Day project and accompanying website, which maintains dozens of online articles encouraging people to come out. A number of these webpages are directed toward specific communities like bisexuals, people of colour, Spanish speakers, transgender people, and allies of the LGBT community. The HRC promotes coming out as a necessary step in eliminating homophobia and transphobia, and maintains at the time of this writing no fewer than seven distinct web articles dealing specifically with coming out as transgender. Yet none of these discussions acknowledge the special issues facing trans people after transition, nor even the notion that coming out as transgender might involve something other than revealing one's gender identity. The HRC equates being out as gay, lesbian, or bisexual with being out as transgender, and the coming out imperative is applied with the same force to all transgender people, pre- and post-transition. One article, entitled 'Coming out as transgender: a lifelong journey' discusses coming out as transgender in terms that recall Liang and Wood's discussion of processuality. While this article does acknowledge that 'being out as transgender is not always easy', it claims that being out is

> the only way to educate others about gender identity and expression. Facing possible rejection and even violence, transgender people must continue coming out to friends, family, co-workers and community members so that they can, in turn, become more accepting and supportive. (Human Rights Campaign 2009b)

It cannot be doubted that the sacrifices made by openly gay and openly transgender people have paved the way for countless others to follow similar paths. However, the fact remains that not all paths are identical. John objected to the assumption that one person's visibility will necessarily be representative of other transgender people's experience. For instance, the growing visibility of transgender-identifying people has created greater room, at least in some contexts, for transgender as a distinct gender identity,[11] but this visibility does not necessarily create greater social acceptance for the identities of trans people like John, who see themselves primarily as men or women and might prefer a certain type of invisibility. Furthermore, the HRC's claim that being openly transgender is the only way to educate people on transgender issues diminishes the significant role that non-transgender people can play in combating transphobia. The mismatch between the ideological stance of the HRC and that of many members of the transgender community demonstrates the problematic nature of treating the LGBT acronym as representing a cohesive community outside, as well as inside, academia, particularly with regard to coming out.

Discussion: characterising the genre

In the preceding analysis, I have argued that the way coming out narratives have been previously characterised fails to account for the coming out stories told by transgender people. Of course, these arguments do not undermine the observations made by Wood and Liang for the communities in which they were working. In fact, my analysis can be seen as providing further support for Wood's claims, in that the features she identifies as marking the processuality of coming out are absent from these transgender narratives in which coming out is not processual in the same sense. However, this chapter does illustrate that Liang and Wood's work has given an incomplete picture of the coming out narrative genre as a whole. There is no reason to suppose that either Liang or Wood assumed the patterns they observed would hold true across the queer community; indeed, Liang's observations about the differences between the narratives of white and Asian-American gay men (Liang 1997:305–7) suggests that she is sensitive to the possibility that expectations for this genre will vary. However, other authors have more overtly assumed uniformity in the coming out experience, making these differences worth noting if only to underscore the frequently forgotten diversity of the LGBT community.

Rather than attempting to synthesise the commonalities across stories told by these diverse communities of speakers, including those whose narratives have yet to be studied from a linguistic perspective (such as bisexuals), I propose that the coming out narrative genre can be characterised more productively along functional, rather than formal, lines. As I have discussed, transgender and homosexual narratives share the task of describing the process of coming to have, and making sense of, a marginalised identity. Coming out narratives are largely about coming to *be*, and they are stories worth telling because of the challenges inherent in coming to embrace a contested identity. These stories all describe how speakers came to understand their feelings of otherness in relation to normative constructs of gender and sexuality, and how this understanding came to be realised socially as an identity. Yet these communities produce understandings of their experiences and identities in different ways, which leaves the coming out narrative to function as a venue for the enactment of local forms of identity work. This is exactly what is happening when, as Gerry described in Excerpt 1, speakers claim that their current gender identity has been present and unchanging since early childhood; through asserting a single and unwavering gender identity, speakers are claiming a kind of authentication that is highly valued in transgender communities. That is, many trans people do not see themselves as women becoming men or vice versa, and may even assert that it is impossible to change one's gender, insofar as gender is conceptualised as an internal, psychological, or even spiritual – rather than social or biological – state.[12] In appealing to this system of identity, a speaker authenticates their gender by invoking an ideological norm given great weight within the transgender community. Another form of community-specific identity work is found in the way that similar experiences might be assigned different meanings by members of different communities. For example, the kind of childhood gender non-conformity that might lead transgender people to claim a lifelong sense of themselves as male or female would almost certainly be interpreted through a different ideological lens by a gay or lesbian speaker.

Beyond enacting and legitimating a particular gender or sexual identity, appealing to locally salient ideologies may accomplish other kinds of social work as well. Most immediately, as in many other sociocultural contexts, performing a narrative according to these kinds of in-group norms can be a source of community solidarity; in this case solidarity can be built not only around shared identification with a gender or sexual category, but also around shared resources and tactics for making sense of, and authenticating, these highly contested identities. While the creation of solidarity is an intuitively obvious function of coming out narratives, and has been speculated on by other scholars such as Liang (1994, 1997), Wood (1997) and Pugh (1998), stories in this genre could potentially act in several other capacities as well. First, it is worth noting that transgender coming out narratives are not always told in in-group settings. I asked each of the participants I spoke with where else they had told similar coming out stories, and the sum of these responses represents quite a diverse variety of contexts: churches, employee diversity training sessions, college classrooms, therapists' offices, and workshops for medical providers. In most of these cases, the job of the narrator is to educate listeners through personal narrative. In some sense, the narratives I collected also served this function in that, as I mentioned earlier, speakers seemed aware of both their immediate (in-group) and eventual broader (out-group) audiences.[13]

Coming out narratives provide ideal opportunities to educate non-transgender listeners because of the way they introduce and provide support for the ideologies of the transgender community through personal experience. Speakers will often talk about their past selves as being subscribers to dominant gender ideologies until learning about the existence of alternative systems. If speakers are persuasive – and their audiences open to being persuaded – an account of the experiences that led the narrator to doubt and ultimately reject those dominant ideologies may be sufficient to cause listeners to question them as well.[14] A similar type of ideological positioning can be observed in the tendency for gay speakers in Liang's study to promote the coming out imperative by casting their former, closeted selves as morally lacking.

Similarly, transgender coming out narratives serve to help new members become culturally competent within the transgender community. The orientation speakers display to their community's generic expectations acts as an important form of socialisation for newly declared transgender people as they begin to shape their own coming out narratives by deciding which experiences are relevant and how to make sense of them. A number of participants in this study explicitly mentioned the importance of exposure to other transgender people's stories in helping them to validate and understand their own experiences.[15] Because of the inseparability of this genre from the dominant ideologies of the community, the socialisation provided by coming out narratives prepares members not only to share their own stories as communicatively competent users of this genre, but also to interact as culturally competent members of the transgender community. Knowing this genre means being familiar with the basic tenets embraced by this group in order to create a legitimate and intelligible space for transgender identities. The striking similarity in the ideologies drawn on by my participants, despite the diversity in the particulars of their identities, testifies to this form of shared knowledge.

The connection between generic and ideological expectations runs so deep that these ideologies may in fact directly shape speakers' expectations of the coming out narrative genre. For example, while Gerry suggested that claiming early childhood awareness of one's adult gender identity is common among transgender speakers, none of the participants in this study made such an assertion. It is entirely possible that the stories Gerry has heard simply differ from those that comprise my data, but the fact that this form of authentication is considered extremely powerful by members of the transgender community suggests that Gerry's idea of a prototypical coming out story may not be based purely on the statistical trends of previously heard narratives. The norms speakers invoke when telling their stories may be based as much on what they imagine an 'ideal' transgender coming out narrative to be as it is on what the majority of such narrators actually say.

However, it is not simply the display of pre-existing norms that occurs in these narratives; each telling becomes part of the body of stories previously heard by listeners, and thus can also represent the negotiation, or even subversion, of the community's expectations. If this were not so, we would wonder why, in the example just discussed, Gerry would invoke such a potentially strong authenticating move only to state that it doesn't apply to her life experiences – that she herself was not aware of a female gender identity as a child. It seems that such a reference would destabilise, rather than support, her claim to a female identity. However, as Briggs and Bauman (1992) have argued, speakers may choose either to minimise or to maximise gaps between generic precedents and their own performances toward accomplishing different rhetorical and interactional ends. In this case, Gerry is maximising and explicitly commenting on one such gap; what might this accomplish, assuming that Gerry did not hope to undermine her identity as a woman? First, it seems that she is proposing that while this claim may be typical of transgender coming out stories, it is not a necessary one. As I mentioned earlier, Gerry's happiness as a woman serves as its own form of authentication of her previous gender dysphoria, and so to call attention to the relatively late development of her awareness of her gender identity is to point out that one can be a 'successful' transsexual without having had this supposedly typical experience. Thus, she is simultaneously referencing a norm and contesting its power, actively reshaping the very generic convention she invokes. This kind of negotiation has been characterised by Bauman and Briggs as a defining quality of performance; because of the heightened reflexivity performance invites from both performers and audiences, a space is created 'that invites critical reflection on communicative processes' (Bauman and Briggs 1990:60), such as this particular ideologically driven generic convention that Gerry invokes. The coming out narrative genre seems to be an ideal setting in which to advance critiques on numerous social levels – against the discourses of powerful members of our society (as Wood 1999 discusses), the mainstream gay and lesbian community, and even the transgender community's own ideological tendencies.

More recently, scholars such as Cameron and Kulick (2003) have challenged linguists studying sexuality to put a greater emphasis on how heterosexuality is produced as a normative social position, rather than focusing primarily on the practices of the sexually marginalised. However, the focus on queer or otherwise non-normative subjectivity that has come to characterise studies of language and sexuality continues to be missing in many ways from the study of language and gender. Although it has been a decade since Kulick (1999) called for more research on the linguistic practices of transgender people and even longer since Bing and Bergvall (1996) made a similar plea, there remains a serious dearth of inquiries on how members of these communities talk. Great insights have clearly been gained from the study of language and gender variance in the forms of Indian *hijras* (e.g. Hall 1997), Tongan *fakaleiti* (e.g. Besnier 2003), Brazilian *travesti* (e.g. Chapter 5, this volume; Kulick 1998) and Nigerian *'yan daudu* (e.g. Gaudio 2009). But it is surprising that a field like language and gender, which very often makes English-speaking women and men its focus, has rarely taken advantage of the potential insights to be gained from the study of how gender is produced and managed discursively by English-speaking transgender people. In this chapter, I have shown how transgender speakers make use of what might be thought of as a queer linguistic practice – the coming out narrative – in ways that distinguish them from sexual minorities like gays and lesbians. Rather than primarily challenging heteronormativity (as Wood 1999 describes in the case of lesbian speakers),[16] transgender people's coming out narratives chiefly act as contexts in which to negotiate ideologies about gender, identity, and authenticity as they circulate on multiple levels of community membership, reflecting transgender people's status as trans, as queer, and as women and men. The study of transgender subjectivities, then, has the potential to shed light both on the workings of gender as a social and ideological phenomenon and on the nature of queerness as a concept that spans both sexual and gender-based marginalisation.

Conclusion

For the wealth of literature that has been published on coming out, little work has been done to reconcile dominant notions of coming out as gay or lesbian with the experiences of those on the margins of the queer community. Indeed, there seems to have been little awareness that such a reconciliation is necessary; gays and lesbians have often been seen as unproblematic representatives of the entire LGBT population. Some authors have gone as far as to reproduce the 'silent T' phenomenon wherein the LGBT acronym is used despite an exclusive focus on issues of sexual orientation. I have argued that how coming out itself is conceptualised must be expanded to fully account for the experiences of transgender people, and that the use of certain lexical items, namely *disclose* and *stealth*, reflect the limitations many trans people perceive in the established coming out discourse. By introducing a distinction between the processes of declaration and disclosure, I have introduced a tool that may enable a more nuanced examination of coming out as transgender. In the case of these narratives, the distinction has enabled and elucidated my argument that transgender coming out narratives differ from those told by gays and lesbians.

Moreover, I have demonstrated that the different forms that coming out narratives take across the communities who make use of this genre reflect the various ways that coming out is experienced by members of these disparate, yet socially and historically linked, groups. For the transgender people in this study, coming out was epitomised – if not characterised exclusively – by the process of declaration, which is complete when a person assumes a social gender role matching their gender identity. For gays and lesbians, on the other hand, the ever-continuing nature of coming out seems to be key. Despite variation in terms of how coming out narratives are enacted by members of these communities, they do seem to be making use of a single genre. Yet this genre is not unified by form or content as much as by function. For both homosexual and transgender speakers, the coming out narrative serves as a site in which speakers authenticate and legitimate highly stigmatised identities. As in many verbal performances, this kind of identity work is realised through the display and negotiation of local norms for the genre, potentially including either the reification or subversion of these conventions. Thus, the capacity of this genre is not only to serve as authentication for the individual's sense of self, nor simply to build solidarity between members of oppressed communities, but to contest the ideologies that sustain the very marginalisation and denaturalisation of queer identities that makes coming out necessary in the first place.

Notes

1 For the remainder of this chapter, I use the term *gender identity* to refer to individuals' perception of themselves as men or women – in other words, the gender with which a person self-identifies. I will use the phrase *gender role* to refer to the gender that a person lives as – for example, whether they wear masculine or feminine clothing, whether they and others make use of masculine or feminine pronouns and other forms of reference, and whether they are perceived to be a man or woman by others. *To transition* is a verb used to refer to the process by which a person changes their gender role through medical, social, and/or legal means. All of this terminology is common place both in transgender communities and in the academic literature on transgender issues at the time of data collection and analysis.

2 This emphasis on processuality can be found in non-linguistic discussions of coming out as well (e.g. Morrow 2006).

3 Although the use of the term *European* as a synonym for *White* has become controversial, here I use it in order to be inclusive of research participants like John, who identified with the European ethnic group *Ashkenazi*, but did not describe himself as *White*. Thanks to Bonnie McElhinny for bringing this terminological issue to my attention.

4 *Genderqueer* is a term that refers to individuals who identify outside of the male/female binary. It includes people who identify as members of a third gender, as non-gendered or bi-gendered, and a virtually limitless number of other identities. However, many genderqueer people live in and even express a strong preference for either a male or female gender role in their everyday lives. Michael, like the other participants in this study, could be described as transsexual from a medical perspective, lives as a man for practical purposes, and sees himself as being genderqueer 'from a male perspective', rather than a female one (cf. Cromwell 1999:130).

5 I thank an anonymous *Gender and Language* reviewer for suggesting these references.

6 See Cromwell (1999:22–4) for a discussion of these terms as they were used during the 1990s; the principal change I have observed since the time of his research is that *transgender* is no longer used in strict opposition to *transsexual* in the way that he describes. Today, many people identify with both terms, or with the ambiguous shortened form *trans*.

7 It is worth noting that the recruiting text for this study invited anyone with a transgender coming out story to participate, regardless of gender identity or status with regard to transition. However, despite the diverse ways in which the participants in this study experienced their identities as trans people, they could each be classified as transsexuals in a medicalised model of identity.

8 Transcription conventions:

[ ]	overlapping speech
(( ))	extralinguistic actions (e.g. laughter, coughing)
=	latching utterances, continued from previous line without pause
-	speech is cut off abruptly
:	lengthened phone
(word)	speech was unclear; transcription represents author's best guess
(xxx)	unintelligible speech

9 This is not to suggest, however, that *being* transgender is not processual, or that it takes place over a discrete period of time. While some individuals do stop identifying as transgender after transition, at least two participants in this study – including Michael – explicitly mentioned that for them, being transgender was a life-long journey.

10 *Gender dysphoria* is a psycho-medical term used for diagnosing Gender Identity Disorder, but is also widely used within the community to describe feelings of discomfort, distress, or sadness in a gender role.

11 This can be seen in, for example, forms and surveys that offer three options for gender: male, female, or transgender.

12 While many people who reject transgender identities also believe that gender cannot be changed, their view is of course quite different from the one I allude to here. The most dominant perspective seems to be that gender is permanently fixed according to one's sex as assigned at birth. In contrast, some people who accept transsexuals as members of their gender of identification may only do so when an individual has had genital surgery. In the latter case, gender is seen as corresponding to genitals, but is also seen as potentially changeable (to the degree that genitals can be surgically modified). Transgender people, on the other hand, may espouse the view that a person's internal, 'true' gender is unchangeable, but what can be changed is an individual's social gender role and/or biological sex.

13 An interesting exception to this was Elizabeth: despite the fact that I advertised my own transgender status in the recruiting text for this project, Elizabeth skimmed the ad and was not aware of this fact until I made reference to it at the end of our interview.

14 I believe that Bacon (1998) underestimates the rhetorical persuasion that takes place during coming out when she says that one need only claim a queer identity to have that identity accepted by a listener. These claims are not always so easily accepted, particularly for transgender people, who are often claiming not (only) to be queer, but to be men or women despite evidence to the contrary.

15 Of course, not everyone finds such solace in the communities they seek out. People of colour, for example, often feel alienated in mostly white transgender communities; likewise, genderqueer-identified individuals frequently object to the way many transgender communities accept, reproduce, and even police the male/female binary. Those who do not feel validated by the ideologies dominant within the transgender community may seek out or form other networks that better address their needs and experiences.

16 Though certainly a number of these speakers also challenged heteronormativity, as my anecdote about John's mother assuming he would only be attracted to women illustrates.

References

Bacon, Jen (1998) Getting the story straight: coming out narratives and the possibility of a cultural rhetoric. *World English* 17: 249–58. https://doi.org/10.1111/1467-971X.00098

Bauman, Richard and Briggs, Charles L. (1990) Poetics and performance as critical perspectives on language and social life. *Annual Review of Anthropology* 19: 59–88. https://doi.org/10.1146/annurev.an.19.100190.000423

Besnier, Niko (2003) Crossing genders, mixing languages: the linguistic construction of transgenderism in Tonga. In Janet Holmes and Miriam Meyerhoff (eds) *Handbook of Language and Gender* 279–301. Malden, MA: Blackwell. https://doi.org/10.1002/9780470756942.ch12

Bing, Janet M. and Bergvall, Victoria L. (1996) The question of questions: beyond binary thinking. In Victoria L. Bergvall, Janet M. Bing and Alice F. Freed (eds) *Rethinking Language and Gender Research: Theory and Practice* 1–30. London: Longman.

Briggs, Charles L. (1986) *Learning How to Ask: A Sociolinguistic Appraisal of the Role of Interview in Social Science Research*. Cambridge: Cambridge University Press. https://doi.org/10.1017/CBO9781139165990

Briggs, Charles L. and Bauman, Richard (1992) Genre, intertextuality, and social power. *Journal of Linguistic Anthropology* 2: 131–72. https://doi.org/10.1525/jlin.1992.2.2.131

Bucholtz, Mary, Liang, A. C., Sutton, Laurel A. and Hines, Caitlin (eds) (1994) *Cultural Performances: Proceedings of the Third Berkeley Women and Language Conference*. Berkeley, CA: Berkeley Women and Language Group.

Cameron, Deborah and Kulick, Don (2003) *Language and Sexuality*. Cambridge: Cambridge University Press.

Chirrey, Deborah A. (2003) 'I hereby come out': what sort of speech act is coming out? *Journal of Sociolinguistics* 7: 24–37. https://doi.org/10.1111/1467-9481.00209

Coon, David W. (2003) *Lesbian, Gay, Bisexual and Transgender (LGBT) Issues and Family Caregiving.* San Francisco, CA: Family Caregiver Alliance.

Corrigan, Patrick W. and Matthews, Alicia K. (2003) Stigma and disclosure: implications for coming out of the closet. *Journal of Mental Health* 12: 235–48. https://doi.org/10.1080/0963823031000118221

Cromwell, Jason (1999) *Transmen and FTMs: Identities, Bodies, Genders, and Sexualities.* Urbana, IL: University of Illinois Press.

De Monteflores, Carmen and Schultz, Stephen J. (1978) Coming out: similarities and differences for lesbians and gay men. *Journal of Social Issues* 34: 59–72. https://doi.org/10.1111/j.1540-4560.1978.tb02614.x

Fields, Jessica (2001) Normal queers: straight parents respond to their children's 'coming out'. *Symbolic Interaction* 24: 165–87. https://doi.org/10.1525/si.2001.24.2.165

Gaudio, Rudolf P. (2009) *Allah Made Us: Sexual Outlaws in an Islamic African City*. Malden, MA: Wiley-Blackwell. https://doi.org/10.1002/9781444310535

Hall, Kira (1997) 'Go suck your husband's sugarcane!' hijras and the use of sexual insult. In Livia and Hall (1997): 430–60.

Human Rights Campaign (2009a) Glossary of terms. Retrieved on 1 February 2009 from www.hrc.org/issues/3336.htm.

Human Rights Campaign (2009b) Coming out as transgender: a lifelong journey. Retrieved on 1 February 2009 from www.hrc.org/issues/transgender/3438.htm.

Hunter, Ski (2007) *Coming Out and Disclosures: LGBT Persons Across the Lifespan.* Binghamton, NY: Haworth Press.

Kulick, Don (1998) *Travesti: Sex, Gender, and Culture among Brazilian Transgendered Prostitutes.* Chicago, IL: University of Chicago Press.

Kulick, Don (1999) Transgender and language: a review of the literature and suggestions for the future. *GLQ: A Journal of Lesbian and Gay Studies* 5: 605–22.

Labov, William (1972) The transformation of experience in narrative syntax. In his *Language in the Inner City* 352–96. Philadelphia, PA: University of Pennsylvania Press.

Liang, A. C. (1994) 'Coming out' as transition and transcendence of the pubic/private dichotomy. In Bucholtz et al. (1994): 409–20.

Liang, A. C. (1997) The creation of coherence in coming-out stories. In Livia and Hall (1997): 287–309.

Livia, Anna and Hall, Kira (eds) (1997) *Queerly Phrased: Language, Gender, and Sexuality*. New York: Oxford University Press.

Markowe, Laura A. (1996) *Redefining the Self: Coming Out as Lesbian*. London: Polity.
Morrow, Deana F. (2006) Coming out as gay, lesbian, bisexual, and transgender. In Deana F. Morrow and Lori Messinger (eds) *Sexual Orientation and Gender Expression in Social Work Practice: Working with Gay, Lesbian, Bisexual, and Transgender People* 129–49. New York: Columbia University Press.
Munt, Sally R., Bassett, Elizabeth H. and O'Riordan, Kate (2002) Virtually belonging: risk, connectivity, and coming out on-line. *International Journal of Sexuality and Gender Studies* 7: 125–37. https://doi.org/10.1023/A:1015893016167
Pugh, William White Tison (1998) 'It's just my job to be "out"': tenure stories of lesbian, gay, and bisexual academics. *Journal of Gay, Lesbian, and Bisexual Identity* 3: 93–112.
Rasmussen, Mary Lou (2004) The problem of coming out. *Theory Into Practice* 43: 144–50. https://doi.org/10.1207/s15430421tip4302_8
Schiffrin, Deborah (1993) 'Speaking for another' in sociolinguistic interviews: alignments, identities, and frames. In Deborah Tannen (ed.) *Framing in Discourse* 231–63. Oxford: Oxford University Press.
Sedgwick, Eve Kosofsky (1990) *The Epistemology of the Closet*. Berkeley, CA: University of California Press.
Seidman, Steven, Meeks, Chet and Traschen, Francie (1999) Beyond the closet? The changing social meaning of homosexuality in the United States. *Sexualities* 2: 9–34. https://doi.org/10.1177/136346099002001002
Whitman, Joy S., Cormier, Sherry and Boyd, Cynthia J. (2000) Lesbian identity management at various stages in the coming out process: a qualitative study. *International Journal of Sexuality and Gender Studies* 5: 3–18. https://doi.org/10.1023/A:1010181416984
Wood, Kathleen M. (1994) Life stories as artifacts of a culture: lesbian coming-out stories. In Bucholtz et al. (1994): 777–86.
Wood, Kathleen M. (1997) Narrative iconicity in electronic-mail, lesbian coming-out stories. In Livia and Hall (1997): 257–73.
Wood, Kathleen M. (1999) Coherent identities amid heterosexist ideologies: deaf and lesbian coming-out stories. In Mary Bucholtz, A. C. Liang and Laurel A. Sutton (eds) *Reinventing Identities: The Gendered Self in Discourse* 46–63. New York: Oxford University Press.

Part III
Unpacking heteronormativity

8

Constructing hegemonic masculinities in South Africa: the discourse and rhetoric of heteronormativity

Russell Luyt
UNIVERSITY OF GREENWICH, UK

This chapter considers how dominant representations of masculinity are (re) produced, and how men's gender identities are constituted, through situated interaction. It highlights the role played by the dominant discourse and rhetoric of heteronormativity in South African (SA) men's gender understanding. This is worthwhile. First, as Connell (1993:600) argues, English-language literature is ethnocentric in its attempt to make sense of masculinities through the experience of '(at most) 5 percent of the world's population of men, in one culture-area, at one moment in history'. Anthropological research has challenged this ethnocentrism somewhat over the last two decades by describing diversity in men's experiences. This study contributes toward accounts of diversity in gender sense-making within a non-Western context. Second, SA provides a rich research site in which to explore such diversity due to its social-cultural plurality, as well as its turbulent political history. Lastly, a focus on heteronormativity among SA men has important social implications, given the link between dominant constructions of men's (hetero)sexuality and homophobia (Msibi 2009), sexual health (Ragnarsson et al. 2008), and sexual violence against women (Jewkes and Morrell 2010) in SA and elsewhere in Africa. The concept of hegemonic masculinity/ies (Connell 1995; Connell and Messerschmidt 2005) provides a useful theoretical framework for this study. This concept has been subject to much discussion. Hegemonic masculinity, a critique of the concept, and its relevance to SA, are briefly considered below.

The notion of hegemonic masculinity has inspired a great deal of research literature (e.g. Cooper 2009; Light and Kirk 2000). It has also, unsurprisingly therefore, stimulated a great deal of theoretical debate (e.g. Hall 2002; Schippers 2007). It was originally defined 'as the configuration of gender practice which embodies the currently accepted answer to the problem of the legitimacy of patriarchy, which guarantees (or is taken to guarantee) the dominant position of men and the subordination of women' (Connell 1995:77). This definition is firmly grounded in social constructionism. Gender is neither believed to be biologically nor psychologically determined (Jefferson 2002). Nor is it merely considered to be a set of social expectations or an identity (Connell and Messerschmidt 2005). It comprises configurations of social practice that are informed by, and inform, existing social conditions (Connell 1993). Luyt (2003), for example, argues that hegemonic masculinity in contemporary SA emphasises the importance of masculine control, (un)emotionality, physicality and toughness, competition, success, responsibility, and (hetero)sexuality.

Hegemonic masculinity never achieves complete consensus or incorporation, is constantly challenged, and changes over time (Connell 1995). For example, the literature testifies to the historical dominance of 'white' men and masculinity in SA. The neo-colonial period, following union[1] in 1910 and up until the first democratic election in 1994, was marked by the ascendancy and decline in the hegemony of 'white' Afrikaner men and masculinity in particular (Swart 2001, 2004).

Challenge and change to the hegemonic ideal is always present. Louw (2001), for instance, describes the emergence of homosexual practices within the settlement of Mkhumbane during the 1950s. Practices of this kind were argued to have developed from within their own 'rules of formation' (Louw 2001:294) and, as such, displayed distinct continuity with traditional social practices. But their emergence occurred under specific conditions of geographical isolation and political upheaval, in which traditional social practices were disrupted. Their potential for challenge was therefore limited.

As the dominant configuration of gender practice at any historical moment (Hearn 2004), the concept of hegemonic masculinity embodies a culturally idealised form which serves the interests of powerful men by legitimating and maintaining patriarchal gender relations. The ascendancy and maintenance of a particular version of masculinity as hegemonic, relies on cultural processes. These include texts, images and ideas (Hall 2002). Representations of the ideal are made familiar through institutions such as the mass media (Connell 1995). For example, television advertising in SA continues to reflect traditional hierarchical relations in society, where men are represented as being dominant vis-à-vis women (Luyt 2011), and 'white' men are represented as exemplars of hegemonic masculinity, while 'black' men are marginalised (Luyt 2012).

The concept recognises two forms of hierarchy in gender relations: one between men and women, as well as one among men. Hierarchical relations among men are acknowledged through terms such as complicit, subordinated and marginalised masculinities (Connell 1987). Relatively few men are able to practice hegemonic masculinity. Furthermore, it is unlikely to mirror the lived reality of even the most powerful (Connell 1995, 2002). It exists as a cultural ideal and is therefore only partially represented in the social practices of individual men (Connell 2002). Most actively support or passively collaborate in maintaining hegemonic masculinity. They do so, despite both their inability to practice it and the concessions that they may make to women in their everyday lives (Connell 1995). On these occasions they are described as being complicit. Complicity is motivated by either fantasy gratification (Connell 1987) or the benefit they collectively accrue through their shared interest in the subordination of women. The latter is described as the patriarchal dividend (Connell 1995). McClendon (1995) provides a useful example of how 'black' men have been complicit in gender oppression, while simultaneously reinforcing their own racial subordination in SA.

Hierarchy between masculinities plays an important role in the functioning of patriarchy, whereby the interests of powerful men are secured (Connell 1987). The notion of subordinated masculinities contributes toward the description of this. Sexuality exists as the most common axis along which hegemonic and subordinate masculinities are distinguished in contemporary Western society and beyond, as this chapter suggests. Heterosexuality is considered a definitive characteristic of masculinity, whereas homosexuality is not. Predictably, effeminate masculinities are also subordinated, given their association with women (Connell 1995).

Donham (1998) describes how during Apartheid, sexual identity in same-sex male relationships within urban 'black' culture was based on a subtle negotiation of the link between heteronormativity, gender and biological sex. A clear distinction was made between the effeminate or passive partner versus the active partner in same-sex male relationships. Effeminate or passive sexual partners were either considered hermaphrodites (i.e. *stabane*) or members of a second female sex. Alternatively, active sexual partners were thought to remain 'real' men. It is interesting to note that men rarely considered themselves as belonging to a mixed or second female sex. However, in a homophobic context, it was more socially acceptable for them to appear as such. *Skesanas*, as they called themselves, dressed as women and adopted a receptive role during sex. Their participation as 'wives' in men's migrant hostels served to reinforce this identity.

The notion of marginalisation describes how gender intersects with other structures such as class, 'race' and sexuality. Marginalised masculinities are patterns of gender practice that develop among men within oppressed groups. These masculinities may share many features in common with hegemonic masculinity. Dominant men determine when these features are authorised as hegemonic (Connell 1995) but such authorisation does not result in the improved authority of these men in society in general (Jefferson 2002).

Sexual success appears to be a key way in which marginalised men may practice 'real' masculinity. For example, Campbell (1997, 2001) notes the sexual promiscuity of 'black' men working in gold mines on the Witwatersrand. Poor and unpredictable working conditions, in combination with low levels of self-efficacy, result in a particular construction of masculinity that encourages multiple unprotected sexual encounters as a means through which they may perform assertive masculinity.

The concept of hegemonic masculinity has undoubted worth. Yet it has also generated critique. It is worthwhile reviewing some key criticisms concerning its arguably inadequate theorisation of concepts such as 'self' and 'subjectivity' in particular.

Wetherell and Edley (1999) underline the utility of Connell's framework for social psychological analysis. Nevertheless, together with others (e.g. Jefferson 2002; Whitehead 1999), they criticise it for its theorisation of the self. Little consideration is afforded the micro-level processes that operate in men's negotiation of identity in relation to hegemonic masculinity. Moreover, there is limited reflection concerning how these processes may result in identity that is complex and contradictory, or even psychically divided and multilayered (Connell and Messerschmidt 2005). In short 'Connell's account of the discursive/ideological field is ... too neat' (Wetherell and Edley 1999:352). Two questions emerge as being especially important:

- *What social norms constitute hegemonic masculinity?* The concept refers to an ideal form of masculinity, but its content remains ill-defined. Its constituent social norms are not consistent across situations, nor do individuals seem to understand it in precisely the same way. Hegemonic sense-making is clearly diverse, complex and often contradictory. This suggests that there may be more than a single hegemonic form at any time and place. Multiple as well as contradictory discursive resources exist for the construction of gender identity (Wetherell and Edley 1999).

- *How is hegemonic masculinity (re)produced?* Answers should extend beyond the suggestion that men conform to social norms. It's implausible to suggest that men may embody complicit or resistant types when few, if any, are able to practice hegemonic masculinity. Furthermore it's questionable whether hegemonic masculinity holds regulatory force when existing only as an unachievable ideal. A psychological account concerning the negotiation of gender subjectivity must be considered (Wetherell and Edley 1999). This should explain how social norms are (re)produced through compliance, or resistance, in everyday interaction (Wetherell and Edley 1999; Whitehead 1999).

A discursive approach, emphasising the importance of language in the (re) production of meaning, might aid the theoretical development of the concept (Whitehead 1999). A number of attempts have been made to understand masculinity using this approach (Speer 2001). In particular, Wetherell and Edley (1999) consider how men's gender identity is constituted through discursive practices, building upon previous work (Edley and Wetherell 1996) where they identify the worth of understanding masculinities as informed by societal discourses (Speer 2001).

These authors suggest that hegemonic masculinity operates at a macro- and micro-level. At the macro-level, it is seen to comprise a set of pre-existing discourses in society. Alternatively, at a micro-level, it is described as individual discursive positioning within these discourses. Wetherell and Edley (1999) extend our understanding of the latter through the notion of imaginary positions. This explains how masculinity is achieved psychologically. It refers to a process in which individuals adopt subjectivities relative to discourses of hegemonic masculinity, through situated psycho-discursive practices. These positions are 'imaginary' in that, although they serve as the basis for identity, they are constantly discursively re-instantiated. Self-positioning merely exists as a discursive strategy in which multiple meanings of masculinity are selectively drawn upon, according to the vagaries of the interactional context. Thus, individual men should not be labelled as particular character types, for example complicit or subordinate (Wetherell and Edley 1999). Rather they 'can adopt hegemonic masculinity when it is desirable; but the same men can distance themselves strategically from hegemonic masculinity at other moments' (Connell and Messerschmidt 2005:841). Situated discursive practices determine how men position themselves at any time, and hence the extent to which they consider themselves, or are described by others, as achieving the masculine ideal. This accounts for those seemingly contradictory occasions in which men simultaneously appear complicit with, as well as resistant to, hegemonic norms (Wetherell and Edley 1999). The banality of gender suggests that these practices are often unconscious. But, at times, they may also be consciously and deliberately deployed.

Although Connell and Messerschmidt (2005) reject the criticism levelled by discursive psychologists that the original formulation of hegemonic masculinity emphasises overarching structures and ideology to the detriment of individual agency, they do acknowledge the value of discursive theorising as it accounts for plurality and contradiction in men's subjectivities. Men are seen to strategically adopt these within situated interaction (Connell 2002). The multiple meanings associated with hegemonic masculinity are also far from problematic when viewed from this perspective, in that numerous related societal discourses are seen to give rise to them (Connell and Messerschmidt 2005).

Connell and Messerschmidt (2005) go on to argue that hegemonic masculinities may be studied empirically at three levels: local, regional and global. Local masculinities are constructed through face-to-face interaction, regional masculinity/ies are constructed at a cultural or societal level, and global masculinity is constructed in transnational settings such as politics, business and media. These three levels are interlinked and reciprocally inform each other. A 'geography of masculinities' goes some way to resolve the appearance of multiple hegemonic masculinities that simultaneously appear independent and interlinked. The meanings associated with local hegemonic masculinities always converge to a degree. This results from their shared representation in a single regional model, as well as their common constitution in relation to women's gender practices. It is clear that global masculinity has power to shape those at a regional and local level. However it is important not to overemphasise the extent to which this is the case. Regional masculinities have an ability to resist and inform the global (Connell and Messerschmidt 2005). This study specifically considers how local and regional representations of hegemonic masculinity are (re)produced, and how men's gender identities constituted, through situated interaction. An attempt is made to account for complexity and diversity in this sense-making across intersecting social categories such as ethnicity and social class. Discourse analysis facilitates study into regional and local representation. It also describes local practices in which individuals discursively position themselves in relation to a shared understanding of the regional ideal.

Exploring masculinities through discourse analysis

Talking to South African men

Ten focus groups were held within the Cape Town metropolitan area. There were approximately six men in each group. An attempt was made to recruit men with varied life experiences in order to achieve multivocality or diversity of perspective. Community gatekeepers facilitated access to participants. Individuals were sampled and grouped on the basis of their ethnicity, as determined by spoken home-language and self-defined 'race', and social class, as established by attained education level. Ethnic categories consisted of Xhosa-'black'; Afrikaans-'coloured'; English-'coloured'; Afrikaans-'white'; and English-'white'. Attained education levels incorporated primary; secondary; and tertiary. Age was not included as a formal sampling criterion. Nevertheless an attempt was made to involve men of different ages in each group. Participants ranged between the ages of 17 and 70 and averaged 32 years of age. Sexuality was likewise not formally sampled, partly due to sensitivities concerning its disclosure.

Focus groups were an appropriate method for data gathering in the current study for two reasons. First, analysis is partly informed by the rhetorical perspective. Data emerging from group discussion is particularly useful when adopting this perspective (Billig 1998). Second, this study embraces a feminist research agenda. Focus groups are said to diminish the power imbalance between the researcher and the researched; to reduce the extent to which the researcher imposes her/his interpretation in the research encounter; and play a potentially positive role in raising critical consciousness among participants (Wilkinson 1998).

Focus groups are sometimes criticised for producing manufactured data. Yet they arguably provide a useful sketch for analysis, where meaning is actively and collaboratively (re)produced through participant interaction. It is recognised that facilitators contribute to the (re)production of meaning through directing discussion toward a topic, and by attending to specific concepts. In this sense data is manufactured. But the purpose of focus group research is neither considered a 'fact-finding mission', as may be the case in their more traditional use, nor a more 'pure' examination of meaning-making through the analysis of 'naturally' occurring social interaction. Rather, focus groups are argued to provide rich and often unexpected data concerning a topic of interest. They allow researchers to ask what participants are doing, as well as to examine the broader representations they draw upon, in specific interactional contexts. Crucially, these contexts are considered specific, but no more so than any other; including the so-called 'naturalistic' (Edley and Litosseliti 2010:157).

The focus group procedure made use of three materials:

- 24 photographic cues selected so as to represent a broad range of masculinities across intersections of age, 'race' and social class, and serving as a pre-verbal aid to participant discussion;

- six vignettes developed in order to represent notions of 'sexuality', 'toughness', 'independence', 'status', 'responsibility' and 'homophobia', which are argued to represent dominant norms of masculinity in contemporary SA (Luyt 2003, 2005); and
- a semi-structured interview schedule.

These materials were included on the understanding that focus groups require active verbal participation from members, and some degree of standardisation across groups. Individuals differ in their exposure to discussion of abstract concepts such as masculinities in SA. It was anticipated that these materials would encourage group debate. While these prompted debate, care was taken to offer a safe environment which facilitated the emergence of issues beyond those introduced by the materials. Discussion was therefore more than simply an artefact of the prompts used, and reflected active negotiation between group members.

Three men facilitated focus group discussion. Each was assigned groups that were of their home language and 'race'. This was considered necessary in order to encourage unhindered discussion. Both assistants had graduate training, and experience in social scientific fields. This included gender studies. Various additional steps were taken to ensure their requisite knowledge of both the research topic and focus group methodology.

Group discussion lasted between 1½ and 2 hours. This took place at suitable locations, and at times amenable to all participants. These locations included a range of community venues, such as scout and school halls. Participants were made aware of standard ethical issues, including their anonymity, the confidentiality of data, and their right to withdraw from the study. Furthermore, groups were informed that discussion would be recorded through the use of video- and audio-recording equipment.

Participant debate was transcribed in full, providing a comprehensive and permanent data record. The analysis undertaken in this study describes discourses at a macro-level as well as their (re)production through micro-level rhetorical devices. It may be argued that a study including a focus on such devices necessitates a detailed transcription method (Potter and Wetherell 2001, 2005). However a highly comprehensive method such as Jeffersonian transcription (Jefferson 1984) was deemed inappropriate. The chosen transcription method was intentionally simple, to avoid confusion during the complicated translation process. Some detail was nonetheless included, for example inaudible discussion and interruptions, in order to maximise the fullness of the text within existing practical constraints (Billig 1998). Although the more traditional conversation analytically oriented reader may be disappointed, it is felt that micro-level analysis did not suffer as a result, given the use of the rhetorical devices introduced below. Indeed, overly fine-grained analysis is debatably inappropriate when applied to data that has undergone translation as a result of the added layer of interpretation that this involves.

The researcher is an English-speaking, heterosexual, 'white' South African, who has obtained a tertiary level of education. Therefore, where required, transcripts were reproduced in English through the procedure of back-translation (Brislin 2000). This procedure attempts to achieve what has been described as lexicon equivalence, in which importance is placed on both the linguistic and semantic features of the text (Neuman 1997; Swartz 1998). Facilitators participated in the translation of their respective focus groups. They did so along with others who were fully bilingual, as well as familiar with the socio-cultural norms of each group.

Developing a discourse analytic technique

A technique of discourse analysis was applied in this study. A discourse may be '... defined as a particular way of talking about and understanding the world (or an aspect of the world)' (Jørgensen and Phillips 2002:1). This understanding is socially mediated (Paechter 2001). Discourses exist as nebulous patterns of meaning, and are characterised by contradiction and fragmentation (Gavey 1997). They are shaped by, and simultaneously shape, broader ideological structures. These structures serve to maintain inequalities in power and privilege in society (Fairclough 1995; Wooffitt 2005). They do so through informing how social institutions, styles of thinking, individual subjectivity (Gavey 1997), and bodies are (re)produced (Paechter 2001). Discourse analysis attempts to identify such patterns of meaning through detailed linguistic examination of texts. These texts may include transcripts of naturally occurring conversations or interviews, existing documents or records, and even descriptions of more general social practices (Gavey 1997). Patterns of meaning are informed by interrelated textual extracts. These allow discourse analysts 'to show systematic links between texts, discourse practices, and socio-cultural practices' (Fairclough 1995:17). In describing discourses, the analyst is able to distinguish discursive resources and practices that individuals use in order to construct an understanding of their world (Gavey 1997), and how these make wider ideologies appear real (Potter and Wetherell 2001). Current discussion will focus on issues of importance to an approach known as discursive psychology (Edwards and Potter 1992). Different theoretical approaches such as rhetoric, ethnomethodology, conversation analysis, and post-structuralism, have contributed to its development (Ballinger and Payne 2000).

Discourse analysis is applied differently within discursive psychology, depending upon its specific theoretical orientation. Edley and Wetherell (1997, 2008) usefully distinguish between *top-down* and *bottom-up* approaches to analysis. The top-down approach draws heavily on the work of theorists such as Foucault (1978) and Marx ([1867–94]1981). It focuses on broad concepts such as ideology and power in order to explore how individuals are constituted or positioned through discourse. Analysis primarily seeks to explore how inequality is maintained through describing dominant discourses (Ballinger and Payne 2000). Emphasis is placed upon the 'distal context'. This includes the broader background features of talk/text, such as the participant's age, ethnicity, 'race' and social class; the sites in which talk occurs; and the socio-cultural and ecological milieu in which it is embedded (Wetherell 2001).

Alternatively the bottom-up approach is informed by the work of theorists such as Sacks ([1964–5]1992) and Garfinkel (1967). It is arguably the dominant approach in discursive psychology at present (Jørgensen and Phillips 2002). Fine-grained analysis of textual features is undertaken in order to describe the action-orientation of talk/text (Edley and Wetherell 1997, 2008). Austin (1962) was the first to identify 'talk as action'. He argued that language not only carries meaning but also force. That is to say, individuals are able to do and achieve things through the use of language. This suggests that analysis should focus on what individuals are accomplishing through talk (Wood and Kroger 2000). Systematic analysis primarily seeks to describe the features of talk/text and, in so doing, explain their function (Ballinger and Payne 2000). It therefore focuses on the 'proximate context'. This includes characteristics of the actual interaction, such as participant understanding surrounding the type of conversation to which they are contributing, the actions made possible through sequences of talk and the roles that participants are assigned or assume (Wetherell 2001).

Thus, a clear tension exists between the top-down approach to discourse analysis, which focuses on broader social and political processes, and the bottom-up approach that focuses on the action accomplished by language use. The current study argues that a combined, or hybrid approach, as applied by Edley and Wetherell (1997) and convincingly recommended by Edley and Wetherell (2008), may well be preferable. The strength of this approach, specifically with respect to this study, is that it 'can not only appreciate gender as a discursive resource, but one that can also understand how discourse shapes people's sense of themselves (and others) as gendered beings' (Edley and Wetherell 2008:166). As such, it facilitates exploration into how local and regional representations of hegemonic masculinity are (re)produced, through attending to differences in its construction across social categories such as ethnicity and social class, as well as considering how men's gender identities are accomplished in situated interaction.

It is important to recognise that a combined approach does not resolve the tension between top-down and bottom-up approaches to analysis. However, it does seek to manage it and, in so doing, account for the fact that individuals are at the same time both the products and the producers of discourse. Discursive psychologists are increasingly adopting this approach (Wilkinson 2001), albeit with different emphases on top-down and bottom-up processes.

The analytic procedure adopted in this study was informed by the existing literature. This incorporates the fundamental assumptions of discourse analysis, as well as important concepts outlined by the rhetorical perspective (Billig 1987). New analytic concepts are also included. It is argued that these usefully extend existing theory. The rhetorical perspective suggests that hegemonic and subordinate discourses[2] emerge respectively through the processes of *categorisation* and *particularisation*. Hegemonic discourses largely appear as stable categories of meaning, but may be disrupted and exposed to controversy through the process of particularisation. Consequently, subordinate discourses emerge to challenge them. In such conditions of controversy, individuals *justify* or *criticise* discourses in order to persuade an audience of their position. In this study the position participants choose to support concerns either the traditional construction of heteronormative masculinity, or an alternative one. However, it is argued here that individuals are doing more than just simply rejecting or supporting a position when they engage in justification and criticism. Luyt (2003:57) has distinguished between 'normative reform' and 'normative revolution'. Normative reform is understood as a specific form of criticism. It is directed against a hegemonic discourse, and holds 'the seeds for future critical challenge' Luyt (2003:57). This 'differs from outright normative revolution where challenge to dominant conceptualisation would find direct confrontation' through the justification of a subordinate conceptualisation Luyt (2003:57). Analytic subtlety can be developed further through the introduction of two additional concepts: *normative preservation* and *normative (re)production*. The first may be understood as a form of justification in support of a hegemonic discourse. The second is best described as a form of counter-criticism. It is directed against a subordinate discourse, and serves one of three functions. It may act to (a) challenge, but not reject, the subordinate discourse; (b) reject the subordinate discourse, but in so doing, not completely support the hegemonic discourse; and (c) reject the subordinate discourse and, in this manner, offer complete support for the hegemonic discourse. Normative reform, revolution, preservation and (re)production might usefully be described as *norm-referencing* rhetorical devices. Such devices serve to warrant the factuality, reality or truth of the discourses they construct. Other common rhetorical devices applied in research include, for instance, 'category entitlements', 'empiricist accounting' and 'vivid description'. In addition to applying norm-referencing rhetorical devices in order to map broader patterns of discursive justification or criticism, this study also provides detailed rhetorical analysis of talk/text through the use of more conventional devices such as *extreme case formulations, consensus claims* and *contrast* (Edwards and Potter 1992:160–62) or *differentiation.*

There are no set procedures for undertaking discourse analysis (Billig 1998). Yet textual coding is frequently mentioned as a necessary preliminary stage. This seeks to reduce the density of text by sorting it into broad categories (Billig 1998; Potter and Wetherell 2001) in an 'inclusive and cyclical' process (Potter 1998:239). An iterative inductive-deductive coding strategy was initially adopted in order to identify broad patterns of meaning. The traditional discourses of masculinity around which discussion had been focused through the aid of vignettes, provided an initial means through which to understand data. This understanding progressively developed through a commitment to inductive processes, where patterns of meaning were identified through interrelated textual extracts. As in other rhetorically guided studies (e.g. Radley and Billig 1996), turn-taking sequences (Hutchby and Wooffitt 1998) served as the unit of analysis.

The coding process contributes only partially to analysis. Indeed some discourse analysts go so far as to claim that it should not be considered part of the actual process of analysis (e.g. Potter 1998; Potter and Wetherell 2001). More fine-grained analysis of text takes place during the writing phase of the report, and is evident in the presentation of findings. It is important to stress that no analysis is ever definitive (Billig 1998). The results presented here are no exception.

The current chapter considers a single discourse and related participant subject positioning that emerged through in-depth analysis: heteronormativity. This may be described as a dominant discourse of regional hegemonic masculinity. Particular emphasis is afforded its underlying traditional/alternative discursive practices of 'performative/intimate (hetero)sexuality' and 'homosexual rejection/acceptance'. The way in which these practices are constructed differs across socio-cultural groups, giving rise to local hegemonic masculinities. Yet their shared constitution in the regional discourse suggests, as is the case in Western society, that sexuality exists as a common axis along which hegemonic and subordinate masculinities are distinguished in contemporary SA society. It seems appropriate therefore to consider the two discursive practices underlying the discourse of heteronormativity.

Findings

Discursive practices of 'homosexual rejection' and 'homosexual acceptance'

Homosexual rejection, or homophobia, may be described as an act of Othering. Individuals are able to secure an identity and reputation as 'real' men through distancing themselves from subordinated homosexuals (Hearn 2004; Reeser 2010). Connell (1992:736) succinctly observes that 'antagonism toward homosexual men may be used to define masculinity'. This understanding is supported through countless research studies (e.g. Cameron 1997; Gough and Edwards 1998). Participant discussion revealed support for the traditional discursive practice of *homosexual rejection* as well as the alternative discursive practice of *homosexual acceptance.*

Traditional discursive practice of 'homosexual rejection'

The traditional discursive practice of *homosexual rejection* surfaced frequently, although not exclusively, in discussion concerning vignette 3. This vignette presents a hypothetical scenario in which 'Bongani' unexpectedly finds his son 'Thandu' kissing another man. He is with his friends at the time, but chooses not to tell any of them what he has just seen.

Extract 1: Xhosa-'black' men with secondary education

P5 … I would not speak about it because speaking about is not going to take away the pain I feel and the embarrassment not only to manhood but to the whole of African humankind … This makes an embarrassment bigger than all embarrassments. This is a pain that you can't explain in words. I think that it is difficult to say: 'No he was right or he was wrong', what I say is that even if I was him, it was not going to be easy to talk about it.

FOCUS GROUP UB1

Participant 5 supports the hegemonic discursive practice of homosexual rejection. His support for this and its construction as normative, is asserted through a number of extreme case formulations (Pomerantz 1986), for example, 'bigger than all embarrassments' (line 5) and 'the whole of African humankind' (lines 3–4). He also positions himself within it by stressing that his son's supposed homosexuality would be shaming to the extent that he would find it difficult to 'talk about it' (line 9) with friends, and it would cause pain he was unable to 'explain in words' (line 6). The co-construction of real 'manhood' (line 3) and heterosexuality is also evident here. But what is particularly interesting is his association between this and 'African' (line 4) culture. An implicit contrast, or 'strategy of differentiation' (Edley and Wetherell 1997:209), is therefore made between 'real' heterosexual African manhood and Other non-African homosexual masculinities. Homosexuality appeared taboo among Xhosa participants to the extent that at times they were found to resist suggestion of its existence:

Extract 2: Xhosa-'black' men with secondary education

```
Int  I hear you saying his father saw him doing something wrong. Are you saying it is wrong for a man to kiss another man or kissing is wrong?
 P3  No, what he was doing is wrong, it is something new and unfamiliar.
 P5  Yes it is unfamiliar that a man kisses another man.
Int  That means…
 P5  It means it is wrong.
Int  When you say it is unfamiliar, it means it is there and it happens?
All  There is nothing like men kissing.
```

FOCUS GROUP UB1

The interviewer introduces an alternative discursive resource, seen in the suggestion that homosexuality 'is there and it happens' (lines 9–10), which challenges the discourse of heteronormativity. In response, participants offer a terse extreme case formulation that 'there is nothing like men kissing' (line 11). This signals their disapproval of the practice, reinforces the co-construction of 'real' masculinity and heterosexuality, and also again implicitly contrasts African culture from problematic or 'wrong' (line 8) Other homosexual cultural practice. That is to say 'it is something new and unfamiliar' (lines 4–5). Their identity claim to 'real' heterosexual African manhood is thus collectively (re)instantiated. Literature, however, suggests that homosexuality is not as alien as these men suggest. For example, evidence indicates that male-male sexuality has a long and continuing history among the Basotho, even though they are often characterised as macho and ardently heteronormative in comparison to other cultural groups in southern Africa (Epprecht 2002). Even so, the occurrence of homosexuality is popularly considered rare if not non-existent among 'black' Africans. The African nationalist movement encourages such thinking, arguing that such behaviour is 'un-African' and merely an imported European phenomenon. Growing regional African nationalism is therefore complicit in perpetuating homophobia among 'black' Africans, where a positive and idealised postcolonial African identity position is constructed against an imagined 'white' Other. In this respect, it is ironic that homophobia may in actuality be considered the true European import (van Zyl 2011). However this hegemonic discursive practice was not only justified through appeals to culture. Normative preservation was achieved differently across groups:

Extract 3: English-'coloured' men tertiary education

Int … kissing a woman. But now he's kissing another guy and suddenly it's not the same thing anymore.
P7 Ah, it wasn't a girl.
P2 It's not normal.
P5 No.
Int For you. But for him?
P5 It might be, but from where I'm standing…
P2 No but, I'm saying, there's no, there's no doubt God …
P1 (Inaudible).
P2 … like, how can I say …
Int He created people.
P2 Yes, in the beginning he didn't create two men, kissing …
P7 Each other.
P2 … and he didn't, and he didn't create a man and a woman kissing. But, still, that's how it started. Why you want to change it now?

FOCUS GROUP UC3

In the extract above, identity work is being accomplished both explicitly and implicitly. Participant 5 explicitly positions himself within the discourse of heteronormativity, recognising that there 'might be' alternatives but not from 'where (he's) standing' (line 7). Participant 2 likewise suggests that homosexuality is 'not normal' and therefore implicitly positions himself within this discourse. Disapproval of homosexuality is justified on theological grounds. '(I)n the beginning', he claims, God 'didn't create two men' (line 13) but rather 'a man and a women' (lines 16–17). Homosexuality is therefore inappropriate in that it transgresses the divine ordinance of heterosexuality. It is relevant to note that theological justification emerged within interaction which was situated in a community church to which group members belonged. Wetherell (2001) highlights the importance of the distal context, such as the site in which talk occurs, when interpreting data. The normality of homosexuality is similarly thrown into question in Extract 4.

Extract 4: English-'white' men with tertiary education

Int You-you-you just. Why, why would; let's, let's just
ask you why? Why, why would it be uncomfortable? I
mean you say it's strange, and we all laugh because
we have some implicit understanding, or certainly
an emotional understanding, of what you're saying;
but why, in-in-in …
P6 Because it's strange.
P2 Because I mean like it's, we-we find it, I mean
we've been programmed, I mean genetically, or so-
called genetically programmed, to like shag the
other s-side of the, the, the equation, we are not
asked, and-and like to see it, it's just, it
doesn't s-seem natural. I mean to-to me it doesn't,
it doesn't, I mean like c-coming from Durban it's
not as prevalent in fucking Durbs, you know what
I'm s, homosexuality. And then coming down here, I
mean, I, I, again I, don't get me wrong I don't
have a problem with it, but it's just, um, it's-
it's just strange to see. Like I go into clubs and
seeing guys kiss is just, is weird.
P6 I think we're all brought up with this; well men,
these days are, we're sort of moving towards that
effeminate kind of way of looking at life. A lot of
this has, I mean it has happened slowly, but, we
still want to be manly you know. We still want to
exude some masculinity. And-and to find you, your
son kissing another man is not masculine, you know
it's, and that's really what makes us men you know,
it's …

FOCUS GROUP UC5.2

In this case participants do not justify their disapproval of homosexuality on the basis of a cultural (e.g. Extracts 1 and 2) or theological argument (e.g. Extract 3), but rather a scientific one. Again, the interactional context appears related to the chosen justification. Discussion took place within a university setting among commerce students. Participant 2 suggests that it 'doesn't seem natural' given that 'we've been programmed ... genetically' to have sex with females who are 'the other s-side of the, the, the equation' (lines 10–11). However, he anticipates criticism, through the disclaimer 'don't get me wrong I don't have a problem with it, but it's just' (lines 17–18). He then moves on immediately to justify his position so as to inoculate himself against accusations of prejudice. The participant underlines he is particularly unaccustomed to homosexuality having recently moved to Cape Town[3] from Durban. As such, it is not that he is homophobic, but rather because homosexuality appears 'strange' (line 19) to him. In doing so, he positions himself within the discourse of heteronormativity.

Participant 6 likewise supports and positions himself within this discourse. This follows initial resistance, seen in his non-elaborative response – 'Because it's strange' (line 7) – to the alternative discursive resource made available by the interviewer who questions why homosexual practice would make men feel 'uncomfortable' (line 2). This questioning again acts to challenge the discourse of heteronormativity. The participant later suggests that 'we're sort of moving toward that effeminate kind of way of looking at life' (lines 2–23) but despite this still have a need 'to be manly' (line 25). Consensus in this position, and hence its implied factuality, is claimed through the use of words such as 'we' (line 24) and 'us' (line 28). In essence he invokes a rehearsed argument that links effeminacy, homosexuality and masculinity (Gough and Edwards 1998; Martino 2008). Connell (1992:736 *emphasis original*) explains that 'To many people, homosexuality is the *negation* of masculinity, and [because femininity is also considered masculinity's opposite] homosexual men must be effeminate'. It is interesting to note that the participant chooses not to suggest that it is heterosexuality that 'makes us men' (line 28). This underlines the observation that heterosexuality acts as a compulsory but hidden social norm (Kitzinger 2001; Rich 1980). Thus, any direct mention of heterosexuality is absent. Homophobia alone adequately marks hegemonic masculinity. Given such staunch support for the hegemonic discursive practice of homosexual rejection, it may seem incongruous to suggest that this participant in fact engages in a process of *normative reform*, albeit unintentionally. He makes a discursive resource available for the critical (re)negotiation of masculinity through appreciation that notions of masculinity are 'sort of moving' (line 22) rather than remaining static. This is not, however, taken up by other participants.

Alternative discursive practice of 'homosexual acceptance'

In Extract 5, the interviewer asks the group whether they could expect a 'negative reaction from others', if their son were found to be homosexual. The alternative discursive practice of *homosexual acceptance* emerges through participants 2's response. He claims that there is little overt prejudice against homosexuality in society:

Extract 5: English-'white' men with tertiary education

```
Int  … but what would you exp, er, expect in terms of,
     er, negative re-reaction from others, if anything?
 P2  None.
Int  None whatsoever?
 P2  Not nowadays. They may think what they want to, but
     certainly you would get no, no hectic reaction,
     your friends would still be your friends, your
     family would still be your family, suddenly
     somebody's just become gay.
```

FOCUS GROUP UC5.1

The participant justifies the subordinate discourse, arguing that homosexuality would receive 'no hectic reaction' (line 6) from others 'nowadays' (line 5), and therefore presents the case that there has been a successful *normative revolution*. The discursive practice of homosexual rejection is claimed to have been displaced by homosexual acceptance. Yet the participant's resistance to the alternative discursive resource made available by the interviewer, who suggests that 'negative re-reaction from others' (line 2) to homosexual practice still occurs, is seen in his short and swift extreme case formulation – 'none' (line 3). This implies that despite his rhetorical strategies, he is aware of homophobia in society. He confirms this later by accepting individuals 'may think what they want to' (line 5) but are expected to censor their prejudice. His argument was also challenged by others:

Extract 6: English-'white' men with tertiary education

P3 I don't know, I, I still think there's quite a lot
of fear...
P1 Oh, obviously.
P3 ... you know, whether it's something subtle or, ah;
certainly my friends they, I-I don't think there
would be huge reaction, but um, amongst his
friends, parents might be, you know, but i-it
depends on the age of-of-of the child, th-the
people respond in a, wherever they are in terms of
coming to, to terms with the fact that, that
someone can be gay, you know, um.

FOCUS GROUP UC5.1

Participant 3's response offers an interesting example of identity work. He accepts the subordinate discursive practice of homosexual acceptance, and clearly positions himself within it. Moreover its factuality is implied by supposed consensus in this position. That is to say, among his 'friends' (line 5). However he criticises participant 2's suggestion that such acceptance is now dominant. He argues, through a strategy of differentiation, that there is still 'quite a lot of fear' (lines 1–2) and that cultural differences will determine the extent to which there is a negative reaction from others. That is to say, a comparison is made between his friends and Bongani's 'friends' and 'parents' (line 7), who presumably differ along socio-cultural lines. He is therefore making a distinction between himself/ his friends, presumably 'white' English men, who are tolerant, versus intolerant 'black' people. Nonetheless, participant 3 seems to be aware of the fact that he making potentially controversial racial claims, as evidenced by the number of repetitions and insecurities in lines 6 to 11.

Discursive practices of 'performative (hetero)sexuality' and 'intimate (hetero)sexuality'

The notion of *performative (hetero)sexuality* is often identified as an important characteristic of hegemonic masculinity (Boyarin 1997; Donaldson 1993). This 'encourage[s] men to be sexually assertive, be always ready to have sex, view sex primarily as pleasurable and recreational, perceive penetration as the goal of sex, control all aspects of sexual activity, and have multiple sex partners' (Bowleg 2004:169). Research evidence supports this notion (e.g. Allen 2003; Grazian 2007). Performative (hetero)sexuality emerged as a traditional discursive practice in this analysis. An alternative conceptualisation surrounding *intimate (hetero)sexuality* also materialised. This highlighted the importance of emotional intimacy over physical performance and pleasure in heterosex. Few research studies observe intimacy as related to the practice of traditional masculinity (e.g. Rogers 2005).

Traditional discursive practice of 'performative (hetero)sexuality'

The traditional discursive practice of *performative (hetero)sexuality* was often, although not only, evident in discussion concerning vignette 5. Participants were asked to discuss a scenario in which 'Henk' had been unable to achieve an erection during a sexual encounter with 'Sara'. A high degree of agreement characterised group discussion where it was frequently argued that failure to perform 'degrades your manliness' (line 5). The co-construction of 'real' masculinity and performative (hetero)sexuality is obvious here:

Extract 7: English-'coloured' men with secondary education

```
Int  Why do you think Henk was right to feel
     embarrassed?
 P7  I don't know. It's just…
 P6  He's a man. Henk, Henk won't… (inaudible).
 P4  It degrades your manliness.
 P3  (Inaudible).
 P5  Ja.
Int  It degrades your manliness. Wha, you're saying?
 P6  Same, it's definitely serious.
Int  Okay and…
 P3  His reputation.
```

FOCUS GROUP UB3

Participants in this extract *preserve* the discursive practice that men should perform during heterosex. To fail is 'definitely serious' (line 9). Participant 3 justifies this position by suggesting that Henk's 'reputation' (line 11) would suffer as a result of his failure. Reputation rests upon normative assumptions concerning the relationship between masculinity and performative (hetero)sex. It entrenches the importance of this relationship among men. Bartky (1990:72) notes:

> In contemporary patriarchal culture, a panoptical male connoisseur resides within the consciousness of most women: They stand perpetually before his gaze and under his judgement. Women lives her body as seen by another, by an anonymous patriarchal Other.

Similarly men find themselves exposed to the gaze of others. Women, as defined by the gender order, reside within each man's consciousness. This serves a self-regulatory function. This is evident in participant 5's imagined situation in Extract 8, where, if he failed to get an erection during sex 'it becomes obvious to her there is a problem about you, when the problem starts you lose confidence and your manhood' (lines 25–7).

Extract 8: Xhosa-'black' men with primary education

P4 But what is important is to talk about it and say, my friend it is the first time I ever experienced this with you so you can't conclude and say I am the one with a problem, you should also observe yourself. Even if you do not reach an understanding you would have talked about it.

P1 I say, this guy is in a problem he didn't expect this and he knows what they say about men who can't do their job (get an erection) when they are supposed to. Now when this happens to you, you become shocked and disappointed that you feel she should just leave you immediately. Don't you think that you would not think about other things like talking?

P6 There is only one thing that I would say, my friend the thing that happened that day confused me as well because it does not usually happen, now I only think how I will be when we meet again.

Int I want to know; according to our own opinion is it embarrassing when a man does not get an erection? Is that a serious embarrassment?

P5 That is an embarrassment because when you invite a woman you know that you are going to work and you are full of confidence. Now when you get embarrassed, it becomes obvious to her there is a problem about you, when the problem starts you lose confidence and your manhood.

FOCUS GROUP UA1

The participant argues that 'when you invite a woman' (lines 22–3) to engage in sex, she expects erectile performance. To imagine anything but is an 'embarrassment' (line 22). Masculinities undergo (re)production under an omnipresent system of patriarchal heterosexual surveillance. This acts upon the individual man. It encourages his practice of dominant gender discourse (Bartky 1990) and related gender identity positioning.

Nonetheless *normative reform* was evident in a limited number of cases. Participant 4 criticises the common suggestion that men 'should just leave' (line 12) when they are unable to perform during heterosex. He argues that at the very least it 'is important to talk about it' (line 1) with the woman. This discursive resource made available by participant 4 holds the potential to challenge the dominant discursive practice that equates 'your manhood' (line 27) to your (penis) 'going to work' (line 23).

Despite the potential for future critical challenge made possible through the willingness to enter into dialogue, participant 4 does not directly challenge the dominant discursive practice, but rather suggests that this may serve as a means by which the woman is forced to accept responsibility for the man's failure. It is argued that the woman 'should also observe [her]self' (lines 4–5). Blaming the women for performative failure in heterosex emerged repeatedly in group discussion.

Alternative discursive practice of 'intimate (hetero)sexuality'

Direct challenge to the hegemonic discourse occurred rarely. But instances of *normative revolution* did appear. Yet this most often took place among historically and materially privileged groups. It is fair to suggest that members of these groups have the greatest power to (re)produce alternative discursive resources that challenge the status quo. Most notably, in Extract 9, participant 3 argued that emotional intimacy takes precedence over physical performance and pleasure in heterosex where 'the whole love aspect of it is very important' (lines 5–6):

Extract 9: English-'white' men with tertiary education

P3 Ja, I would imagine that there are some people who are who are quite selfish in the whole, the whole thing, um. Ja, I'm-I'm very cons-conservative; I wouldn't say conservative; I'm-I'm quite, I-I don't believe in casual sex, so, y-you know the whole love aspect of it is very important, an-and the, the soul side of it, and that kind of thing, so; there are people who are, are shallow in that regard, in their views, more likely than others, and so, I accept that.

Int So do you, are you saying that those issues that make it less important for someone to view sex as instrumental rather than…

P3 I thought they'd probably end-up being more important, you know, whereas for me it's just part of the whole thing, really. For some it might be a huge, if it's just a physical thing, then a physical malfunction is a problem; whereas if it's an emotional everything thing, more than it is a physical side of things, well, ooh I've got to go all work it out.

FOCUS GROUP UC5.1

The participant positions himself favourably within the discursive practice of intimate (hetero)sexuality through a strategy of differentiation. He argues 'that there are some people who are who are quite selfish in the whole, the whole thing' (lines 1–3). He goes on to justify and hence warrant its factuality through two rhetorical strategies. Firstly, he draws upon the notion of conservatism in order to suggest that his position is safeguarding traditional and hence consensual and esteemed values. This is curious in that the present study, as well as the existing literature cited above, indicates that these values are, in fact, non-traditional. Secondly, he argues that individuals who consider performance and pleasure as overarching goals in heterosex 'are shallow' (line 8). It is only for these individuals that 'physical malfunction is a problem' (line 18).

Finally, and more generally, it is interesting to note the extent to which participant discussion supports the previously noted observation that heterosexuality acts as a compulsory but hidden norm in society (Kitzinger 2001; Rich 1980). Sex, for participants, implicitly referred to heterosex. This highlights the overlap between the traditional discursive practices of performative (hetero)sexuality and homosexual rejection. The heterosexual norm partly structures internal hegemony within society. Hegemonic masculinity is defined against subordinated homosexuality (Cheng 2007; Connell 1995).

Conclusion

This study describes the (re)production of local and regional representations of hegemonic masculinity, together with the constitution of men's gender identity through situated social practices. It points toward the importance of heteronormativity in defining hegemonic masculinity in SA, and examines how this is variably (re)produced in interactions among different groups of men. This extends the existing literature (e.g. Cameron 1997; Kiesling 2006; Kitzinger 2006) seeking 'to understand how heteronormativity is produced and reinforced in everyday interactions' (Kitzinger 2008:121) across societies.

The emergent discourse of heteronormativity was described. This, together with its underlying discursive practices of 'homosexual rejection' and 'performative (hetero)sexuality', constitutes a dominant discourse of regional hegemonic masculinity. Two further related alternative discursive practices were also described: 'homosexual acceptance' and 'intimate (hetero)sexuality'. These practices may otherwise be described as contributing toward a subordinate discourse of regional hegemonic masculinity, and thereby resisting the dominant definition of masculinity.

Discourse was defined as dominant in so far as it appeared taken for granted (Edley 2001) by most participants. In comparison, subordinate discourse appeared to differ in that it was not taken for granted. Local hegemonic masculinities were variably informed by discursive practices, as well as by the arguments around which they were constructed. Diversity in local hegemonic sense-making emerged across intersecting social categories such as ethnicity and social class. Group comparison demonstrated this well. For example, in the analysis above, the discursive practice of homosexual rejection was justified variably on the basis of cultural, theological and scientific arguments by Xhosa-'black', English-'coloured' and English-'white' men respectively. Divergent support across social groups for discursive practices and their component arguments indicates some of the crisis tendencies currently being resolved among men in the SA gender order. For example, the challenge posed by ascendant 'black' African masculinity, constructing itself against an imagined inferior Other, yet marginalised in 'white' men's rhetoric. The interests of some men were also clearly privileged over others. The dominant discourses of masculinity tend to serve the interests of young heterosexual men who espouse a female sexual object choice, and are best able to perform heterosex.

The results therefore confirm the notion that multiple hegemonic masculinities can exist. These occur at the local level, and appear independent as well as interlinked. The meanings associated with local hegemonic masculinities converge to a degree as a result of their shared constitution in regional discourse. This accounts for complexity, contradiction and diversity in hegemonic discourse. But these features were also evident in situated social practice. Men's gender identities were continually (re)constituted through complex practices. More specifically, individuals were found to strategically adopt subjectivities within situated interaction. This was the case in, for example, Extract 9. The participant positioned himself as conservative. This was somewhat contradictory in that it served to justify the subordinate and hence non-traditional discursive practice of intimate (hetero)sexuality. Yet, in justifying the subordinate discourse through this rhetorical strategy, he was able to legitimately position himself within it. Identities were therefore constituted through available discursive resources. Participants were most likely to position themselves within accessible local hegemonic representations. It is therefore important to stress the degree to which self-positioning exists as a discursive strategy. Multiple meanings surrounding masculinity are selectively drawn upon, according the vagaries of the interactional context. For example, in Extract 3, the interactional context of a church likely contributed toward participants drawing upon theological justification for homosexual rejection. Contexts were largely defined in this study through homogenous focus groups, pre-selected so as to represent a broad range of men in society, and defined on the basis of ethnicity and social class. These appear as particularly important axes of social difference in contemporary SA as evidenced in discussion. For example, as was evident in Extract 9, direct challenge to the hegemonic discourse most often took place among historically and materially privileged groups (e.g. 'white' men with high levels of education) who have the greatest power to challenge the status quo. Masculinities therefore seemingly continue to be constructed around category differences that were salient in the country's past. This is clearly seen in the various strategies of differentiation employed by the participants.

A technique of discourse analysis that considers the rhetorical aspects of text was adopted. This highlights the extent to which practices of both compliance and resistance contribute toward the (re)production of masculinities. Participants overwhelmingly engaged in complicit practices in support of the hegemonic discourse of heteronormativity. This was seen in numerous instances of normative preservation. But challenge to this discourse, seen in normative reform and revolution, was also evident in a limited number of cases, thus making change possible. This usefully exposes the complexity, contradiction, diversity and inherent tensions in hegemonic sense-making. The technique incorporates the fundamental assumptions of discourse analysis in addition to important concepts outlined by the rhetorical perspective. The description of the four norm-referencing rhetorical devices, namely normative preservation, reform, revolution and (re)production, arguably provides added theoretical subtlety and analytic strength, in addition to other more commonly applied devices. Lastly, the analysis sought to emphasise both macro- and micro-level analyses in order to highlight that individuals are both the products and the producers of discourse.

This study's greatest strength resides in its providing insight into how the notion of hegemonic masculinities may be reciprocally analysed – socio-culturally through discourse, and psychologically through subjectivity. Yet there are other aspects that deserve further attention. The study did not explore the psychic dimensions of gender identity (Jefferson 2002). As suggested, this may include consideration surrounding whether gender identity is psychically divided and multilayered, and whether men experience tensions as a result of often complex and contradictory identities. Moreover greater consideration should surround the extent to which gender relations are (re)produced through discursive as well as material practices. The notion of embodiment remains a useful starting point in this regard (Connell and Messerschmidt 2005). Finally, few studies have considered the extent to which global masculinity shapes that at a regional and local level. Goswami's (2008:344) concept of 'compulsory heteroimperial masculinity' serves as an interesting starting point for further study into the global (re)production of heteronormativity and hegemonic masculinities. More work should be undertaken in this area.

Notes

1 The Union of South Africa originated through the amalgamation of the two Boer republics of the South African Republic (Transvaal) and the Orange Free State, as well as the two British colonies of the Cape and Natal, under a single system of government (see Beinhart 2001).

2 The concepts of 'dominant', 'hegemonic' and 'traditional discourses', as well as 'alternative' and 'subordinate discourses', are considered interchangeable in the current study.

3 Cape Town is considered as the 'gay capital' of Africa (see Visser 2003).

References

Allen, L. (2003) Girls want sex, boys want love: resisting dominant discourses of (hetero) sexuality. *Sexualities* 6: 215–36. https://doi.org/10.1177/1363460703006002004

Austin, J. (1962) *How to Do Things with Words*. Cambridge, MA: Harvard University Press.

Ballinger, C. and Payne, S. (2000) Discourse analysis: principles, applications and critique. *British Journal of Occupational Therapy* 63: 567–72. https://doi.org/10.1177/030802260006301202

Bartky, S. L. (1990) *Femininity and Domination: Studies in the Phenomenology of Oppression*. New York, NY: Routledge.

Beinart, W. (2001) *Twentieth-Century South Africa*. Oxford: Oxford University Press.

Billig, M. (1987) *Arguing and Thinking: A Rhetorical Approach to Social Psychology*. Cambridge: Cambridge University Press.

Billig, M. (1997) The dialogic unconscious: psychoanalysis, discursive psychology and the nature of repression. *British Journal of Social Psychology* 36: 139–59. https://doi.org/10.1111/j.2044-8309.1997.tb01124.x

Billig, M. (1998) Rhetorical and discursive analysis: How families talk about the royal family. In N. Hayes (ed.) *Doing Qualitative Analysis in Psychology* 39–54. Hove: Psychology Press.

Bowleg, L. (2004) Love, sex, and masculinity in sociocultural context: HIV concerns and condom use among African American men in heterosexual relationships. *Men and Masculinities* 7: 166–86. https://doi.org/10.1177/1097184X03257523

Boyarin, D. (1997) *Unheroic Conduct: The Rise of Heterosexuality and the Invention of the Jewish Man*. Berkeley, CA: University of California Press.

Brislin, R. W. (2000) Back-translation. In A. E. Kazdin (ed.) *Encyclopedia of Psychology* 359–60. Washington, DC: American Psychological Association. https://doi.org/10.1037/10516-122

Cameron, D. (1997) Performing gender identity: young men's talk and the construction of heterosexual masculinity. In S. Johnson and U. H. Meinhof (eds) *Language and Masculinity* 4–64. Oxford: Blackwell Publishers.

Cameron, D. and Kulick, D. (eds) (2006) *The Language and Sexuality Reader*. London: Routledge.

Campbell, C. (1997) Migrancy, masculine identities and AIDS: the psychosocial context of HIV transmission on the South African gold mines. *Social Science and Medicine* 45: 273–82. https://doi.org/10.1016/S0277-9536(96)00343-7

Campbell, C. (2001) 'Going underground and going after women': masculinity and HIV transmission amongst black workers on the mines. In Morrell (2001): 275–86.

Cheng, C. (2007) Marginalized masculinities and hegemonic masculinity: an introduction. *Journal of Men's Studies* 7: 295–315. https://doi.org/10.3149/jms.0703.295

Connell, R. W. (1987) *Gender and Power: Society, the Person and Sexual Politics*. Cambridge: Polity Press.

Connell, R. W. (1992) A very straight gay: masculinity, homosexual experience, and the dynamics of gender. *American Sociological Review* 57: 735–51. https://doi.org/10.2307/2096120

Connell, R. W. (1993) The big picture: masculinities in recent world history. *Theory and Society* 22: 597–623. https://doi.org/10.1007/BF00993538

Connell, R. W. (1995) *Masculinities*. Cambridge: Polity Press.

Connell, R. W. (2002) On hegemonic masculinity and violence: response to Jefferson and Hall. *Theoretical Criminology* 6: 89–99. https://doi.org/10.1177/136248060200600104

Connell, R. W. and Messerschmidt, J. W. (2005) Hegemonic masculinity: rethinking the concept. *Gender and Society* 19: 829–59. https://doi.org/10.1177/0891243205278639

Cooper, A. (2009) 'Gevaarlike transitions': negotiating hegemonic masculinity and rites of passage amongst coloured boys awaiting trial on the Cape Flats'. *Psychology in Society* 37: 1–17.

Donaldson, M. (1993) What is hegemonic masculinity? *Theory and Society* 22: 643–57. https://doi.org/10.1007/BF00993540

Donham, D. L. (1998) Freeing South Africa: the 'modernization' of male-male sexuality in Soweto. *Cultural Anthropology* 13: 3–21. https://doi.org/10.1525/can.1998.13.1.3

Edley, N. (2001) Conversation analysis, discursive psychology and the study of ideology: a response to Susan Speer. *Feminism and Psychology* 11: 136–40. https://doi.org/10.1177/0959353501011001007

Edley, N. and Litosseliti, L. (2010) Contemplating interviews and focus groups. In L. Litosseliti (ed.) *Research Methods in Linguistics* 155–79. London: Continuum.

Edley, N. and Wetherell, M. (1996) Masculinity, power and identity. In M. Mac-an-Ghaill (ed.) *Understanding Masculinities: Social Relations and Cultural Arenas* 97–114. Buckingham: Open University Press.

Edley, N. and Wetherell, M. (1997) Jockeying for position: the construction of masculine identities. *Discourse and Society* 8: 203–17. https://doi.org/10.1177/0957926597008002004

Edley, N. and Wetherell, M. (2008) Discursive psychology and the study of gender: a contested space. In Harrington et al. (2008): 161–73.

Edwards, D. and Potter, J. (1992) *Discursive Psychology*. London: Sage Publications.

Epprecht, M. (2002) Male–male sexuality in Lesotho: two conversations. *The Journal of Men's Studies* 10: 373–89. https://doi.org/10.3149/jms.1003.373

Fairclough, N. (1995) *Critical Discourse Analysis: The Critical Study of Language*. London: Longman.

Foucault, M. (1978) *The History of Sexuality*, vol. 1 (trans. R. Hurley). Harmondsworth: Penguin.

Garfinkel, H. (1967) *Studies in Ethnomethodology*. Englewood Cliffs, NJ: Prentice-Hall.

Gavey, N. (1997) Feminist poststructuralism and discourse analysis. In M. M. Gergen and S. N. Davis (eds) *Toward a New Psychology of Gender* 49–64. New York: Routledge.

Goswami, N. (2008) Autophagia and queer transnationality: compulsory heteroimperial masculinity in Deepa Mehta's *Fire*. *Signs* 33: 343–69. https://doi.org/10.1086/521052

Gough, B. and Edwards, G. (1998) The beer talking: four lads, a carry out and the reproduction of masculinities. *Sociological Review* 46: 409–35. https://doi.org/10.1111/1467-954X.00125

Grazian, D. .(2007) The girl hunt: urban nightlife and the performance of masculinity as collective activity. *Symbolic Interaction* 30: 221–43. https://doi.org/10.1525/si.2007.30.2.221

Hall, S. (2002) Daubing the drudges of fury: men, violence and the piety of the 'hegemonic masculinity' thesis. *Theoretical Criminology* 6: 35–61. https://doi.org/10.1177/136248060200600102

Harrington, K., Litosseliti, L., Sauntson, H. and Sunderland, J. (eds) (2008) *Gender and Language Research Methodologies*. Basingstoke: Palgrave Macmillan.

Hearn, J. (2004) From hegemonic masculinity to the hegemony of men. *Feminist Theory* 5: 49–72. https://doi.org/10.1177/1464700104040813

Hutchby, I. and Wooffitt, R. (1998) *Conversation Analysis: Principles, Practices and Applications*. Cambridge: Polity Press.

Jefferson, G. (1984) Transcription notation. In J. Atkinson and J. Heritage (eds) *Structures of Social Interaction* ix–xvi. New York: Cambridge University Press.

Jefferson, T. (2002) Subordinating hegemonic masculinity. *Theoretical Criminology* 6: 63–88. https://doi.org/10.1177/136248060200600103

Jewkes, R. and Morrell, R. (2010) Gender and sexuality: emerging perspectives from the heterosexual epidemic in South Africa and implications for HIV risk and prevention. *Journal of the International AIDS Society* 13: 1–11.

Jørgensen, M. and Phillips, L. (2002) *Discourse Analysis: As Theory and Method*. London: Sage Publications. https://doi.org/10.4135/9781849208871

Kiesling, S. F. (2006) Playing the straight men: displaying and maintaining male heterosexuality in discourse. In Cameron and Kulick (2006): 118–31.

Kitzinger, C. (2001) Sexualities. In Unger (2001): 272–85.

Kitzinger, C. (2006) Speaking as a heterosexual: (How) does sexuality matter for talk-in-interaction. In Cameron and Kulick (2006): 169–88.

Kitzinger, C. (2008) Conversation analysis: technical matters for gender research. In Harrington et al. (2008): 119–38.

Light, R. and Kirk, D. (2000) High school rugby, the body and the reproduction of hegemonic masculinity. *Sport, Education and Society* 5: 163–76. https://doi.org/10.1080/713696032

Louw, R. (2001) Mkhumbane and new traditions of (un)African same-sex weddings. In Morrell (2001): 287–96.

Luyt, R. (2003) Rhetorical representations of masculinities in South Africa: moving towards a material-discursive understanding of men. *Journal of Community and Applied Social Psychology* 13: 46–69. https://doi.org/10.1002/casp.706

Luyt, R. (2005) The Male Attitude Norms Inventory–II: a measure of masculinity ideology in South Africa. *Men and Masculinities* 8: 208–29. https://doi.org/10.1177/1097184X04264631

Luyt, R. (2011) Representation of gender in South African television advertising: a content analysis. *Sex Roles* 65: 356–70. https://doi.org/10.1007/s11199-011-0027-0

Luyt, R. (2012) Representation of masculinities and race in South African television advertising: a content analysis. *Journal of Gender Studies* 21(1): 35–60. https://doi.org/10.1080/09589236.2012.639176

Martino, W. J. (2008) Male teachers as role models: addressing issues of masculinity, pedagogy and the re-masculinization of schooling. *Curriculum Inquiry* 38: 189–223. https://doi.org/10.1111/j.1467-873X.2007.00405.x

Marx, K. ([1867–94]1981) *Capital: A Critique of Political Economy*, vol. 1–3. Harmondsworth: Penguin Books.

McClendon, T. V. (1995) Tradition and domestic struggle in the courtroom. *International Journal of African Historical Studies* 28: 527–61. https://doi.org/10.2307/221173

Morrell, R. (ed.) (2001) *Changing Men in Southern Africa*. Pietermaritzburg: University of Natal Press.

Msibi, T. (2009) Not crossing the line: Masculinities and homophobic violence in South Africa. *Agenda* 80: 50–54.

Neuman, W. L. (1997) *Social Research Methods: Qualitative and Quantitative Approaches*. Boston, MA: Allyn & Bacon.

Paechter, C. (2001) Using poststructuralist ideas in gender theory and research. In B. Francis and C. Skelton (eds) *Investigating Gender: Contemporary Perspectives in Education* 41–51. Buckingham: Open University Press.

Pomerantz, A. (1986) Extreme case formulations: a way of legitimizing claims. *Human Studies* 9: 219–29. https://doi.org/10.1007/BF00148128

Potter, J. (1998) Discursive social psychology: from attitudes to evaluative practices. *European Review of Social Psychology* 9: 233–66. https://doi.org/10.1080/14792779843000090

Potter, J. and Wetherell, M. (2001) Discourse analysis. In J. A. Smith, R. Harré and L. van Langenhove (eds) *Rethinking Methods in Psychology* 80–92. London: Sage Publications.

Potter, J. and Wetherell, M. (2005) *Discourse and Social Psychology: Beyond Attitudes and Behaviour*. London: Sage Publications.

Radley, A. and Billig, M. (1996) Accounts of health and illness: dilemmas and representations. *Sociology of Health and Illness* 18: 220–40. https://doi.org/10.1111/1467-9566.ep10934984

Ragnarsson, A., Onya, H. E., Thorson, A., Ekström, A. M. and Aarø, L. E. (2008) Young males' gendered sexuality in the era of HIV and AIDS in Limpopo Province, South Africa. *Qualitative Health Research* 18: 739–46. https://doi.org/10.1177/1049732308318373

Reeser, T. W. (2010) *Masculinities in Theory: An Introduction*. Oxford: Wiley-Blackwell. https://doi.org/10.1002/9781444317312

Rich, A. (1980) Compulsory heterosexuality and lesbian existence. *Signs* 5: 631–60. https://doi.org/10.1086/493756

Rogers, A. (2005) Chaos to control: men's magazines and the mastering of intimacy. *Men and Masculinities* 8: 175–94. https://doi.org/10.1177/1097184X04265319

Sacks, H. ([1964–5]1992) *Lectures on Conversation*. Oxford: Basil Blackwell.

Schippers, M. (2007) Recovering the feminine other: masculinity, femininity, and gender hegemony. *Theory and Society* 36: 85–102. https://doi.org/10.1007/s11186-007-9022-4

Speer, S. A. (2001) Reconsidering the concept of hegemonic masculinity: discursive psychology, conversation analysis and participants' orientations. *Feminism and Psychology* 11: 107–35. https://doi.org/10.1177/0959353501011001006

Swart, S. (2001) 'Man, gun, and horse': hard right Afrikaner masculine identity in post-Apartheid South Africa. In Morrell (2001): 75–89.

Swart, S. (2004) 'Men of influence': the ontology of leadership in the 1914 Boer Rebellion. *Journal of Historical Sociology* 17: 1–30. https://doi.org/10.1111/j.0952-1909.2004.00224.x

Swartz, L. (1998) *Culture and Mental Health: A Southern African View*. Cape Town: Oxford University Press.

Unger, R. K. (ed.) (2001) *Handbook of the Psychology of Women and Gender*. Hoboken, NJ: John Wiley & Sons.

Van Zyl, M. (2011) Are same-sex marriages unAfrican? Same-sex relationships and belonging in post-apartheid South Africa. *Journal of Social Issues* 67: 335–57. https://doi.org/10.1111/j.1540-4560.2011.01701.x

Visser, G. (2003) Gay men, tourism and urban space: reflections on Africa's 'gay capital'. *Tourism Geographies* 5: 168–89. https://doi.org/10.1080/1461668032000068261

Wetherell, M. (2001) Debates in discourse research. In M. Wetherell, S. Taylor and S. J. Yates (eds) *Discourse Theory and Practice: A Reader* 380–99. London: Sage Publications.

Wetherell, M. and Edley, N. (1999) Negotiating hegemonic masculinity: imaginary positions and psycho-discursive practices. *Feminism and Psychology* 9: 335–56. https://doi.org/10.1177/0959353599009003012

Whitehead, S. (1999) Hegemonic masculinity revisited. *Gender, Work and Organization* 6: 58–62. https://doi.org/10.1111/1468-0432.00069

Wilkinson, S. (1998) Focus groups in feminist research: Power, interaction, and the co-construction of meaning. *Women's Studies International Forum* 21: 111–25. https://doi.org/10.1016/S0277-5395(97)00080-0

Wilkinson, S. (2001) Theoretical perspectives on women and gender. In Unger (2001): 17–28.

Wood, L. A. and Kroger, R. O. (2000) *Doing Discourse Analysis*. Thousand Oaks, CA: Sage Publications.

Wooffitt, R. (2005) *Conversation Analysis and Discourse Analysis: A Comparative and Critical Introduction*. London: Sage Publications. https://doi.org/10.4135/9781849208765

9

Online constructions of metrosexuality and masculinities: a membership categorisation analysis

Matthew Hall
ULSTER UNIVERSITY, UK

Brendan Gough
LEEDS BECKETT UNIVERSITY, UK

Sarah Seymour-Smith
NOTTINGHAM TRENT UNIVERSITY, UK

Susan Hansen
MIDDLESEX UNIVERSITY, UK

- *Gastrosexual*: 'A male, aged 25–44, upwardly-mobile and aware of and passionate about global cuisine, and he cooks to impress and seduce' (PurAsia 2008:3).
- Übersexual: 'A man with a type of masculinity that combines the best of traditional manliness (strength, honor, character) with positive traits traditionally associated with females (nurturance, communicativeness, cooperation)' (Salzman et al. 2005:167).
- *Metrosexual*: 'A young man with money to spend, living in or within easy reach of a metropolis – because that's where all the best shops, clubs, gyms and hairdressers are' (Simpson 2002:2).

The common theme across these contemporary categories, also present in previous incarnations such as the 'Dandy' of the Eighteenth Century and the 'new man' of the 1980s, is men's participation in historically feminised practices (Coad 2008:22–4). Many of these changes have been spurred on by media representations of men, which have contributed to the increasing visibility of men's bodies (Gill et al. 2005). Where once female bodies dominated style magazines, newspapers and televisions, men's bodies are now just as likely to feature. The launch of men's lifestyle magazines in the 1980s (e.g. *GQ*) and other mass market men's publications (e.g. *Men's Health*), along with billboard images (e.g. actor Djimon Hounsou donning his Calvin Klein underwear on the side of the Ritz Carlton Hotel in Hong

Kong), have helped to firmly establish the presence of the men's bodies as objects to be eroticised and consumed (Gill et al. 2005). Greater visibility of men's bodies has led some men at least to 're-evaluate their appearance, re-position themselves as consumers of fashion and style products, and ultimately re-construct their idea of what it is to be male' (Harrison 2008:56).

Such forays into hitherto feminine identity territory have led some to wonder if conventional or 'hegemonic'[1] (Connell 1995) forms of masculinity have been superseded or modernised (see MacInnes 2001). However, social science scholars do seem to agree that these new developments are producing interesting places of slippage where traditional and distinct gendered ways of being are potentially undermined and contested (Whitehead and Barrett 2001). For example, Simpson's (2005) research interviewed men working in employment areas traditionally seen as feminine such as nursing, primary school teaching and hairdressing. These interviewees reported experiences of abuse and challenges to their sexual orientation and 'manliness' (Simpson 2005:366–76). As is common with men in women-dominated professions, these men also reframed aspects of their job in more conventionally masculine ways, citing skill acquisition, management, a focus on specialisms (e.g. male nurses working in accident and emergency) or the management of sports teams (Simpson 2005:373).

So despite rumours of demise, it would seem that hegemonic masculinities still wield power even in situations where men are ostensibly taking up feminised positions and practices. This claim is supported by research, which looks at men in other feminised contexts. For example, Gough (2007) examined various UK mass-market newspaper representations of men and diet, and identified enduring constructions of men as uninterested in healthy eating, with a supposed preference for bulk and red meat-based dinners. Even those newspaper articles which featured 'metrosexual' men sampling new cooking deployed masculinised metaphors (e.g. hunting and gathering), and ultimately rejected nutritional advice. In the realm of beauty products too, men are increasingly being targeted, in the previously taboo terrain of cosmetics. For example, Harrison's (2008) semiotic analysis of male mascara advertising on the internet found that interest for male mascara and other cosmetic products is increasing, although she noted that advertisers reframed similar women's products such as mascara and eyeliner in masculine ways ('manscara'; 'guy-liner'). It is clear from her work and others (de Visser 2008; Hill 2006) that some men are orienting to contemporary identities (e.g. 'metrosexual') and practices (e.g. applying make-up), which have traditionally been associated with femininity. To date, however, the literature has featured little direct engagement with how men orientate to and negotiate emergent category membership in the company of other men (or women). One apparent reason for this absence is that modern gendered identity categories are easily dismissed as inconsequential, or even as marketing fabrications (Coad 2008:26–32). But we don't yet know how men ascribe to modern identity categories such as 'metrosexual', or how men's discursive practices link to masculine identity in this context.

An obvious place to access suitable data featuring self-ascribing metrosexuals is the internet, since it is routinely associated with freedom of expression, critiques of established off-line social and personal practices, and the creation of alternative online communities and identities, such as specific sexual fantasy groups and gamers (Slouka 1995). The opportunities afforded by information and communication technologies via the compression of time and space allows instantaneousness for the user and, since the user is not physically present in cyberspace (therefore it is easier to withdraw from problematic situations by exiting an online session, as opposed to a face-to-face interaction), new forms of identity and self-expression are able to thrive (Turkle 1997). New forms of male identity such as the 'metrosexual', sometimes ridiculed and marginalised in off-line society, are arguably more easily claimed online in an age of almost universal access to cyberspace (Kollock 1999).

Although marginalised identities may be more easily claimed online, computer-mediated communication still creates the same 'real' identities as those expressed in offline communications by relying on the same references to space, embodiment, time and shared experiences (Greenfield and Subrahmanyam 2003; Coyle and MacWhannell 2002). For example, research on suicide forums (Horne and Wiggins 2009), eating disorders (Winzelburg 1997) and sexual abuse (Moursand 1997) all showed similarities to offline identity construction via the disclosure of shared experiences, knowledge, meanings, characteristics and activities with those who have membership entitlement within the electronic space.

Given these apparent similarities our study thus examines metrosexual 'talk' within a distinct and popular format – the internet discussion forum – an electronic bulletin board where forum members begin threads for discussion, building bonds and reaching other interested parties. We focus on how forum members achieve identities for themselves, each other and absent others through the same process of membership categorisation as found in offline contexts (Vallis 2001).

Method

Analytic approach

We draw on membership categorisation analysis (MCA) (Baker 1997; Hester and Eglin 1997; Jayyusi 1984; Sacks 1972, 1992[2]; Schegloff 2007; Stokoe 2003; Wowk 1984) as an analytical apparatus, since its central concern is to examine how people go about categorising and negotiating social identities, realities, social ordering, social relationships and moral activity (Jayyusi 1984). Sacks demonstrated in his now well-cited example 'The baby cried. The mommy picked it up' (Sacks 1992:236) that we hear the baby as the baby of the mother because they form part of a collection of categories (membership category device) called 'family'. We also hear these categories as going together because they have some 'rules of application'. For example, the 'economy rule' states that a single category is sufficient for some inferences to be made, such that 'mommy' infers caring for a child (Sacks 1992:40–41). Categories are also governed by a 'consistency rule', which means that for some given population, all members can be categorised in the same way (Sacks 1992:238–9). Categories can also be 'duplicatively organised' to produce complete units like 'husband and wife' (Sacks 1992:240). Complete units like these are also 'standardised relational pairs' in which members have duties and obligations to each other (e.g. love and support). Often categories are 'hierarchically organised' whereby 'mommy' would be ranked higher than 'baby'. And finally, categories are associated with specific actions (category-bound activities) and characteristics (natural predicates).

Although categories have these features, why, as Schegloff (2007:469) puts it, 'should one *care* all that much about these terms and their deployment?' He points out that their importance for study is due to their 'inference richness' and so they store huge amounts of culturally rich common-sense knowledge (e.g. social norms, morals etc) within them. Such common-sense knowledge about each category is often slow, or even not revised. Those who contravene category norms may be seen as a 'phony' (Sacks 1992), 'an exception', 'different', or even a defective member of the category' (Schegloff 2007:469), or indeed re-categorised (Speer 2005:119–20).

The importance of this common-sense knowledge for members and non-members is that it allows for sense making of the everyday social world via value assessments of people's activities (Wowk 1984). For example, Widdicombe and Wooffitt's (1990) interviews with self-identified 'punks', 'rockers', 'gothics' and 'hippies' showed that genuine and non-genuine group identity assessments centred on things like members' knowledge and commitment to the identity category, time as a member, fully participating in the activities, embracing characteristics and so on. Those that failed such assessments were frequently thought of as inauthentic or not 'real' members.

In order to for us to see how such things come into play within a stretch of talk, Baker (1997:142–3) suggests working through three analytical steps:

1. Locate the central categories that are named and/or implied by their activities in the talk.
2. Focus on the activities and predicates associated with each category.
3. Look at how members produce categories, activities and predicates connections for the implied social actions. That is, the 'descriptions of how categories of actors do, could or should behave.'

Applying these steps to 'metrosexual talk' then, we will show how men participating in activities like self-adornment, fashion and grooming, conventionally held to be for members of the category 'women' (Edwards 2003), justify and negotiate their actions.

Data

The Internet boasts a variety of computer mediated communication opportunities such as blogs, chat rooms and MUDs (multiuser domains). Our analysis focuses on a distinct and popular format – the Internet discussion forum – an electronic bulletin board where members of the website can begin threads for the purpose of discussion, building bonds and reaching other interested groups. Online data where the category 'metrosexual' was explicitly taken up (and also disavowed) was identified from an extensive search and cataloguing of Internet forums. Like Miller (2006:105) we encountered 'metrosexuality' in western Europe, Australia, South Asia, Latin America, Africa and the US. 'Metrosexuality' has also infiltrated other globally available languages such a Italian, German and Spanish, and discussed on local forums (e.g. http://foros.univision.com/foros; http://forum.thiazi.net). However, due to our limited foreign language knowledge we chose to focus on predominantly on Western, English-speaking forums. These appeared on a variety of sites such as men's online lifestyle magazines (e.g. AskMen), gaming sites (e.g. Rangerboard), social networking sites (e.g. Facebook), local community boards, and many others. We also encountered many forums discussing metrosexuality as a topic and activities claimed to be metrosexual, such as 'shaving chest hair' and wearing 'makeup'. We considered the 'metrosexual' data from these sites for their length, depth and clarity of discussions. The majority of the forums only contained limited (e.g. 4–7) metrosexual posts. However, members' contributions from the MacRumours forum thread 'Metrosexuals?' (http://forums.macrumors.com/showthread.php?t=163687) stood out for the sustained attention to the matter at hand, richness in detail and diversity of members' perspectives, and so we decided to focus on this dataset. The extracts we focus on are part of a much larger (65 posts) and ongoing discussion by the MacRumours forum members to the thread 'Metrosexuals?, the main thrust of which was the product of a day and a half's discussion in November 2005 (accessed 30 April 2008).

Forum contributors access the MacRumours website for Apple news, Apple Rumours and to participate in community, social and intellectual discussions, ranging from '*Seriously considering a handgun ...*' to '*God The Ultimate Human Meme - Intrinsic, Integral, or Irrelevant?*' Typically on such discussions the electronic dialogue flows for a while before participants withdraw as they presumably go about their daily activities, and then later dialogue re-opens. The data in our study is extracted from a much larger and ongoing discussion by the MacRumours forum members to the thread 'Metrosexuals?' We discounted some of the later contributions of this forum thread, because although they contained relevant material on metrosexuality, discussions were often short-lived or fragmented, quickly switching to other unrelated topics. This particular section of the MacRumours forum thread aside, the site features detailed and dedicated discussion of metrosexuality and its predicates along with, and in relation to, other relevant categories such as homosexuality, heteronormative masculinity and femininity – the focus of this chapter.

We present the written text of the extracts in their original form, including spelling mistakes and vernacular expressions. In line with conventional transcription conventions (Jefferson 1984) we have included line numbers for analytical purposes, but have removed members' avatars and signatures for ease of presentation and analysis.

Analysis

Throughout the MacRumours 'Metrosexuals?' thread, contributors defined metrosexuality largely in terms of men who are consumers of fashion, grooming and beauty products. Those disavowing metrosexuality, however, structured their arguments and criticisms in relation to what Connell (1995:223) calls the 'symbolism of difference' i.e. the symbolic opposition of femininity and masculinity that leads to perceptions of 'gender-appropriate' activities (see also Edwards 2003:141–2). With this in mind, we focus here on five extracts featuring discussions of metrosexuality in relation to other categories (e.g. women, homosexuals, preppy, übersexual and other more conventional men).

The analysis will centre on the following three main points of interest. The first centres on sexuality, and specifically the boundary work needed to establish a distinction between metrosexuality and homosexuality, and a connection between metrosexuality and heterosexuality. The second focuses on the negotiation of candidate metrosexual-bound activities and predicates contra other masculine categories. The final point of interest considers the various distancing strategies employed by self-ascribing metrosexuals to negotiate category membership. It will be suggested that metrosexuality is being situated in relation to a perceived hierarchy of masculinities, and also in relation to notions of discrete sexes.

Metrosexuality contra homosexuality

Focusing on sexuality and the boundary work needed to establish a distinction between metrosexuality and homosexuality, we begin our analysis with the initial sequence of electronic talk from the MacRumours 'Metrosexuals?' thread.

Extract 1

Simplistic 26 November 2005, 01:48 am

Any other metrosexuals in here? I know I'm not the only one.
Embrace your self-loving nonsense.

Lacero 26 November 2005, 01:49 am

Your 7th post and *this is it*?
What does it matter, anyway?

Simplistic 26 November 2005, 01:54 am

It doesn't matter. That's not the point. Just asking. And I'm bored...

---

homerjward 26 November 2005, 01:56 am
Ref: Lines 5–6

don't worry, Lacero's just echoing edesignuk's first comment[3] in this thread (asking whether there were any gay people at this forum) btw, lacero edesignuk didn't italicize "is it" and he flipped the two clauses in the 2nd sentence.

Lacero 26 November 2005, 01:57 am
Ref: Line 5–6

sorry if i come off sounding like a jerk, i dont mean to at all, and indeed, Welcome to the forums i just dont understand the need to ask this question i guess, but thats probably because im a ditz (and proud of it too)

---

sjpetry 26 November 2005, 01:58 am

How about any closet metros?

Simplistic 26 November 2005, 02:02 am

I used to be in the closet about it. It was so annoying. Whenever I'd do something dainty I'd get weird looks from my parents. Eventually they stopped caring and I was tweasing my eyebrows without a care in the world!

Seasought 26 November 2005, 02:03 am

I don't believe I am.
I'm not terribly liberal.
I'm not really into fashion (though I have my own eccentricities).
I would hope I have a reasonable sense of taste.
I am hetero, however.

---

mad jew 26 November 2005, 02:11am

I wear collared shirts and I don't drink beer...

Simplistic 26 November 2005, 02:11 am

I like the attention I get from being the way I am. Like, I have this attitude that is like, "Hey, ladies. I look good and I don't even know it… or do I?" So the girls think, "Hmm, that guy looks good, but he doesn't look too full of himself. Let me go talk to him." It's good.

Right on, jew. I don't drink nor smoke. I hate drinking and smoking would only be cool if it didn't have the nasty side affects.

---

mkrishnan 26 November 2005, 02:14 am

I am, I am! Although, I need a manicure, and I haven't seen my hair stylist in a longer amount of time than any time since I moved here. *le sigh*[4]

Simplistic's opening 'Any other metrosexuals in here?' (line 1) makes the category 'metrosexual' relevant. However, his suggestion that metrosexuality is a relevant topic of discussion prompts *Lacero* to respond by similarly echoing a previous post in another forum thread 'GayWay – the gay and lesbian discussion', culminating in the dismissive 'What does it matter, anyway? (line 4). *Lacero*'s response indicates that some sort of normative code may be breached if this topic is discussed because it may potentially be a 'non-tellable' (West and Garcia 1988). That is, dispreferred conversational pursuits (e.g. women's personal feelings) or non-tellable topics (e.g. homosexual behaviour). But what kind of 'non-tellable' at this point in the text is unclear, although we do get a sense of it from *Simplistic*'s 'Embrace your self-loving nonsense' (line 2), which suggests male vanity or narcissism. These category predicates, as Edwards (2003:141–2) tells us, are 'antithetical if not an outright oxymoron' for conventional men. *Lacero*'s post therefore, can be read as perhaps attempting to steer forum members away from discussing a potentially delicate category. *Simplistic* appears to read *Lacero*'s post in this way a by downplaying his investment in the topic, presenting his motivation as mundane: 'I'm bored' (lines 5–6). However, Homerjward's subsequent support to *Simplistic* ('don't worry': line 7) and critique of *Lacero*'s inaccurate echoing of *edesignuk*'s previous post ('btw, lacero edesignuk didn't italicize "is it" and he flipped the two clauses in the 2nd sentence': lines 9–10) elicits an apology from *Lacero* (line 11), who then accounts for his dismissiveness of metrosexuality by categorising himself as a 'ditz' (line 14) (scatterbrain). What *Homerjward*'s response and Lacero's subsequent apology achieve is to re-open a space for metrosexuality to be discussed.

Sjpetry seizes this opportunity by asking the question 'How about any closet metros?' (line 15). By invoking the category-bound activity of being in the 'closet' we are immediately provided with an association to other potentially relevant categories (e.g. gay men and women not disclosing their sexuality; see Silverman 1998:75). *Sjpetry*'s question does the work of suggesting that there are similarities between homosexuality and metrosexuality. The potential similarities of these two categories provides us with a clearer picture of why metrosexuality could be seen as breaching normative masculine codes of conduct (e.g. heterosexuality) (Connell 1995) and occupy a 'troubled subject position' (Wetherell 1998).

Simplistic's subsequent post serves as a non-challenging response to sjpetry and presents as light-hearted self-mockery 'I used to be in the closet about it' (line 16). On the other hand, his display of unconventional predicates 'something dainty' (line 17) and 'tweasing my eyebrows' (lines 18–19), which reportedly elicited 'weird looks from (his) parents' (lines 17–18) who 'eventually stopped caring and I was tweasing my eyebrows without a care in the world!' (lines 17–19), also allows him to orientate his category-bound predicates as courageous, autonomous and individual in relation to conventional masculine norms. In short, *Simplistic* subtly positions himself as a 'gender-rebel' (Gill et al. 2005; Wetherell and Edley 1999), and in doing so masculinises himself and makes participating in these potentially demeaning activities (in relation to heteronormative masculinity) seem heroic and alternative (Wetherell and Edley 1999:350).

Simplistic's reframing of his 'metrosexual' activities as masculine has not yet dispelled metrosexual associations with homosexuality as implied by *sjperty* (line 16), as evidenced by *Seasought*'s (and later *Simplistic*'s) subsequent posts. *Seasought*'s non-ascription to metrosexuality ('I don't believe I am': line 20) is followed by a short list that can be read as containing both presumed 'metrosexual' and 'non-metrosexual' predicates, or 'contrast categories' (Hester and Eglin 1998:138; Smith 1978). That is, omitting the adverb 'not' from the first two items implies metrosexual predicates – I am terribly liberal and I am really into fashion (lines 21–2). The third item, 'a reasonable sense of taste', if read in conjunction with Edwards (2003:141–2) 'antithetical' claim about male style and vanity (see above), also suggests that 'although metrosexuals are into fashion they do not have a sense of taste'. This tells us that metrosexual fashion is different, and perhaps distasteful, to more conventional men. But why would metrosexuals adopt non-normative category-bound activities and predicates, which have the potential to undermine their masculine identity? *Seasought*'s ascription to heterosexuality at the end of his post – 'I am hetero, however' (line 25) – provides a clue.

Through asserting his heterosexuality, *Seasought* directs us back to the associations between metrosexuality and homosexuality previously produced by *Sjpetry*. Since sexual orientation cannot be ascertained for certain, these claims must rest on the assumption that the category-bounded activities of metrosexuality and homosexuality are alike or similar. And in a society that recognises gender binaries and heteronormativity as the standard, metrosexuality and homosexuality must both have predicates that are considered feminine (Edwards 2003; Harrison 2008; Simpson 2005).

Simplistic displays awareness of this conflation of the two categories, and responds with a heteronormative masculine defence: 'I like the attention I get from being the way I am' (line 27). *Simplistic*'s shifting categorisations of the type of women who give him attention, from 'ladies' (line 28) to 'girls' (line 29) is an interesting piece of rhetorical work. The selection of one category over another within the device 'gender' which includes the categories 'ladies' and 'girls' carries important implications for how the text is read. Edwards (1998:25) argues that these categories carry 'potentially useful conventional associations with age, marital status, and potential sexual availability'. Stokoe (2003:331) suggests that when the category 'girl' is invoked, it 'suggests frivolity, a lack of authority and purpose' whereas 'lady' infers asexuality'. *Simplistic*'s post first describes the attention he gets as from 'ladies' but then selects the replacement category, 'the girls'. The switch from 'ladies' to 'girls' functions to position him as not just visually appealing to the opposite sex but also sexually appealing to them. This 'category, predicate and task' (Hester and Eglin 1997) serves to counter accusations of homosexuality from 'being the way I am' (line 27) as a member of a 'disjunctive' category (Schegloff 2007:469) and works to reconfigure metrosexual membership in heterosexual terms.

Simplistic's post can also be seen as a critique of conventional masculinity by setting up the contrast pair (Smith 1978) – looking good/not looking good. The activity serves to hold conventional men and their masculinities accountable for their disinterest in self-presentation (in this case predicated on a pragmatic anti-fashion attitude to appearance – see Edwards 2003) in terms of inferior self-respect. His critique goes a step further in his references to *mad jew* (line 26) who previously offered: 'I wear collared shirts and I don't drink beer' as potential metrosexual predicates. Implied in this statement is that these category-bounded activities potentially belong to the category 'metrosexual' rather than more conventional masculinities. *Simplistic*, as a self-ascribed 'metrosexual', picks up on 'drinking' (line 32) as a more conventional masculine category predicate along with 'smoking' (line 32) (see Edwards 2003). These contrastive pairs form part of the set of modifications that are administered by metrosexual members to be able to recognise that someone involved in grooming and personal adornment for heterosexual reasons is 'metrosexual' and not any other 'masculine category'.

Simplistic's remasculinisation of his metrosexual activities and critique of conventional masculinities' disinterest in self-presentation elicits an eager self-ascription to metrosexuality by *mkrishnan* 'I am, I am!' (line 35).What is also implied in his post is that mkrishnan's subsequent comment, which claims non-participation in two metrosexual bounded activities ('I need a manicure, and I haven't seen my hair stylist': lines 35–6), is that frequency of grooming activities may be a factor for metrosexual membership. Similarly to Vallis's (2001) study of internet chat rooms and Widdicombe and Wooffitt's (1990) interviews of with self-identified 'punk's, 'rockers', 'gothics' and 'hippies', this may also provide a means for other self-ascribing metrosexuals (and non-metrosexuals) in the forum to accord in-group status. That is, to police members relationships to self-presentation practices despite their positive orientations to metrosexuality.

Thus, so far, drawing on the three-step process of Baker (1997:142–3), the categories 'metrosexual' and 'homosexual' have been made relevant and equated in the talk, and since 'homosexual' is a marginalised category (Whitehead and Barrett 2001), the normative category 'heterosexual men' is implied. This means that the two marginalised categories with the bounded predicate 'self-presentation' elicit moral judgements (Jayyusi 1984) in order for members to be able to make sense of the social world. That is, all men must position themselves, and are positioned, in relation to 'hegemonic' norms (Connell 1995). Non-normative activity participation therefore, requires metrosexuals to re-orientate membership in line with heterosexual norms (e.g. sexual prowess). However, although forum members have provided some clues as to metrosexual category-bound activities and predicates, we don't yet have a clear understanding of the category's parameters. It is the negotiation of these that the analysis will now turn to.

Negotiating category-bound activities

Since 'metrosexual' is a relatively new identity category, forum members negotiated candidate identity characteristiscs. The following two sequences of talk were the first sustained attempts to define what exactly constituted 'being metrosexual'.

Extract 2

Raggedjimmi 26 November 2005, 09:12 am

```
I don't know what I am. a blend of country boy and metrosexual perhaps? God knows. I don't drink, I like outdoors activities, I like fashion, I like to be clean, smell nice etc, im very eccentric. I'm my own style I suppose
```

---

mkrishnan 26 November 2005, 09:26 am
Ref: Lines 95–98

```
Let's see if you classify as a Manchester Metrosexual, do you:
-Hang out in Living Room/Canal Street
-Have a mullet/fin
-Shop frequently in Flannels/Diesel
-Think 'distressed' is still in
-Go to tanning salons/apply St Tropez
If you tick 4/5 then you can probably say yes
```

---

clayj 26 November 2005, 09:43 am

```
What we really need is a list of things that qualify you as a metrosexual.
I'll start it off:
- You wash with anything beyond bar soap and shampoo in the shower.
- You get a manicure and/or a pedicure more than once a decade.
- You've EVER been called 'pretty boy'.
- You apply any sort of skin conditioning lotion on a semi-regular basis.
- You spend more than 10 minutes a day grooming.
- You pay more than $30 for a haircut.
```

```
- You have hair coloring applied. (Exception: Eliminating grey
doesn't make you metrosexual, it just makes you insecure about
getting old. Adding 'accents' to your hair DEFINITELY makes you
metrosexual.)
- You wear ornately decorated shirts. (Usually these are button-down
shirts with excessively-complicated designs and/or paisley.)
- If a woman calls you a metrosexual, you are.
```

Drawing on Hester and Eglin's (1997) 'category, predicate and task' we can see that *Raggedjimmi*'s specific task in his opening his post is to find out from other forum members, with presumably more category identity knowledge than him, whether he belongs in any of the three distinct categories 'country boy', 'metrosexual' (line 95) or individualist ('my own style': lines 96–7). One way for others to assign category membership is to offer candidate category-bound activities (see Vallis 2001:90), such as 'I don't drink, I like outdoors activities, I like fashion, I like to be clean, smell nice etc, im very eccentric' (lines 96–7). However, *Mkrishnan* or *Clayj* do not undertake a category assignment of *Raggedjimmi*. Instead, both respondents provide quite distinct and extensive, if not humorous, lists of metrosexual category-bound activities and predicates for which *Raggedjimmi* (and other forum members) could orientate to and self-ascribe. Jefferson's (1991:68) work on listing suggests that hearers (and speakers) are able to use lists as an 'orientated-to-procedure'. In other words, it provides the hearer with a means to discursively position themselves in relation to the items on the list. Moreover, it also provides a means for other forum members, whether metrosexual or not, to accord group status and police members' positive orientations to metrosexuality (Widdicombe and Wooffitt 1990; see also Vallis 2001 for other online, non-metrosexual examples).

Mkrishnan's response seems to poke fun at *Raggedjimmi*'s request for category categorisation by his ironic question 'Let's see if you classify as a Manchester Metrosexual' (line 99). One reasonable prerequisite of metrosexuality is 'living in or within easy reach of a metropolis' (Simpson 2002:2), and *Raggedjimmi*'s reference to 'country boy' provides for a possible hearing that he is a non-urban dweller and specifically not a 'Manchester Metrosexual'. Furthermore, one feature of the device 'types' (e.g. 'types of metrosexual' implied by *Raggedjimmi*'s 'my own style' and *mkrishnan*'s 'Manchester Metrosexual') is that such characterisations can elicit humour (Benwell and Stokoe 2006:198; Vallis 2001:95). That is, it serves as a distancing strategy for category members (e.g. *mkrishnan*, Extract 1) which separates them from those aspiring to or uncertain of their metrosexual category membership (e.g. *Raggedjimmi*, Extract 2). In other words, 'real' metrosexuals would not need to ask for membership clarification. Therefore, *mkrishnan*'s deployment of 'humour' implicates *Raggedjimmi* as a disjunctive category member or 'phony' (Sacks 1992:581). *Clayj*, on the other hand, rather than distancing other forum members from possible membership ascription, orientates the talk back to a more serious level 'What we really need is a list of things that qualify you as a metrosexual. I'll start it off' (lines 106–7).

Clayj offers an extensive nine-part list featuring fashion and grooming activities (lines 108–22), which serves as a resource to normalise these activities as category-generated features of metrosexual membership. Like *Seasought*'s post (Extract 1) –reading each item in the negative (e.g. You don't' etc.) – also provides a resource for defining (for *clayj*) the category-bound activities of conventional men. Moreover, *Clayj*'s list items are perhaps also a partial recycling of the candidate activities provided in previous sequences in the talk (see Jefferson 1991:89) – *Simplistic*'s 'tweasing my eyebrows', *Seasought*'s ' fashion' and *Raggedjimmi*'s 'fashion' and personal hygiene 'I like to be clean, smell nice etc'. Frequently implied activities grouped around the category 'metrosexual' reinforce the tie between 'metrosexuality' and the predicate 'concern with self-presentation'. Yet as Edwards (2003:141–2) has pointed out, activities such these are conventionally tied to the category 'women'. Therefore, like *Simplistic*'s fourth post (Extract 1), *clayj* culminates his post by making reference to categorisation by women. This may suggest that women are experts on identification of the types of activities metrosexuals perform, and/or serve, like *Simplistic*'s post, as a warrant for warding off potential accusations of homosexuality by justifying these activities as undertaken for heterosexual prowess, thereby effectively re-masculinising these predicates.

The posts presented in Extract 2 provide a clearer insight into specific metrosexual-bounded activities and predicates, centred on notions of self-presentation. However, also evident from *mkrishnan*'s post was the in-group and out-group policing of category membership through the deployment of 'humour', thus also giving a clear indication that 'metrosexual', along with other categories such as 'homosexual', is a marginalised category. That is, like the analysis of Extract 1, metrosexuality presents as at odds with conventional men and masculinity, such that justification for non-normative activities need to be hedged in heteronormative ways. A similar manoeuvring tactic is also evident in the following extract. However, what is also interesting about this extract is the discussion that centres on whether men's concern for self-presentation is only an attribute of metrosexuality.

Extract 3

CompUser 26 November 2005, 10:02 am

My friend (who is a girl) always calls me metro all the time. I don't know how it does but it seems to be frequently. She also has called me a 'Perfect, pretty boy'. Apparently its a good thing according to her.

I don't use special soaps and lotions. Nor do I go off and a manicures and such. She makes this judgment because I wear more expensive cloths such as ones from mainly Abercrombie & Fitch, Polo, and J. Crew, probably considered 3 prime examples of preppy stores. Most of my shirts are either Polo, Long sleeve polo, rugby, or button down. I only have about 4-5 long sleeve non colored shirts.

Plymouthbreezer 26 November 2005, 11:37am
Ref: Lines 127–137

142 Hah, me too! Lots of girls (and guys) call me 'really preppy' and a
143 few less have called me metro. I guess it's because I have
144 obsessive compulsive disorder, and am quite eccentric by many
145 kids standards. I'm an artist, love theater and acting, dress nicely,
146 enjoy expensive things (I use Macs...Lol), have a good friend
147 who's gay, I hate George Bush, and tend to get along with girls
148 who never seem to want to go out with me - and all of which
149 usually goes hand in hand with being either gay or metrosexual.
150 But, I'm not gay, so I guess I must be metro, although I hear the
151 correct term thesedays is 'Ubersexual.'
152 Anyway, it's frustrating when people call me gay (not that I have a
153 problem with homosexuals at all) just because I am... Uhh... More
154 'refined' then most kids (I'm 15, 16 next month) today.

CompUser's relays the category work undertaken by his 'friend (who is a girl)' (line 127) 'always calls me metro all the time'. Like *Simplistic*'s post (Extract 1), the significance of invoking the category 'girl' (see Stokoe 2003:331) sets any following talk in heteronormative terms and wards off potential charges of effeminacy or homosexuality. Further warrant for this can be garnered from *CompUser*'s claim that this 'girl' calls him 'Perfect, pretty boy' (line 129), which introduces attractiveness as a metrosexual attribute as identified by 'women'. But, this disrupts conventional modes of looking where '*men look at women and women watch themselves being looked at*' (Berger 1972:47). Talk of male attractiveness risks charges of effeminacy even though heterosexuality has already been implied. *CompUser* deals with this by offering the disclaimer: 'Apparently it's a good thing according to her' (lines 129–30). In other words, he distances himself from his friend's categorisation. Distancing can also be deduced from his invoking of the category 'preppy' implied from his consumption choices e.g. shopping in 'preppy stores' (line 135), and activities e.g. 'I don't use special soaps and lotions. Nor do I go off and a manicures and such' (lines 131–2). As we saw in Extracts 1 and 2 (e.g. *clayj*'s list), conventional men and masculinities disassociate with grooming practices and fashion (also see Edwards 2003). Therefore *CompUser* achieves distance from metrosexuality by his professed disinterest in grooming activities, while at the same time also disassociating himself from conventional men's disinterest in fashion. In other words, his task (Hester and Eglin 1997) in implying membership of the category 'preppy' is to positions him as a man with self-respect via his activities (clothing consumption), while at the same time retaining conventional gender demarcation in the realm of grooming.

Plymouthbreezer responds to *CompUser* with recognition of being positioned in a similar way (lines 142–3). Interestingly, *Plymouthbreezer* accounts for other's categorisation of him as metrosexual or 'really preppy' by categorising himself as having mental health issues ('obsessive compulsive disorder', line 144), which accounts for his unconventional 'eccentric' behaviours. Being 'eccentric' was also a category invoked by *Seasought* (Extract 1, line 23), and *Raggedjimmi* (Extract 2, line 97) which also works as a disclaimer for their participation in typically feminised activities (Edwards 2006). For *Plymouthbreezer*, this strategy also allows him to justify his lack of success with girls 'who never seem to want to go out with me' (line 148). Understanding that his activities may be perceived as homosexual ('all of which usually go hand in hand with being gay or metrosexual', lines 148–9), *Plymouthbreezer* explicitly wards off such charges with 'I am not gay, so I guess I must be metro' (line 150), followed by a re-categorisation of himself as possibly 'ubersexual' (line 151) (see Salzman et al. 2005:167). Moving back and forth between the various categories to which he partially ascribes – 'Lots of girls (and guys call me 'really preppy' (line 142), 'so I guess I must be metro' (line 150) and 'Ubersexual' (line 151) – directs our attention back to the difficulty those who participate in non-conventional category-bounded activities face in constructing a suitable or coherent gendered identity. This also clearly demonstrates the difficulty those ascribing to media and marketing produced categories have in collectively stabilising the meaning of what constitutes membership of those categories. Indeed, the media and marketing origins of metrosexuality are made explicit in the following extract. What is also interesting about the following extract is how those origins can be used as disclaiming and distancing strategies.

Distancing strategies

Given the potential for 'metrosexual' to be interpreted as 'homosexual' as we showed in Extract 1, many forum participants deployed distancing strategies to inoculate against potential charges of 'homosexuality'.

Extract 4

Daveway 26 November 2005, 12:28 pm

I would be lying to myslef if I didn't raise my hand to this. I think
my cousin got me caught into the whole metro thing. I remember
seeing a story on 60minutes about it.
Anyways I admit to the hair, expensive clothing, tweasers,
shaving, more than one kind of soap, and various face washes.
I can't stand to wear last years clothing, loose clothing, and t-shirts
w/ baseball cap worn everywhere is NOT my style. I go for
distressed jeans, button down shirt, and jacket.
Why is it bad to care how you look?

Daveway's ascription to 'metrosexuality' (line 174) presents metrosexuality as a contemporary media and marketing produced masculine identity. Warrant for this can be garnered from his reference to metrosexuality being discussed as a topic on the US Columbia Broadcasting System (CBS) television newsmagazine. 'I remember seeing a story on 60minutes about it' (lines 175–6), and his list of consumption-based activities e.g. 'expensive clothing', 'various face washes' (lines 177–81). As we have seen in the previous posts (also see Edwards 2003), there is a risk in ascribing to these category-bound activities and predicates – being charged with effeminacy, narcissism or homosexuality. *Daveway* deals with this, in part, by attributing some responsibility for his actions to his cousin (lines 174–5) 'my cousin got me caught into the whole metro thing' (lines 174–5) and CBS's broadcast (lines 175–6) (see Silverman 2006 for how texts influence the way people see the world and how they should act). His discursive work therefore can be seen to legitimise and position metrosexuality as a popular identity, while at the same time serving as a distancing strategy from a potentially troubled identity – 'Why is it bad to care how you look?' (line 182) – that sits in contrast to conventional masculinity (Wetherell 1998).

As with Extracts 1 and 2, *Daveway*'s listing of category-bounded activities (lines 177–81) discredit more conventional heteronormative masculine features: 'wear[ing] last years clothing, loose clothing, and t-shirts w/ baseball cap worn everywhere' (lines 179–80). These category-bound activities serve to question normative masculine disinterest in self-presentation and act as a critique of its presumed low level of self-respect. Gill et al.'s (2005:54–6) semi-structured interview research with British men found that self-respect was a specific masculine characteristic cherished by their participants. Those men who failed to demonstrate self-respect were frequently criticised. *Daveway*'s orientation to self-respect via self-presentation practices positions metrosexuality in more conventional masculine terms. Furthermore, like *Simplistic* (Extract 1), *Daveway* can also be seen as a 'gender-rebel' (Gill et al. 2005; Wetherell and Edley 1999) for his non-normative category-bound activities and predicates.

In the final extract, the contributor explicitly draws upon the marketed aspect of metrosexuality to define membership. It should be recalled that in Extract 3 *CompUser* was not ascribing to metrosexuality and had in fact disavowed membership based on his non-participation in grooming activities (lines 131–2), even though his friend had reputedly positioned him as metrosexual (line 127). However, in Extract 5 *CompUser* presents uncertainty over which category applies to him: 'really preppy' or 'metrosexual' (line 361). At this point Matt steps in to offer advice based on the consumption of specific brands.

Extract 5

CompUser 27 November 2005, 04:29 pm

```
361  Is some one consided 'really preppy' such as I also metro?
```

Matt 27 November 2005, 04:41 pm
Ref: Line 357

```
362  well, you're doubting your fashion sexuality are you not?
363  if there is a doubt, the answer is always yes
364  just posting in this thread made you metro…welcome…
365  i am definitely metro …
366  professional shampoo/conditioner/hair gel…
```

```
algae facial treatments and other nice skin moisturizers…
PowerBook G4
shop at Banana Republic, Diesel, Calvin Klein, Armani
Exchange…boxer briefs manicures/pedicures
Tumi backpack
Prada and Gucci eyewear
Pottery Barn furniture (ultra suede comforter = the ticket)
wow…it feels good to be out of the…uhhh walk-in closet
girls love metros…who doesn't like invites to shop with them at
victoria's secret
```

Matt opens his post with a fascinating mixture of references to *CompUsers* queries about fashion and broader references to sexuality ('fashion sexuality', line 362). The purpose in using humour at the outset denies other contributors the ability to hold him completely accountable for his subsequent metrosexual ascription (line 365). As previously noted, a 'stylish' man can pose problems for those invested in hegemonic masculinities (Edwards 2003), and so 'ambiguous masculinities' such as metrosexuality, which contravene the 'symbolism of difference' (Connell 1995:223) are often deployed with humour, which serves as a distancing strategy (Benwell 2003:156).

Matt continues by affirming *CompUser*'s ascription to metrosexuality and claims that 'just posting in this thread made you metro…welcome…' (line 364). This can be read as either: metrosexuals would only discuss metrosexuality in a forum about metrosexuality, or that purchasers of Apple Mac computers (those who participate in MacRumours threads) are by virtue of their consumption, 'metrosexual'. The more likely interpretation is that *Matt* is referring to the consumption of Apple hardware 'PowerBook G4' (line 368), which lays the ground for his subsequent list of consumer brands for category identification (lines 368–73) (Silverman 2006). Listing apparent metrosexual brands gives contributors yet another device in which to orientate to metrosexuality (Jefferson 1991:68), and at the same time normalises the consumption practices of metrosexuals. Noticeable also is that *Matt* concludes his post by making reference to 'girls' (line 375), a strategy also previously employed by *Simplistic* (Extract 1) and *Clayj* (Extract 2) in order to reframe metrosexuality in masculine ways that draw on self-respect and sexual prowess.

Concluding remarks

Our analysis clearly indicates that there is a lot at stake for self-ascribing metrosexuals – as is the case for anybody ascribing to a marginalised identity (Edwards 2006). The power of established gendered knowledge clearly makes it difficult to identify with and invest in emerging and potentially subversive categories like metrosexual – we know that members of alternative categories risk being castigated as 'defective or 'phony' (Sacks 1992). Our data highlights the continued force of hegemonic masculinities, since on the one hand metrosexuality was critiqued and rejected as non-masculine (hence accusations of homosexuality, effeminacy and narcissism), while on the other self-identifying metrosexuals invoked conventional masculinity signifiers in the process of their identity work (heterosexual prowess, self-respect etc.). Metrosexual avowal walks a fine line between rejecting traditional masculinised practices (e.g. disinterest in appearance) and invoking other masculinised ideals (e.g. autonomy, self-discipline).

As well as highlighting the gendered discursive resources informing identity construction, our analysis also attended to the discursive practices used in this process. We saw, for example, the deployment of listing (Jefferson 1991) as a strategy for orienting to metrosexuality, allowing contributors to move towards and against the metrosexual label in dynamic ways. We also saw the use of terms such as 'style' and 'fashion', which facilitated a temporary identification with metrosexuality – one that could be discarded if critique becomes excessive. The use of irony and humour was also widespread (see Benwell 2004), again providing inoculation against charges of effeminacy or vanity. Attention to discursive practices as well as resources thus illuminates the shifting and sophisticated manoeuvres involved in claiming and rejecting metrosexual (and masculine) identities.

Our analysis then moves beyond media representations of metrosexuality (Simpson 1994, 2002) and the analysis of magazine masculinities (e.g. Edwards 2006; Benwell and Stokoe 2006) by offering insights into the dynamics of metrosexual (dis-)identification. Further, our analysis underlines the continued influence of hegemonic masculinities in the construction (and rejection) of supposedly 'new', 'modern' or 'alternative' forms of masculinity. We question claims about the deconstruction of, or resistance to, culturally embedded masculine signifiers and the idea that conventional or 'hegemonic' (Connell 1995) forms of masculinity are, or have been, superseded (MacInnes 2001). Yet what does appear to be evident is that some masculinities now appear to be modernised in line with changes in contemporary consumption practices.

This analysis fits with other work which maintains that men's forays into hitherto feminised domains (beauty, health, care etc.) is invariably accompanied by a masculinised reframing (or even critique) of the practice in question (see Harrison 2008; Gough 2007; Gill et al. 2005; Edwards 2003), and/or an assertion of one's masculinity credentials with respect to other domains (see e.g. de Visser 2008). This work implies that hegemonic masculinities (Connell 1995; Connell and Messerschmidt 2005) remain culturally available and influential for (some) men (with reference to sexual performance, self-respect, autonomy etc.) – but this is not to suggest that the meanings around such masculinities are fixed, or that their deployment is predictable or mechanistic. Rather, our analysis foregrounds the complex and dynamic ways in which masculinities are negotiated in the context of metrosexuality, and further advertises the value of attending to discursive resources and practices in this field (see also Wetherell and Edley 1999).

Notes

1 Hegemonic masculinity is a normative masculinity, which is the current most honoured way of being a man in a given context, even though most men do not enact it. However

all men are required to position themselves in relation to hegemonic forms, which can also be deployed to legitimate the subordination of women and marginalised men (Connell and Messerschmidt 2005:832).

2 Sacks developed MCA in a series of lectures from 1963–4, which were published in 1972 and 1992.

3 This remark is about a mirrored comment made by edesignuk in the forum 'GayWay – the gay and lesbian discussion' (aka Any Gays Here?) in which edesignuk posted 'Your 1st post, and *this* is it? 😁 Anyway, what does it matter?'

4 A phrase commonly used by bloggers to express feelings of frustration (see www.urbandictionary.com/define.php?term=le sigh).

References

Baker, C. (1997) Membership categorization and interview accounts. In D. Silverman (ed.) *Qualitative Research: Theory, Method and Practice* 130–43. London: Sage.

Benwell, B. (2003) Ambiguous masculinities: heroism and anti-heroism in the men's lifestyle magazine. *The Sociological Review* 51(S1): 151–68.

Benwell, B. (2004) Ironic discourse: evasive masculinity in the British men's lifestyle magazines. *Men and Masculinities* 7(1): 3–21.

Benwell, B. and Stokoe, E. (2006) *Discourse and Identity*. Edinburgh: Edinburgh University Press.

Berger, J. (1972) *Ways of Seeing*. London: Penguin.

Coad, D. (2008) *The Metrosexual: Gender, Sexuality, and Sport*. New York: SUNY Press.

Connell, R. W. (1995) *Masculinities*. Cambridge: Polity.

Connell, R. W. and Messerschmidt, J. W. (2005) Hegemonic masculinity: rethinking the concept. *Gender and Society* 19(60): 829–59. https://doi.org/10.1177/0891243205278639

Coyle, J. and MacWhannell, D. (2002) The importance of 'morality' in the social construction of suicide in Scottish newspapers. *Sociology of Health and Illness* 24(6): 689–713. https://doi.org/10.1111/1467-9566.00314

de Visser, R. O. (2008) 'I'm not a very manly man': qualitative insights into young men's masculine subjectivity, *Men and Masculinities* (24 January): 1–5.

Edwards, D. (1998) The relevant thing about her: social identity categories in use. In C. Antaki and S. Widdicombe (eds) *Identities in Talk* 15–33. London: Sage.

Edwards, T. (2003) Sex, booze and fags: masculinity, style and men's magazines. In B. Benwell (ed.) *Masculinity and Men's Lifestyle Magazines* 132–46. Oxford: Blackwell. https://doi.org/10.1111/j.1467-954X.2003.tb03607.x

Edwards, T. (2006) *Cultures of Masculinity*. London: Routledge.

Gill, R., Henwood, K. and McLean, C. (2005) Body projects and the regulation of normative masculinity. *Body and Society* 11(1): 37–62. https://doi.org/10.1177/1357034X05049849

Gough, B. (2007) 'Real men don't diet': an analysis of contemporary newspaper representations of men, food and health. *Social Science and Medicine* 64(2): 326–37. https://doi.org/10.1016/j.socscimed.2006.09.011

Greenfield, P. M. and Subrahmanyam, K. (2003) Online discourse in a teen chatroom: new codes and new modes of coherence in a visual medium. *Applied Developmental Psycholog*, 24: 713–38. https://doi.org/10.1016/j.appdev.2003.09.005

Harrison, C. (2008) Real men do wear mascara: advertising discourse and masculine identity. *Critical Discourse Studies* 5(1): 55–74. https://doi.org/10.1080/17405900701768638

Hester, S. and Eglin, P. (eds) (1997) *Culture and Action: Studies in Membership Categorization Analysis.* Washington, DC: University Press of America.

Hill, D. B. (2006) Feminine heterosexual men: subverting heteropatriarchal sexual scripts? *The Journal of Men's Studies* 14(2): 145–59. https://doi.org/10.3149/jms.1402.145

Horne, J. and Wiggins, S. (2009) Doing being 'on the edge': managing the dilemma of being authentically suicidal in an online forum. *Sociology of Health and Illness* 31(2): 170–84. https://doi.org/10.1111/j.1467-9566.2008.01130.x

Jayyusi, L. (1984) *Categorization and the Moral Order*. New York: Routledge & Kegan Paul.

Jefferson, G. (1984) Transcription notation. In J. Atkinson and J. Heritage (eds) *Structures of Social Interaction* ix–xvi. New York: Cambridge University Press.

Jefferson, G. (1991) List construction as a task and a resource. In G. Psathas (ed.) *Interactional Competence* 63–92. New York: Irvington Publications.

Kollock, P. (ed.) (1999) *Communities in Cyberspace*. London: Routledge.

MacInnes, J. (2001) The crisis of masculinity and the politics of identity. In S. M. Whitehead and F. J. Barrett (eds) *The Masculinities Reader* 311–29. Cambridge: Polity Press.

Miller, T. (2006) A metrosexual eye on queer guy. *Lesbian and Gay Studies* 11(1): 112–17. https://doi.org/10.1215/10642684-11-1-112

Moursand, J. (1997) Sanctuary: social support on the internet. In J. E. Behar (ed.) *Mapping Cyber- space: Social Research on the Electronic Frontier* 53–78. Oakdale, NY: Dowling College Press.

PurAsia (2008) The emergence of the gastrosexual. Retrieved on 21 July 2008 from www.gastrosexual.com/EmergenceoftheGastrosexual.pdf.

Sacks, H. (1972) On the analysability of stories by children. In R. Turner (ed.) *Ethnomethodology* 216–32. Harmondsworth: Penguin Education.

Sacks, H. (1992) *Lectures on Conversation*. Oxford: Blackwell.

Salzman, M., Matathia, I. and O'Reilly, A. (2005) *The Future of Men*. Basingstoke: Palgrave Macmillan.

Schegloff, E. A. (2007) A tutorial on membership categorisation. *Journal of Pragmatics* 39: 462–82. https://doi.org/10.1016/j.pragma.2006.07.007

Silverman, D. (1998) *Harvey Sacks: Social Science and Conversation Analysis*. Cambridge: Polity Press.

Silverman, D. (2006) *Interpreting Qualitative Data: Methods for Analysing Talk, Text and Interaction*, 3rd edition. London: Sage.

Simpson, M. (1994) Here come the mirror men. *The Independent* (15 November). Retrieved on 12 October 2017 from www.marksimpson.com/here-come-the-mirror-men.

Simpson, M. (2002) Meet the metrosexual. Retrieved on 4 January 2008 from http://dir.salon.com/story/ent/feature/2002/07/22/metrosexual/index2.html.

Simpson, R. (2005) Men in non-traditional occupations: career entry, career orientation and experience of role strain. *Gender, Work and Organisation* 12(4): 363–80. https://doi.org/10.1111/j.1468-0432.2005.00278.x

Slouka, M. (1995) *War of the Worlds: Cyberspace and the High-Tech Assault on Reality*. New York: Basic Books.

Smith, D. (1978) K is Mentally Ill: the anatomy of a factual account. *Sociology* 12: 23–53. https://doi.org/10.1177/003803857801200103

Speer, S. (2005) *Gender Talk: Feminism, Discourse and Conversation Analysis*. Hove: Routledge. https://doi.org/10.4324/9780203321447

Sproull, L. and Kiesler, S. (1991) *Connections*. Cambridge, MA: MIT Press.

Stokoe, E. H. (2003) Mothers, single women and sluts: gender, morality and membership categorization in neighbour disputes. *Feminism and Psychology* 13: 317–44. https://doi.org/10.1177/0959353503013003006

Turkle, S. (1997) *Life on the Screen*. London: Phoenix.

Vallis, R. (2001) Applying membership categorization analysis to chat-room talk. In A. McHoul and M. Rapley (eds) *How to Analyse Talk in Institutional Settings: A Casebook of Methods* 86–99. London: Continuum.

West, C. and Garcia, A. (1988) Conversational shift work: a study of topical transitions between men and women. *Social Problems* 35(5): 551–75. https://doi.org/10.2307/800615

Wetherell, M. (1998) Positioning and interpretative repertoires: conversation analysis and post-structuralism in dialogue. *Discourse and Society* 9(3): 387–412. https://doi.org/10.1177/0957926598009003005

Wetherell, M. and Edley, N. (1999) Negotiating hegemonic masculinity: imaginary positions and psycho-discursive practices. *Feminism and Psychology* 9(3): 335–56. https://doi.org/10.1177/0959353599009003012

Whitehead, S. M. and Barrett, F. J. (2001) *The Masculinities Reader*. Cambridge: Polity Press.

Widdicombe, S. and Wooffitt, R. (1990) 'Being' versus 'doing' punk: on achieving authenticity as a member. *Journal of Language and Social Psychology* 9(4): 257–77. https://doi.org/10.1177/0261927X9094003

Winzelburg, A. (1997) The analysis of an electronic support group for individuals with eating disorders. *Computers in Human Behaviour* 13(3): 393–407. https://doi.org/10.1016/S0747-5632(97)00016-2

Wowk, M. T. (1984) Blame allocation, sex and gender in a murder interrogation. *Women's Studies International Forum* 7(1): 75–82. https://doi.org/10.1016/0277-5395(84)90087-6

10

A bit too skinny for me: women's homosocial constructions of heterosexual desire in online dating

Kristine Køhler Mortensen
UNIVERSITY OF COPENHAGEN, DENMARK

Introduction: homosocial aspects of desire

Researchers within the field of language and sexuality (e.g. Bucholtz and Hall 2004; Cameron and Kulick 2003a) have debated the methodological difficulties in investigating a phenomenon such as desire in linguistic and interactional analysis, as it is most often understood as an internal state of the individual's body and mind. As Eckert states:

> We tend to view desire ... as an individual, private, thing. It is desire, in other words, that brings the mystification into the study of sexuality, and it is in contemplating desire that we are inclined to fall into an asocial and naturalized view of sexuality. The challenge, then, is to adopt an approach that focuses on the social mediation of desire. (Eckert 2002:100)

At the same time as desire is considered to be an individual experience, the enactment and negotiation of desire is commonly portrayed as the exclusive interaction between two mutually desiring participants – a man and a woman. However, studies of adolescent girls demonstrate that numerous participants are involved in the act of planning, negotiating and establishing heterosexual romantic relations (Eckert 2011; Kotthoff 2008). Thus, the negotiation is not merely constituted by two romantic partners, but also includes subsidiary participants who co-act in the process of constructing certain persons as acceptable and attractive objects of desire. Homosocial constructions of desire have primarily been examined among adolescent girls and young men in offline settings (Georgakopoulou 2007; Kiesling 2005) and in literary studies (Sedgwick 1985). As the Internet becomes a key social context for people seeking romantic partner, the question of how subsidiary participants take part in online flirtation emerges. Scholarly approaches to online dating practices have focused on interaction and self- and other-presentation among users online, whereas homosocial aspects of such practices (i.e. how user's social networks take part in the process of finding, assessing and communicating with potential partners) remain under-studied.

This article examines how heterosexual online dating may also involve homosocial activities. Based on audiovisual recordings, analyses show how homosociality frames heterosexual desire construction. The article addresses two questions:

- How is female heterosexual desire for online-mediated men and male bodies enacted in talk in a homosocial context?
- How can desire be understood as a phenomenon established and negotiated by social actors beyond those involved in the romantic act?

By use of the concept of stance-taking (Du Bois 2007) it is demonstrated how homosocially related participants assess male objects according to affiliation on the interpersonal level. It is argued that, in this case, acts of desire are collaborative undertakings, as the production of heterosexual desire is generated through homosocial bonding.

Heterosexual desire and homosociality in interaction

Since digital communication technologies have entered the domestic sphere (Baron 2008), making computers and smartphones an integrated part of the individual's social life, romantic practice is now partly enacted in online contexts. Thus, online dating practices are rich fields of desire production as members continuously, through various modes, articulate and negotiate sexual and romantic wants (e.g. Chapter 11, this volume; Jones 2012).

Within the field of language and sexuality, desire has been theorised with inspiration from psychoanalysis and poststructuralist understandings of power, contributing an emphasis on social and linguistic manifestations (Cameron and Kulick 2003a). In a few words, desire may be understood as that 'which we lack but want' (Kiesling 2005:699).[1] The desire constructed by the women in this study may be broadly termed as a 'desire for a romantic partner', which, broken down, consists of attraction to a complex cluster of aspects (e.g. specific physicality, sexual behaviour, social skills and affectivity) according to which a potential partner is valued.

In her groundbreaking book *Between Men* (1985), literary theorist Eve Kosofsky Sedgwick offers the term *homosocial desire* as a concept for understanding how desire is constructed in social contexts. Desire is a dialogic phenomenon; a social relation rather than an inner individual state. Sedgwick argues that desire operates in a triangular form in such literary themes as marriage arrangements and male rivalry concerning a woman. In these situations, two men are linked in a homosocial relation via a woman. By drawing a line to connect the male subjects in this literal love triangle, Sedgwick highlights the desire established between them. The female object is a conduit for this. Thus, Sedgwick's work illustrates the patriarchal structures of society in which women are traded as commodities and vehicles for the males' reciprocal desires. Sedgwick uses *homosocial desire* as a blanket term for all forms of desire within same-gender interaction, ranging from erotic desires at one end of a continuum, to social desires at the other (Sedgwick 1985:2). This paper focuses on two interrelated aspects of homosocial desire: *heterosexual desire* (i.e. sexual and romantic desire directed at the opposite gender) and *homosociality* (i.e. the interactional negotiation of both heterosexual and homosocial desire in same-gender contexts).

Not surprisingly, given its origin in masculinity studies, research into the concept of homosocial desire within language, gender and sexuality has been deployed primarily in analyses of men's interaction (Kiesling 2005, 2011; Milani and Jonsson 2011). A body of sociolinguistic work on girls and women talking desirously about boys and men also exists, but is not explicitly framed in terms of homosocial desire, but rather by such concepts as friendship and connection among female peers (Eder 1993; Georgakopoulou 2007; Kotthoff 2008; Mortensen 2010). As Kiesling (2002, 2005, 2011) points out, heterosexual desire is a widely used resource for performing homosocial desire. While the women also use heterosexual desire as a resource for forging a homosocial relation, this article aims to understand how stance-taking in homosocial interaction creates a framework for the construction of heterosexual desire. As demonstrated, the women's desire for homosocial engagement makes them adjust and negotiate their expressions of heterosexual desire.

Taking desirous stances

In the present study, I map Sedgwick's triangular model of homosocial desire onto the linguistic model of the stance triangle (Du Bois 2007), since the process of desire construction in this context is ultimately carried out by taking desirous stances towards male objects. According to Du Bois, stance-taking comprises the explicit act of expressing one's stance towards a stance object, while at the same time it includes acts of subject positioning and intersubjectivity. Any type of stance is enacted dialogically and always includes three simultaneous aspects: evaluation, positioning, and alignment (Du Bois 2007:169). This triangular model allows us to understand how stances of shared desire create social bonds between subjects in interaction. The stances taken by the women in the present case function as the projection of desire onto online male bodies while at the same time establishing solidarity in the homosocial relation. The most outspoken way of doing stance in this context is through assessment talk, defined by Goodwin and Goodwin (1992:154) as 'evaluating in some fashion persons and events being described within talk'. The online dating site constitutes an environment that invites assessment talk, as participating in the site's activities partly consist in assessing other members. Through assessment sequences, users articulate and negotiate specific romantic/erotic preferences. By observing the objects being assessed, the assessables, and how these are evaluated either positively or negatively, it is possible to understand what is being viewed as desirous in this context. Additionally, turn-by-turn analysis of how interpersonal stances are achieved through alignment and affiliation (Stivers 2008) gives concrete insight into how desire is generated through homosocial bonding.

In this study, the women's stances may be understood as elements in the process of heterosexual female identity construction. According to Thurlow and Jarworski (2011:245) social identity may be conceptualised as the accumulation of stances taken over time. Bucholtz (2009:2) points out that stances do not directly index specific identity categories such as gender or sexuality, but are better understood as interactional moves for constructing personas. The stances taken by the women in the present study should not be interpreted as direct indicators of the identity category of 'heterosexual woman'. Rather, they are part of the activity of developing coordinated erotic taste. Arguably, this activity feeds into a broader construction of identity, as it is carried out repeatedly in various contexts, accumulating positions that in interplay with larger macro-level ideologies produce solid heterosexual identities.

While stance-taking has recently been investigated in relation to online environments (Jones, Schieffelin and Smith 2011; Walton and Jaffe 2011; Kang and Chen 2014), such studies focus purely on the online mode. Likewise, although online media have been accorded a great deal of attention in recent research, online dating is still under-investigated. Within the tradition of language, gender and sexuality studies, a majority of the existing work focuses on gay men's online dating and erotic activities (e.g. Canakis 2010; King 2011; Milani 2013). Most existing research on heterosexual online dating has a main focus on textual self- and other-presentation in dating profiles (e.g. Ellison, Heino and Gibbs 2006; Jacobs 2010; Frohlick and Migliardi 2011). The interactional aspect of online dating has not gained as much attention in the literature, perhaps due to challenges regarding the collection of naturally occurring data with informed consent.[2] However, a few researchers have examined the interactional strategies of users in heterosexual and gay dating chat rooms, based on interactional data (Adams-Thies 2012; Del-Teso-Craviotto 2008; Jones 2005; King 2011).[3]

In the present study, I focus on interaction both online on the dating site and offline in front of the screen, in order to examine how shared stance-taking at the micro level of turn-by-turn interaction shapes the construction of desire.

Browsing together

As part of a larger project on language and heterosexual desire, I carried out ethnographic fieldwork among female users of online dating. From observations and interviews, it appeared that engaging in each other's online dating activities was a widespread practice. Most commonly, such activities would consist of showing specific male profiles to each other – an activity that increased throughout my fieldwork as the shared accessibility to dating sites enhanced via smartphone applications.[4] More rarely, collective dating activities would involve recommending male users to friends, if they were considered to be a better match for a friend. Following up on this observation, I asked two female friends to record their shared engagement in online dating activities. The recording was initiated by me, but it documented a common everyday activity when spending time together.

This paper focuses on the conversation between Louise and Stine (both names are pseudonyms). The women were aged 29 and 30, respectively, at the time of the study, and had been close friends since their teenage years. Both were experienced online daters, with profiles on and off the largest Danish dating site, www.dating.dk. The women's way of spending time together involved regular meetings and weekly phone calls in which they, among other things, would talk about personal romantic and erotic activities. The recording was carried out one evening at Louise's apartment home. Throughout most of the recording, the women were logged onto Stine's account. At the end of the conversation they briefly logged onto Louise's account and then returned to Stine's. During the conversation, the women browsed through 43 male profiles – 34 while logged onto Stine's profile and 9 while logged onto Louise's profile.

The recording was made using the screen-tracking software Hypercam. This software enables the researcher to audio record face-to-face offline interaction, as well as visually tracking the screen and the cursor movements of the simultaneous online interaction. The excerpts in this article are represented as multimodal transcriptions in order to capture spoken conversation, cursor movements and screen activity. This type of audiovisual online and offline data offers a unique opportunity to look at the construction of heterosexual desire, while also providing insight into how simultaneous homosocial interaction plays into this process. It has been pointed out in studies within computer-mediated communication that a strict distinction between online and offline modes cannot be upheld since participants treat the two modes as intertwined; users give social meaning to online activities in offline contexts, and vice versa (Barton and Lee 2013; Ellison, Steinfield and Lampe 2006; Stæhr 2014). The recorded Hypercam data offers an insight into how online and offline modes are synthesised in immediate interaction. Being able to analyse face-to-face interaction simultaneously with screen activity provides a basis for understanding how participants manage interaction with multiple participants and in multiple modes at the same time. Moreover, access to both cursor movements and spoken conversation opens up a perspective on how online media are read and given meaning, since the data demonstrates which online functions are operated by the users and which features on the screen are given value. In the transcription of the excerpts, mouse activity is documented, since working the mouse in this context is an important interactional resource. Mouse manoeuvres generate points of attention and arguments in the verbal interaction, and thus they become a medium for turn-taking (cf. Raudaskoski 2003). As it will become evident in the analysis, talk and cursor acts are entirely integrated, since talk manages attention on the screen and cursor movements manages talk. Therefore, online and offline interaction cannot be distinguished as two aspects deriving from two different places, but must be viewed as one complex context of multimodal interaction.

The dating site as a frame for desire construction

Recent statistics from Denmark show that around 500,000 people out of a total population of 5 million make use of online dating services (Danske Medier 2012). www.dating.dk is the oldest and largest dating site in Denmark, founded in 1995 and hosting approximately 100,000 users. The site primarily serves heterosexual

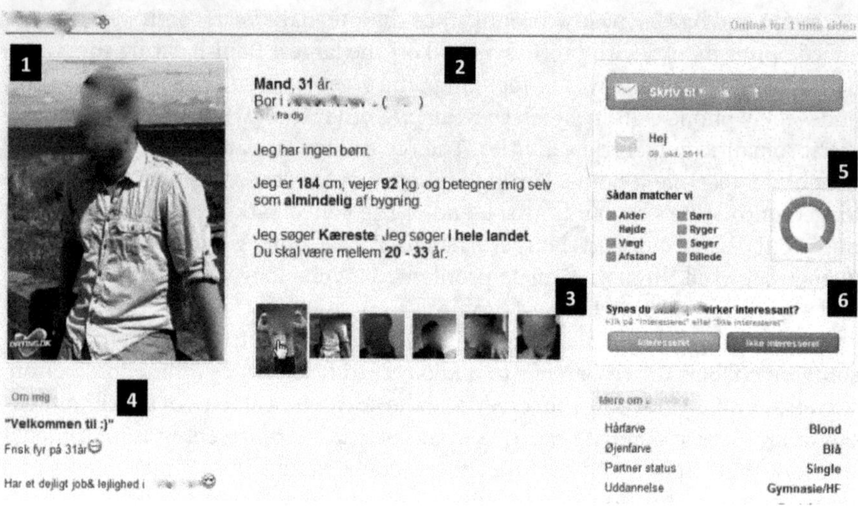

Figure 1: Male personal profile on www.dating.dk.

users and offers membership that allows users to create a personal profile, view others' profiles, and be viewed by others. To be able to contact other users, a paying membership of 219 Danish kroner (around 40 US dollars) is required.

On entering the site, the women are presented with a row of male users who fit their predefined search criteria. Figure 1 depicts a male profile as viewed through Stine and Louise's accounts. The dating site interface enables the multimodal display of the user, involving photographs, written text and graphic elements.

The display of the male user is divided into several parts, featuring a clear information hierarchy. A profile photo features prominently as the largest element in the layout (1). A short list of facts has a central position in the profile, informing the reader of physical characteristics, geographical location, children status and preferred type of relationship (2). Below, a previewed list of additional photos appears (3), which the reader can click on to enter a photo album with further visual information. The actual profile text in which the profile owner describes himself in a continuous text appears as the last section and requires the reader to scroll down to view the full text (4). The women's reading paths generally follow the structure laid down by the site – that is, they first orient towards the large profile photo, and then typically access the photo album (3). Hence, the site's information hierarchy plays a dominant role in determining to which aspects of the objects desire is attached. The profile design clearly serves to categorise looks and physical attributes as prominent aspects of a romantic partner. Only few users act against the visual focus of the profile by simply not uploading any photos to their profile. However, in such cases Stine and Louise reject the profile owner without even reading the text. This corresponds to information from other users who, when interviewed, reported that they had remarkably more success in getting in touch with other users when they uploaded photos to their profiles.

The profile view further offers a line of matching options and interactive choices, of which the women make use of the 'Perfect Match' scheme (5) and the interested/not-interested function (6). The match scheme helps the visitor to quickly assess whether she is compatible, according to predefined preferences (age, height, weight, body, smoking habits, geographical proximity, children status, preferred type of relationship, and whether the profile includes photos). If all predefined categories fit each party's preferences, the display will show a full green circle with a blinking golden star. Once again, the site's predefined parameters for a 'perfect match' influence what users may be oriented towards when defining the right partner. However, the site offers an additional service for individual preferences via an advanced search function in which preferred details of appearance, career and lifestyle can be entered. The 'interested/not-interested' function is used as a channel for initial contact, as it allows the reader to inform the profile owner of her interest without having to send a personal email. The function is applied by clicking either the color-coded green 'interested' or red 'not interested', whereupon the reader – if interested – will be listed among other interested visitors on the profile owner's account, as seen in Figure 2.

This is the most favoured communicative function among the women. It is the first option they are oriented towards when they enter their accounts, and they keep returning to this list. This is a simplified and very binarised way of expressing potential desire, or the lack thereof, and as such restricts the users in terms of the ways that they can categorise each other. Rather than spending time and emotional energy on producing a free text via an email, the interested/not-interested option appeals to users, as they can quickly test reciprocal interest. The simple selection enhances the number of users who can be communicated with, thereby creating an efficient means of communication. Additionally, the function seems to encourage a pick-and-choose attitude, since saying yes or no is operated through a simple click on an icon.

In the following, the women's shared reading and assessments of the male profiles will be examined. The analysis focuses on how they construct and negotiate shared desire, knowing that the architecture of the dating site plays into the desire that they are able to produce.

Figure 2: List of interested visitors on Stine's profile.

Non-desire, desire and adjustments

In the analysis I demonstrate how the participants, through stance-taking practices, engage in the activities of doing non-desire, desire and adjustment of desire. The analysis of this article falls into three sections. First, I focus on how non-desire is co-constructed through collaborative format tying (Goodwin 2006) and distinction (Bucholtz and Hall 2005). Second, I explore how initial non-desire can be negotiated into shared desire. Finally, I examine how individual desire is adjusted to ensure affiliation in the homosocial relation.

Constructing shared heterosexual non-desire

Most of the conversation between the women is characterised by the joint achievement of stances on the male users they browse through. The composite nature of these stances suggests that the construction of non-desire is just as important an online dating activity as the construction of desire. The excerpt below demonstrates how the women co-construct negative assessments of a male object.

Excerpt 1

See the appendix to this article for a guide to transcript notation used for all excerpts.

	Speaker	Turn	Mouse movements	Screen
1	LOU:	°ej undskyld° men er han ikke en lille bitte smule bælgøjet **°excuse me° but isn't he a little bit pop-eyed**		
2			Stine holds the mouse still throughout the following 28 turns.	
3	STI:	jo **yes**		
4		så er det li- han har sgu da lidt- et meget rundt hoved **then it's just- he's really got a bit- a very round head**		
5	LOU:	@[@@] 		
6	STI:	[@] @		
7		han [mangler da-] **isn't he [lacking-]**		
8	LOU:	[uden at være] tyk **[without being] fat**		
9	STI:	mang[ler] **lack[ing]**		
10	LOU:	[så er] han faktisk meget- **[he's] actually quite-**		
11	STI:	mangler han ikke lidt kindben **isn't he lacking a bit of cheekbone**		
12		og lidt [ø:h] **and a bit of [u:h]**		
13	LOU:	[KÆBE] **[JAW]**		

14		han mangler kæbe **he's lacking jaw**		
15	STI:	og kæbe **and jaw**		
16	LOU:	men han mangler også kindben **but he's also lacking cheekbones**		
17		og så lidt **and then a bit**		
18		ej jeg ve:- °også lidt retardo øjne° **argh I do:n't- °and then a bit retardedo eyes°**		
19	STI:	ja **yes**		
20	LOU:	kukkuk((animated)) **cuckoo ((animated))**		
21	STI:	@ @[@@ @@@]	Stine presses the "not interested" icon and the page changes to the next profile on the list.	DETAIL
22	LOU:	[@@ @@@]@		

Louise starts out by assessing the man negatively, according to his looks (i.e. his eyes; turn 1). Initially, she lowers her voice noticeably while expressing an attention getter: 'ej undskyld' ('excuse me') – signalling that what follows may challenge general rules of politeness. Thus, the derogatory adjective ('bælgøjet', 'pop-eyed') has been prepared for and thereby potentially mitigated. The only other instance of 'undskyld' in the conversation appears just before a similarly derogatory utterance. Interestingly, this use of mitigation suggests that a participation framework specific to the ongoing activity is at work. Since they are, at the moment of talking, logged onto Stine's profile, Louise has reason to refrain from exercising epistemic stance authority (Heritage and Raymond 2005) – in this context, refraining from producing radical first-turn assessments, especially negative ones. In other words, she avoids downgrading candidates that Stine might approve of, and vice versa.

It should be noted that in previous assessments of 11 other men, Louise has shown no reluctance whatsoever to offer immediate negative comments. In this case she does not, thus potentially making this man a special case. So it may be argued that by lowering her voice and mitigating her assessment, she potentially draws attention to this candidate.

What follows, consequently, is an evaluation of a series of attributes. Stine introduces another assessable – the man's head being 'round' (turn 4). This observation sets off simultaneous laughter and thereby affective affiliation (turns 5–6).

In following turns (7–17), the women further construe the male object as laughable and deviant by pointing to several deficiencies in his facial features (jaw, cheekbones). This is accomplished through rapid interaction containing, for example, overlapping turns (7–8, 9–10, 12–13) and co-produced turns (11–13). In adolescent girls' assessment talk, Goodwin observes, overlapping turns are a 'way the participants can display that their minds are together' (Goodwin 2006:202). In the excerpt, another means to obtain this effect is the continuous use of 'lidt' ('a bit') – Stine in turns 4, 11 and 12, and Louise in turns 17 and 18. Overall, the women obtain full affiliation in that every candidate object of assessment (jaw, cheekbones, etc.) is readily acknowledged or topped (turns 11–18).

In turn 18, Louise draws a full circle by returning to the eyes. She emphasises her initial observation, using an even more degrading term 'retardo øjne' ('retardo eyes'), hinting at a person with disabilities. And she lowers her voice. Whispering indicates a change of mode and may thus be considered an act of intimacy in this context. This build-up of affective affiliation is ultimately acted out in turns 20–22 with ridicule and mutual laughter. Finally, Stine clicks the 'not-interested' icon thus ending the assessment activity. This move is fitted into the women's laughter and it may therefore be regarded in parallel with a spoken turn contributing to the ongoing interaction.

By comparing the man to a person with disabilities, he is positioned as an unsuitable object for desire under heteronormative ideologies. Research within disability studies has shown that both the media and broader ideologies depict disabled men and women as asexual (Gartner and Joe 1987; Haller 2000). Since gender and sexuality are intrinsically bound together, the man is not only desexualised, but also demasculinised (Robertson 2004), thus exposed to an overall marginalisation in the heterosexual marketplace (Eckert 2011). As the women metaphorically 'dissect' the male object, they align in the assessment that every part of his physical appearance is unsuitable for desire. Thus, this could potentially be interpreted as an abilist act tying into and reproducing larger ideologies for which bodies can be attached with desire.

Tied to the women's positioning of the other is an oppositional positioning of themselves as normative and attractive subjects within the same heteronormative ideology. In their collaboratively produced assessment, they affirm each other's positions as abled heterosexual women and recognise their co-performed non-desire as normative. By co-constructing stances and by drawing on encompassing ideologies of disability as asexual, the women highlight their difference from the man (cf. Bucholtz and Hall 2005). This demonstrates how non-desire functions as an important element in producing heterosexual desire in homosociality, as it works to link the women together and develop coordinated erotic taste.

Constructing shared heterosexual desire

Even though non-desire takes up a major part of the women's browsing activity, non-desire can also be negotiated into desire. Male users' desirousness or the lack thereof is not simply decided upon once and for all, but developed and modified throughout and by means of the interaction. As Stine and Louise are interacting via various modes with the profiles of the male users – photos, personal profile texts, and textual facts about various characteristics such as occupation, body type and geography – they negotiate shared desire according to this information, as well as in relation to each other. The following analysis demonstrates how the women build changing assessments, thus demonstrating that stance is an accomplishment of the interaction.

In the second excerpt, the women first align in a negative assessment of a male user. Later, the assessment is moderated and turned into a positive assessment. After having gone through the automatically generated matches, the women turn to the visitor's list, which is an overview of users who have visited Stine's profile. Here they click into a profile in order to review the photos and information.

Excerpt 2a

	Speaker	Spoken language	Mouse movements	Screen
1	LOU:	okay der får du sgu da **okay there you really get some**		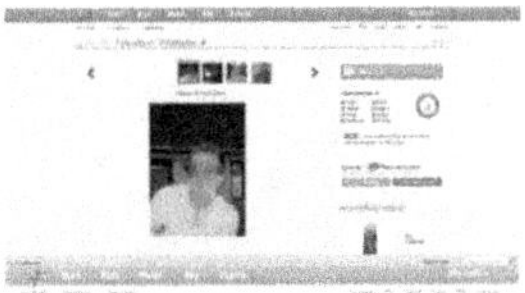
2		kindben eller kæbe eller et eller andet **cheekbone or jaw or something**	Louise clicks on the first photo in the photo album and the photo changes.	
3		[til gengæld] også noget af en næse **[on the other hand] also a bit of a nose**		
4	STI:	[og næse] **[and nose]**		
5		**(1.37)**	Louise clicks on the next photo.	
6		men er næs- en stor næse ikke også betyder det ikke også noget andet **but isn't nos- a big nose also a sign of something else**		
7	LOU:	han [ser sgu da <u>sød</u> ud] **he [looks really <u>sweet</u>]**	The photo changes - delayed response to the previous click.	
8	STI:	[han er- meget <u>sød</u> ud] **[he's- looks quite <u>sweet</u>]**		
9		(4.64)	Louise clicks on the next photo. Louise clicks back to the profile overview.	

10 	 **%eng**	nå hvad skriver han **well what does he write**	Louise scrolls down to the man's profile text and moves the mouse across the text. 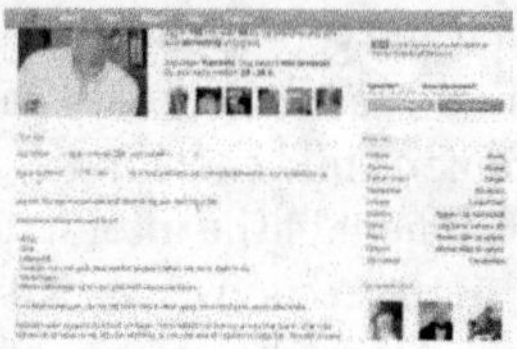
		00:11:30 – 00:12:44: OMITTED, the women read through the man's profile text and search through his photo album	
11	LOU:	@@[@@@@@@@ ej prøv lige at se hans næse der] **@@[@@@@@@@ oh just take a look at his nose there]**	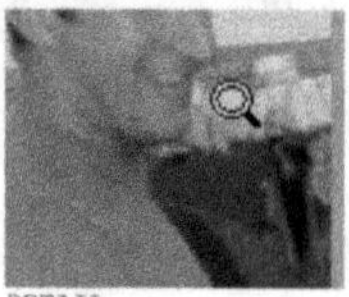 Louise moves the mouse towards the man's nose. DETAIL
12	STI:	[@@@@det er bare om at bytte rundt på noget @@@] **[@@@@ it's just about switching something around @@@]**	
13	LOU:	**[@@@@@@@@@@@]**	
14	STI:	**[@@@@@@@@]**	Louise moves the mouse to the photo album index and clicks on the next photo. 
15		**[@]**	
16	LOU:	**[@]**	
17		**@@@ @[@]**	
18	STI:	[ej] det ved jeg ikke **[oh] I don't know**	Louise clicks on the next photo. 
19		**(1.4)**	
20		[ej det eddermame en Günther han har] **[oh it's a freaking Günther he's got]**	
21	LOU:	[ej den er den er eddermame stor] **[oh it's freaking big]**	
22		**(2.0)**	Louise clicks on the next photo. 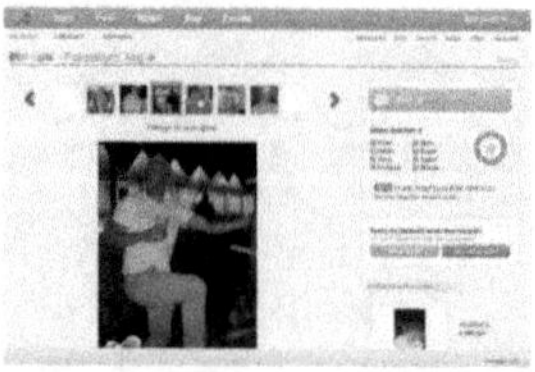

23		forfra er [han altså-] **from the front[he's really-]**	Louise clicks on the next photo.	
24	STI:	[hvad hvad] var hans højde og sådan noget egentlig **[what what] was his height and so on by the way**	Louise clicks on the next photo.	
25			Louise clicks on the next photo.	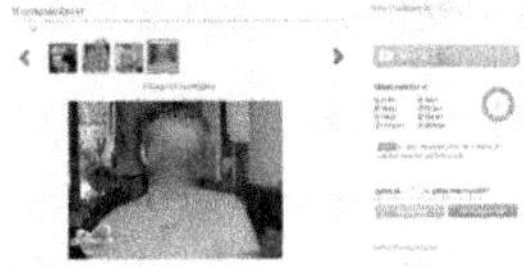
26		han ser da rimelig ø:h **he looks quite u:h**	Louise moves the mouse to the man's username and clicks on it - leads back to the profile overview.	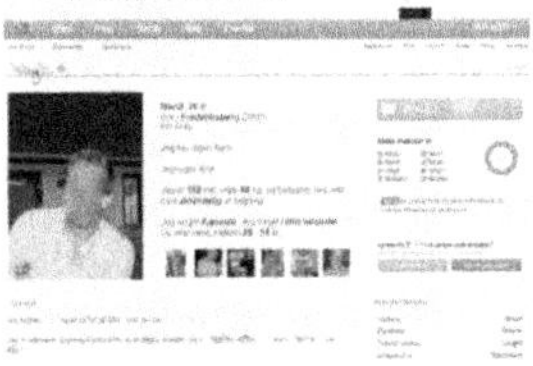
27	LOU:	han ser rimelig stor ud **he looks quite big**		
28	STI:	rimelig stor ud ja **quite big yeah**		
29	LOU:	næ det er han ikke engang det er sgu meget normalt **no he's not really it's really pretty normal**	Louise drags the mouse to the information about the man's height and weight.	
30		**(1.39)**		
31	STI:	årh næsten en halvfems alligevel **oh well still almost one ninety**		
32	LOU:	jo jo men men og så ø:h rent vægtmæssigt **yeah yeah but but and then u:h in terms of weight**	Louise moves the mouse across the physical information and marks height and weight.	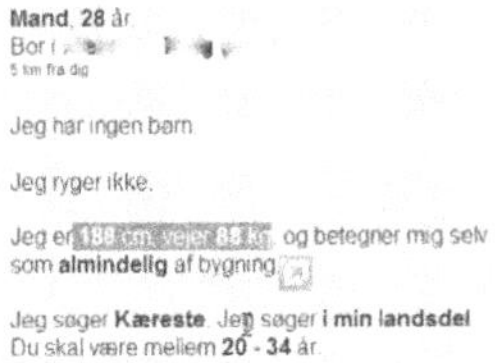 Mand, 28 år Bor i 5 km fra dig Jeg har ingen børn Jeg ryger ikke. Jeg er 188 cm, vejer 88 kg og betegner mig selv som **almindelig** af bygning Jeg søger **Kæreste**. Jeg søger **i min landsdel** Du skal være mellem **20 - 34** år. DETAIL
33	STI:	ja **yes**		
34	LOU:	det er da sådan meget nor- altså **it's well quite nor- really**		
35		**(1.55)**		
36		*normalt* ***normal***		

As in the first excerpt, the assessables in this sequence are primarily the male user's physical body parts. From turns 1–3, the man is assessed positively, in contrast to the male user in the previous example, but this is eventually moderated into aligning negative assessments of his nose (turns 4–5). The size of the man's nose continues as a topic of conversation throughout the excerpt (turns 12–25), but in between, as they search through the man's profile, the women co-construct more positive assessments of his general looks (turns 8–9) and his body type (turns 27–42).[5]

Aligning assessments are produced on several levels. In turns 8–9, they accommodate syntactically as Stine changes the structure halfway through to match Louise's. Stine seems to set out to utter the expression 'han er sød' ('he is sweet'), but then changes the wording to match Louise's 'han ser sød ud' ('he looks sweet'). Later, the women use similar prosodic and lexical features to create affiliation. In response to a photo they say, in overlap: 'ej det eddermame en Gynter han har' ('wow it's a freaking Günther he's got') and 'ej den er (.) den er eddermame stor' ('wow it's freaking big'). The turns are synchronised with 'ej' ('wow') – in itself an explicitly affective exclamative and here almost shouted out. Wordings are practically repeated in overlap and with identical prosody. Furthermore, deployment of identical intensifiers displays reciprocity. Thus, the women create affective affiliation in turn taking, lexis, syntactics and prosody.

The physical focus of Louise and Stine's assessment talk is further reflected in their use of the mouse. In this example, the mouse becomes a part of the offline body by serving as a virtual index finger that can play out gestural moves (turn 12). The cursor touches the virtual male face, pointing out the features talked about, in this case the nose. Through both virtual touch and discussion of the size of the man's nose, and the relation between his height and weight, his body is made almost touchable and physically present. Here, the women incorporate the mouse into their activity and make use of it for interactional purposes, both by stressing specific utterances and by drawing attention to specific details of the men's appearance. In addition, the mouse is the tool by which they can act upon their desire, since clicking on certain icons such as the 'interested' icon serves as a desirous act, in that it sends a message to the man in order to indicate romantic/erotic interest.

Shared enactment of desire

After negotiating the man's desirousness and affiliating aligning in a mostly positive assessment, Louise urges Stine to actively approach the man, which, in turn, is developed into a shared 'plan to act on' their constructed desire.

Excerpt 2b

37		der er perfect match ((blød stemme)) **there's a perfect match ((soft voice))**	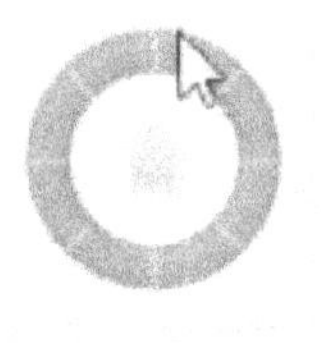 Louise moves the mouse to the "perfect match" scheme. DETAIL
38		**(1.25)**	
39		og han er online ((blød stemme)) **and he's online ((soft voice))**	Louise draws the mouse back to the profile photo.
40		sikker på du ikke er interesseret **sure you're not interested**	Louise draws the mouse towards the center of the page and further up to the right corner.
41		ej jeg må hellere lade være med at styre musen **no I'd best not control the mouse**	
42	STI:	nej øh øh hvis bare tryk interesseret men [hvis du:-] **no uh uh if just press interested but [if you:-]**	
	LOU:	[°det er din°]	
43		**[°it's yours°]**	
	STI:	han skriver så svarer du **he writes then you'll**	
44		**answer**	
45		**(2.19)**	
46	LOU:	det er I orden **that's OK**	The mouse is moved to the "interes-ted" icon, and clicks 

After agreeing on a man's desirousness the women have to decide whether to approach and express their interest by clicking on the interested icon and thereby initiating contact. In this case, Louise is the vehicle for reaching a decision on this matter. Through simultaneous linguistic and cursor acts, she draws Stine's attention to the fact that the man is a 'perfect match' and that he is online, thereby implying that communication in real time is a possibility (turns 37, 39). At this point, she deploys prosody by softening her voice, perhaps to create a more intimate and confidential, maybe even romantically loaded, atmosphere. Here, Louise's performed desire is interactionally channeled into Stine's. As they are logged onto Stine's account, Stine will appear as the sender of any information about romantic interest, even though Louise may be the one to operate the mouse.

After a pause with no response from Stine, Louise takes up another strategy, withdrawing from her attempts to convince Stine to approach the man: 'ej jeg må hellere lade være med at styre musen' ('no I'd best not control the mouse'; turn 41). Here, it is made clear that by controlling the mouse Louise is able to actively act upon her own desire for the man, on behalf of Stine. Regarding the system of turn-taking, the mouse control (or the lack thereof) may be viewed as a turn, which regulates who is speaking when. She thereby offers Stine the opportunity to take control of the mouse and choose whether to approach the man or to move on to the next man on the list. Stine responds by rejecting the offer, instead engaging Louise further in the enactment of desire by instructing her to answer if he returns the interest with an email (turns 51, 53). Through this utterance, she abstains from the option to express her desire individually and instead actively engages Louise in potential future romantic activity. This explicit wish for co-enacting desire demonstrates that the homosocial context does not simply frame the activities preceding heterosexual interaction between Stine and the male user. It also comes to frame the potential future heterosexual interaction, as Stine pre-engages Louise in future correspondence with the man.

Taking desirous stances does not always function as a more or less agreeing process. Discrepancies between individually constructed desires do appear in the data. The following example demonstrates how personal stances are adjusted in order to maintain affiliation in the homosocial relation.

Negotiating and adjusting desire

In excerpt 3 the women are searching through the list of who has visited Stine's profile in the past. Here, Stine specifically draws attention to a male user that she has seen on some earlier occasion and found desirable. She begins with a presentation of the man, in which she assesses him positively. As Louise does not align completely, Stine adjusts her initial evaluation.

The excerpt demonstrates more generally how the construction of affiliation in the homosocial relation comes to frame the desire that Stine can produce towards the specific man.

Excerpt 3

	Speaker	Turn	Cursor movements	Screen
01	STI:	nu skal jeg vise dig en jeg synes var meget sød **now I'll show you someone who I thought was pretty sweet**	Stine clicks on the "next-page" icon in the lower right-hand corner.	
02		ham der **this guy**	Stine points to the man's face on the photo and clicks on it so that they enter the man's profile.	 DETAIL
03	LOU:	nå XXX((mandens brugernavn)) ((oplæsnings stemme)) **huh XXX ((the male's username)) ((reading voice))**		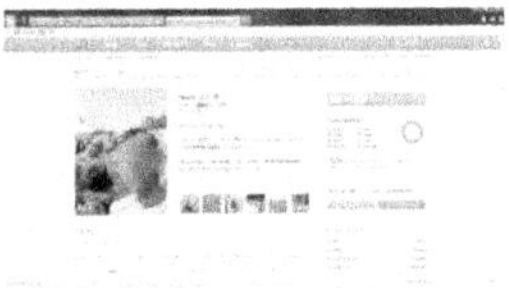
04		°ja° **°yes°**	Stine scrolls down the page.	
05	STI:	HAN ser sød ud **HE looks sweet**	Stine points to the second photo in the photo album and clicks to enter the man's photo album.	 DETAIL
06		nu skal jeg vise dig her **now I'll show you here**		
07		BOM KØNT ansigt hvad **BOM ((onomatopoeia)) HANDSOME face huh**	Stine circles the cursor twice around the man's face and then moves towards the upper right part of the page.	 DETAIL
08		ikke så meget hår på hovedet men- **not too much hair on the head but-**	Stine moves back to the photo and points to the man's hair, then moves back towards the upper right part of the page.	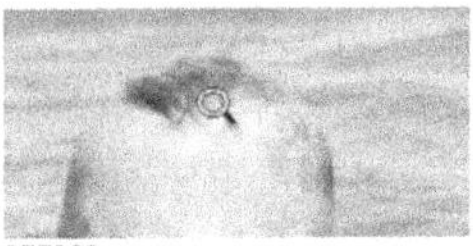 DETAIL
09		ja **yes**		
10	LOU:	men det er heller ikke håret der- **anyhow it isn't the hair that's-**	Stine clicks to the next photo.	

11	STI:	BOM LÆKKERT ANSIGT **BOM HOT FACE**	Stine clicks to the next photo.	
12		[JE:P] wakeboard **[YE:S] wakeboard**	Stine clicks to the next photo.	DETAIL 
13	LOU:	[ja det er fedt<X hvor er vi bare ikke X> ((mumlende stemme))] **[yes it's cool <X how we just aren't X> ((mumbling voice))]**		
14	STI:	lidt lidt tynd til mig jeg kan godt lide der er lidt mere **a bit a bit too skinny for me I like when there's a bit more**	Stine clicks to the next photo.	
15	LOU:	jeg skulle lige til at sige hvor vil du lave en doughnut på ham **I was just about to say where are you going to make a doughnut on him**	Stine clicks to the next photo.	DETAIL 
16	STI:	@@@ balden **@@@ the buttock**	Stine clicks to the next photo.	

Stine opens by introducing – both through talk and cursor manoeuvres – an assessable (the man) and taking an evaluative lead towards him with her personally accountable positive assessment (turn 1). The mouse click serves to introduce a new visual topic filling the spot opened by 'en' ('someone') in the verbal turn – specifying by pointing the cursor to the man's face. Thus, the mouse manoeuvre emphasises visually the argument presented in the verbal turns. This goes for the excerpt from beginning to end. As Stine has viewed this man on an earlier occasion, the women are not exploring him together and thereby do not possess the same epistemic stance authority (Heritage and Raymond 2005). Here, Stine takes the role of the presenter, with expertise on the assessable that precedes Louise's. Prior to this viewing, Stine has categorised the man as attractive and the following joint exploration of him serves as an attempt to engage Louise equally in the desirous stance. This is done as a 'guided tour' through the man's photo album, in which Stine repeats and develops her positive assessment by shifting from a personally accountable past-tense formulation to a declarative present tense, making the evaluation of the man's desirousness relevant in the current situated context (turn 5). Following, she uses a tag question to downgrade her stance authority, and thereby indicates similar rights available to Louise (turn 7). In the path of her assessment series, she moves from more general comments on the man's looks to tuning in on his face, drawing attention to it with the cursor (turn 7), thus demonstrating that, in this context, a face in itself may count for the person in total. Throughout her presentation, an accompanying strong affective involvement is build up by onomatopoeia, emphatic stress and increased volume (turns 5, 7, 11, 12).

Louise engages in the positive assessment production, but with strong discrepancies in affective involvement. Typically, second assessment production includes upgrade or same evaluation (Pomerantz 1984). However, Louise's responses throughout appear disengaged and are characterised by delay through preface, low volume, mumbling voice and unfinished turns (3, 4, 10, 13). This response pattern stands in stark contrast to the previous excerpts in which assessments were co-produced through quick format tying, upgrades and repetitions.

In response to Louise's lack of expressed desire, Stine incorporates alternative assessables, which she assesses negatively (e.g. hair and body type; turns 8, 14). The target lines appear when Stine draws attention to the man's body type, which consequently receives a changed and affectively engaged second assessment from Louise in the form of a critical joking question 'hvor vil du lave en doughnut på ham' ('where are you going to make a doughnut on him'; turn 15). In this context, doughnut refers to a roll of fat on the stomach around the navel that, when squeezed together, resembles a doughnut. On several occasions during the conversation the women state that they like men who are 'bigger' and not overly muscular. To be able to make 'a doughnut' in this context, therefore, refers to this particular physical desire. By orienting towards previous affiliating erotic taste, Louise manages to strengthen the homosocial relation that, in this case, is potentially threatened by an imbalance in erotic preferences.

In the above analysis, an assessable is introduced as attractive by one participant. Yet since the other participant does not recognise the performed desire and agree explicitly, the initial evaluator starts to incorporate more critical commentary, pointing out particular body features as problematic. This adjustment of desire illustrates the influence of the homosocial relation on what kind of desire is possible in this particular context. The desire for homosocial affiliation in this case very clearly frames the heterosexual desire that is produced.

Conclusion

Inspired by Sedgwick's (1985) development of the notion of desire, this article has examined heterosexual desire construction through the lens of homosociality. By discovering homosocial interaction as a setting for the social production and negotiation of romantic and erotic desire, the above analysis has demonstrated how homosociality comes to frame heterosexual desire.

As Stine and Louise engage in the activity of assessing men as desirous objects they build consensual versions of what attractive and unattractive men are like. The production of corresponding interpersonal stances demonstrates the importance of a third party's approval of the object of desire and how a lack of affiliation is dealt with by downgrading the initial desire. As Sedgwick argues, the object mainly becomes desirable through the desire of a same-gender participant – and then, on the other hand, loses its attractiveness if it is not recognised in the homosocial relation. Thus, homosociality influences what kind of desire is possible. This phenomenon highlights the need to include homosocial contexts in order to arrive at a full analysis of how shared desire construction and negotiation play into and shape the romantic and sexual lives of women and men.

In the online dating context, part of being a heterosexual woman is to recognise and execute a physically focused desire in which appearance and, in particular, physical features are at the centre of the evaluation. As the analysis demonstrates, the physical focus is further refined and emphasised by the women as they reduce male users to fragmented body parts (e.g. jawlines, cheekbones, noses or hair), pinpointed with the help of the cursor. This foregrounding of traditional male physicality can potentially be seen as a contestation on the women's part of a hegemonic desire system in which heterosexual men generally value partners according to physical attributes and women according to socio-economic status (Coupland 1996). This is further supported by the fact that the women generally respond with immediate rejection to pure textual profiles that do not feature any visual representations of the male. However, the physically oriented desire is established from the outset by the website design and the general activity of online dating, which by its nature requires assessments of appearance. Thus, the women may simply buy into an established romantic and sexual economy in which the building blocks for hegemonic masculine appearance (e.g. strong jawlines, or noses as symbols for genitals) have the highest value. As Eckert (2002:109) points out, physical attraction is a 'social course of learning', and the process of reading and assessing online dating profiles can thus be seen as a way for the women to accommodate and negotiate what female heterosexual desire looks like.

The shared practice of attaching desire to male objects may be described as an inversion of Sedgwick's desire triangle – a way for women to turn the tables and exercise the right to use patriarchal power in the same way as it has predominantly been ascribed to men. The women take up the position of desiring subjects who bond through a shared desire for particular men presented on the dating site. The men thus function as commodities in a consumption process in which heterosexual desire and non-desire can be performed. Furthermore, these same male commodities take on the function of inter-linking the women, acting as a conduit for their social desire towards each other. Paradoxically, the male objects that connect the women in the homosocial relation will eventually interrupt the homosociality, if a romantic heterosexual relationship is formed. As much as the women work to bond in their shared desire, this same desire production works to dissolve their homosocial intimacy.

The inversion of the triangular model may challenge female objectification, but does not as such question the objectification and sexualisation of the body itself. In this sense, heterosexual online dating sites such as the one discussed in this article should not be perceived as a field giving rise to new and hitherto unseen forms of desire construction, but rather as a sustained arena for multifaceted and highly homosocially influenced desire constructions.

Appendix: transcription conventions

(number)	timed pause
[word]	overlap
@	laughter, each token marks one pulse
°word°	low volume
WORD	high volume
word	whisper
word	stress
<X words X>	uncertain transcription
word-	unfinished word or sentence/broken off
wo:rd	extension of word
XXX	anonymisation
((word))	comment

Notes

1 This simplified definition serves as a starting point for thinking about desire, but should not elude one from considering the more complex workings of desire and its relation to power. For further discussions, see Harvey and Shalom (1997) and Cameron and Kulick (2003b).

2 Mortensen (2015) elaborates on the topic of the collection of intimate data.

3 All scholars focus on chat rooms, which in the case of Danish online dating services are a form of communication that is losing its popularity. For instance, the most used dating service in Denmark, www.dating.dk, does not even offer the option of participation in general chat room interaction, but solely offers personal emails and private chats.

4 Since I conducted the major part of my fieldwork in 2011–12, online dating has advanced rapidly in line with general digital development. The most striking change was the launch of the application Tinder, which works as a simple application that connects to a member's Facebook account and smartphone GPS. Thus, users are supplied with quick and accurate information on a potential partner's social network and geographical proximity. More than 150,000 Danes are currently using Tinder. My ongoing observations of the dating culture among research participants and my own personal network show that the convenience and constant access to the online dating market provided by smartphone applications, has increased the homosocial activity of co-assessing potential romantic partners.

5 Stine's utterance in turn 13, 'det er bare om at bytte rundt på noget' ('it's just a question of switching something around'), refers to previous turns in which she has been comparing the male user's name to a sexual term. This adds to the sexual innuendo that she continuously brings into the evaluation.

References

Adams-Thies, B. (2012) Fluid bodies or bodily fluids: bodily reconfigurations in cybersex. *Journal of Language and Sexuality* 1(2): 179–205. https://doi.org/10.1075/jls.1.2.03ada

Baron, N. S. (2008) *Always on: Language in an Online and Mobile World*. Oxford: Oxford University Press. https://doi.org/10.1093/acprof:oso/9780195313055.001.0001

Barton, D., and Lee, C. (2013) *Language Online: Investigating Digital Texts and Practices*. Abingdon: Routledge.

Bucholtz, M. (2009) From stance to style: gender, interaction, and indexicality in Mexican immigrant youth slang. In A. Jaffe (ed.) *Stance: Sociolinguistic Perspectives* 146–70. Oxford: Oxford University Press. https://doi.org/10.1093/acprof:oso/9780195331646.003.0007

Bucholtz, M. and Hall, K. (2004) Theorizing identity in language and sexuality research. *Language in Society* 33(4): 469–515. https://doi.org/10.1017/S0047404504334020

Bucholtz, M. and Hall, K. (2005) Identity and interaction: a sociocultural linguistic approach. *Discourse Studies* 7(4–5): 585–614. https://doi.org/10.1177/1461445605054407

Cameron, D. and Kulick, D. (2003a) *Language and Sexuality*. New York: Cambridge University Press. https://doi.org/10.1017/CBO9780511791178

Cameron, D. and Kulick, D. (2003b) Introduction: language and desire in theory and practice. *Language and Communication* 23(2): 93–105. https://doi.org/10.1016/S0271-5309(02)00047-2

Campbell-Kibler, K., Podesva, R. J., Roberts, S. J. and Wong, A. (eds) (2002) *Language and Sexuality: Contesting Meaning in Theory and Practice*. Stanford, CA: CSLI Publications.

Canakis, C. (2010) Eroticing male homo-subjectivities in online personals. In C. Canakis, V. Kantsa and K. Yiannakopoulos (eds) *Language and Sexuality (Through And) Beyond Gender* 143–70. Newcastle upon Tyne: Cambridge Scholar Publishing.

Coupland, J. (1996) Dating advertisements: discourses of the commodified self. *Discourse and Society* 7(2): 187–207. https://doi.org/10.1177/0957926596007002003

Danske Medier (2012) *Danskernes brug af internettet*. Copenhagen: Danske Medier.

Del-Teso-Craviotto, M. (2008) Gender and sexual identity authentication in language use: the case of chat rooms. *Discourse Studies* 10(2): 251–70. https://doi.org/10.1177/1461445607087011

Du Bois, J. (2007) The stance triangle. In R. Englebretson (ed.) *Stancetaking in Discourse: Subjectivity, Evaluation, Interaction* 139–82. Amsterdam: John Benjamins. https://doi.org/10.1075/pbns.164.07du

Eckert, P. (2002) Demystifying sexuality and desire. In Campbell-Kibler *et al.* (2002): 99–110.

Eckert, P. (2011) Language and power in the preadolescent heterosexual market. *American Speech* 86(1): 85–97. https://doi.org/10.1215/00031283-1277528

Eder, D. (1993) 'Go get ya a French!' Romantic and sexual teasing among adolescent girls. In D. Tannen (ed.) *Gender and Conversational Interaction* 17–31. New York: Oxford University Press.

Ellison, N. B., Heino, R. D. and Gibbs, J. L. (2006) Managing impressions online: self-presentation processes in the online dating environment. *Journal of Computer-Mediated Communication* 11(2): 415–41. https://doi.org/10.1111/j.1083-6101.2006.00020.x

Ellison, N., Steinfield C. and Lampe, C. (2006) Spatially bounded online social networks and social capital: the role of Facebook. Retrieved on 14 May 2012 from www.ucalgary.ca/files/stas341/Facebook_ICA_2006.pdf

Frohlick, S. and Migliardi, P. (2011) Heterosexual profiling. *Australian Feminist Studies* 26(67): 73–88. https://doi.org/10.1080/08164649.2010.546329

Gartner, A. and Joe, T. (1987) Introduction. In A. Gartner and T. Joe (eds) *Images of the Disabled, Disabling Images* 1–7. New York: Praeger Publishers.

Georgakopoulou, A. (2007) Positioning in style: men in women's jointly produced stories. In P. Auer (ed.) *Style and Social Identities: Alternative Approaches to Linguistic Heterogeneity* 393–418. Berlin: Mouton de Gruyter.

Goodwin, C. and Goodwin, M. H. (1992) Assessment and the construction of context. In A. Duranti and C. Goodwin (eds) *Rethinking Context: Language as an Interactive Phenomenon* 147–90. Cambridge: Cambridge University Press.

Goodwin, M. H. (2006) *The Hidden Life of Girls: Games of Stance, Status, and Exclusion*. Malden, MA: Blackwell. https://doi.org/10.1002/9780470773567

Haller, B. (2000) If they limp, they lead? News representations and the hierarchy of disability images. In D. O. Braithwaite and T. L. Thompson (eds) *Handbook of Communication and People with Disabilities: Research and Application* 273–88. Mahwah, NJ: Lawrence Erlbaum Associates.

Harvey, K. and Shalom, C. (1997) *Language and Desire: Encoding Sex, Romance and Intimacy*. London: Routledge.

Heritage, J. and Raymond, G. (2005) The terms of agreement: indexing epistemic authority and subordination in talk-in-interaction. *Social Psychology Quarterly* 68(1): 15–38. https://doi.org/10.1177/019027250506800103

Jacobs, K. (2010) Lizzy Kinsey and the adult friendfinders: an ethnographic study of internet sex and pornographic self-display in Hong Kong. *Culture, Health and Sexuality* 12(6): 691–703. https://doi.org/10.1080/13691058.2010.481332

Jones, G. M., Schieffelin, B. B. and Smith, R. E. (2011) When friends who talk together stalk together: online gossip as metacommunication. In Thurlow and Mroczek (2011): 26–47. https://doi.org/10.1093/acprof:oso/9780199795437.003.0002

Jones, R. H. (2005) 'You show me yours, I'll show you mine': the negotiation of shifts from textual to visual modes in computer-mediated interaction among gay men. *Visual Communication* 4(1): 69–92. https://doi.org/10.1177/1470357205048938

Jones, R. (2012) Constructing and consuming 'displays' in online environments. In S. Norris (ed.) *Multimodality in Practice: Investigating Theory in Practice through Methodology* 82–96. Abingdon: Routledge.

Kang, M. A. and Chen, K. H. Y. (2014) Stancetaking and the Hong Kong girl in a shifting heterosexual marketplace. *Discourse and Society* 25(2): 205–20. https://doi.org/10.1177/0957926513515587

Kiesling, S. F. (2002) Playing the straight man: displaying and maintaining male heterosexuality in discourse. In Campbell-Kibler *et al.* (2002): 249–66.

Kiesling, S. F. (2005) Homosocial desire in men's talk: balancing and re-creating cultural discourses of masculinity. *Language in Society* 34(5): 695–726. https://doi.org/10.1017/S0047404505050268

Kiesling, S. F. (2011) The interactional construction of desire as gender. *Gender and Language* 5(2): 213–39. https://doi.org/10.1558/genl.v5i2.213

King, B. W. (2011) Language, sexuality and place: the view from cyberspace. *Gender and Language* 5(1): 1–30. https://doi.org/10.1558/genl.v5i1.1

Kotthoff, H. (2008) Konversationelle Verhandlungen Des Romantischen Marktes: Adoleszente Freundinnen Am Telefon. *Jugendsprache* 42: 39–78.

Milani, T. M. (2013) Are 'queers' really 'queer'? Language, identity and same-sex desire in a South African online community. *Discourse and Society* 24(5): 615–33. https://doi.org/10.1177/0957926513486168

Milani, T. M., and Jonsson, R. (2011) Incomprehensible language? Language, ethnicity and heterosexual masculinity in a Swedish school. *Gender and Language* 5(2): 241–69. https://doi.org/10.1558/genl.v5i2.241

Mortensen, K. K. (2010) 'Kan I Kende Dem Drenge?': Sexistisk Sprogbrug Og Kønsidentitet Bland Fire Unge, Danske Kvinder. *Københavnerstudier i Tosprogethed* 56: 61–81.

Mortensen, K. K. (2015) Informed consent in the field of language and sexuality: the case of online dating research. *Journal of Language and Sexuality* 4(1): 1–29. https://doi.org/10.1075/jls.4.1.01mor

Pomerantz, A. (1984) Agreeing and disagreeing with assessments: some features of preferred/dispreferred turn shapes. In J. M. Atkinson and J. Heritage (eds) *Structures of Social Action* 57–101. Cambridge: Cambridge University Press.

Raudaskoski, P. (2003) User's interpretations of a computer tutorial: detecting (causes) of misunderstandings. In C. L. Prevignano and P. J. Thibault (eds) *Discussing Conversation Analysis: The Work of Emmanuel A. Schegloff* 109–40. Amsterdam: John Benjamins. https://doi.org/10.1075/z.118.07rau

Robertson, S. (2004) Men and disability. In J. Swain, S. French, C. Barnes and C. Thomas (eds) *Disabling Barriers - Enabling Environments*, 2nd edition, 75–80. London: Sage Publications.

Sedgwick, E. K. (1985) *Between Men: English Literature and Male Homosocial Desire*. New York: Columbia University Press.

Stæhr, A. (2014) *Metapragmatic Activities on Facebook: Enregisterment across Written and Spoken Language Practices*. Working Papers in Urban Language and Literacies 124. London: King's College London et al. Retrieved on 12 October 2015 from www.academia.edu/6172932/WP124.

Stivers, T. (2008) Stance, alignment and affiliation during story telling: when nodding is a token of preliminary affiliation. *Research on Language in Social Interaction* 41(1): 31–57. https://doi.org/10.1080/08351810701691123

Thurlow, C. and Jarworski, A. (2011) Banal globalization? Embodied actions and mediated practices in tourists' online photo sharing. In Thurlow and Mroczek (2011): 220–50. https://doi.org/10.1093/acprof:oso/9780199795437.003.0011

Thurlow, C. and Mroczek, K. (eds) (2011) *Digital Discourse: Language in the New Media*. Oxford: Oxford University Press. https://doi.org/10.1093/acprof:oso/9780199795437.001.0001

Walton, S. and Jaffe, A. (2011) 'Stuff white people like': stance, class, race, and internet commentary. In Thurlow and Mroczek (2011): 199–219. https://doi.org/10.1093/acprof:oso/9780199795437.003.0010

Part IV

Gender, sexuality and space

11

Normal straight gays: lexical collocations and ideologies of masculinity in personal ads of Serbian gay teenagers

Ksenija Bogetić
UNIVERSITY OF BELGRADE, SERBIA

Introduction

Questions of male speech behaviour have long been a key topic in language-oriented investigations of gender. Central to this discussion is the notion of masculinity, with scholars stressing the variability of masculine identities and the multiple roles that language can play in their construction. Looking at diverse heterosexual contexts, a number of studies have provided rich accounts of the ways that men draw on cultural discourses of gender in order to construct socially valued masculine identities (Cameron 1997; Coates 2003; Kiesling 2002, 2005; Pascoe 2007, 2010). The concept of 'hegemonic masculinity' (Connell 1995) has been especially useful for theorising the most dominant or most desired form of masculinity in society. However, little work has been done to explore how hegemonic masculinity is linguistically performed within non-heterosexual male groups, or how this form of masculinity relates to non-hegemonic masculinities. The present article seeks to address these issues, by examining linguistic collocation patterns in a corpus of gay Serbian teenagers' personal ads.

In contrast to existing research (e.g. Hayes 1981; Gaudio 1997; Baker 2002) that has revealed how hegemonic masculinity and heterosexuality are in marginalised groups challenged through linguistic practice, replaced by local values of gendered behaviour, the present analysis demonstrates how ideologies of hegemonic masculinity and hegemonic heterosexuality figure prominently among Serbian gay teenagers. These ideologies closely reflect cultural ideals of manhood in Serbia, a setting caught between national tradition and globalisation where sexuality has become a hotly debated issue. In brief, language in the teenagers' ads is shown to provide a subtle, but salient resource through which the construct of appropriate masculinity is perpetuated, while the cultural stigma associated with homosexuality is shifted to non-masculine gay men, through a process I term *recursive marginalisation*. The content of the ads further illustrates the ways that ideology works to constrain the linguistic representation of desire, as exemplified in the desire-laden genre of personal ads. Moreover, the focus on gay youth identities, which remain underexamined in language and sexuality research, contributes to a fuller understanding of the linguistic construction of sexually marginalised identities.

The article also aims to make a methodological point by demonstrating that collocation analysis offers a productive means for understanding ideology, as lexical co-occurrence may shed new light on complex webs of identities, discourses and social representations in a community. Collocation patterns potentially index deeply rooted cultural meanings, as suggested by several scholars in previous research (e.g. Baker et al. 2008; Hunston 2002), and can also reflect social stereotypes (Romaine 2001; Mills 2008). However, most of the existing studies only briefly address collocation, and there are as yet few detailed analyses of collocations in their social and cultural context. The present article is intended to contribute to this line of inquiry, by providing a qualitative analysis of collocations, supplemented with corpus linguistic methods of quantitatively analysing recurrent language patterns. As I demonstrate below, collocation analysis offers a fruitful tool for investigating gender ideologies, revealing the ways that Serbian gay teenagers draw on shared cultural knowledge and ideological resources available in their community in order to construct a specific kind of gay identity modelled on the basis of socially desirable masculine identities.

Previous research

Language and sexuality

While sexuality was in earlier language and gender research mainly subsumed into gender, it has more recently come to be recognised as a separate theoretical concept, encompassing issues of both desire and identity (Keith and Shalom 1997; Cameron and Kulick 2003; Bucholtz and Hall 2004; Cameron 2005). Nevertheless, the relationship of sexuality and gender remains a central point of interest. Gender becomes especially salient in social representations of non-normative sexual identities, which are based not only on sexual practice, but also on their perceived deficiencies with regard to femininity and masculinity (Cameron and Kulick 2003).

An important question for the sociolinguistic study of sexuality, then, is how the construction and negotiation of sexual identity and desire are affected by and reflect social attitudes in specific cultural contexts. There is now substantial research focusing on how queer varieties may work to challenge or recreate gender and sexual ideologies (e.g. Gaudio 1997; Lucas 1997; Boellstorff 2004). Central to this understanding is the notion of hegemony. With regard to gender and sexuality, hegemonic or hierarchical relations referring to the dominance of men over women have been most widely discussed in feminist-inspired scholarship (e.g. Cameron 1992; Spender 1980; Mills 2008). Furthermore, hegemonic relations operate between different forms of masculinity itself (Connell 1995), most typically involving dominance of heterosexual over homosexual masculinities. Much research on language and sexuality is thus centred on the concepts of hegemonic masculinity and hegemonic heterosexuality (Kiesling 2002;

Boellstorff 2004), looking at how non-normative sexual identities are negotiated in relation to the mainstream identities. In relation to this, however, it must also be observed that recent years have seen the rise of more nuanced understandings of hegemonic masculinity, with an eye to avoiding one-dimensional treatments of hegemony and hierarchy. Connell and Messerschmidt (2005) thus argue that the understanding of hegemonic masculinity should incorporate a more holistic understanding of gender hierarchy, recognising not only the power of dominant groups, but also the agency of subordinated groups, along with the mutual conditioning of gender dynamics and other social dynamics. Despite these reformulations, the fundamental initial aspects of the concept of hegemonic masculinity have been retained and continue to exert a strong influence on the thinking about gender and social hierarchy, most notably in stressing the plurality of masculinities, the hierarchy of masculinities, and the idea that the hierarchy of masculinities is a pattern of hegemony, not a pattern of simple domination based on force.

Hegemonic masculinity and heterosexuality are particularly salient in the social world of adolescence, where concerns over peer status are at a premium (Thurlow 2001). Achieving an appropriate heterosexual, masculine identity among youth centrally revolves around the repudiation of homosexuality, effected through various linguistic activities such as ritual homophobic name-calling (Pascoe 2007). Although there is now a growing body of research on language, sexuality and power in youth groups, it is mostly limited to explorations of homophobia in high-schools, mainly in Anglophone societies (e.g. Leap 1993; Pascoe 2007, 2010), and little is known about how the gay teenagers themselves understand their situation, or how they negotiate identities in different interactional settings. The present study aims at addressing this gap, by looking at the interplay between language use and sexuality among teenagers in the telling material of online personal ads, in the less explored cultural context of Serbia.

Personal ads and the encoding of desire

A relatively novel and constantly evolving site for the study of youth language and sexuality is provided by the growing medium of internet communication. Among numerous online settings popular among teenagers, personal ad websites are an especially salient context for constructions of romance and desire. The genre of online personals also provides a specific frame for language use and self-expression, and is hence a rich source of insights both for the study of register and for the sociocultural study of sexuality.

Most existing research on personal ads uses data from print media, though linguistic analyses of the genre remain relatively scarce. Bruthiaux (1994) describes the language of the ads as a simplified register, structured to convey a 'maximal amount of maximally appealing information about the writer' (Bruthiaux 1994:139). In gender studies, a common discourse-oriented approach has been to compare the language of men's and women's personals, resulting in rather stereotypical accounts of gender differences: men typically focus on physical traits, while women are more concerned with personality and interpersonal relationships (e.g. Hatala and Prehodka 1996; Groom and Pennebaker 2005). However, a growing number of scholars have come to acknowledge personal ads as a fruitful site for studying sexuality and desire. Celia Shalom (1997) thus focuses on newspaper ads of gay and straight men and women, showing how the private search for desired partners is taken into the public domain, establishing specific communication between writer and reader. Anna Livia (2002) specifically examines this search for partners in lesbian print ads. Her analysis points to common exclusions in the ads based on gender presentation, where butches and masculine women are disliked, while the feminine look is prized. In the few studies that also look at gay men's ads, similar emphases on stereotypical gender characteristics have been noted (Thorne and Coupland 1998; Baker 2003).

While the main function and linguistic structure of such personal ads remain largely unchanged over time, the social context in which they are placed has been dramatically affected by the rise of internet communication. For one thing, communication via ads is no longer limited to those living in the same geographical location or having access to the same print publication. Relationships can be made beyond the boundaries of regions, countries or continents, allowing unprecedented connections between 'the most intimate and the most distant' (Slevin 2000:113). Users can browse the ads anonymously and cheaply, without leaving the comfort of their own homes. With regard to content, rather than just transferring print to digital form, internet ads also allow for more detailed personal profiles, hyperlinks to websites and searchable global databases (Gudelunas 2005). While in these respects personal ad sites are similar to other computer-mediated modalities (e.g. chatrooms: Jones 2005; del-Teso-Craviotto 2008; Chapter 12, this volume; or cybersex: Jones 2008), they differ from other online settings by virtue of their inherent anticipation and targeting of offline face-to-face encounters (Shaw 1997). In this way, personal ads represent a unique mediation between online and offline social worlds.

Not surprisingly, much of the appeal of such mediation is reserved for sexually marginalised groups, whose sexuality carries physical or social risk in the real world. Online ads fora offer a safe and friendly environment for building relationships that may extend beyond communication via ads. They have important advantages over the print medium, being more dynamic, more accessible and with a larger number of authors and readers. Moreover, as Gudelunas (2005) points out, while many people may be reluctant or unable to pick up a local gay print newspaper, the internet allows them to browse ads anonymously at home. These features of online ads may be especially alluring to gay teenagers and high-schoolers, who interact in particularly homophobic social settings (Thurlow 2001; Leap 1993).

In the present study online personal ads are found to be a valuable site for investigating the interrelations of language and sexuality among marginalised youth, by looking at the linguistic properties of ads written by Serbian gay teenagers. The underlying idea is that in understanding how sexuality and desire are represented in language use, lexical phenomena deserve special attention, as they can shed light on locally salient concepts and values. In this respect, patterns of lexical collocation are especially revealing, as they point to wider cultural meanings (Romaine 2001).

Bringing collocation analysis into sociolinguistic research

Corpus linguistic methodology places emphasis on quantitative, objectively verifiable language patterns, but its techniques are not necessarily incompatible with more contextualised analyses. Methods grounded in corpus linguistics, such as collocation analysis, have a lot to offer to sociolinguistic and discourse-analytic research. A number of scholars have recently acknowledged this, calling for synergising corpus linguistic methods with other discourse-oriented frameworks (Baker et al. 2008), and the promising impact of such calls has been attested by the growing number of studies that adopt these potentially complementary methodologies (e.g. McEnery 2006; Bondi 2007; King 2009; Chapter 12, this volume).

One strand of linguistic research where corpus analysis of collocation can be especially valuable is the study of ideology. As Hunston (2002) points out, repeated collocations implicitly reflect social meanings which can even be in direct opposition to what is claimed overtly. Furthermore, words that collocate with particular linguistic items have an influence over the meaning of those items. As Romaine puts it: 'connotations of words do not arise from words themselves but from how they are used in context. The meanings of words are constructed and maintained by patterns of collocation. Collocations transmit cultural meanings and stereotypes which have built up over time' (Romaine 2001:160). The key properties of collocation articulated in this statement – its construction of word connotations and its reflection of deeply-rooted cultural meanings – well capture what makes collocation a fruitful object of analysis in sociocultural linguistics. Repeated collocation patterns in language use both reflect and reproduce cultural ideologies, uncovering social attitudes that may be invisible in the propositional content of the text.

Given its impact on word meaning, collocation is an important vehicle for the discursive presentation of social groups (Baker et al. 2008). In language and gender research, several authors have addressed the role of collocations in the presentation of gender identities. Ideologies of gender are uncovered, for example, in Romaine's (2001) corpus findings on the pejorative collocates of the lexeme *spinster* (*gossipy, nervy, sex-starved, ineffective* etc.) or in Mills's (2008) observations on sexism in the use of phrases like *career woman* or *divorcée* whose meaning is affected by their typically negative collocates. While these authors emphasise that collocations can index deeply-rooted and often hidden stances, discourses and ideologies, there are as yet few studies that specifically deal with collocations from a sociolinguistic or gender perspective. The present article is aimed at addressing this gap, by demonstrating how collocation patterns can point to gender and sexual ideologies among sexually marginalised teenagers.

Context, data and methodology

Serbia: 'We live where we live'

The collected corpus is rich with references to the social circumstances of Serbia, in which the authors take a largely negative stance towards their home country. Some illustrative examples include, for instance, those with more implicit allusions to the difficulties of gay adolescents in Serbia (e.g. *Zao mi je sto je ovo jedini nacin da upoznam nekog ok ali zivimo gde zivimo* 'I am sorry this is the only way to meet someone but we live where we live') or those with sociohistorical references (e.g. *Rodio sam se nekada davno, u bedaku, odvratnom bedaku, kada je cika Sloba dosao na vlast i razjebao nam sve sto smo imali* 'I was born in misery, disgusting misery, when uncle Sloba [Slobodan Milošević, ex-president of Serbia/Yugoslavia] came into power and fucked up all we had'). Such mentions of the writers' home country are common in the corpus, often invoking an inherent opposition of Serbia to an idealised non-Serbian or Western context.

The real-life circumstances behind these comments are rather complex and go beyond ideologies of sexuality. Admittedly, the position of LGBT people in Serbia has changed significantly over the past two decades, both in the legal and social spheres. Same-sex sexual acts have been decriminalised, and the issue of LGBT human rights is nowadays very present in the public discourse. There is a growing number of activist groups, as well as several queer publications, internet websites and queer party events, mostly in the capital city. Nevertheless, sexual minorities are reported to be one of the most discriminated against social groups in the country (Anmeghichean and Salo 2007), as well as frequent victims of violence. According to a recent pilot survey conducted in three major cities in Serbia, 72 per cent of the LGBT respondents have suffered violence because of their sexual orientation, and more than half of them suffered violence more than once (reported in Anmeghichean and Salo 2007). In general, the public discourse in Serbia is shaped by heteronormative views, which is especially salient in the social construction of men's gender role. Some authors see the dominant ideas of masculinity as further impacted by the war in ex-Yugoslavia, which resulted in more emphasised ethnic identity and nationalist traditionalism that continue to have a profound presence in the public sphere. In such circumstances, the desirable identity of the Serbian man emerges as being patriotic, manly, a strong guardian of the family and nation, while different masculine identities are typically dismissed as deviant (Milićević 2006). The church has also been a prominent actor in social change, contributing to the patriarchal and traditionalist cultural politics (Miglbauer 2008). In the religious discourse on sexuality, gay men tend to be constructed as mentally ill, in need of help to be cured and returned to the right paths of fatherhood and family life. Moreover, some statements of church officials have been taken to provide direct legitimisation for violence against non-heterosexual individuals (e.g. *Drvo koje ploda ne rađa siječe se i u oganj baca.* 'A tree with no offspring is cut and thrown into the fire', a statement by Amfilohije Radović of Serbian Orthodox Church, September 2010, prior to the first Pride Parade in Belgrade). What is common to both the political and religious discourses, however, is the construction of homosexuality as a disease of the West, which threatens Serbian traditional and family values. One notable result of this situation is that sexuality has become so hotly debated not just because of the dominant sexual conceptualisations, but also because it has been embedded in the wider conflicting discourses of national identity, tradition, globalisation and economic progress.

Similar stances towards masculinity and sexuality have been projected onto the teenage community. The high-school environment tends to embrace the traditional values of masculinity and toughness in men, often also conceptualised as a significant component of national identity. The practice of 'pairing off' (Eckert 2002) in heterosexual couples is a prerequisite to gaining acceptance and social status. Open statements of homosexuality are uncommon, and they typically result in social exclusion, stigmatisation, as well as physical abuse by peers. The ad-writers in the corpus often explicitly orient to this social reality, with a tendency to see homophobia as essentially 'Serbian', though these attitudes to masculinity and homosexuality among youth in many ways resemble those already documented in the United States and the UK (e.g. Pascoe 2007, 2010; Thurlow 2001). However, they have been made more urgent and arguably more violent in the Serbian high-school context as the tensions over sexuality, family, tradition and national identity spill into the adolescent realm.

The internet then serves as a safe place to be gay for Serbian youth. For many of the otherwise isolated teenagers, web portals like the one analysed here provide a significant site for obtaining information and connecting with others, without any physical or face risk. Importantly, the internet offers a specific place for identity construction. Computer-mediated communication is especially attractive for young people, as it allows them to establish online identities that reflect their desired personae and the ways in which they wish to be perceived by others. Moreover, the possibility of staying anonymous makes the online space much more suitable for exploring one's sexuality and some issues that would probably never be raised in face-to-face communication. In this study I draw on such online personal ads to conduct a linguistic analysis of sexual and gender identities and ideologies, using the material from a popular website GaySerbia.

GaySerbia

The data used in this study consist of 200 personal ads taken from the GaySerbia web portal, collected in the period of 2008–9. In total, the corpus consists of 8145 tokens and 2496 types. Only ads written by young men between 16 and 19 years of age, who specified seeking male partners, were considered. The pseudonyms were anonymised, and the invented examples try to preserve some overall stylistic properties of the nicknames (combinations of letters and numbers, double letters, initial-like names etc.).The initial sample included over 250 ads, or over 80 per cent of ads total for this age group (2009 total: 301), but those that contained only the default personal statistics were excluded from the analysis.

The GaySerbia web portal is the most popular dating and entertainment website for the Serbian LGBT community. Apart from the personal ads section, visitors

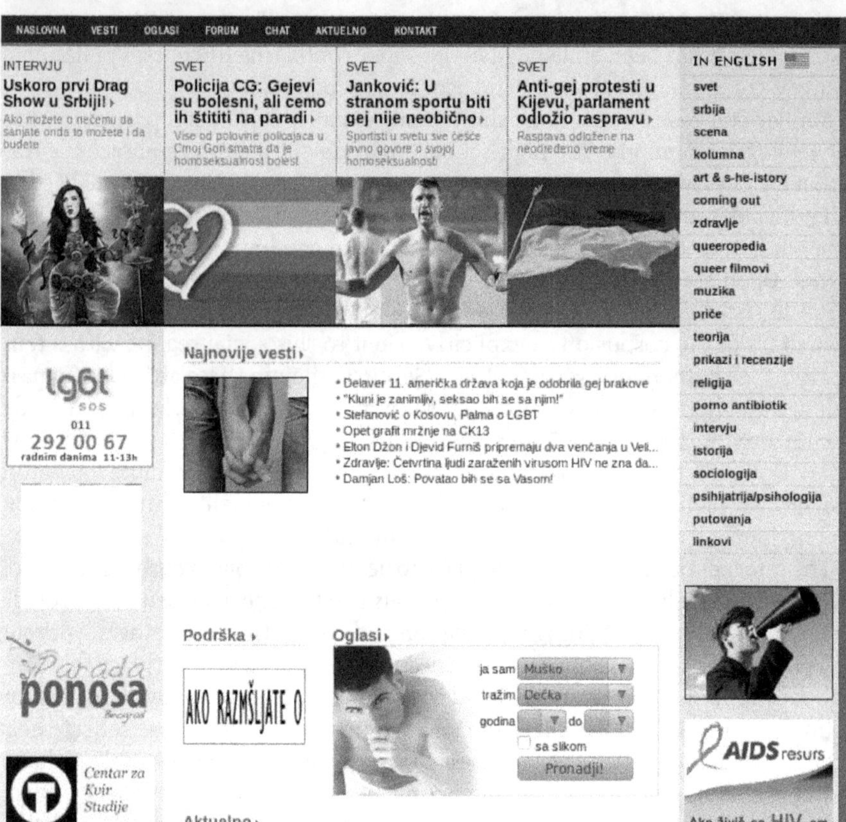

Figure 11.1 GaySerbia homepage.

can communicate in a chat room or on the forum. The site also offers news and articles on current queer events, movies and music, as well as a selection of readings from the fields of sociology, history and psychology. The ads, however, are among the central elements of the site and graphically take a visible place on the home page. In order to post or read ads, authors must first register at the site; registration is free and involves no minimal age requirements. To access the ads page, users specify their own gender and the preferred gender of the partner (only the male/female binary is offered; it is also possible to choose 'women seeking men' or 'men seeking women', though few ads are posted in these categories, mainly by/for transgender individuals), with the optional choice of partner's age, country of residence and purpose of meeting (friendship, love, sex). In a basic list containing posters' pseudonyms, age and (sometimes) photo, the users click on the pseudonym to open a specific ad. On each ad page, formulaic personal statistics (height, hair/eye colour etc.) are first given, followed by the text of the ad below. At the end of each user's ad page, there is the optional statement *Koga tražim ...*

Kako tebe zamišljam ... 'Who I'm looking for ... How I imagine you ...', prompting a continuation of the textual ad, though writers often choose to ignore this section and describe desired partners in the first textual ad segment. It is not obligatory to fill in all sections, but the majority of authors provide the personal statistics and a textual ad (one or both parts). It is these textual ads that are subjected to linguistic analysis here.

Methodology

The present study combines discourse analysis with corpus linguistic methods. The underlying idea behind this choice of methodology is that while the two approaches differ in emphasis, they are by no means uncomplementary. On the contrary, certain problems associated with corpus-linguistic techniques, such as the tendency to disregard context, are removed when these techniques are united with discourse analysis, allowing the quantitative findings to be contextualised with regard to social, political or cultural factors. Following Baker (2010), it is here assumed that there is no reason why corpus linguistic analyses should be limited only to corpus methods, without regard to wider contextual elements. Similarly, discourse-analytic study can significantly benefit from corpus linguistic techniques, which provide quantitative evidence for discourse-related observations. As noted by Partington, corpus technology can help to 'reinforce, refute or revise a researcher's intuition and show them why and how much their suspicion was grounded' (Partington 2003:12). This analysis employs one particular corpus-linguistic technique – collocation analysis, which is found useful in demonstrating relationships between the words of interest, and more broadly in analysing discourses and ideologies.[1]

However, one initial problem in any study of collocation is posed by choosing the appropriate definition of the term and deciding what to count as collocation. Most commonly, collocation is defined as 'the occurrence of two or more words within a short space of each other within a text' (Sinclair 1991:170), in a broad sense drawing on Firthian early descriptions of collocation as 'the company a word keeps' (Firth 1957:11). However, when we try to apply such general definitions and arrive at a precise operationalisation of collocation, a variety of different definitions is found. Some researchers, like Harris (2006), see collocations as sequences of adjacent words. Others (e.g. Sinclair 1991) do not take adjacency as a significant factor, but use the term more broadly for words that occur in proximity to one another. In such approaches, the emphasis is on the tendency of words to appear close to one another, or as Hunston (2002:68) puts it, 'to be biased in the ways they co-occur'. In a further definition Susan Hunston describes collocation more specifically as the statistical tendency of the co-occurrence of words. Importantly, this brings us to another major point of divergence in the understanding of collocation – statistical and non-statistical definitions.

The use of statistics for the extraction of collocation has some obvious advantages. Statistical significance tests help to establish more-than-random word co-occurrences and they make measurements more reliable (Hunston 2002). Such statistical methods, sometimes termed *collocation-via-significance* (McEnery and Hardie 2012), remove certain potential problems in the identification of collocation, such as the tendency to obtain the usually less telling function words (conjunctions, prepositions, articles, etc.), as in analyses solely based on frequency (Baker 2010). On the other hand, many practitioners have recently pointed out that complex statistical procedures are often not necessary or even appropriate in identifying collocation. Stubbs (1995) justifies this point by showing the list of collocates for the node 'cause' in a large corpus - words like *accident, alarm, concern, confusion, damage, harm*, with no positive examples and only a few neutral examples, noting that it is perfectly clear to the human analyst that the collocates found are semantically related. In other words, the pattern is perfectly clear without further statistical manipulation. In such non-statistical techniques (i.e. *hand-and-eye* techniques, or *collocation-via-concordance*, to use the terms of McEnery and Hardie 2012), examples and recurrent patterns are identified by the linguist, who scans the individual concordance lines. In this way a more prominent role is given to the human analyst, allowing the identification of a wider range of patterns and properties that may be missed in an automated analysis.[2] The stance is further justified by certain problems associated with statistical calculations of collocation. For instance, Stubbs (2001) observes that often when a collocation is identified the co-occurrence levels found are likely to be far above those that we could expect by chance, and it consequently makes little sense to cite probability levels. Conversely, results that do not reach significance levels may still well be of interest to the researcher (Stubbs 1995). Another practical problem has been posed by the choice of statistical software, as it has been demonstrated that different programs used to calculate collocation yield significantly different collocate lists (for examples see Hunston 2002; McEnery and Hardie 2012).

The present analysis adopts non-statistical, *collocation-via-concordance* methods. Given the topic specificity and the small size of the corpus, as well as some observed difficulties with statistical calculation of collocations, hand-and-eye techniques were found to be appropriate and more practical. Computer software (AntConc) was used to provide sorted concordance lines, keywords and collocates, and collocation was based on raw frequencies. Adjacency is not taken as a criterion, and collocations are defined as words occurring *in proximity* to one another. Only collocates occurring within the same sentence were considered, as words in proximity but in separate sentences are not suggestive of any associations.

As a starting point, the general word frequency count was performed in order to identify some keywords and lexical patterns. As the present study is specifically concerned with lexical elements denoting masculinity and non-masculinity, five lexemes were selected on the basis of frequency (occurring at least 10 times in the corpus) and subjected to analysis.

- *fem* 'fem'
- *nefem* 'non-fem'
- *feminiziran* 'effeminate'

- *nefeminiziran* 'non-effeminate' and
- *muževan* 'manly'.

An overall collocation analysis was performed for these five lexemes, with the window span limited to four words to the left and right of the node (following Sinclair 1991). In this process, the collocates obtained in AntConc were annotated in order to overcome difficulties associated with the complex inflectional morphology of Serbian. More specifically, the lemmatisation of individual collocate forms was performed to accurately sort out all the inflected case forms of the same words (which made it possible to examine the frequency of collocate lemmas). Following this basic collocate analysis, further analysis focused specifically on adjectival and nominal collocates. This decision was motivated by the need to eliminate the less telling function words that were obtained in a basic collocate analysis (e.g. *and, the*) and to examine association patterns between specific personal properties and the five words selected. As the adjectival and nominal collocates were found to exhibit a notable tendency to form coordinate phrases, such phrases were also examined in detail. Coordinated words occurring in the same syntactic function were found to be of interest, as they were expected to bear more relation than lexemes solely occurring next to each other in a linear sequence. Finally, separate analysis was performed to classify the coordination collocates of the five node adjectives into specific semantic groups, and the groups were ranked by frequency.

In addition, the adjective *normalan* 'normal' which was initially found to feature prominently among the keywords in the corpus and among the collocates of *nefem* 'non-fem', *nefeminiziran* 'non-effeminate' and *muževan* 'manly', was submitted to analysis and is analysed in a separate section.

Analysis

The word frequency search yielded some useful results regarding the lexical patterns in the ads (see Appendix 1). Expectedly, top content words include those referring to positive characteristics whether physical (*zgodan* 'handsome', *lep* 'pretty', *sladak* 'cute') or psychological (*normalan* 'normal', *iskren* 'frank'). Strikingly, the adjective *normalan* 'normal' was the third most frequent content word in the corpus, followed by *nefem* 'non-fem'.

While such word frequency lists may provide useful information about the lexicon of the personal ads genre, the present study is specifically concerned with lexical elements denoting masculinity and non-masculinity. For the purpose of this analysis five such lexemes were selected on the basis of frequency: *fem* 'fem', *nefem* 'non-fem', *feminiziran* 'effeminate', *nefeminiziran* 'non-effeminate' and *muževan* 'manly'. These cover the majority of the words used for denoting masculinity and lack of masculinity (less frequent lexemes include *muško* 'man, manly', *ženskast* 'womanish', and some general pejorative words for gay men such as *tetka* 'auntie'). In this respect, the corpus does not exhibit much stylistic variation and lexical creativity, possibly due to genre conventions and the practice of recycling

Table 11.1 Top adjectives by frequency.

	Lexeme	Gloss	Number of tokens
1.	*normalan*	normal	59
2.	***nefem***	**non-fem**	**47**
3.	*zgodan*	handsome	38
4.	***fem***	**fem**	**26**
5.	***feminiziran***	**effeminate**	**26**
6.	*lep*	good-looking	25
7.	*sladak*	cute	21
8.	***nefeminiziran***	**non-effeminate**	**19**
9.	*uni*	uni /sex role/	18
10.	*iskren*	frank	18
	...		
17.	***muževan***	**manly**	**10**

the previously used words and phrases of others, as evident in the notable similarities between many ads. Four of the five words listed above are also among the most frequent adjectives in general (Table 11.1). *Nefem* and *fem* are especially high on the list; their longer equivalents *nefeminiziran* and *feminiziran* are somewhat less frequent, possibly due to the tendency to use shortened lexical forms in ads (Bruthiaux 1994). The fifth, *muževan* 'manly', is slightly less prominent, though it also has a notable frequency in the adjectival category (ranked 17th).

Importantly, the five adjectives selected for analysis are typically found in repeated collocations with other, often value-laden lexemes. In the following analysis, collocation patterns are shown to involve frequent repetitions of linguistic items, meanings and associations, which indirectly index gender ideologies and attitudes towards sexuality in this community. The analysis shows that words denoting effeminacy are typically collocated with negative traits, and those denoting non-effeminacy and masculinity are collocated with positive traits.

Collocation

Among the general collocates of the five adjectives selected for analysis, one notable pattern is the tendency for *fem* 'fem' and *feminiziran* 'effeminate' to collocate with negative-form verbs and particles. These include merged negative forms of the copular verb *biti* 'to be' *nisam/nisi/nije* 'am not/are not/is not', as well as *ne* 'not', *ni* 'neither', or *niti* 'nor' (see Appendix 2). The following are some examples (ad writer's age is given in brackets).

Example 1

> *Sladakk (18): Tražim momka do 20g s kim bih prvi put probao seks sa muškarcem. Samo da* ***nisi feminiziran*** *i debeo. Piši na mail-*
>
> Sladakk (18): Looking for a guy up to 20 years of age, with whom I would have sex with a man for the first time. As long as you'***re not effeminate*** and fat. Email me at-

Example 2

Dane (19): ***Nisam fem,*** *mrzim femaste momke, okej sam, malo lud al nadam se da vam nece smetati.*

Dane (19): I **am not fem,** I hate femmy guys, I'm okay, a little crazy but I hope you won't mind.

Example 3

Niki (16): Normalan sam, ***nisam feminiziran,*** *volim sex sa starijim momcima, i intimno druženje.*

Niki (16): I am normal, I'**m not effeminate,** I like sex with older guys and intimate friendship.

In these concise ads, all three writers stress non-effeminacy in self-description or in the description of the ideal partner. Moreover, in Example 2 Dane's negation of being fem is followed by a strong evaluative stance *mrzim femaste momke* 'I hate femmy guys', that serves both to construct his own identity and to discourage any 'femmy' guys from responding. The negation of effeminacy shown in the collocation patterns can also be understood as part of a general trend in the ads to emphasise what one is not, rather than on what one is, with the typically negated features mainly involving effeminacy. An additional analysis of the use of *fem* and *feminiziran* in context reveals remarkable consistency: in the entire corpus, there are only two examples where these adjectives occur with no collocated negative particle, both involving a rather defensive stance (*ok sam, iako sam pomalo fem* 'I'm ok, though I'm a little fem'; *Fem, da, po ponašanju i nesvesno, tako da nema šta kome da smeta* 'fem, yes, in behaviour and subconsciously, so nobody should have a problem with that'). These exceptions suggest that being fem is in this community treated as problematic, needing to be accounted for somehow.

Collocates of *nefem* 'non-fem', *nefeminiziran* 'non-effeminate' and *muževan* 'manly', on the other hand, are harder to classify and do not yield much relevant information. Overall, an apparent problem with this sort of basic collocate analysis is that it yields a number of function words, copular verbs and so on that are not very telling for analytic purposes. It was thus more useful to examine adjectival and nominal collocates, as the type of collocation that can reveal most about what kind of person, personal properties and behaviours are associated with being masculine and non-masculine in this community.

Adjectival and nominal collocates revealed more striking patterns – *nefeminiziran, nefem* and *muževan* tend to be predominantly collocated with words of positive connotation, and *fem* and *feminiziran* are collocated with pejorative nouns and adjectives,[3] many of which are frequently repeated (Examples 4 and 5; for a detailed list of adjectival and nominal collocates, see Appendix 3).[4]

Example 4

mastermind (16): Decko van scene, lep, lepo gradjen, urban, nefem.

mastermind (16): A guy outside of the scene, good-looking, well-built, urban, non-fem.

Example 5

> *Sava (17): Ako ima neki normalan mlađi dečko iz Bga za druženje i nešto više nek se javi na PM, sa ovim profilima se ne smaram često. Ne gubim vreme na svakakve likove koji zalaze ovde, stop pedofilima i feminiziranim kretenima.*
>
> Sava (17): If there's any normal younger guy from Bg [Belgrade] for hanging out and something more, contact me by PM, I don't bother with these profiles often. I don't waste time with all kinds of guys that come here, stop paedophiles and effeminate idiots.

The author in Example 4 provides a pithy description of himself, collocating adjectives that denote positive physical characteristics and potentially desirable traits of urbanity and modernity. The final adjective *nefem* 'non-fem' takes on the positive connotation from its preceding collocates and is understood as another appealing characteristic of the author. Additionally, being 'outside of the [gay] scene' indicates disinterest in gay culture and presumably preoccupation with more conventional masculine pastimes. In the second example, the author concisely articulates what he wants, adopting a more aggressive stance in the final sentence. Mentioning *svakve likove koji zalaze ovde* 'all kinds of guys that come here' he voices his despite for the GaySerbia dating pages and implicitly denies any sense of the site as a virtual community. His sentence structure further suggests that these 'guys' include pedophiles and effeminate men. The stop-format used here appears in several ads as a way of saying who is not to reply; it is presumably a feature of the ads genre, not used in everyday speech. The value-laden phrase *feminizirani kreteni* 'effeminate idiots' is indexical of the author's attitude towards effeminate men, who are directly discouraged from replying. This particular noun phrase is repeated several times in the corpus, pointing to common attitudes possibly reproduced via reading and reusing wordings of others.

A notable trend that emerges from this analysis of adjectival and nominal collocation is the tendency for collocates to form coordinate phrases, as in Example 4. As determined by examining concordance lines, the lexemes *fem, nefem, feminiziran, nefeminiziran* and *muževan* mostly form relations of coordination with their collocates. In total, a striking 74% of instances of these lexemes include coordination (Table 11.2).

Table 11.2 Frequency of occurrence in coordination.

Word	**Occurrence in coordination**
fem	38% (10/26)
nefem	81% (38/47)
feminiziran	81% (21/26)
nefeminiziran	95% (18/19)
muževan	80% (8/10)
TOTAL	74% (95/128)

Collocates in coordination

All instances of coordinate phrases analysed involved *i* 'and', *ili* 'or' as coordinators, or were asyndetic (without coordinators). The analysis shows that terms in this type of coordination do not necessarily share semantic properties, though they tend to share evaluative meaning. Coordinate phrases constructed in this way are often strikingly long (Examples 6 and 7).

Example 6

bAngel (17): Trebas da si ***nefeminiziran, sharmantan, pricljiv, dobar, veseo i normalan,*** *da me volis takvog kakav sam, nista drugo nije bitno.*

bAngel (17): You should be **non-effeminate, charming, talkative, good, cheerful and normal,** like me the way I am, nothing else matters.

Example 7

dulkemali (18): Kazu bitno je ono iznutra i slazem se ja, ali tebra nije da iko voli ***glupe, ruzne, feminizirane, perverzne, isfolirane*** *likove i to ...*

dulkemali (18): They say what's inside is important, but dude it's not like anybody likes **stupid, ugly, effeminate, perverted and fake** guys and that ...

The common tendency to use coordinate phrases and create long coordination chains can be attributed to the inherent linguistic properties of personal ads as a genre, such as simplified syntax due to spatial constraints. Listing coordinated positive characteristics of the self and the desired and undesired characteristics of the partner provides a good strategy for squeezing the maximum amount of crucial information into limited space. Both authors above use such coordination chains to effectively describe their likes and dislikes. The first ad is composed solely of coordinated desired characteristics of the partner, with non-effeminacy followed by a range of diverse, but largely positive characteristics. The second author takes a more evaluative stance, listing numerous negative coordinated properties along with *effeminate*, while also drawing heavily on 'generalized perspectives' (Linell 2009:102) such as *kazu ...* 'they say ...' and *nije da iko voli ...* 'it's not like anybody likes ...'. The ad also involves the discourse particle *tebra* 'dude', created from the more common *brate* through the process of syllable permutation characteristic of youth slang in Serbia, Croatia and Bosnia (called *šatrovački*; e.g. Rizzolo 2006). In the present ad *tebra* indexes youth, coolness and a laid-back stance, but also gives the ad an interactional feel, as though the author was directly conversing with the reader. Additionally, though by no means limited to use by men, the Serbian *tebra* is typically associated with heterosexual masculinity (similar to the English *dude*; Kiesling 2004).

As the examples show, coordinate phrases involve a firm associative link between the elements, which often get the same evaluative judgement. Additionally, words affect the meanings of other words with which they are coordinated. In line with this view, the analysis of coordination in the corpus gives a clear insight into the dominant values of the ads. The adjective *feminiziran* 'effeminate', for instance, is rarely used on its own, but is typically found in coordination with nouns and adjectives denoting negative physical attributes, as well as undesirable psychological traits. As in Example 7 above, its otherwise neutral meaning is affected by its negative collocates. A more detailed observation of the coordinate elements occurring with the properties of being effeminate or non-effeminate reveals an invariable formula: words denoting effeminacy are consistently coordinated with negative traits, while those denoting non-effeminacy are coordinated with positive traits (Examples 8–12; see also Appendix 4).

Example 8

SM (18): Što se izgleda tiče, mogo bih da kažem da sam ***zgodan i nefeminiziran****, mada mi izgled i nije toliko bitan.*

SM (18): As far as looks are concerned, I could say that I'm **handsome and non-effeminate**, though looks don't matter that much to me.

Example 9

Novak (19): Ako si ***zgodan i muževan****, imaš manje od 25 godina i živis u Beogradu, kontaktiraj me na mejl i posalji sliku.*

Novak (19): If you're **handsome and masculine**, less than 25 years old and living in Belgrade, contact me by email and send a photo.

Example 10

Shvrle (17): ... Tebe zamišljam kao lepog mladog i pametnog dečka koji nije ***feminiziran ili isfoliran****, koji zna šta hoće.*

Shvrle (17): ... I imagine you as a handsome young and smart guy who's not **effeminate or fake**, who knows what he wants.

Example 11

Andrej (19): Voleo bih da upoznam nekog ko je normalan, da nije ***feminiziran i perverzan****, mogu i stariji.*

Andrej (19): I'd like to meet someone who's normal, not **effeminate and perverted**, older guys are ok too.

Example 12

Ivan (19): Koga tražim? Ne nekog ***perverznog, feminiziranog, lažljivog, prevrtljivog*** *... već šarmantnog, slatkog i veselog.*

'Ivan (19): Who am I looking for? Not someone **perverted, effeminate, lying, two-faced** ... but someone charming, cute and cheerful.

In the first two examples non-effeminacy is associated with positive physical traits and effeminacy with negative physical characteristics. The ad writers provide concise descriptions of the self or partner, emphasising good looks and masculinity as the absolute minimal requirements. Unlike these two ads, Examples 10 and 11 illustrate the coordination of *feminiziran* 'effeminate' with negative personality traits, such as being fake or perverted. Example 12 involves a coordination of *feminiziran* with a set of negative attributes (*feminiziranog, lažljivog, prevrtljivog* 'perverted, lying, two-faced'), which are placed in direct opposition to the traits of being *šarmantan, sladak* and *veseo* 'charming, cute and cheerful'. A number of diverse coordinations of these and similar types are repeated throughout the ads, producing some almost fixed forms (e.g. *normalan i nefeminiziran* 'normal and non-effeminate', *zgodan i nefeminiziran* 'handsome and non-effeminate'). As the given examples show, associations go beyond physical attributes to include a whole range of other traits.

It is apparent from the above examples that certain properties are repeated in coordinate phrases with the target lexemes. When these coordinate collocates were classified into semantic groups, certain predominant categories were identified (e.g. ATTRACTIVE, NORMAL). Classification into semantic groups also removed the observed potential problems relating to the semantic prosody of individual words. The most frequent semantic groups are shown below; the semantic groups are given in boldface low caps, with the number of instances in brackets followed by examples from the ads:

This list of categories covers the majority of lexical items coordinated with the given adjectives in the corpus. These frequently repeated collocations are indicative of the ad-writers' attitudes and values, clearly pointing to the desirability of masculinity, as well as to a widespread stigmatisation of effeminacy within this community. The most frequent semantic groups of collocates coordinationed with *fem* and *feminiziran* thus include not only UGLY, but also those related to perversion, insanity or dirtiness. Such patterns essentially evoke the discourses of mental instability or filthiness that feature prominently in the dominant conceptualisations of homosexuality in Serbia. On the other hand, ATTRACTIVE is the top category in coordinations with all three adjectives denoting masculinity, followed by NORMAL, CLEAN and HONEST. The social significance of these collocation patterns is further addressed in the Discussion.

Collocations with normalan 'normal'

The adjective *normalan* 'normal' has featured prominently in the findings discussed above. It is the third most frequent content word in the corpus, the top adjective by frequency, and among the very top adjectival/nominal collocates of *nefeminiziran* and *nefem* (Appendix 3). Despite having a rather vague meaning, it apparently refers to an important property of the self or the desired partner to be mentioned. A possible explanation for the this adjective's frequency may be that it reflects attempts of distancing from the 'abnormality' ideologically associated with homosexuality; it is also possible to interpret it in its less common meaning,

Table 11.3 Most common semantic groups of words coordinated with the target lexemes.

fem **'fem'**	***feminiziran*** **'effeminate'**	***nefem*** **'non-fem'**	***nefeminiziran*** **'non-effeminate'**	***muževan*** **'manly'**
UGLY **(5)** *ružan* 'ugly' *gabor* 'dog'	DISHONEST **(15)** *lažljiv* 'lying' *neiskren* 'untruthful' *prevrtljiv* 'two-faced'	ATTRACTIVE **(30)** *zgodan* 'handsome' *lep* 'good-looking' *seksi* 'sexy' *sladak* 'cute'	ATTRACTIVE **(8)** *zgodan* 'handsome' *lep* 'good-looking' *lepuškast* 'good-looking' *seksi* 'sexy'	ATTRACTIVE **(9)** *zgodan* 'handsome' *seksi* 'sexy'
PERVERTED **(3)** *perverzan* 'perverted' *perverznjak* 'pervert'	PERVERTED **(7)** *perverzan* 'perverted' *promiskuitetan* 'promiscuous'	NORMAL **(10)** *normalan* 'normal'	NORMAL **(4)** *normalan* 'normal'	NON-FEM **(6)** *nefem* 'non-fem' *nefeminiziran* 'non-effeminate'
DIRTY **(2)** *prljav* 'dirty, filthy' *neuredan* 'untidy'	UGLY **(6)** *ružan* 'ugly' *rugoban* 'ugly' *gabor* 'dog'	CLEAN/TIDY **(9)** *čist* 'clean' *uredan* 'tidy'	SMART **(3)** *pametan* 'smart' *bistar* 'bright'	EXPERIENCED **(1)** *iskusan* 'experienced'
DISHONEST **(2)** *neiskren* 'dishonest' *lažljiv* 'lying'	INSANE **(5)** *poremećen* 'demented' *nenormalan* 'abnormal'	SMART **(4)** *pametan* 'smart' *inteligentan* 'intelligent' *obrazovan* 'educated'	CLEAN/TIDY **(2)** *čist* 'clean' *uredan* 'tidy'	NORMAL **(1)** *normalan* 'normal'
INSANE **(1)** *bolesnik* 'sicko'/deranged/	OLD **(4)** *star* 'old' *mator* 'old'	DISCREET **(4)** *diskretan* 'discreet'	BIG **(1)** *krupan* 'big'	DECENT **(1)** *pristojan* 'polite'

as a word denoting an 'ordinary' man (though this again entails opposition to someone 'not ordinary').

The social meaning of this adjective becomes clearer when we observe the lexical items with which it collocates. It has already been shown that *normalan* is among the most frequent collocates of *nefem* 'non-fem' and *nefeminiziran* 'non-effeminate'. However, the issue can be approached from the opposite angle – examining the most frequent collocates of *normalan* itself. The results show that *nefem* is *normalan*'s top adjectival/nominal collocate (Appendix 5), followed by vague words like *tip* 'guy', as well as *nefeminiziran* 'non-effeminate', and the adjective *strejt* 'straight' discussed in more detail below. A further examination of concordance lines shows that *normalan* tends to co-occur with various other lexems, phrases or clauses emphasising masculinity or non-effeminacy, such as *potpuno nefem dečko koji je pre svega normalan u glavi* 'a totally non-fem guy who's above all normal in the head' or *trebaš biti muško, i normalan* 'you should be a man, and normal', as well as heterosexual behaviour *normalan sam dečko, imao sam devojke* 'I'm a normal guy, I've had girlfriends'. Coordinations like *normalan i nefeminiziran* 'normal and non-effeminate' / *normalan i nefem* 'normal and non-fem' become especially common (Examples 13–16).

Example 13

Miki (16): Normalan, nefeminiziran dečko, za druženje i nešto više. Pišite na mail.

Miki (16): A normal, non-effeminate guy, for friendship and something more. Write to my email address.

Example 14

Dušan (17): I dalje se nadam da ovde mogu upoznati nekog normalnog i nefeminiziranog dečka. Stop stariji perverznjaci.

Dušan (17): I still hope I can meet a normal and non-effeminate guy here. Stop older perverts.

Example 15

VR (17): Uni sam, 17 cm, tražim nekog ko je diskretan, o.k; trebaš biti muško, krupan, nefem, relativno obdaren i normalan dečko.

VR (17): I'm uni, 17cm, looking for someone discreet, ok; you should be a manly, big, non-fem, relatively large and normal guy.

Example 16

Gagi (19): Maksimalno da imaš 35 god normalnog str8 izgleda, da imaš kola za ostalo ćemo se dogovoriti.

Gagi (19): Maximally you should be 35, of normal str8 look, have a car, we'll arrange everything else.

Miki's ad in Example 13 illustrates a common form, in which the writer offers a brief self-description and invites further communication by email. Being *normalan* 'normal' and *nefeminiziran* 'non-effeminate' are the only properties of the self that the author finds necessary to disclose at this point. Dušan's ad (Example 14) contains a similar example of the typical collocations with *normalan*. After expressing his wish to meet a vaguely described *normalnog i nefeminiziranog dečka* 'normal and non-effeminate guy', he uses the *stop-* format to discourage 'abnormal' older perverts from replying. In Example 15, the ad shows the collocation of *normalan* with a wider range of properties, though traits of masculinity and sexual potency again feature prominently.

Example 16 illustrates a related tendency that deserves some elaboration: the linking of the adjective *normalan* with heterosexual-like appearance and behaviour. The ad is somewhat formal in tone, demanding among other things that the respondent should be of 'normal str8 look'. The English-influenced spelling of *str8* is less formal and stands in contrast to the otherwise more serious style of the ad, indexing youth, modernity and belonging to global gay culture. The association of *normalan* and *str8* sheds light on the author's attutudes towards non-straight/gay look, which is implicitly constructed as not only unwanted, but abnormal. Such associations are repeated several times in the corpus, making *strejt* 'straight', in its various spelling forms (*strejt, straigt, streight, str8*), one of the most common adjectival collocates of *normalan* (see Appendix 5).

'Normal straight gays' and the collocation of opposites

A striking pattern revealed in the examination of the usage of *normalan* is the coining of the phrase *normalan strejt gej* 'normal straight gay'. This collocation features in several ads as the description of the self or the desired partner (Examples 17 and 18).

Example 17

Jovke (16): Voleo bih da upoznam normalne strejt gejeve do 20 godina.

Jovke (16): I'd like to meet normal straight gays not older than 20.

Example 18

KG333 (19): Volim normalne muškarce, što znači da se ponašaju kao normalan straight gay, ne feminizirane, i kojima seks nije jedina glavna stvar u životu.

KG333 (19): I like normal men, which means that they act like a normal straight gay, who are not effeminate, and for whom sex is not the single most important thing in life.

In the first ad, Jovke concisely describes the type of person he would like to meet. Apart from age, Jovke's criterion for potential partners entail being *normalni strejt gejevi* 'normal straight gays'. The category is introduced in a matter-of-fact tone that presupposes the term's familiarity, despite being rather oxymoronic and unusual outside of this community. The form of the coinage does not correspond to the term *straight-acting* in English, though it is somewhat similar in meaning. Example 18 is particularly revealing, as the author directly defines *normalne muškarce* 'normal men' as those who act like heterosexuals and who are not effeminate. The collocation *normalan straight gay* thus frames heterosexuality as the norm, without challenging it in any way.

Moreover, this collocation of semantic opposites has consequences for meaning. Bringing the antonyms *straight* and *gay* into a single noun phrase erases the otherwise presupposed opposition between the two, extending their meanings beyond the diametrically opposite poles of sexual identity. *Straight* here takes on the whole array of meanings related to typical heterosexual-like masculine behaviour, as opposed to non-masculinity and effeminacy. In this way, gay men can be called 'straight', if they possess socially valued straight characteristics in all aspects of behaviour except sexual practice. Additionally, the typical collocation with *normalan* clearly shows the positive ideological value of the term 'straight gays'. On a broader level, this collocation demonstrates that in this community straight look and behaviour are valued as natural and 'normal'. Crucially, the construction of a separate category of 'normal straight gays' allows community members to position themselves as closer to this norm and to locate gay male sexuality within the realm of standard Serbian conceptualisations of masculinity.

Discussion

The preceding analysis of the collocations of lexemes denoting masculinity and non-masculinity has revealed some notable patterns of co-occurrence, indicative of the sexual and gender ideologies among the ad-writers. For instance, the tendency for words denoting effeminacy to be used in negation, collocated with negative particles and verb forms, points to the common practice of distancing from non-masculine characteristics, while also highlighting such characteristics as unwanted in potential partners. Further, adjectival and nominal collocates are particularly revealing, showing how effeminacy becomes associated with various negative terms, while masculinity and non-effeminacy are typically collocated with positive attributes. Such collocations are illustrative of the dominant gender representations among the writers, and contribute to creating a cohesive community in which effeminacy is marginalised and masculinity prized.

An especially frequent form of collocation that has emerged from the analysis is coordination, possibly due to the constraints of the personal ads genre. Authors tend to use long coordination chains as the most efficient way of communicating key information about the self or desired partner, while keeping syntactic complexity at a minimum. The analysis of coordinate phrases has confirmed strong patterns of co-occurence of effeminacy with negative traits and masculinity with positive traits. A detailed picture of such association patterns is obtained when examining the most frequent general meanings coordinated with the lexemes in question. At first glance, it appears difficult to see the common semantic relationship between the given adjectives – for instance, how being effeminate relates to properties like perversion or dishonesty. However, the frequency of these collocations, some of which function almost as fixed terms, points to deeper ideological meanings. The negative traits coordinated with effeminacy precisely involve the typical representations of homosexuality in the public discourse in Serbia. For instance, arguments centred around perversion or dirtiness are particularly common in popular debates, while those related to abnormality and insanity feature prominently in religious discourse. The language of the ads reveals the influence of such associations, which can be viewed as a reflection of dominant social attitudes, though here shifted only to one subgroup of gay men: effeminate gay men.

Collocations involving the adjective *normalan* 'normal' reveal a similar adoption of heteronormative discourse, with the concept of 'normality' primarily linked to masculinity and heterosexual traits. A particularly illustrative example of this tendency is the construction of the term *normalan strejt gej* 'normal straight gay', featuring as a distinct category in the ads. The social meaning of the term can only be understood through the processes of opposition and differentiation, involving implied contrast with some 'abnormal gay guy', a gay man who does not possess the socially desirable 'straight' characteristics. The phrase *strejt gej*, which is rather oxymoronic outside of this community, is based on shared cultural knowledge within the group that allows the ad readers to interpret the term and, more importantly, its social meaning.

Crucially, the patterns of collocation found in the analysis point to a subtle strategy by which the social stigma associated with homosexuality is in this gay youth community discursively shifted only to one subgroup, effeminate homosexuals. This process is evocative of Irvine and Gal's (2000) notion of recursivity, whereby an opposition that is salient at some level of relationship is projected onto another level. Language patterns in the ads show how the wider social opposition between negatively conceptualised effeminate (and gay) characteristics and positively conceptualised masculine (and heterosexual) traits is transferred into a local online gay community. In this way, intergroup oppositions are projected inward into intragroup oppositions. By adopting such oppositions and constructing a subgroup of aberrantly gendered 'others', the ad writers are able to indirectly index the normativity of their own gay selves. This is what provides suitable ground for distancing from socially marginalised gender and sexual identities and for positioning one's own identity as closer to the traditional model of masculinity. The ad writers' efforts to describe themselves and their desired partners as typical, masculine men points to their acceptance of the dominant social understanding of masculinity and provides a path for gay men to come as close as possible to the cultural ideal of a man, in looks, behaviour, attitude, values and activities, with the sole difference lying in sexual behaviour. The outcome of this tendency can be termed *recursive marginalisation*, through which insufficiently masculine gay men are stigmatised both in the heterosexist society and in the intragroup context.

Recursive marginalisation and the stigmatisation of the constructed deviant 'other' support the idea of sexual and gender (and other) identities as intersubjectively constituted and inherently relational, rather than being the property of isolated individuals (Bucholtz and Hall 2004). From the perspective of theorising masculinity, this study also confirms the view that masculinity cannot be analysed on its own, but that it acquires social meaning only when understood as the opposite of non-masculinity, or femininity (Coates 2003; Kiesling 2006). The analysis of linguistic and collocational patterns in the ads reveals how masculine, normative identities are built within the gay community by drawing on an opposition with the subordinated categories of effeminate gay men. The process of social differentiation or distinction (Bucholtz and Hall 2004), central to the ad writers' construction of their own masculine selves, underscores the intersubjective nature of sexual and gender identities.

The phenomenon of recursive marginalisation has implications beyond gender and sexuality. This concept highlights the way that core members of any socially marginalised group can also be positioned as marginal within that group, by virtue of being viewed as the most typical representatives of a socially delegitimised identity. On the other hand, such linguistically mediated positioning simultaneously works to preclude stereotypicalisation and erasure (Irvine and Gal 2000), in which identities inconsistent with the dominant representations (e.g. masculine gay men) tend to be rendered invisible by ideology.

Further, these findings also have implications for the understanding of desire as projected in language. The linguistically constructed recursive opposition between repudiated effeminacy and desirable masculinity highlights the complex ways that desire intersects with culture, ideology and identity. Overall, the ad-writers are shown to mould their representations of desire according to what is socially valued, although there may well be a huge discrepancy between such representations and the actual experience of desire. Oppositions evident in language patterns centrally reflect the tension between the expression of desire for non-normative intimate relationships and the efforts to claim a normative, socially valued gender identity. Investigating how such tensions between the intimately erotic and the culturally prescribed are negotiated through linguistic practice may provide a fruitful avenue for further research.

Conclusions

Collocation analysis proved to offer a productive avenue for investigating cultural meanings and associations. In this respect, the combination of qualitative discourse analytic methods and corpus linguistic techniques was found to be particularly gainful. As the patterns of collocation were contextualised and further observed qualitatively, they offered a window into the dominant gender ideologies of the teenage ad writers.

The marginalisation of effeminate gay men and the upholding of stereotypical masculinity can be seen as linked to the more traditional Serbian conceptualisations of 'real men', and the associations of inappropriate masculinity with insanity and perversion are certainly evocative of the representations of homosexuality in religious and public discourses more broadly. On the other hand, this presentation of sexual subjectivities and expectations is not very different from what has been observed in similar dating ads in Anglophone contexts (Thorne and Coupland 1998; Baker 2003). A parallel can also be drawn with preferences for stereotypical femininity in lesbian dating ads, as found by Livia (2002). What nevertheless distinguishes this analysis from the majority of previous studies is that it focuses on sociocultural and sexual identities articulated by gay adolescents, a group that has been little studied in existing research. Here, the findings must thus further be understood in the context of school and family influences, peer pressures, as well as the more prominent tensions between modernity and tradition.

On the whole, the language practices in gay teenagers' personal ads confirm the view that 'sexuality is not just about sex' (Eckert 2002:109) but is socially structured and thus imbricated in cultural norms and power relations. The ad-writers are shown to perpetuate the hegemonic discourses of gender in Serbia. However, they simultaneously exhibit some resistance to existing social representations, by constructing gay male sexuality as not necessarily outside of the realm of hegemonic masculinity. The multifaceted web of subordination and resistance illustrated in the present study has important implications for sociolinguistic scholarship on gender and sexuality, highlighting the intersection of linguistic practice, desire, identity and power. Only when these are understood as interlaced and mutually constitutive can we hope to achieve an adequate understanding of the social and linguistic construction of sexuality.

Appendix 1 Most frequent content words

1.	*voleti*	to like	101
2.	*tražiti*	to search	62
3.	*normalan*	normal	59
4.	*nefem*	non-fem	47
5.	*imati*	to have	45
6.	*seks*	sex	44
7.	*zgodan*	handsome	38
8.	*ok*	ok	36
9.	*javiti se*	to contact	32
10.	*godina*	age/years	31
11.	*fem*	fem	26
12.	*feminiziran*	effeminate	26
13.	*lep*	good-looking	25
14.	*dečko*	guy	24
15.	*sladak*	cute	21
16.	*nefeminiziran*	non-effeminate	19
17.	*druženje*	hanging out	18
18.	*uni*	uni /sex role/	18
19.	*iskren*	frank	18
20.	*misliti*	to think	17

Appendix 2 Most frequent collocates of the five target lexemes

Fem

1.	*i*	and	27
2.	*(ne) biti*	(not) to be	21
3.	*da*	that	14
4.	*biti*	to be	10
5.	*ne*	not	10
6.	*tip*	guy	6
7.	*ni*	neiter	5
8.	*u*	in	4
9.	*ili*	or	3
10.	*niti*	nor	3

Feminiziran

1.	*i*	and	22
2.	*(ne) biti*	(not) to be	15
3.	*da*	that	10
4.	*ne*	not	7
5.	*biti*	to be	6
6.	*perverzan*	perverted	5
7.	*isfoliran*	fake	4
8.	*koji*	which	4
9.	*samo*	just	4
10.	*ja*	I	3

Nefem

1.	*i*	and	21
2.	*zgodan*	handsome	15
3.	*biti*	to be	15
4.	*normalan*	normal	10
5.	*da*	that	10
6.	*do*	by	9
7.	*za*	for	8
8.	*dečko*	guy	8
9.	*ja*	I	8
10.	*neko*	someone	7

Nefeminiziran

1.	*i*	and	18
2.	*biti*	to be	12
3.	*da*	that	6
4.	*dečko*	guy	5
5.	*normalan*	normal	5
6.	*uredan*	tidy	4
7.	*neko*	someone	3
8.	*zgodan*	handsome	3
9.	*čist*	clean	2
10.	*izgledati*	to look	2

Muževan

1.	*i*	and	8
2.	*biti*	to be	5
3.	*nefem*	non-fem	5
4.	*zgodan*	handsome	5
5.	*tip*	guy	4
6.	*za*	for	3
7.	*ja*	I	2
8.	*samo*	only	2
9.	*seks*	sex	2
10.	*tražiti*	to search	2

Appendix 3 Most frequent adjectival/ nominal collocates of the five target lexemes

Fem

1.	*tip*	guy	6
2.	*debeo*	fat	2
3.	*dečko*	guy	2
4.	*perverzan*	perverted	2
5.	*ružan*	ugly	2
6.	*seks*	sex	2
7.	*sladak*	cute	2
8.	*veza*	relationship	2
9.	*život*	life	2
10.	*bolesnik*	sicko	2

Feminiziran

1.	*perverzan*	perverted	5
2.	*isfoliran*	fake	4
3.	*kreten*	idiot	3
4.	*lik*	guy	3
5.	*normalan*	normal	3
6.	*debeo*	fat	2
7.	*glup*	stupid	2
8.	*iskompleksiran*	mixed up	2
9.	*matorac*	old guy	2
10.	*napaljen*	horny	2

Nefem

1.	*zgodan*	handsome	15
2.	*normalan*	normal	10
3.	*dečko*	guy	8
4.	*uredan*	tidy	6
5.	*muževan*	masculine	5
6.	*ok*	ok	5
7.	*godina*	age/years	4
8.	*lep*	good-looking	4
9.	*lik*	guy	4
10.	*momak*	guy	4

Nefeminiziran

1.	*dečko*	guy	5
2.	*normalan*	normal	5
3.	*uredan*	tidy	4
4.	*zgodan*	handsome	3
5.	*čist*	clean	2
6.	*lep*	good-looking	2
7.	*seksi*	sexy	2
8.	*sladak*	cute	2
9.	*star*	old	2
10.	*tip*	guy	2

Muževan

1.	*nefem*	non-fem	5
2.	*zgodan*	handsome	5
3.	*tip*	guy	4
4.	*seks*	sex	2
5.	*bulja*	ass	1
6.	*debeo*	fat	1
7.	*dečko*	guy	1
8.	*diskrecija*	discretion	1
9.	*duženje*	hanging out	1
10.	*iskusan*	experienced	1

Appendix 4 Most frequent collocates in coordination of the five target lexemes

Fem

1.	*ružan*	ugly	2
2.	*bolesnik*	sicko	1
3.	*debeo*	fat	1
4.	*fetišist*	fetishist	1
5.	*gabor*	dog	1
6.	*lažljiv*	lying	1
7.	*neiskren*	dishonest	1
8.	*neuredan*	untidy	1
9.	*perverzan*	perverted	1
10.	*perverznjak*	pervert	1

Feminiziran

1.	*perverzan*	perverted	5
2.	*isfoliran*	fake	4
3.	*debeo*	fat	2
4.	*iskompleksiran*	mixed up	2
5.	*ružan*	ugly	2
6.	*gabor*	dog	1
7.	*glup*	stupid	1
8.	*kreten*	idiot	1
9.	*lažljiv*	lying	1
10.	*mator*	old	1

Nefem

1.	*normalan*	normal	10
2.	*zgodan*	handsome	10
3.	*uredan*	tidy	7
4.	*diskretan*	discreet	4
5.	*lep*	good-looking	4
6.	*ok*	ok	3
7.	*aktivan*	active	3
8.	*muževan*	masculine	3
9.	*sladak*	cute	3
10.	*čist*	clean	2

Nefeminiziran

1.	*normalan*	normal	4
2.	*lep*	good-looking	2
3.	*seksi*	sexy	2
4.	*bistar*	bright /smart	2
5.	*čist*	clean	1
6.	*dobar*	good	1
7.	*inteligentan*	intelligent	1
8.	*krupan*	big	1
9.	*lepuškast*	good-looking	1
10.	*muškarac*	man	1

Muževan

1.	*nefem*	non-fem	5
2.	*zgodan*	handsome	4
3.	*iskusan*	experienced	1
4.	*mišićav*	muscular	1
5.	*muškarac*	man	1
6.	*napucan*	muscular	1
7.	*nefeminiziran*	non-effeminate	1
8.	*normalan*	normal	1
9.	*pristojan*	decent	1
10.	*seksi*	sexy	1

Appendix 5 Most frequent adjectival and nominal collocates of normalan 'normal'

Normal

1.	*nefem*	non-fem	10
2.	*dečko*	guy	9
3.	*lik*	guy	9
4.	*nefeminiziran*	non-effeminate	6
5.	*seks*	sex	6
6.	*gej*	gay	5
7.	*ok*	ok	4
8.	*strejt*	straight	4
9.	*lep*	good-looking	3
10.	*muškarac*	man	3

Notes

1 It should be acknowledged here that the use of the term 'discourse' is always somewhat problematic given its multiple definitions in linguistics and other disciplines. The majority of these definitions emphasise the understanding of discourse as 'language in use' (e.g. Brown and Yule 1983), but there is a vast body of work that stresses what discourse is beyond language in use. The term is thus also used to imply particular linguistic regularities or types of language in use, such as political discourse, religious discourse, etc. The present chapter adopts a further understanding of discourse in the Foucauldian sense, as 'practices which systematically form the objects of which they speak' (Foucault 1972:49). Nevertheless, as observed by Baker (2006), it is in practice difficult to consider this meaning of discourse without taking into account the other meanings, and all these meanings of discourse are unavoidably evoked in the analysis.

2 The importance of researcher's intuitions is well acknowledged by the proponents of statistical approaches as well (see McEnery and Hardie 2012).

3 It would here pay to conduct a separate analysis of semantic prosodies (Louw 1993) in order to obtain more evidence of positive or negative connotations of the collocates, but the lack of a balanced general corpus of contemporary Serbian makes this task unfeasible. However, with the majority of the examples common-sense judgements are sufficient to observe positive or negative terms (e.g. *stupid*, *ugly*, *idiot*; *handsome*, *good-looking*), and, similarly to Stubbs's arguments on collocation (Stubbs 1995), we can assume that no further statistical examination is necessary to show a semantic pattern. The number of examples provided throughout the chapter should make these patterns more transparent to the reader.

4 The lists of collocates naturally also contain some examples that could be considered neutral (*tip* 'guy', *dečko* 'guy').

References

Anmeghichean, M. and Salo, A. (2007) EU support for LGBT people in neighbouring countries: is it (good) enough? In I. Dubel and A. Hielkema (eds) *Urgency Required* 273–80. The Hague: Humanist Institute for Cooperation with Developing Countries (Hivos).

Baker, P. (2002) *Polari: The Lost Language of Gay Men*. London: Routledge. https://doi.org/10.4324/9780203167045

Baker, P. (2003) No effeminates please: a corpus-based analysis of masculinity via personal adverts in *Gay News/Times* 1973–2000. In B. Benwell (ed.) *Masculinity and Men's Lifestyle Magazines* 243–61. Oxford: Blackwell. https://doi.org/10.1111/j.1467-954X.2003.tb03614.x

Baker, P. (2006) *Using Corpora in Discourse Analysis*. London: Continuum.

Baker, P. (2010) *Sociolinguistics and Corpus Linguistics*. Edinburgh: Edinburgh University Press.

Baker, P., Costas G., Khosravinik,M., Krzyzanowski, M., McEnery, T. and Wodak, R. (2008) A useful methodological synergy? Combining critical discourse analysis and corpus linguistics to examine discourses of refugees and asylum seekers in the UK press. *Discourse and Society* 19(3): 273–306. https://doi.org/10.1177/0957926508088962

Boellstorff, T. (2004) Gay language in Indonesia. *Journal of Linguistic Anthropology* 14: 248–68. https://doi.org/10.1525/jlin.2004.14.2.248

Bondi, M. (2007) Key-words and emotions: a case study of the Bloody Sunday enquiry. In N. Fairclough, G. Cortese and P. Ardizzone (eds) *Discourse and Contemporary Social Change* 407–32. Bern: Peter Lang.

Brown, G. and Yule, G. (1983) *Discourse Analysis*. Cambridge: Cambridge University Press. https://doi.org/10.1017/CBO9780511805226

Bruthiaux, P. (1994) Me Tarzan, you Jane: linguistic simplification in personal ads register. In D. Biber and E. Finegan (eds.) *Sociolinguistic Perspective on Register* 136–54. Oxford: Oxford University Press.

Bucholtz, M. and Hall, K. (2004) Theorizing identity in language and sexuality research. *Language in Society* 33: 501–47. https://doi.org/10.1017/S0047404504334020

Cameron, D. (1992) *Feminism and Linguistic Theory*. Basingstoke: Macmillan. https://doi.org/10.1007/978-1-349-22334-3

Cameron, D. (1997) Performing gender identity: young men's talk and the construction of heterosexual masculinity. In S. Johnson and U. Meinhof (eds) *Language and Masculinity* 47–64. Oxford: Blackwell.

Cameron, D. (2005) Language, gender, and sexuality: current issues and new directions. *Applied Linguistics* 26(4): 482–502. https://doi.org/10.1093/applin/ami027

Cameron, D. and Kulick, D. (2003) *Language and Sexuality*. Cambridge: Cambridge University Press. https://doi.org/10.1017/CBO9780511791178

Coates, J. (2003) *Men Talk: Stories in the Making of Masculinities*. Oxford: Blackwell. https://doi.org/10.1002/9780470755617

Connell, R. (1995) *Masculinities*. Cambridge: Polity Press.

Connell, R. and Messerschmidt, J. (2005) Hegemonic masculinity: rethinking the concept. *Gender and Society* 19(6): 829–59. https://doi.org/10.1177/0891243205278639

Del-Teso-Craviotto, M. (2008) Gender and sexual identity authentication in language use: the case of chat rooms. *Discourse Studies* 10: 251–70. https://doi.org/10.1177/1461445607087011

Eckert, P. (2002) Demystifying sexuality and desire. In K. Campbell-Kibler, R. Podesva, S. Roberts and A. Wong (eds.) *Language and Sexuality: Contesting Meaning in Theory and Practice* 99–110. Stanford, CA: Center for the Study of Language and Information.

Firth, J. R. (1957) A synopsis of linguistic theory 1930–1955. *Studies in Linguistic Analysis* (Special Volume, Philological Society): 1–32.

Foucault, M. (1972) *The Archaeology of Knowledge*. London: Routledge & Kegan Paul.

Gaudio, R. (1997) Not talking straight in Hausa. In A. Livia and K. Hall (eds) *Queerly Phrased* 416–29. New York: Oxford University Press.

Groom, C. and Pennebaker, J. (2005) The language of love: sex, sexual orientation, and language use in online personal advertisements. *Sex Roles* 52(7–8): 447–61. https://doi.org/10.1007/s11199-005-3711-0

Gudelunas, D. (2005) Online personal ads: community and sex, virtually. *Journal of Homosexuality* 49: 1–33. https://doi.org/10.1300/J082v49n01_01

Harris, A. (2006) Revisiting anaphoric islands. *Language* 82(1): 114–30. https://doi.org/10.1353/lan.2006.0037

Hatala, M. N. and Prehodka, J. (1996) Content analysis of gay male and lesbian personal advertisements. *Psychological Reports* 78: 371–4. https://doi.org/10.2466/pr0.1996.78.2.371

Hayes, J. (1981) Gayspeak. In J. Chesebro (ed.) *Gayspeak: Gay Male and Lesbian Communication* 45–57. New York: Pilgrim.

Hunston, S. (2002) *Corpora in Applied Linguistics*. Cambridge: Cambridge University Press. https://doi.org/10.1017/CBO9781139524773

Irvine, J. and Gal, S. (2000) Language ideology and linguistic differentiation. In P. Kroskrity (ed.) *Regimes of Language: Ideologies, Polities and Identities* 35–84. Santa Fe, NM: School of American Research Press.

Jones, R. (2005) 'You show me yours, I'll show you mine': the negotiation of shifts from textual to visual modes in computer-mediated interaction among gay men. *Visual Communication* 4: 69–92. https://doi.org/10.1177/1470357205048938

Jones, R. (2008) The role of text in televideo cybersex . *Text and Talk* 28(4): 453–73. https://doi.org/10.1515/TEXT.2008.022

Keith, H. and Shalom, C. (1997) *Language and Desire: Encoding Sex, Romance and Intimacy*. London: Routledge.

Kiesling, S. (2002) Playing the straight man: displaying and maintaining male heterosexuality in discourse. In K. Campbell-Kibler, R. Podesva, S. Roberts and A. Wong (eds). *Language and Sexuality: Contesting Meaning in Theory and Practice* 249–66. Stanford, CA: Center for the Study of Language and Information.

Kiesling, S. F. (2004) Dude. *American Speech* 79(3): 281–305. https://doi.org/10.1215/00031283-79-3-281

Kiesling, S. (2005) Homosocial desire in men's talk: Balancing and re-creating cultural discourses of masculinity. *Language in Society* 34: 695–726. https://doi.org/10.1017/S0047404505050268

Kiesling, S. (2006) Hegemonic identity-making in narrative. In A. De Fina, D. Schiffrin and M. Bamberg (eds) *Discourse and Identity* 261–88. Cambridge: Cambridge University Press. https://doi.org/10.1017/CBO9780511584459.014

King, B. (2009) Building and analysing corpora of computer-mediated communication. In P. Baker (ed.) *Contemporary Corpus Linguistics* 301–320. London: Continuum.

Leap, W. (1993) Learning gay culture in 'a desert of nothing': language as a resource in gender socialization. *High School Journal* 77(1–2): 122–32.

Linell, P. (2009) *Rethinking Language, Mind and World Dialogically*. Charlotte, NC: Information Age Publishing.

Livia, A. (2002) Camionneuses s'abstenir: lesbian community creation through the personals. In K. Campbell-Kibler, R. Podesva, S. Roberts, and A. Wong (eds.) *Language and Sexuality. Contesting Meaning in Theory and Practice* 191–206. Stanford, CA: Center for the Study of Language and Information.

Livia, A. and Hall, K. (eds) (2002) *Queerly Phrased*. New York: Oxford University Press.

Louw, B. (1993) Irony in the text or insincerity in the writer? The diagnostic potential of semantic prosodies. In Baker, M., Francis, G. and Tognini-Bonelli, E. (eds) *Text and technology: In honour of John Sinclair*, Philadelphia and Amsterdam: John Benjamins, 157–76. https://doi.org/10.1075/z.64.11lou

Lucas, I. (1997) The color of his eyes: Polari and the Sisters of Perpetual Indulgence. In Livia and Hall (1997): 85–94.

McEnery, T. (2006) *Swearing in English: Bad Language, Purity and Power from 1586 to the Present.* London: Routledge.

McEnery, T. and Hardie, A. (2012) *Corpus Linguistics: Method, Theory and Practice.* Cambridge: Cambridge University Press.

Miglbauer, M. (2008) 'In Serbia at least I never heard that someone as a man decided to go on maternity leave but I can tell you that I will have no problem with that': gendered professional identities, gendered discourses and their effects on employees in postsocialist globalised workplaces. Paper presented at IGALA 5, Victoria University of Wellington, Wellington, New Zealand, 3–5 July.

Milićević, A. (2006) Joining the war: masculinity, nationalism and war participation in the Balkans war of secession, 1991–1995. *Nationalities Papers* 34: 265–87. https://doi.org/10.1080/00905990600766487

Mills, S. (2008) *Language and Sexism.* Cambridge: Cambridge University Press. https://doi.org/10.1017/CBO9780511755033

Partington, A. (2003) *The Linguistics of Political Argumentation: The Spin-Doctor and the Wolf-Pack at the White House.* London: Routledge. https://doi.org/10.4324/9780203218259

Pascoe, C. J. (2007) *Dude, You're a Fag: Masculinity and Sexuality in High School.* Berkeley, CA: University of California Press.

Pascoe, C. J. (2010) Dude, you're a fag: adolescent masculinity and the fag discourse. In I. Beattie, R. Arum and K. Ford (eds) *The Structure of Schooling: Readings in the Sociology of Education* 391–400.

Rizzolo, O. (2006) The syllable is not a valid constituent: evidence from two Serbo-Croatian language games. *Formal Approaches to Slavic Linguistics* 15: 264–82.

Romaine, S. (2001) A corpus-based view of gender in British and American English. In M. Hellinger and H. Bussmann (eds) *Gender across Languages: The De/construction of Gender Roles through Language Variation and Change* 153–76. Amsterdam: John Benjamins. https://doi.org/10.1075/impact.9.12rom

Shalom, C. (1997) 'That great supermarket of desire: attributes of the desired other in personal advertisements. In K. Harvey and C. Shalom (eds) *Language and Desire* 186–203. London: Routledge.

Shaw, D. (1997) Gay men and computer communication: a discourse of sex and identity in cyberspace. In Steve G. Jones (ed.) *Virtual Culture: Identity and Communication in Cybersociety* 133–45. London: Sage.

Sinclair, J. (1991) *Corpus, Concordance, Collocation.* Oxford: Oxford University Press.

Slevin, J. (2000) *The Internet and Society.* Malden, MA: Polity Press.

Spender, D. (1980) *Man Made Language.* London: Routledge.

Stubbs, M. (1995) Collocations and semantic profiles: on the cause of trouble with quantitative studies. *Functions of Language* 2(1): 23–55. https://doi.org/10.1075/fol.2.1.03stu

Stubbs, M. (2001) *Words and Phrases.* Oxford: Blackwell.

Thorne, A. and Coupland, J. (1998) Articulations of same-sex desire: lesbian and gay male dating advertisements. *Journal of Sociolinguistics* 2(2): 233–57. https://doi.org/10.1111/1467-9481.00042

Thurlow, C. (2001) Naming the 'outsider within': homophobic pejoratives and the verbal abuse of lesbian, gay and bisexual high-school pupils. *Journal of Adolescence* 24(1): 25–38. https://doi.org/10.1006/jado.2000.0371

12

Language, sexuality and place: the view from cyberspace

Brian W. King
CITY UNIVERSITY OF HONG KONG

> Place is security, space is freedom; we are attached to the one and long for the other. (Tuan 1977:3)

> Place can be as small as the corner of a room or as large as the earth itself: that the earth is our place in the universe is a simple fact of observation to homesick astronauts ... (Tuan 1974:245)

Place merits a central focus in the investigation of language and sexuality (whether online or offline). Disregarding place means ignoring its social foundations as well as what Sidnell (2003:328) refers to as 'practices of speaking which weave gender into the seen-but-unnoticed backdrop of everyday life'. One purpose of this article will be to explore this notion of interwoven place and gender while experimenting with the inclusion of sexuality in the weave. Places, like social categories, are no longer assumed to have fixed characteristics (Valentine 2002:145). In fact it has become a common sense notion that places are socially constructed, and the *language* of social relations and identity is inherently spatial (Bell et al. 1994:31). We do not perform identities and form communities with spaces and places serving as boxes around us or static backdrops;[1] rather our understandings of our surroundings are intermingled with our understandings and impressions of our 'selves' and others as we struggle to strike a 'visible presence' in the world (Skeggs et al. 2004:1839). Place is also relevant online, for the word 'cyberspace'[2] has become an ever-present term used to describe 'where' we 'go' when we interact with others through means of communication provided by the internet. All of cyber*space* has been imbued with a place-like character when in truth it is more similar to a big magazine or newspaper than a place; it is linguistic in its nature, from the codes used in computer programs to the words which appear on one's screen (Cicognani 1998:19). Then again it has territorial hues that traditional information media lack, and this 'geographicalisation' is foundational. By analysing the purely linguistic performance of sexualised places online, the hope is to also gain insight into the role that language plays in the creation of offline places.

The main aim of this paper is to investigate the ways in which social relations are often in dialog with places, adapting to one another along a reformulating path (Natter and Jones III 1997:149). Focussing on genders and sexualities, I ask two main questions:

- Through talk in cyberspace, how are places performed, in dialog with the performance of gendered and sexual subject positions?
- How are these places, genders, and sexualities performed as queer?

In order to address these questions I draw on a corpus of online talk-in-interaction. The data comprises text-only, typed conversations from 'chat rooms' in which participants perform masculinities while expressing sexual desire for masculine others. In the process of analysing these texts, I keep an eye to the participants' 'identities' and their 'identifications' (a psychoanalytic concept) (Cameron and Kulick 2003:138–9). Although speakers are not always conscious of the tools that they use to perform identities, they are conscious of the ways in which they are presenting themselves (i.e. their identities). Identifications, on the other hand, refer to ways in which people are transformed through 'assimilation' of aspects of an 'other' through (largely unconscious) disavowals and rejections that are shown through inconsistencies, contradictions, and silences. Identifications can augment or disrupt identity performances. In the course of the analysis I demonstrate how the study of language and sexuality is enhanced by concurrent attention to place, gender, sexual identity, and sexual identification during analysis.

I consider these issues as part of more general goals. First, I want to 'include space ... as a central analytic tool' (Blommaert 2005a:140), so as to explore how the 'where' of sexuality relates to linguistic performances of sexual desires and sexual identities. Interesting questions arise when one considers that sexuality (in terms of both identities and sexual subject positions) is not exclusively about what we *say* and *do* but is also influenced by *where* we are as well as how we feel (Kawale 2004:577). Language and sexuality research is further enabled by paying attention to situational place. It is here, at the site of interaction, where performative citations imbue visible, audible, and/or tangible spaces with meaning, often converting them into places (i.e. more familiar spatialities). These places do not pre-exist their performance; rather their construction is ongoing and unstable, hence they can be sexualised and gendered through sexual subject positions. We sexualise our bodies in ways that are influenced by the social understandings we 'take from' and 'build into' the places around us (see also Browne, Lim and Brown 2007:4). We become sexual subjects within these places rather than being *a priori* sexualised subjects (Waitt 2006:776), with our ability to feel sexy or sexually aroused in a certain place hinging partly upon reiterations of sexualised places that have been 'felicitous'. To put it another way, this is why certain locations fail to be understood as sexual by some people, yet are eminently 'sexualisable' to others, or to the same people at other times. Therefore, to ignore the 'where' of language and sexuality limits analysis. It would be similar to conducting a study of the discourses of sales interactions at a garage sale while failing to consider that 'garage' spatiality might result in different discourses from that of a 'shop'.

The language that is used in sales will incorporate elements of garage spatiality, and garage spatiality will be influenced by the discourses of sales. Hence the goal is to 'wield' place as a tool in the analysis of sexualised discourse, while simultaneously wielding discourse as a tool in the analysis of sexualised place.

Second, along the way I aim to explore definitions of 'place' as used thus far in sociolinguistic literature and problematise the prevalent association of the term 'place' with large-scale social relations (e.g. neighbourhoods and regions). This conflation is in danger of becoming reified in sociolinguistic literature, largely as a result of the regional focus of variationist sociolinguistics. For example, Johnstone (1999:517) has found the concept of 'place' useful in demonstrating that speakers 'ground aspects of their identities' in places. One might just as logically ask then, how aspects of places (socially understood locales) are grounded in the identities of speakers who interact there? More in line with the latter question, Modan (2007:317) focuses in her research on the discursive construction of a neighbourhood (a social space), an approach more in line with the present study. Significantly, although expressing some reservations concerning the conflation of social space with place, and any erasures that this might precipitate, Modan has decided to continue using the term 'place', stating that it is common in the field, and echoing Cresswell (2004:10) in suggesting that place and social space serve similar functions:

> When humans invest meaning in a portion of space and then become attached to it in some way (naming is one such way) it becomes a place. Although this basic dualism of space and place runs through much of human geography since the 1970s it is confused somewhat by the idea of social space – or socially produced space – which, in many ways, plays the same role as place [citing Lefebvre [1974]1991; Smith 1991].

In order to emphasise that 'social spaces' can be states, neighbourhoods, bars, rooms, parks, farms, closets, online chat rooms, radio shows, and telephone connections (the list could go on), I will continue to use the word 'place' in reference to all such spatial entities. I have chosen to concur in order to emphasise that the issues and processes I address in this article are not separable from 'place' and discourse as explored at the neighbourhood level (Modan 2007) or at the level of towns (Johnstone 1990), cities (Johnstone, Andrus and Danielson 2006) and states (Johnstone 1999).[3]

My misgivings spring from the fear that collapsing 'socially produced space' into place as the term has thus far been used in sociolinguistics (i.e. to refer to macro-spatial entities such as neighbourhoods and states) tends to erase what Collins and Slembrouck (2005:191) call '*small-scale spatial relations* ... the situation, the site and arena of face-to-face exchange'. By this, they mean our immediate surroundings (e.g. an office, or the corner of a room). It also erases what I will call *ephemeral social spaces* (both physical and online). Ephemeral social spaces are those which are 'familiar' to none (or few) who are involved in their ongoing construction (hence not yet places necessarily) but rather spaces of social exploration. What familiarity they have (or gain) for people is achieved via the performative citation of other places which are more familiar. In this sense, an online chat room that is familiar to a given participant might be a *place* to that person (however metaphorically), but the ephemeral nature of online chat rooms and the tendency for a high turnover of participants might make this 'place' status tenuous for many. It seems more productive to think of online chat rooms as places which are always being performatively constructed and which do not pre-exist their performance. This idea is explored further below.

Triangle of space

The guiding framework for this investigation is the 'triangle of space', which Gotved (2006) has developed and theorised, inspired by the insights of Henri Lefebvre ([1974]1991). She builds upon his heuristic division of socially produced space into three categories: spatial practice, representations of space, and spaces of representation.[4] 'Spatial practice' is the actual space that we perceive and our movements through it (hence the 'practice' element); it provides us with the possibilities of navigation; it is that which must be socially understood and mapped out. 'Representations of space' are conceptions of space based on dominant systems of knowledge – 'the space of scientists, planners, urbanists, technocratic subdividers and social engineers' (Lefebvre [1974]1991:38). These are not 'lived' spaces, but office-based conceptions of space which reflect the interests of those endowed with the power to impose them. Finally, 'spaces of representation' are lived spaces, born of understandings gained through interpersonal interaction, and the site of possible resistance by those not endowed with such power. These three categories work together, influencing one another to socially produce space. There is not adequate space here to explain these abstract concepts fully; instead I now turn to Gotved's interpretations of Lefebvre's model.[5]

Lefebvre's hypotheses are not without critics (see, for example, Unwin 2000), and there are some problems with the clarity of his concepts, but Gotved acknowledges these limitations while using his theories as a starting point. Her adaptation of Lefebvre's framework (for the exploration of *online* spatiality) is useful for this study because it adapts and interlinks Lefebvre's three dimensions (see previous section):

- Spatial practice, which Gotved reframes as the spatial nexus formed by the 'visible' dimension of online chat room spatiality (the screens of the user interface).
- Representations of space, which Gotved reframes as the '(re) constructive' dimension (in this study the spatialising of sexuality/gender via the room metaphor).
- Spaces of representation, which Gotved reframes as the 'practice' dimension (in this study the sexualising/gendering of spatiality through participant interaction).

Modan (2007) has also adapted Lefebvre's three-sided model, finding his ideas of social space production useful in her analysis of an urban community as place.[6] Modan reinterprets Lefebvre in her own way, pointing out that *spaces of representation* and *representations of space* are more clearly understood if one combines them into one category (representation), a category which she subsequently divides into the mental and the symbolic in order to facilitate analysis. This move is still compatible with Gotved's triangle because reconstructive spatiality contains the symbolic (metaphors and that which they cite) and the mental (how those citations are received and interpreted). Practice spatiality also contains the symbolic (interaction and that which small-d discourse cites) and the mental (how those citations are received and interpreted). Gotved's triangle of space will thus form the theoretical backbone of this investigation because it is useful to maintain Lefebvre's original heuristic separation in this case, for the reason that the participants are both the architects of online place and its users. Any separation between the symbolic and mental will be backgrounded despite its usefulness in Modan's offline work. Discussing Gotved and Modan together however helps to emphasise the continuum of spatiality which bridges online and offline experiences and places.

Visible spatiality (inspired by Lefebvre's spatial practice category) is the location of interaction, but this is not only about the physical. It starts with what the participants in a chat room can see on their screens. It is the ontological, computer-coded dimension of online reality, which Gotved has separated from the epistemic aspects of online social life (Gotved 2006:479). Working with online spatiality, Gotved has found it more useful to heuristically separate practice into its own category ('practice spatiality' below) while maintaining Lefebvre's focus on ontological space and its possibilities for navigation (keeping these aspects in visible spatiality). Despite the possible confusion this might cause because of Lefebvre's original terminology, this separation is useful in the online environment. Dodge and Kitchin (2001:142) observe that it is the chat 'client' (i.e. the software that links chat participants) that 'provides the spatial structure of chat through its interface design'. This is not to say that the spatiality of chat is determined by the interface entirely; in fact despite being 'where' the communication takes place, the interface is only the beginning and is a relatively narrow aspect of online spatiality (Gotved 2006:480). However, as *linguistic landscapes* research has begun to demonstrate, the visible built environment around us often contains (or is inscribed with) language and can have considerable influence on the perceived character of a place (Backhaus 2007). This is a point also brought to light in Scollon and Scollon's (2003) phenomenological analyses of language and place, a study which acknowledges the importance of interaction to place creation but has not yet explored that dimension. Like these landscapes, the computer interface not only provides a place for interaction; rather it can contain linguistic cues which interact with language in the other dimensions of place.

Another of those dimensions is *(re)constructive spatiality* (inspired by Lefebvre's representations of space). Gotved (2006:479) defines this dimension as the creation of a 'recognisable' spatiality through representations such as metaphors and images, a process in which online communication evokes the feeling of three dimensions 'behind the screen'. Even in the material world, visible, audible, and/or tangible surroundings gain meaning through metaphors and images that refer to familiar places. Metaphors transform unfamiliar surroundings into recognisable places, and the same is true in cyberspace. Sidnell (2003:327) asserts that 'settings' and 'context' achieve recognisability through practices of talk-in-interaction rather than serving as backdrops to that interaction. I would like to take the liberty of applying that insight to place, for without linguistic interaction computer interfaces and spatial metaphors have limited meaning.

This leads naturally to Gotved's *practice spatial dimension* (inspired by Lefebvre's spaces of representation). This is the dimension of the model in which *social interaction* between participants complements the visible and (re)constructive dimensions in order to perform and weave together social constructs such as sexualities, genders, and places on an ongoing basis. As explained in the paragraph on visible spatiality (above), this use of the term 'practice' differs from Lefebrve's term 'spatial practice' in that Gotved has separated out the epistemological aspects of Lefebvre's practice theorising and placed them here. The visible and reconstructive spatial dimensions gain social meaning in tandem with social interaction. Without it, although visible spatialities can still be seen (whether bricks and mortar, words on a page, or pixels on a screen), limits are placed on their meaning potential (for examples in the urban built environment, see Blumen 2007; Conlon 2004). In order to investigate the linguistic performance of sexualised places, a corpus of chat-room data was exploited. The next section briefly outlines how that corpus was conceived and collected, before analysing the data using Gotved's tri-partite model.

Corpus creation and word categories

The following section briefly outlines the methods used to acquire the data as well as a few of the practical realities faced while compiling the corpus and preparing it for computational analysis (although the quantitative aspects are not the focus here).[7] Between 27 October and 29 November 2005, data were gathered from the 'public' spaces of queer chat rooms. At no time did I record the type of one-on-one chatting referred to as private by the portal site providing the chat rooms (let alone record it).[8] In a recent article by del-Teso-Craviotto (2008) in which she describes her approach to the gathering of online chat room data, I was struck by the similarities between our approaches although we were unaware of one another's work at the time. Like del-Teso-Craviotto, I did not participate in chatting while it was being recorded. Instead, I spent considerable time participating in the chat rooms beforehand, becoming familiar with the type of interactions which took place there. I then 'lurked' (entered but failed to interact) in five or six rooms at one time, leaving them running for several hours. Then the resulting texts of the conversations were copied and pasted into word processing files, storing them for future processing. As del-Teso-Craviotto (2008:254) points out, this method of data collection sometimes raises ethical concerns, but in this particular study it was possible to contact participants via e-mail, and permission to add their conversations to the corpus was gained (for details on how this was managed, see King 2009). Although the contents were not monitored, this gathering procedure was not random because attention was paid to various chatting circumstances (described in more detail below). That procedure was also dictated largely by the anonymous, spontaneous and often ephemeral nature of online communication.

Geographic locations specified for the rooms, as well as the time of chatting, were carefully considered during data collection, and the data was taken from rooms named after locations in the USA and Australia. Those countries were chosen so as to include one country from North America and one from elsewhere, and there were abundant data available for these two countries. They are both large territories, so data was gathered from locations in diverse regions. This was an attempt to avoid a skewing of data based on regional dialect within one nation (e.g. Texas). I also tried not to collect a disproportionate amount of data from rooms named for large urban centres. As Cameron and Kulick (2003:85) have pointed out, too often rural queer perspectives have been elided from language analyses in the past, so I attempted not to repeat this error. The data were gathered seven days a week at various times (afternoon, evening, and late at night) in order to avoid an overabundance of topics or styles that might dominate on certain days or at certain times of the day/night. Data collection was limited to a one-month period.

It is reasonable to assume that these rooms were populated mostly by participants located in the USA and Australia. The participant profiles allowed access to detailed information about who was chatting in these rooms. There are 1332 participants whose words appear in the corpus. Commonly one has no information at all about the corporeal selves of the people chatting in an online chat-room. In this case (as with Shaw 1997), many of these men were hoping to meet other men in the offline world, so they created profiles, often containing photos and detailed information about themselves.[9]

In the context of the original study (King 2006), decisions needed to be made concerning how to analyse the corpus. In order to discover which words were present in the data, a word list was created using Wordsmith Tools 4. In that process, Wordsmith produces a list of all the words present, tallying a count of each word. Although more frequent words are usually considered to be of great interest in such word lists, it is common in corpora to find 'hapax legomena' (words found only once), as many as forty per cent in most cases (Kennedy 1998). Being so rare in the data, these words are often ignored, but they may prove useful when categorised carefully into 'word categories' (Baker 2004:352–3). To form word categories for analysis, words from the lists are placed into categories, grouping them based on the ways they are used in discourse. For that reason, the decision was made to categorise together words in the generated list that would serve as useful lexical markers; that is, words which point to sections of the corpus in which the performative construction of queer social constructs takes place. By returning to the original source text, every incidence of a word was checked in order to ensure that it was used in a way that was appropriate for the word category. These categories were based partly on my own observation and partly on analyses by other researchers of language use by gay men (including Baker 2005; Cameron and Kulick 2003; Chauncey 1994; Harvey 2000). The word category *Camp Names*, which is featured in this article, emerged through this form of analysis as did other word categories, which will not be analysed here, including:

- feminised vocatives (e.g. use by men of terms like 'sweetie' and 'darling' to refer to other men);
- camp use of French (e.g. He has a certain je ne sais quoi!);
- gender inversions (e.g. referring to a man as 'she' or 'girl');
- reappropriations (e.g. queen, fag); and
- whore-stigma gender inversions (e.g. referring to a man as a 'slut' or 'hussy').

'Camp' here refers to a sensibility and style of speaking, one often associated with effeminacy/femininity due to its ability to expose the theatricality of gender; a theatricality that masculinity tends to be cushioned from due to its unmarked status (Halberstam 1998:238). In defining the character of camp, it is useful to look at the opinions of gay interviewees in a New Zealand study by Brickell and Taylor (2004), in which ideologies around campness and effeminacy emerge. These men view camp as a resource to draw upon in practice, and regard it positively if it is 'done' in moderation, an opinion which points to a covert ideological stigmatisation of effeminacy. They believe camp is not the same as effeminacy because doing camp is (at some level) a self-conscious choice; something that can be turned on and off. Camp is a practice-based resource, whereas effeminacy is seen to be more intrinsic or unconscious. This definition of camp as grounded in practice is useful here because during analysis Camp Names will not be treated as a manifestation of an intrinsic quality of any one participant; rather they are seen to be a manifestation of camp used as a resource. Finally, the interviewees' descriptions of camp are summarised as consisting of affectations, forms of exaggeration, and inversions of value systems (Brickell and Taylor 2004:147). This definition resonates with Keith Harvey's camp talk framework, in which he delineates camp into four rhetorical strategies: parody, ludicrism, inversion, and paradox (Harvey 1998, 2000a, 2000b). Cameron and Kulick (2003:99) have altered the focus of Harvey's framework in order to bring it more in line with a focus on the effects of utterances. Rather than viewing these categories as strategies, they position camp talk as language that *produces the effects* of parody, ludicrism, inversion, and paradox. They also make the valid point that it is a resource available to all (a point which resonates with the opinions expressed above) and not tied exclusively to gay male identities (however useful it might sometimes be for producing them). One might ask to what end someone could take advantage of camp talk's ability to produce those four effects. This study demonstrates one such use of camp's effects as a resource for the manipulation of power relationships, a reworking of subject positions which helps to shape these online places as queer. In fact Camp Names were chosen as a word category for analysis because of their importance to the construction of queer spatialities as well as their relative frequency.[10] Nicknames in online chat provide cues about who people claim to be, and chat participants are aware of this fact. As a result, they '...actively manipulate these meanings to entice the kind of communication in which they are most interested' (Waskul 2003:40). As will be seen below, manipulations of names in these chat rooms (by their owners and their interlocutors) indeed prove to be tied to both camp and to place performance as part of Gotved's practice spatial dimension.

Camp Names is a label inspired by *camp culture* in New York, according to the historical account of Chauncey (1994). Examples of Camp Names that Chauncey gives are Toto (named after the little dog in Wizard of Oz) and Maxine (instead of Max) and Blossom (merely for its feminine ring). A man's use of a Camp Name at that time indexed a public queer identity, certainly, but more importantly it 'marked his transition from the straight world to the gay [world]' (Chauncey 1994:51). We see that Camp Names historically have been directly involved with the (re)creation of queer spatiality. Similar but not identical to Chauncey's model, included in this category are name exclamations (e.g. JOHHHHNNNNYYYY!!), which also relate to Harvey's *camp talk* parody, in which the use of 'catty femininity' by gay men (like 'screechy' greetings) challenges assumptions about how men talk. Name diminutives have also been included, that is suffixes added to names (connoting smallness, daintiness, or babiness) and feminisations of names. For example, the hypothetical nickname *bigbear* might be changed to *bigbearette*, or perhaps *shane2231* might change to *shaniqua* (an oblique reference to pop divas) or to *shaneypoo*. There are diverse examples in the data, but tokens classified as Camp Names for this study are all transformations of online nicknames in one of the above ways. All the names have been changed to protect the online identities of the participants; however, effort was made to create new names that retain the spirit of the original and to convert them in like manner. Example 1 below is taken from a section of the corpus in which we see Camp Names appearing in a particularly dense fashion.

Example 1: Camp Names in use

No.	Nickname	Turn
1	Silverback	hey North
2	Moonlit	i messed up...
3	Silverback	why Moony?
4	Silverback	hey Dan
5	Moonlit	the 'X' button
6	Dancoast	hey Silver
7	Dima	Moonybabes
8	Silverback	ohhh
9	Dima	Rainbeau Bright
10	Moonlit	Dimalover

```
11  STUDbeau      DIIIIMMMMIIEEEEEE!!
12  Moonlit       Beaupeep
13  Dima          Beau Derek
14  STUDbeau      Danni Costalittle
15  Silverback    DimDims
16  OvrhdCAM      gnight… it's dinnner time…
17  Dancoast      Beaubutante
18  Silverback    bye Cam
19  Silverback    hugs
```

At this moment, several participants are arriving and leaving at the same time, and an elaborate greeting and farewell ritual unfolds. In lines 1 and 4, *Silverback* is greeting newcomers to the room whose names have appeared in the list of those 'present' (see A in Figure 12.2 below). He fails to use Camp Names to refer to them, but in line 3 he responds to *Moonlit*'s 'I messed up' using a diminutive name (Moony) which is a rather mundane version of a Camp Name. *Dima* then chimes in with an elaboration (Moonybabes) as a greeting for *Moonlit*, and greets *STUDbeau* as Rainbeau Bright (a reference to a children's doll marketed to girls). In line 10, *Moonlit* returns the gesture, calling him Dimalover and *STUDbeau* uses a screechy Camp Name in line 11. This leads to a string of Camp Names that evoke storybook girls (Beaupeep), models (Beau Derek), drag-queen-like names (*Dancoast* = Danni Costalittle), and young 'society girls' (Beaubutante). Performatively these moves cite gay stereotypes, as is often the case with camp (Campbell 2004:89; Désert 1997:25), and in this case that citation contributes to a performance of gay in-group solidarity (as evidenced by *Silverback*'s 'hugs' in line 19). These identity-related functions of Camp Names are important but are merely one aspect of their use in these chat rooms, as further analysis shall demonstrate.

Visible Spatiality – What you see is not all that you get

Following the sequence of events that participants follow as they log into chat rooms, it makes sense to start with what can be seen on the screen. Woodland ([1995]2000:425) rightly asserts that without meaningful interaction, places for online chat would be precluded in spite of the interface provided, but this visible spatial dimension warrants a brief look because it is where we first see that place 'matters' as part of chat room interaction. Figures 12.1 and 12.2 show two portions of the visible spatiality of the chat rooms in this study.

In the case of the chat client where the data were collected, Figure 12.1 is the first 'window' that appears when someone chooses to participate in a chat room conversation.[11] I have enclosed the label of this particular window *'Chat Room List'* in a black rectangle (see top left corner). By way of this label we see that the metaphor of 'room' appears in the visible dimension. As will be seen later, this metaphor is taken up by the participants on an ongoing basis, contributing to the sense that chat is taking place in a 3D spatiality – a kind of 'room'. Near the middle of this window (in a grey rectangle) there is a 'button' which says 'Enter Room'. Above the *Enter Room* button (in the white box) is a list of available 'rooms', which

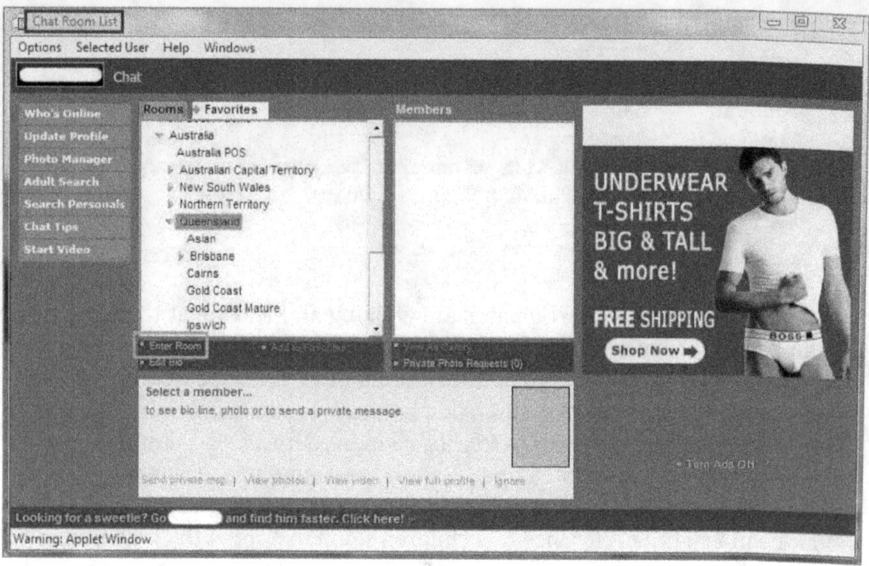

Figure 12.1 Chat client – initial window.

are named after cities such as Brisbane and Cairns. So we see that the 'room' metaphor is again and again encountered as one navigates these screens in search of an online chatting experience. By highlighting one of these 'rooms' and clicking the *Enter Room* button, one passes to a screen like the one displayed in Figure 12.2.

Once this screen has been reached, the chat can begin. Letter C in Figure 12.2 indicates the typing box in which a chat participant types contributions to the ongoing conversation. The ongoing conversation appears as a 'scrolling script' in the large white box above the typing box, with new contributions appearing at the bottom and older ones disappearing out the top. As long as one keeps the window open, one can scroll up to read the older contributions. Letter B indicates the nicknames of participants that appear beside their contributions (blurred for privacy). Every time the chat client receives a contribution from a participant, it is displayed here, followed by a colon and some space, and then their typed words (e.g. jon3245: Hi everybody!). This scrolling script is 'where' the communication can be found (Gotved 2006:480; see also Yates 1996:46). Letter A indicates the list of nicknames of those who have entered the room. The participants are 'here in the room' if their names appear in this list. The interface, then, carries with it certain spatial arrangements that have a direct bearing on how the communication unfolds. For example, the ubiquitous presence of nicknames as a result of the script format (see also Shaw 1997:134) gives *names* central importance, a fact which becomes more salient during participant interaction. Because the interface always remains in the participant's field of view, the visible spatial dimension is not readily separable from the (re)constructive dimension and its metaphors. Participants interact with the user interface and the room metaphor in dynamic ways. They are influenced in their language use by these spatial dimensions.

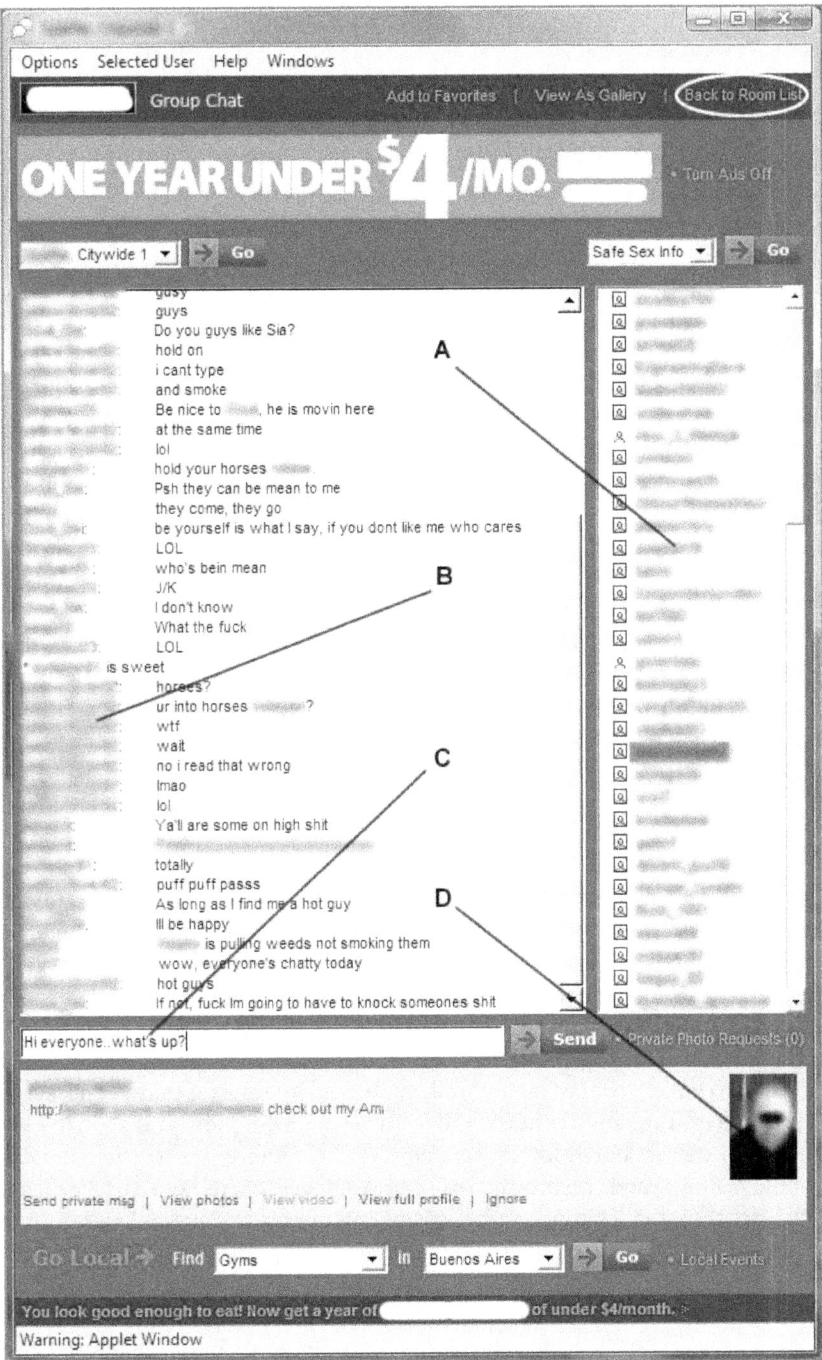

Figure 12.2 Chat client – chatting interface window. A = list of those present; B = contributor's name; C = typing field; D = image displayed by contributor.

Elements of both dimensions call forth place and sexuality in a dialogic relationship that sets the stage for social interaction and its meaning-making potential.

(Re)constructive Spatiality – I need (a) room to move

Online places have arisen from the use of metaphors of place and require an act of shared imagination in order to be experienced as places. The effect of these metaphors is to create a fundamental sense of place; to interact with others online is to have a geographic experience (Taylor 1997:190). This tendency of cyberspace to feel geographical (albeit metaphorically) is reinforced indirectly by Brown (2000:15) who insists that spatial metaphors are lived in very material ways. His argument is that making a clear-cut separation between the metaphorical and material is 'specious' because discourse and its metaphors are inescapable (see also Lakoff and Johnson [1980]2003:3). It is partly through metaphors that performative citations call forth recognisable places.

Along these lines, Gregson and Rose (2000:441) make the important point that places do not pre-exist their performance, an insight they have gained partly by studying 'car boot' sales. At these sales, people meet in their cars at shifting locations in order to sell their used items. Unconventional locations are performed as shopping places – places of commerce – through the language (among other behaviours) of the participants as they assume various familiar subject positions of seller and consumer. The performative citing (or indexing) of these subject positions aids in performances of commercial place *instead of* other types of places. From a performative point of view, one could say that discourses and their metaphors cite past performances in order to 'materialise' places, making tangible places (such as coffee shops) to some extent virtual. Online places (such as chat rooms) likewise cite past performances of places, importing the offline or 'material' world in discursive form.[12] In this way, the material/metaphorical binary is seen to be a reified heuristic division. To ignore the ongoing metaphor of *DISCOURSE as ROOM* would be to overlook the ways in which the shared imaginary of a room helps to shape the performances of genders and sexualities unfolding 'there' and how the gendered and sexualised discourses used 'there' produce the metaphorical room as a certain type of place.

Certainly the appearance of the word 'room' on the interface has a performative effect in which 'rooms' are evoked, evidenced by the fact that as the 'script' scrolls and real-time interaction unfolds, the room metaphor is taken up by participants. The effect partly arises from periodic bald references to 'the room' (see Example 4, line 4) and the prolific use of phrases such as 'in here' to refer to the participants' shared location (a phrase which is spread throughout this corpus). Table 12.1 is a sample of random, unconnected concordance lines taken from the corpus, showing examples of the use of 'in here'.

What I hope to demonstrate by including these examples is that the word 'here' alone would suffice were the participants not aware of the spatiality of the interaction. However, because that would fail to evoke the sense that the participants are 'in' a three-dimensional place, the phrase 'in here' is frequently

Table 12.1 Concordance lines for the term 'in here'.

ASqu: hands what are you doing	**in here**	tonight? Lol
ASqu: Hey Chazie are you awake	**in here**	?
ASqu: Nothing happens	**in here**	cbt. . nothing nothing nothing…
Red4bear2: surely not	**in here**	:P
Red4bear2: thought all the boys	**in here**	all had happy successful relationships
looose: these faggots are feral	**in here**	looose: bobbyD needs to piss on a few
pj: gee its boring	**in here**	tho pj: god sometimes u cant get a word in
beachdude234: gets very confusing	**in here**	whos talking to who
TeachersPet: welcome to the new faces	**in here**	TeachersPet: and the old ones without faces
beat7 : lotta five and six faces	**in here**	
beat7 : really exciting	**in here**	kinkypupdan: exciting as chasing my tail
UrbanUrsa: quiet	**in here**	UrbanUrsa: no one talking much
TeachersPet: bent wot u doing	**in here**	TeachersPet: u lost?
Jiz Jar: boring	**in here**	Jiz Jar: u must all be wanking
chuckblake69: is it always so quiet	**in here**	? beat7 : lurkers n deceivers
jondkilda: hey beat7 think anyone	**in here**	actually wants sex?

chosen, suggesting that spatiality indeed matters in these chat rooms. Bear in mind that this is merely one among a plethora of such spatialising phrases. The city-identified names of the chat rooms are also performative, citing offline locations and lending a sense of place to the experience. As Rheingold (1993:63) has expressed, people offline have a 'strongly shared mental model' of place whereas those online depend on individual imagination for this shared sense. When one enters the *Honolulu Room*, the presence of the word Honolulu might or might not make the chat experience feel more Hawaiian, but it becomes part of a web of place metaphors. What is more, the 'roomness' of the place being performed bears itself out in a feeling of three dimensions during interaction which precipitates discursive bodies. Place and embodiment are interrelated because 'having a body always implies being somewhere, as well as this 'somewhere' not making sense apart from embodied positions, trajectories, [and] traversals (Sundén 2003:92). Evidence for the precipitation of discursive bodies can be seen in Example 2.

Example 2: Precipitation of discursive bodies

No.	Nickname	Turn
1	StudzRround	hey hey everyone
2	Carmichael	that's better, StudzRnd, but I still want a personal kiss :-)
3	StudzRround	yeah and I want a big chocolate cake
4	Carmichael	*scowls @ StudzRround
5	Carmichael	no chocolate hazelnut torte for StudzRnd
6	StudzRround	no but a homemade German Chocolate Cake would do nicely…
7	StudzRround	and bring some milk too
8	Carmichael	I'm still scowling, StudzRround
9	Stretcharmstrong	HMMMm… German Choco Cake
10	SamIam	you scowl in your sleep Car
11	Moonlit	mm@ German Chocolate Cake
12	Carmichael	I think you're right, SamIam

13	Moonlit	*will bottom for German Chocolate Cake…
14	StudzRround	with lots and lots of iceing
15	StudzRround	lol Moonie… you will bottom for anything
16	Carmichael	*goes back to his corner
17	Moonlit	not for anchovies. .
18	SamIam	Studdiekins. . people who live in glass houses… .

In line 4, *Carmichael* responds to *StudzRround*'s playful snub (line 3) by 'scowling' at him. Throughout the corpus, those who write about what they do with their bodies often write it in the way it appears here, with an asterisk and a 'stage direction' style rather than speech style (see also Rellstab 2007; Werry [1996]2004). This kind of discursive embodiment is where we see the room metaphor's indirect influence through its 3D spatiality. Carmichael 'goes back to his corner' in line 16, showing once again that the 'room' is helping to produce this embodied environment. The link between place and embodiment features throughout the rest of this discussion.

Practice spatiality – giving meaning to metaphor

It is through interaction that subject positions start to influence the sexualisation of places, places partly grounded in those subject positions. In this case, queer places emerge from slippage in the citation of subject positions and their power relationships, citations which draw on heteronormative models. Throughout this section, micro-analysis will focus on gendered and sexual subject positions; it must be remembered, though, that these subject positions (and their manipulation) cannot be separated from the ongoing production of the room. The practice dimension remains joined to the reconstruction of the room. Referring back to Example 2 we have already seen Carmichael's body materialise as part of the room. By scowling and scuttling off into corners, his discursive embodiment has not enhanced the sexualisation of the room as a place, but it will soon become clear that sexualisation and the materialisation of bodies often accompany one another in these chat rooms.

In this exchange, participants are engaging in what has been labelled 'verbal duelling' and observed as a socialising behaviour in [heteronormative], male homosocial environments (Dundes, Leach and Özkök 1972). Such sparring and taunting among these participants suggests identification with that sort of male-male social bonding. To reiterate this model is a masculine identity performance for these chatters, yet it is a queer masculinity. Looking at straight-identified men, Heasley (2005:310) defines 'queer masculinity' as having 'the potential to disrupt traditional images of the hegemonic heterosexual masculine'. It is interesting, then, that nickname choices by participants in these chat rooms often appear to be grounded in iconic constructions of masculinity (e.g. StudzRround). As the often overtly masculine nicknames continually scroll up the screen, heteronormatively masculine subject positions are indexed (through the use of the term stud, for example). However, each time one of these names is converted to a Camp Name as part of language play, there is slippage in the reiteration of masculine subject positions, and masculinity is queered. After the typing of one more line, the original masculine nickname returns in the scrolling script beside that participant's contribution, yet masculinity has been problematised. Bodies and subject positions slip away from heteronormativity, contributing to a performance of queer place. The connection between bodies and spatiality is crucial. *Carmichael* has said in line 2 that he still wants a kiss from *StudzRround* who playfully rebuffs *Carmichael* in line 3 by typing 'yeah, and I want a big chocolate cake' (the implication being that we all want various things that we cannot have). *Carmichael*'s notion of receiving a kiss from *StudzRround* suggests once again that the chat room has three-dimensional spatiality and embodied co-presence of interlocutors. Inseparable from this three-dimensionality, the interaction which follows partly shapes how place is performed. A discussion ensues of chocolate cake, and in line 12, *Moonlit* claims (in a stage-direction style aside) that he 'will bottom for German Chocolate Cake'. This is a reference to sexual subject positions that are common gay male stereotypes: 'top' (dominant, penetrator) and 'bottom' (submissive, penetrated). *Moonlit* suggests that receiving chocolate cake would be adequate motivation for him to 'bottom', but significantly he presents this as a marked position for him (something he needs to be bribed to do). So, in fact, he claims the sexual subject position 'top' as part of a performance of masculinity (a conscious identity move). Furthermore, with its evocation of the role of sexual penetrator, claiming the 'top' role shows a perhaps less conscious identification with the heteronormative sexual subject position 'man' (a desirable position in this chat room). The role of heteronormativity is not immediately transparent here, but I would like to suggest that it is akin to the role played by homosexuality in Cameron's (1997) analysis of frat boy conversation. It is a 'danger that cannot be acknowledged' (Cameron and Kulick 2003:122) that must be dealt with in interaction.

In these chat-rooms, participants interacting in typed conversation rely on shared cultural models in order to send and receive signals of desire and identity. Kiesling (2006:262) defines these models as 'Discourses' (in the Foucauldian sense) 'distilled' from the culture into a more concrete form. This top/bottom dyad indexes a heteronormative cultural model analysed by MacKinnon (1982:541) in her phrase *'Man fucks woman: subject, verb, object'*. Although MacKinnon's analysis had a different focus from this study, that phrase captures the notion that women are the *object* or the *recipient of action* in heteronormative talk about sex. The transitive form of the verb 'to fuck' can be interpreted quite broadly as 'to instigate and control sexual interaction' without losing its patriarchal message that men control sex. It is interesting to observe that *StudzRround* responds by suggesting that in fact *Moonlit* will 'bottom for anything' (line 15), placing him in a pejorative subject position heteronormatively reserved for women (i.e. easy or slut). This move queers *Moonlit*'s gender and disempowers him while empowering *StudzRround* by allowing him to disavow the 'woman' subject position. Kiesling ([2002]2006) documents the use of a similar strategy by heterosexual men in the homosocial (single gender) environment of a fraternity in the USA. He identifies the assigning of a women's or a gay male role to a man as a way to subordinate him and disempower him through questioning his masculinity. My purpose here is not to suggest that heteronormativity is inherently and always sexist. As Jackson (1999:164) points out 'it cannot ... be assumed that heteronormativity and male domination always articulate with each other in predictable ways'. In fact the normalising force of heteronormativity also has negative effects on heterosexual men (see Kimmel 2001). Rather, heteronormativity here refers primarily to what Jackson (1999:145) calls the 'penetrative norm' by which men's penises penetrate women's vaginas, a norm captured by Mackinnon's 'man fucks woman' model. As the analyses in this study demonstrate, when used as a tool in power relations, these models are often sexist in tone, likely reflecting gender hierarchies in society. However, non-sexist discourses can still be profoundly heteronormative in their erasure of non-heterosexual subjectivities (see Yep 2003).

Camp Names in Example 2 could also be achieving the disempowerment of participants (at least at the level of playful verbal sparring), particularly in response to identifications with heteronormative sexual subject positions, but also in response to more conscious identity performances. *SamIam*, for instance, intercedes in *StudzRround*'s disavowal by converting his nickname to a Camp Name (*Studdiekins*). This move indexes gay stereotypes, contributing to a gay identity performance for *SamIam* and to the disempowerment of *StudzRround* by converting his name to a form which ceases to index a masculine subject position (via 'stud'). The separation of sexual subject positions by *Moonlit* and *StudzRround* into sharply defined roles of penetrated and penetrator threatens to cite heteronormative sexual place, but the countermoves (which involve gay identity performances and identifications with sexual subject positions) result in queer place through slippage, and heteronormative place is not reiterated despite the heteronormative baggage of the language being used. Example 3 provides further examples.

Example 3: penetrator and penetrated

No.	Nickname	Turn
1	Nobodeez	Wuzzat… very nice black and white pic in ur profile ;-)
2	Wuzzat	thanks Nobbiebabes :D
3	Wuzzat	have a look at my gaydar… . they aer better and in colour
4	PeA	hey Nobodeez
5	Nobodeez	I did that too Wuzz ;-)
6	Nobodeez	heya PeA :-) how goes it?
7	Wuzzat	hehe cheers np :D
8	Torpedo24	tee-hee
9	Too_guyish_1980	IM ME WUZZ
10	Mh_club	* Mh_club doesnt drink
11	Torpedo24	*blinx*

```
12  Wuzzat       * Wuzzat doesn't do drugs either
13  torpedo24    ill make u drink bitch *inserts penis into
                 Mh_club's orafice*
14  mh_club      * feels a slight sensation… looks up and
                 slaps Torpedorella
```

In this section of chat, the room becomes sexualised and place emerges as queer through the identities and identifications of the participants. In line 5, *Wuzzat* thanks *Nobodeez* for complimenting his pic (photo) and transforms *Nobodeez*' name into a Camp Name (*nobbiebabes*). This Camp Name transformation indexes gay stereotypes through parody as part of a gay identity performance for *Wuzzat*, a move which augments queer slippage in the performance of place (see analysis of Example 1). In line 10, *Mh_club* suddenly suggests in an aside that he 'doesn't drink'. *Torpedo24*'s response is to say 'I'll make you drink bitch' and insert his penis in *Mh_club*'s (discursive) orifice. Once again the power relations of subject positions interact with the performance of bodies, which are closely tied to the room metaphor (see last section).

The identifications and identity performances in these two lines are complex. Following Halberstam (1998), masculinity is treated in this study as a construct uncoupled from male bodies; a subjectivity available to all during identity performance. Yet 'male' bodies (within a western cultural context at least) tend to be the only legitimate frames upon which to hang masculinity (Haywood and Mac An Ghaill 2003:116). Analysis of these chat rooms reveals that male bodies are indeed performed in dialog with masculinity and online places, while female bodies are conspicuous only in their absence. Male bodies are called forth and sexualised as part of the sexualisation of the room, with *Torpedo24*'s possession of a penis (and position as sexual aggressor) indexing 'man' as a sexual subject position due to heteronormativity. Through citation of the 'man fucks woman' cultural model, *Torpedo24*'s use of language indexes heteronormative (and in this case sexist) sexual subject positions, leading to a sexual subject position for *Mh_club* that would heteronormatively be reserved for women (bitch, penetrated, submissive). *Mh_club* first resists *Torpedo24*'s masculine identity performance by implying that *Torpedo24*'s penis is so small that he can barely feel it. Even more relevant to our focus here, he transforms *Torpedo24*'s name into a Camp Name (*torpedorella*). This move demonstrates *Mh_club*'s own identification with the 'man' subject position because he resists being placed in the disempowered 'woman' position. He does so by way of a Camp Name conversion for *Torpedo24* and the act of slapping (a feminised form of violence). These responses also index gay stereotypes through camp inversion and lead to a gay identity performance. This identity move further queers the subject positions, and the sexualising of bodies (and thus place) emerges as queer rather than heteronormative. Example 4 contains one more extract from much later in the same conversation.

Example 4: paradox of male-male attraction

No.	Nickname	Turn
1	Insouth_bi	hi all
2	Buff_furry_fifty	is there a storm coming over
3	Spunky25	*wanders back in naked
4	Buff_furry_fifty	this is a boys room
5	Buff_furry_fifty	anyone want some cock as entree this arvo
6	Mh_club	nibblies buffette?
7	Buff_furry_fifty	bit more than that
8	BondsRbeaut65	lol . . More like a buffet!… only a bit more ?
9	Buff_furry_fifty	just actualoly
10	Heavenhemlock34	who want to play with my cock?

The primary exchange in this section of conversation is somewhat opaque because of the online chatting forum in which turns are displayed in the order the system receives them. The (re)constructive room spatiality is evoked by Spunky25, who 'wanders back in naked' and contributes to a sexualising of bodies and spatiality. *Buff_furry_fifty*'s statement 'this is a boys' room' (line 4 – likely in response to *Insouth_bi*'s 'bisexual' nickname) augments this effect through a bald reference to the room spatiality. We see the male body being called forth in turns 5 and 10 ('cock'). Once again, these turns place multiple participants in the sexual subject position 'man' by indexing heteronormative, binary models of bodies in which possession of a cock precludes placement in the 'woman' sexual subject position. Being placed at the receiving end of male attraction creates a paradox because of citations of the 'man fucks woman' cultural model. To clarify, in turn 5, *Buff_furry_fifty* makes a sexual advance, placing other participants in the subject position 'woman. ' In turn 6, *Mh_club* responds to *Buff_furry_fifty*'s comparison of his own 'cock' to an 'entrée' by suggesting that it is just 'nibblies' (i.e. smaller than an entrée). He also transforms *Buff_furry_fifty*'s nickname into a Camp Name by adding '-ette' to the first syllable (buffette). This use of a Camp Name serves as a gay identity performance on *Mh_club*'s part and serves as resistance to 'man fucks woman' subject positions, disempowering him by questioning his masculinity.

Conclusions

This study demonstrates that Gotved's adaptation of Lefebvre's model can be fruitfully applied while investigating how sexualised and gendered places are performed online. By separating out the visible, the metaphorical and the interactive while emphasising their interdependency, provision is made for the investigation of how online spaces (new, exciting, and often ephemeral) can become places (recognisable, safer, and functional). The model allows the researcher to view the process of place formation as performative, and thus grounded in interaction and power. To treat place as performative is a move compatible with space/place theory, and so is the view that place is performed in practice:

> The work of Seamon, Pred, Thrift, de Certeau and others show us how place is constituted through reiterative social practices – place is made and remade on a daily basis. Place provides a template for practice – an unstable stage for performance. Thinking of place as performed and practiced can help us think of place in radically open and non-essentialised ways where place is constantly struggled over and reimagined in practical ways. (Cresswell 2004:39)

Although Cresswell fails to refer to performativity here, the idea that place is 'made and remade on a daily basis' on an 'unstable stage' is clearly compatible with the assertion that place is performative. Other analysts have hinted at the performative nature of place through discourse (e.g. Baynham 2003:349; Leap 1999:115; Modan 2007:310), and Morrish and Leap (2007:34–5) have begun to explore understandings of sexual geographies through narratives about built environments (lending significance to the importance of place to sexuality). To my knowledge, performances of places as sites of interaction (which demonstrate the importance of *sexuality to place)* remain under-researched. Without tools for linking space and interaction, it would be difficult to take up Blommaert's challenge (2005a) to include space as a tool in discourse analysis. In fact, throughout the process of using the triangle of space model, I repeatedly realised that what Gotved was proposing for cyberspace is equally applicable to the offline world. Indeed, as Modan (2007) has also shown, Lefebvre's three-sided model can be applied to built environments.

Gotved's practice spatial dimension is where performative citations call forth subject positions and their power relations, and where the co-constitutive relationship between place, sexual identities/identifications, genders, and discursive bodies unfolds. It is also where heteronormative place is intercepted and precluded through a mix of slippages, and queer places can emerge. In reference to heteronormativity, Gregson and Rose (2000:437) are critical of other studies (in particular Bell et al. 1994) which seem to suggest that heterosexual place is always 'there' as a kind of default sexualisation of place that can only be infiltrated by non-heteronormative performances and subject positions. The key point for the present analysis is that queer places are constructed *instead of* heteronormative ones. However, hegemonic heteronormativity is not easily ignored, making itself felt in the discourses of sexual subject positions which are not easily separated from cultural models.

The room metaphor bridges the online and offline worlds, giving these rooms a three-dimensional feeling which results in the materialising of discursive bodies. The user interface interacts with the metaphor, and in the process sexuality is woven into the fabric of the place. At the same time, primarily during interaction, the room becomes sexualised and gendered, contributing to the sexualisation of bodies. From one point of view, camp is used as a linguistic resource to produce gay subject positions, as paralleled by Chauncey (1994:105) and Kiesling ([2002]2006:122). This gay identity discourse also serves as a form of resistance to the 'man fucks woman' cultural model that arises from the paradox of being (or at least playing the role of) a man who is the target of a man's sexual advances. It is double-edged because heteronormativity produces the sexual subject position 'woman' at the receiving end of male sexual desire (a disempowered position) and the sexual subject position 'man' at the sending end. Masculinity is also potentially bound to the 'sending' position. Indeed, being sexually desirable in these rooms is dependent upon discursively locating oneself squarely in the sexual subject position 'man' while performing masculine gender. Still, how can one occupy both positions at once (under the thumb of heteronormative discourses) and so perform both masculine, manly attractiveness and desire for other masculine men at the same time?

The use of camp by the participant in the receiving position has two simultaneous effects. Addressing someone using a Camp Name, for example, reduces the masculine power of the 'sending' participant by indexing a feminised subject position for him (a strategy learned in other male homosocial environments perhaps) (Kiesling [2002]2006:128–9). At the same time, this use of camp by the recipient *queers* masculinity and sexual subject positions through the performance of stereotyped gay behaviour. This stance tacitly acknowledges the received disempowerment that is taking place while refusing to comply: a disempowering position is seen to have a power of its own. As in Barrett ([1995]2006:163) this conscious production of a stereotype 'appropriates and reworks' domination. In this web, *queer* places (rather than exclusively *gay* places) are performed through the preclusion of heteronormatively sexualised and gendered performances of place. Places are provided *in* which communities (however defined) might form or *to* which they might temporarily or permanently relocate, adding their distinctiveness to performances of places and gaining some distinctiveness from those performances. It is also a 'space' in which random individuals come and go (similar to a bar, for example), performing non-normative sexual identities and/or desires with widely varying levels of investment either in those concepts or in any 'communities' that might be under construction. Participants become sexual while slipping into 'queer space'.

Notes

1 See also Baynham (2003) and LeVine (2007).
2 Cyberspace as a term was initially taken from the novel *Neuromancer* (Gibson 1984).
3 Blommaert (2005b), in his analysis of Ras Pakaay's radio programme in Cape Town, South Africa, also maintains a regional focus.
4 As Modan (2007:323) and Gotved (2006:485) point out, Shields (1998) has modified the original translation into English (by Donald Nicholson-Smith) by changing the name of the third category, making it less confusing.
5 Here I owe acknowledgement to Modan (2007) and Gotved (2006) for their lucid explanations of Lefebvre's categories.
6 If one looks at space at a 'micro' level, it becomes clear that communities (and their practices) interact with various 'sites and arenas of face-to-face exchange' (Collins and Slembrouck 2005:191). To neglect how place is produced through talk and how it influences talk is to overlook a vital element of the context of any community of people regardless of how one defines community.

7 For a more detailed explanation of the compilation, annotation, and quantitative analysis of this corpus, please refer to King (2009).
8 The ethical and practical decisions that I made concerning how (and whether or not) to go about gathering the data, appear in greater detail in King (2009).
9 For details of participant demographics, please refer to King (2009).
10 The quantitative facet of the study attempted to discern just who was using the word categories and in what contexts (see King 2006, 2009).
11 The white elliptical shapes (which appear on the left near the top and bottom) are spots where I have purposely obscured the name of the website for ethical reasons.
12 For an analysis of online performances of place in which offline erotic locations are cited in order to construct a sexualised atmosphere, see King (forthcoming).

References

Backhaus, Peter (2007) *Linguistic Landscapes: A Comparative Study of Urban Multilingualism in Tokyo*. Clevedon: Multilingual Matters.

Baker, Paul (2004) Querying keywords: questions of difference, frequency and sense in keywords analysis. *Journal of English Linguistics* 32(4): 346–59.

Baker, Paul (2005) *Public Discourses of Gay Men*. London: Routledge. https://doi.org/10.1177/0075424204269894

Barrett, Rusty ([1995]2006) Supermodels of the world unite! Political economy and the language of performance among African-American drag queens. In Deborah Cameron and Don Kulick (eds) *The Language and Sexuality Reader* 151–63. London: Routledge.

Baynham, Mike (2003) Narratives in space and time: beyond 'backdrop' accounts of narrative orientation. *Narrative Inquiry* 13(2): 347–66. https://doi.org/10.1075/ni.13.2.07bay

Bell, David, Binnie, Jon, Cream, Julia and Valentine, Gill (1994) All hyped up and no place to go. *Gender, Place and Culture* 1(1): 31–48. https://doi.org/10.1080/09663699408721199

Blommaert, Jan (2005a) *Discourse: A Critical Introduction*. Cambridge: Cambridge University Press. https://doi.org/10.1017/CBO9780511610295

Blommaert, Jan (2005b) In and out of class, codes and control: globalization, discourse and mobility. In Mike Baynham and Anna De Fina (eds) *Dislocations/Relocations: Narratives of Displacement* 128–43. Manchester: St Jerome.

Blumen, Orna (2007) The performative landscape of going-to-work: on the edge of a Jewish ultraorthodox neighborhood. *Environment and Planning D: Society and Space* 25(5): 803–31. https://doi.org/10.1068/d76j

Brickell, Chris and Taylor, Ben (2004) What it means to be a gay man. In Lynne Alice and Lynne Star (eds) *Queer in Aotearoa New Zealand* 145–64. Palmerston North, NZ: Dunmore Press.

Brown, Michael (2000) *Closet Space: Geographies of Metaphor from the Body to the Globe*. London: Routledge.

Browne, Kath, Lim, Jason and Brown, Gavin (eds) (2007) *Geographies of Sexualities: Theory, Practices, and Politics*. Aldershot: Ashgate Publishing.

Cameron, Deborah (1997) Performing gender identity: young men's talk and the construction of heterosexual masculinity. In Sally Johnson and Ulrika Meinhoff (eds) *Language and Masculinity* 47–64. Malden, MA: Blackwell.

Cameron, Deborah and Kulick, Don (2003) *Language and Sexuality*. Cambridge: Cambridge University Press.

Campbell, John Edward (2004) *Getting it on Online: Cyberspace, Gay Male Sexuality and Embodied identity*. Binghamton, NY: Harrington Park Press.

Chauncey, George (1994) *Gay New York: Gender, Urban Culture, and the Making of the Gay Male World, 1890–1940*. New York: Basic Books.

Cicognani, Anna (1998) On the linguistic nature of cyberspace and virtual communities. *Virtual Reality* 3(1): 16–24. https://doi.org/10.1007/BF01409794

Collins, James and Slembrouck, Stef (2005) Editorial: Multilingualism and diasporic populations: spatializing practices, institutional processes, and social hierarchies. *Language and Communication* 25(3): 189–95. https://doi.org/10.1016/j.langcom.2005.03.006

Conlon, Deirdre (2004) Productive bodies, performative spaces: everyday life in Christopher Park. *Sexualities* 7(4): 462–79. https://doi.org/10.1177/1363460704047063

Cresswell, Tim (2004) *Place: A Short Introduction*. Oxford: Blackwell.

Del-Teso-Craviotto, Marisol (2008) Gender and sexual identity authentication in language use: the case of chat rooms. *Discourse Studies* 10(2): 251–70. https://doi.org/10.1177/1461445607087011

Désert, Jean-Ulrick (1997) Queer space. In Gordon Brent Ingram, Anne-Marie Bouthillette and Yolanda Retter (eds) *Queers in Space: Communities | Public Places | Sites of Resistance* 17–26. Seattle, WA: Bay Press.

Dodge, Martin and Kitchin, Rob (2001) *Mapping Cyberspace*. London: Routledge.

Dundes, Allan, Leach, Jerry W. and Özkök, Bora (1972) The strategy of Turkish boys' verbal duelling rhymes. In John J. Gumperz and Dell Hymes (eds) *Directions in Sociolinguistics: The Ethnography of Communication* 130–60. New York: Holt, Rinehart and Winston.

Gibson, William (1984) *Neuromancer*. London: HarperCollins.

Gotved, Stine (2006) Time and space in cyber social reality. *New Media and Society* 8(3): 467–86. https://doi.org/10.1177/1461444806064484

Gregson, Nicky and Rose, Gillian (2000) Taking Butler elsewhere: performativities, spatialities and subjectivities. *Environment and Planning D: Society and Space* 18(4): 433–52. https://doi.org/10.1068/d232

Halberstam, Judith (1998) *Female Masculinity*. Durham, NC: Duke University Press.

Harvey, Keith (1998) Translating camp talk: gay identities and cultural transfer. *The Translator* 4(2): 295–320. https://doi.org/10.1080/13556509.1998.10799024

Harvey, Keith (2000a) Describing camp talk: language/pragmatics/politics. *Language and Literacy* 9(3): 240–60. https://doi.org/10.1177/096394700000900303

Harvey, Keith (2000b) Gay community, gay identity and the translated text. *TTR: Traduction, Terminologie, Rédaction* 13(1): 137–65.

Haywood, Chris and Mac An Ghaill, Mairtin (2003) *Men and Masculinities*. Philadelphia, PA: Open University Press.

Heasley, Robert (2005) Queer masculinities of straight men: a typology. *Men and Masculinities* 7(3): 310–20. https://doi.org/10.1177/1097184X04272118

Jackson, Stevi (1999) *Heterosexuality in Question*. London: Sage.

Johnstone, Barbara (1990) *Stories, Community and Place: Narratives from Middle America*. Bloomington, IN: Indiana University Press.

Johnstone, Barbara (1999) Uses of Southern-sounding speech by contemporary Texas women. *Journal of sociolinguistics* 3(4): 505–22. https://doi.org/10.1111/1467-9481.00093

Johnstone, Barbara, Andrus, Jennifer and Danielson, Andrew E. (2006) Mobility, indexicality, and the enregisterment of 'Pittsburghese'. *Journal of English Linguistics* 34(2): 77–104. https://doi.org/10.1177/0075424206290692

Kawale, Rani (2004) Inequalities of the heart: the performance of emotion work by lesbian and bisexual women in London, England. *Social and Cultural Geography* 5(4): 565–81. https://doi.org/10.1080/1464936042000317703

Kennedy, Graeme (1998) *An Introduction to Corpus Linguistics*. London: Longman.

Kiesling, Scott F. ([2002]2006) Playing the straight man: displaying and maintaining male heterosexuality in discourse. In Deborah Cameron and Don Kulick (eds) *The Language and Sexuality Reader* 118–31. London: Routledge.

Kiesling, Scott F. (2006) Hegemonic identity-making in narrative. In Anna De Fina, Deborah Schiffrin and Michael Bamberg (eds) *Discourse and Identity* 261–87. Cambridge: Cambridge University Press. https://doi.org/10.1017/CBO9780511584459.014

Kimmel, Michael S. (2001) Masculinity as homophobia: fear, shame and silence in the construction of gender identity. In Stephen M. Whitehead and Frank J. Barrett (eds) *The Masculinities Reader* 266–87. Cambridge: Polity Press.

King, Brian W. (2006) A corpus-based investigation into the discourses of men in online queer space. Master's dissertation, University of Leicester, UK.

King, Brian W. (2009) Building and analysing corpora of computer-mediated communication. In Paul Baker (ed.) *Contemporary Corpus Linguistics* 301–20. London: Continuum.

King, Brian W. (Forthcoming) *Location, Lore and Language: An Erotic Triangle*. https://doi.org/10.1075/jls.1.1.06kin

Lakoff, George and Johnson, Mark ([1980]2003) *Metaphors We Live By*. Chicago, IL: University of Chicago Press. https://doi.org/10.7208/chicago/9780226470993.001.0001

Leap, William L. (1999) Sex in 'private' places: gender, erotics, and detachment in two urban locales. In William L. Leap (ed.) *Public sex/gay space* 115–40. New York: Columbia University Press.

Lefebvre, Henri ([1974]1991) *The Production of Space* (trans. Donald Nicholson-Smith). Oxford: Blackwell.

LeVine, Philip (2007) Sharing common ground: the role of place reference in parent–child conversation. In Deborah Tannen, Shari Kendall and Cynthia Gordon (eds) *Family Talk: Discourse and Identity in Four American Families* 263–82. New York: Oxford University Press.

MacKinnon, Catharine (1982) Feminism, Marxism, method and the state: an agenda for theory. *Signs* 7(3): 515–44. https://doi.org/10.1086/493898

Modan, Gabriella Gahlia (2007) *Turf Wars: Discourse, Diversity, and the Politics of Place*. Oxford: Blackwell. https://doi.org/10.1002/9780470773970

Morrish, Liz and Leap, William (2007) *Sex Talk: Language, Desire, Identity and Beyond*. In Helen Sauntson and Sakis Kyratzis (eds) *Language, Sexualities and Desires: Cross-Cultural Perspectives* 17–40. New York: Palgrave Macmillan.

Natter, Wolfgang and Jones III, John Paul (1997) Identity, space, and other uncertainties. In Georges Benko and Ulf Strohmayer (eds) *Space and Social Theory: Interpreting Modernity and Postmodernity* 141–61. Oxford: Blackwell.

Rellstab, Daniel H. (2007) Staging gender online: gender plays in Swiss internet relay chats. *Discourse and Society* 18(6): 765–87. https://doi.org/10.1177/0957926507082195

Rheingold, Howard (1993) *The Virtual Community: Homesteading on the Electronic Frontier*. Boston, MA: Addison Wesley.

Scollon, Ron and Scollon, Suzie Wong (2003) *Discourse in Place: Language in the Material World*. London: Routledge. https://doi.org/10.4324/9780203422724

Shaw, David F. (1997) Gay men and computer communication: a discourse of Sex and identity in cyberspace. In Steve G. Jones (ed.) *Virtual Culture: Identity and Communication in Cybersociety* 133–45. London: Sage.

Shields, Rob (1998) *Lefebvre, Love and Struggle*. London: Routledge.

Sidnell, Jack (2003) Constructing and managing male exclusivity in talk-in-interaction. In Janet Holmes and Miriam Meyerhoff (eds) *The Handbook of Language and Gender* 327–52. Oxford: Blackwell. https://doi.org/10.1002/9780470756942.ch14

Skeggs, Beverley, Moran, Leslie, Tyrer, Paul and Binnie, Jon (2004) Queer as folk: producing the real of urban space. *Urban studies* 41(9): 1839–56. https://doi.org/10.1080/0042098042000243183

Smith, Neil (1991) *Uneven Development: Nature, Capital, and the Production of Space*, 2nd edition. Oxford: Blackwell.

Sundén, Jenny (2003) *Material Virtualities: Approaching Online Textual Embodiment*. New York: Peter Lang.

Taylor, Jonathan (1997) The emerging geographies of virtual worlds. *The Geographical Review* 87(2): 172–92. https://doi.org/10.2307/216004

Tuan, Yi-Fu (1974) Space and place: humanistic perspective. *Progress in Geography* 6: 211–52.

Tuan, Yi-Fu (1977) *Space and Place: The Perspective of Experience*. Minneapolis, MN: University of Minnesota Press.

Unwin, Tim (2000) A waste of space? Towards a critique of the social production of space.... *Transactions of the Institute of British Geographers* 25(1): 11–29. https://doi.org/10.1111/j.0020-2754.2000.00011.x

Valentine, Gill (2002) Queer bodies and the production of space. In Steven Seidman and Diane Richardson (eds) *Handbook of Lesbian and Gay Studies* 145–60. London: Sage. https://doi.org/10.4135/9781848608269.n10

Waitt, Gordon R. (2006) Boundaries of desire: becoming sexual through the spaces of Sydney's 2002 gay games. *Annals of the Association of American Geographers* 96(4): 773–87. https://doi.org/10.1111/j.1467-8306.2006.00811.x

Waskul, Dennis D. (2003) *Self-Games and Body Play: Personhood in Online Chat and Cybersex*. New York: Peter Lang.

Werry, Christopher C. ([1996]2004) *Linguistic and Interactional Features of Internet Relay Chat*. In Geoffrey Sampson and Diana McCarthy (eds) *Corpus Linguistics: Readings in a Widening Discipline* 340–52. London: Continuum.

Woodland, Randal ([1995]2000) Queer spaces, modem boys and pagan statues. In David Bell and Barbara Kennedy (eds) *The Cybercultures Reader* 416–31. London: Routledge.

Yates, Simeon J (1996) Oral and written linguistic aspects of computer conferencing. In Susan C. Herring (ed.) *Computer-Mediated Communication: Linguistic, Social and Cross-Cultural Perspectives* 29–46. Amsterdam: John Benjamins. https://doi.org/10.1075/pbns.39.05yat

Yep, Gust A. (2003) The violence of heteronormativity in communication studies: notes on injury, healing, and queer world-making. *The Journal of Homosexuality* 45(2–4): 11–59. https://doi.org/10.1300/J082v45n02_02

13

Homophobia as moral geography

William L. Leap

FLORIDA ATLANTIC UNIVERSITY, USA; AMERICAN UNIVERSITY, USA

In spite of the apparent openness and acceptance that circulates around images of homosexuality in the public media, the threat of sexually based verbal and physical assault continues to haunt the everyday experiences of same-sex identified women and men in US society. Experiences of verbal and physical assault are something that same-sex identified men spoke about frequently during interviews and informal conversations connected with an ongoing study of DC area sexual geography (Hersker 2002; Hersker and Leap 1996; Leap 1999, 2002, 2009; Viteri 2008a, 2008b).[1] In some of those stories, narrators positioned themselves as if they were 'innocent victims' caught up in experiences of trauma and violence over which they had no control. In other cases, narrators framed the experiences of trauma and violence as if they were events in the journey of 'mythic hero' en route through an unknown and dangerous terrain in his quest for safety, apotheosis and, ultimately, resurrection/return (compare Campbell 1949:245–6). In those instances, rather than invoking images of helplessness and a loss of agency, the story-telling allowed narrators to proclaim courage, endurance and fortitude in the face of verbal and physical adversity.

This foregrounding of the 'hero' rather than as 'victim' is not a categorical feature of the narratives collected from same sex identified men during this research, and in this chapter I am interested in understanding why some DC area men would describe experiences of sexual assault in such seemingly self-serving terms.

I am also interested in how we can situate these men's storytelling (and the research project itself) within the changes in DC area urban geography that were taking place during the research period (1995–2006). Massive reconstruction projects, including a rebuilding of the city centre so that tourist-friendly entertainment centres replaced the stagnant commercial core, and the planned displacement of residents from nearby low-income neighbourhoods, were literally reinventing the DC landscape during this time. The effects of these changes unfolded unevenly and incompletely across the urban terrain, leaving many of DC's neighbourhoods with newly built structures adjacent to original businesses and abandoned buildings and with commercial and residential profiles reflecting an equally diverse accumulation.

These changes and their effects on the urban landscape were not unique to the Washington DC context during this period, of course. They were (and continue to be) part of a worldwide program of urban restructuring that reflects the particular agenda of capital and labour in the current neoliberal moment (di Leonardo 2008). One theme in this neoliberal agenda positions the accumulation of resources, not merely their consumption, as the immediate goal of a productive economy, while noting that sites of production are now pluralised and decentralised (Harvey 1989:189–97, 2005:178–9). Another theme in this neoliberal agenda questions 'whether municipal governments or proprietary developments – shopping malls and industrial parks as well as gated communities – are the most efficient institutions for the provision of basic goods and services' (Low 2003:20) and strongly favours private sector initiatives or public/private sector partnerships as the way to answer that question. The neoliberal agenda also promotes a new form of subjectivity, one that 'normalizes the logics of individualism and entrepreneurialism, equating individual freedom with self-interested choices, making individuals responsible for their own well-being and redefining citizens as consumers and clients' (Leitner et al. 2007:2). This chapter also investigates how one can link these changes in economic and urban landscape and in subjectivity to the ways sexual assault is narrated.

Homophobia as moral geography

Understandably, the restructuring of a neighbourhood raises questions about the rights of place: who belongs in the 'new' if still not fully formed urban setting and who does not. Faced with these conditions in her study of gentrification in DC's Mount Pleasant neighbourhood, linguistic anthropologist Modan argues that urban subjects develop statements of moral geography as ways of answering this question. These statements show 'how you fit in and that you fit in to the given terrain and confirm that you and given landscape are well matched' (Modan 2007:91). In Modan's description, long-term residents of the Mt. Pleasant neighbourhood demonstrate their rights to place by invoking ('imagining') a general contrast between urban and suburban space amplified by additional contrasts: safety vs. danger, ethnic diversity vs. 'white' homogeneity, fearlessness and fearful people, masculinity vs. femininity, strong local networks vs. weak networks and law-and-order sentiments. They situate Mt. Pleasant within the urban side of the binary, and explain the decline of the neighbourhood in terms of the intrusion of 'suburban' elements into the 'urban' neighbourhood terrain (Modan 2007:88–136.)

As reflected in the stories of interest to this chapter, the moral geography shaping same-sex identified men's narratives showing 'where [they] fit in and that [they] fit in' is not oriented around an urban vs. suburbia contrast, but the narrators' efforts to position themselves, as sexual subjects and urban residents, in relation to the changing dynamics of race, class and privilege now unfolding in the DC area. In certain ways, the parallel with the neoliberal subjectivity described by Leitner et al. (2007) above would be unavoidable. But if that happened, the statements of moral geography would no longer reflect the historical immediacy of place so much as a sense of personal investment that is aligned with much broader economic and social (that is to say, neoliberal) interests. Descriptions of the narrator's sense of DC sexual geography would cease to be statements about Washington DC and, perhaps, cease to be statements about sexuality.

So my purpose in this chapter is to show how same-sex identified men's stories about sexually based verbal and physical assault experience also make statements of moral geography in the sense of Modan's argument. And I specifically want to explore the detail of the moral statement which these men present in their stories when they position themselves as the heroic survivors of assault, rather than as its victims.

Suggesting that DC area same-sex identified men may use narratives of homophobic experience as sites of narrative conceit underscores Bryant and Vidal-Ortiz's insistence that researchers pay careful attention to 'the effects of the discourses of homophobia ... in order to reveal unintended and sometimes less than liberatory consequences that taken-for-granted understandings and uses of homophobia may engender' (Bryant and Vidal-Ortiz 2008:391). As they note, while not disregarding the 'very real material consequences' which 'structured anti-homosexuality' may produce, discursive responses to those material consequences also have their own circulation and material consequences. So while not denying the seriousness of homophobia as a form of violence, and agreeing that there are reasons to think about homophobia as a form of 'sexual prejudice', 'heterosexism', or 'hate crime' in some instances (Cramer 2002; Franck 2002; Herek 2004; Pascoe 2007; Pharr 1998), Bryant and Vidal-Ortiz (2008:392) want us to take note of 'the ways that homophobia as a conceptual tool and discursive resource *itself* engenders sets of effects' (emphasis in original). It is these sets of effects that I engage in this chapter, as I explore homophobia as moral geography, using details of homophobic narratives to disclose what same-sex identified men have to say about 'how [they] fit in and that [they] fit in' to the Washington DC's urban terrain.

Describing 'gay city'

The narratives examined in this chapter are drawn from interviews with 85 DC area same-sex identified men collected in the Washington DC area during the period 1995–2006. The interviews were part of a larger project designed to explore what I have elsewhere termed 'gay city' (Leap 2009:204–10). This term refers to the understandings of the urban terrain that same-sex identified men develop as they engage the city as sexual subjects and as urban residents. In Modan's (2007) phrasing, these understandings constitute statements of moral geography, and as such, they are deeply connected to the respondents' lived experiences in the urban setting. For that reason, gay city is in no sense a uniform construction; it is deeply inflected across racial, ethnic, class, age and other social boundaries. To the extent that gay city reflects shared understandings of the urban terrain, those understandings are shared unevenly.

There is one point of general consensus, however: the spatial geography of gay city is quite different from those presented in DC-focused gay tourist materials, gay newspapers and gay-oriented commercial advertising (Hersker 2002:50–83; Leap 2002:49–56). For example, the men interviewed for this project insist that DC has no 'gay ghetto', 'gayborhood', or other residential or commercial centre. Instead, they describe gay city as decentralised and broadly diffused, incorporating individual sites located throughout the District's boundaries and, in some men's accounts, locations in nearby northern Virginia and Maryland.[2] But it also excludes major segments of the terrain lying inside the District's boundaries, since many areas have no gay commercial locations (bars, dance clubs, restaurants), no identifiable cruising areas, or other sites with predetermined 'gay' associations.

To be part of gay city in Washington DC is to be engaged in acts of point-to-point movement – moving between sites of certainty or mobbing in search of them. In some cases, movement takes the subject into areas of the city that may be unfamiliar or areas that the subject might otherwise have no reason to visit. In others, movement takes the subject into familiar terrain, but at unfamiliar moments of the day or night. The unexpectedness of movement lends a sense of excitement to urban gay experiences but also prompts the anticipation of danger. And for these reasons, men interviewed for this project repeatedly began to place themselves at distance from areas of city that they used to enjoy, and for similar reasons began to report feeling disconnected from 'gay city' as a whole.

Disconnection is not a feature of DC gay geography that is placed on display in the tourist materials and other publications describing DC area gay geography. But 'disconnected' was the term of choice in this discussion for many of the men interviewed for this project, regardless of racial, ethnic or socioeconomic background. Importantly, disconnection invited story-telling. Some respondents explained why they felt disconnected from particular locations (see Robbie's story in Example 5 below), and others explain why they still frequented sites to which they no longer had any sense of personal attachment. In that case, as they explained, being disconnected from their terrain of movement made descriptions of movement more mysterious, adventurous and, thereby, more heroic. So here, some of the unevenness in responses began to unfold.

To capture the differences between the respondents' descriptions of the urban gay terrain and the depictions in the commercial publications, the starting point for the interviews was a respondent-centred map-drawing task. Drawing maps allowed respondents to create an on-paper depiction of DC-area gay geography as they *image*-ine it. Besides being useful data in their own right, the details of each depiction provided the basis for the follow-up questions guiding discussion during the remainder of each interview.

The format for collecting the maps was as follows: after explaining the purpose of the interview and securing the necessary indications of respondent consent, the researcher handed the respondent a blank piece of paper and a pencil and asked him to 'draw a map of Washington DC as a gay city'. The researcher then withdrew from the work area so the respondent could pursue the map drawing task on his own. The researcher returned after five to eight minutes, and began the tape-recorded discussion by asking the respondent to 'tell me about your map'. All of the men interviewed for this project drew maps in some form, and all of them were willing to talk about the images they had drawn. Place identifications and descriptions flowed into stories about personal experiences. Frequently researcher and respondent began exchanging stories about gay life in the DC area, making the 'interview' more of a two-way conversation than a respondent-centred monologue. Some of the stories of homophobic invective and violence discussed below were told in this context. The 60–90-minute interview period moved by quite rapidly, and some of the men wanted to schedule a second appointment so that the interview conversation could continue.

'Moving through and beyond the facts' to find the heroic message

As I have suggested, the stories about homophobic experiences collected in the gay city research project describe the object of homophobic assault as a victim or as a heroic figure. It is possible that that the research process – and, particularly, a data-gathering strategy that asked respondents to talk about themselves – encouraged autobiographic reflections framed in heroic terms. Interestingly, however, Myslik's (1996) study of gay men's perceptions of safety and violence in Washington DC's Dupont Circle area elicited stories in which gay men consistently described themselves as victims, not as heroes (Example 1 below is taken from Myslik's project). Myslik conducted his research in the early 1990s, just before the interviews for the gay city project began, and the difference in timeframe may have influenced how respondents claimed subject position in each case, as I explain in the final section of this chapter. If so, then narrative texture may have been influenced by research context, rather than the process of inquiry.

If so, that is not surprising. Personal narratives like the ones collected in the gay city research project never provide an objective, accurate rendering of the real-life experience on which they are based. Contextual details along with a host of additional factors ensure that personal narratives become imaginary renderings of real conditions of existence, in the sense of Althusser's discussion of ideology (Althusser 1971:164).[3] Moreover, while 'the order of events in [a] narrative can be taken to mirror the order of events in some postulated real world' (Linde 1993:68), the audience usually becomes aware of those events out of sequence through the speaker's use of false starts, flashbacks, abrupt scene-shifting, addition of forgotten details or other narrative devices – all of which underscores the *constructed*, rather than literal, nature of the narrative presentation. Add to this processes like *retrospective narratisation* (Kleinman 1988:50–51) which allow speakers to emphasise certain features of the past, and to downplay other features, so that they can make a point about the lessons they have learned from personal experiences while telling stories to others, and it is easy to see that personal narratives are constructed, fabricated documents, whose fictive qualities leave little room for presentations of objective, unbiased presentation.

This, says oral historian Alessandro Portelli, is what makes the information presented in personal narrative so valuable to the researcher. Introducing one of his essays on Italian village life during the Second World War, Portelli (1991:2) writes: 'The oral sources used in this collection are not always reliable in point of fact. [Yet,] rather than being a weakness, this is, however, their strength: errors, inventions and myths lead us through and beyond facts to their meanings.'

David James addressed the same issue in relation to his construction of an oral history of the Peron years in Argentina. Paying attention to the 'subjective, textual quality of oral testimony' allows us to look beyond the detail of the text and 'to approach the issues of agency and subjectivity in history' (James 2000:14).

Likewise, the goal in this study of homophobia as moral geography is to move 'through and beyond facts' and to 'approach issues of agency and subjectivity' associated with stories about verbal and physical assault collected during the gay city research project. These stories engage issues of agency and subjectivity in several ways; there is no single genre dictating the terms of the homophobic narrative. Of interest here are the stories that describe conditions of danger and violence as moments of heroic experience, and then use the heroic moment, rather than the stance of victimhood, to make statements about moral geography, while invoking examples of homophobic experience to strengthen the heroic argument and the moral position that it conveys.

Danger and violence as heroic experiences

The first story (Example 1) comes from Myslik's (1996) study of gay men's perceptions of DC area spaces of safety and danger. Myslik interviewed 50 white gay men between the ages of 23 and 48 for his project. Seventy per cent of the men he interviewed lived near Dupont Circle, an area that was home to several of DC's popular gay entertainment venues. Consistent with that point, while the remainder of the men that Myslik interviewed lived elsewhere, they visited the Dupont Circle area frequently. As was the case for the area's gay residents, they also described Dupont Circle as a centre point of their personal gay geography and considered Dupont Circle to be 'our territory', a place over which they 'have some sense of belonging or social control' (Myslik 1996:168).[4]

Gay people were not a majority group in the Dupont Circle area, however, and many of the men that Myslik interviewed reported that the area was unsafe for gay men. Nearly all of the men surveyed were aware that anti-gay violence occurred frequently in the Dupont Circle neighbourhood and most expected that they would become the target of such violence (Myslik 1996:166). They all knew stories like Example 1, Dan's description of an incident where he was attacked by four men 'wearing high school football jackets' who 'beat [him] up pretty bad'.

***Example 1:* They beat me up pretty bad**
Speaker: Dan
Interviewer: Wayne Myslik
Source: Myslik (1996: 156)

It was late at night. I was walking to my car. At first they followed me in their car for a couple of blocks. I tried to lose them. Then they cut me off and got out of the car and chased me down. They kept screaming 'rich faggot'. I think there were four of them. They were wearing high school football jackets. They beat me up pretty bad.

While Dan's remarks were brief, he offers enough information to suggest that this was not an accidental encounter, but something which involved deliberate action on the part of the men who pursued him. That is, they 'followed [Dan] in their car' then 'cut [him] off' and 'chased him down'. The pursuit unfolded over several blocks and Dan 'tried to lose them' but was ultimately not successful: 'they beat me up pretty bad'.

Dan's claims to agency in this passage emphasise his attempts to avoid danger when circumstances outside of his control made danger inevitable. The assailants' references to 'rich faggot' reflects associations between gay men, affluence and urban residence which either indexes the restructuring of the Dupont Circle area just beginning to be attested at the time of this event or metaphorise the assailants' anger over sexual visibility by linking sexuality to privilege. Either way, the repetition of the phrase suggests that the usage was not accidental and unintentional.

Nothing in this passage identifies the location of this event, however. Since Myslick and Dan had agreed that Dupont Circle geography was the focus of interview discussion, repeated references to the specifics of location were not required during story-telling. They do not appear in Dan's example nor are they found in the other examples of homophobic violence discussed in Myslik's essay. Instead, those examples, like Dan's, focus attention on the violent acts and on those who initiated them. Similarly, those examples present the narrator as someone who may have tried valiantly to avoid the inevitability of violent assault but, as here, someone who ultimately became its victim.

Some of the narratives collected during the gay city project also de-emphasised the particulars of location while foregrounding details of violence. This was not the usual format for story-telling in these interviews, however. Gay city geography under discussion in this project was not limited to predetermined locations like Dupont Circle. Because the men framed discussions of gay city geography in terms of movement from site to site, the location of a particular event could not be taken for granted and often had to be named before the events could be discussed – even if references to location were pushed into the sidelines after the site was identified.

But even when place is named, questions of agency and responsibility remained open to negotiation, as Fred's story (Example 2) will suggest. Fred is a DC-area gay-identified African American man in his mid-thirties, whose enthusiasm for exploring the city, by day and by night, has made him one of the more valuable contributors to the project database. Overall, he told me, he sees DC as a safe place for openly gay black men to live, provided, he explains, 'you don't force people to know about your business'. In Example 2, he describes one of the few times that he came face to face with physical violence while living in the DC area.

Example 2: How I was supposed to do that, with this guy's arm around my neck... ?

Speaker: Fred Anderson

Interviewer: William Leap

What happened was, I was walking in this open area near Broad Branch Road and the bike path. I had gone up a hill and I was walking on a flat dirt trail, with low brush on one side and a hill on the other side. No one in sight. It was a warm July afternoon, and the sky was blue and no clouds. I was amazed by how beautiful, beautiful everything was for a DC summer day. I heard some running sounds behind me, and then someone grabbed me and put an arm around my throat and pulled me backwards and pushed me face down onto the ground. He kept an arm around my neck and pushed something sharp into my side. Someone else - not the person who was holding me - yelled something like 'faggot' or 'fag' or something, grabbed my backpack, and then shouted 'give us your wallet'. And I thought 'how was I supposed to do that, with this guy's arm around my neck and whatever pushed into my side?' But I reached back and pulled at my pocket. And the guy holding me released the sharp thing and pushed my hand away and pulled my wallet out of my pocket. Then he squeezed my neck hard, so I was gasping to breathe. And he got up and kicked me hard in the side of the stomach, and said, 'stay down, don't look up and don't get up until we are gone'. I heard them run back the way they came. I remember waiting a minute, trying to breathe. I got up, and the first thing I thought about was my cell phone was gone, and then I remembered that my keys were still in my pocket. I could get into my apartment once I got home. But they had my wallet so they knew where I lived. Shit, I thought, this is what you get when you leave work and go walking in Rock Creek Park on a weekday afternoon.

Notice how he names the site in lines 1–3, and describes the local terrain in lines 3–6. These remarks provide a rationale for distraction, and may be Fred's way of explaining why he did not notice the assailants until just before the physical assault began (lines 6–8). Fred's description of the assault is not as tersely worded as was Dan's description. Even so, once Fred began to describe the assault, the specifics of location disappeared from the narrative. The violent events described in Fred's story, as in Dan's, could take place in any urban location where, due to the relative isolation of the site or the lateness of the hour, passers-by are not otherwise in evidence.

The interesting feature of Fred's narrative lies in the final evaluation statements, lines 21–2. We do not know if this is how he actually responded to the events in the aftermath of the assault. But his remarks express his reaction when he revisited the event during the narrative moment. The significance of his 'this is what you get' evaluative statements (line 30) is examined below. For the moment, note that as the evaluative remarks are introduced into the discussion of verbal and physical assault, the focus of discussion moves away from the assaults and returns to comments about the particulars of location: Rock Creek Park is once again named (line 31). Moreover, while Fred had presented himself throughout the body of the narrative as very much the object of violence and very much unable to break free from the victim's stance, Fred positions himself quite differently in the coda. Instead of the powerless, passive figure presented in the preceding lines, Fred is now reflexive, active, assertive, and willing to assume some degree of personal responsibility for the events his story-telling has just detailed.

Chester's recollection in Example 3 contains a similar narrative shift, with the actions of those who initiated violence once again upstaged by the actions of the narrator as the storyline unfolds. Chester, a gay-identified white DC resident in his mid-fifties, told me many stories about DC's 'gay scene' in the years before the late 1960s and early 1970s (the years associated with the 'Stonewall' rebellion and the beginnings of the 'gay liberation' period). During the early 1960s, Chester was working a summer job in the gymnasium on a local university campus, while he attended a two-month enrichment programme for gifted high-school seniors. Chester already knew he was sexually attracted to men, but he had not found opportunities to act on his desires while living in his home town in West Virginia during the 1950s and early 1960s. One afternoon, he heard some college athletes talking very matter-of-factly in the gym's locker room about going downtown and 'rolling people'.[5] And this conversation immediately caught his attention.

***Example 3:* There were people somewhere in this town walking around**
Speaker: Chester Christian
Interviewer: William Leap

```
Hhhhhh, yes. [pause] Ummmmm, it was by, I was a
student here during the summer. I was working with
a couple of the athletes who were being sort of
sponsored by a guy I always thought was gay. And
they were talking about going downtown and rolling
people. And I was, I didn't know what they were
talking about. And I said 'What are you talking
about?' And they looked at me, dumb high school
kid doesn't know nothing. He says, 'Oh yeah, we go
down, uh, walk around a little bit, couple of
queers come by, um we let them get sort of
friendly and then we take 'em somewhere and then we
just roll 'em'. What do you mean roll 'em?' 'Oh,
```

you know, strong arm them, get some money off of
them'. I said, 'You gotta be kidding'. But the
thing stuck in my mind that there were people
somewhere in this town walking around.

According to Chester's description of this incident, he was at first startled by the athletes' matter-of-fact-description of this practice: 'You gotta be kidding' (line 15), and that the athletes recognised this reaction as naivety: 'they looked at me, dumb high school kid doesn't know nothing' (line 8–9). Nevertheless, as the remainder of his remarks suggests Chester was not so naïve. He listened carefully to the athletes' stories about their participation in acts of homophobic violence. He erased (Irvine and Gal 2000:38) or at least suspended the associations between homophobic violence and place, which were established through his citations of reported speech. Then he confirmed from the remaining details of those citations that '[gay] people ... in this town somewhere were walking around' (lines 16–17) and he could find them if he went 'downtown'.

And that is what Chester did, according to the next segments of the story that Chester told me. He went downtown on a Saturday afternoon and he wandered around, exactly as the athletes described in lines 8–10, ending up at Lafayette Square near the White House. After sitting on a park bench for a short period of time, he met a man who became his first gay friend in the DC area and, after a few months, his lover for ten years.

Taken together, Fred's and Chester's stories resemble stories like Dan's (Example 1) to the extent that they specify those who were responsible for moments of verbal or physical assault without making clear details of location. However, unlike Example 1, these stories are not static constructions. They are narratives in formation, and their references to agency may be eclipsed by references to location or to the speaker's own assertion of agency in the face of assault, information that moves the texture of the narrative into new directions once it is introduced.

In Example 4, note how Zane describes his visits to the gay entertainment zone in the Navy Yard area in southeast DC in the late 1970s. Zane is a gay-identified white man in his late fifties and a long-time DC resident. He refers here to the cluster of sites south of the US Capitol building that were shut down, as of 2002, and their buildings demolished to accommodate the construction of the Washington Nationals' baseball stadium.[6] He spent many minutes describing the interior spaces and how much fun people had dancing and socialising with their friends at these sites. Then he paused, and his voice shifted in tone as he began to talk about the conditions in the surrounding neighbourhood.

***Example 4:* People we knew made it to the bars**
Speaker: Zane Clark
Interviewer: William Leap

... All of those discos and bars were in a, a, in a
poorer, black section of town. They were having a

```
real balancing act because one of the dark sides of
the disco scene down there was car vandalisation,
people being robbed and brutalised for their money,
and their goods and clothing, that sort of thing.
One of my trips which I had with a group down
there was pelting with either beer bottles or
rotten vegetables, when I was going to the Pier one
night, having the car pelted. Because at that
time, going down one of the streets, there were
abandoned, vacant project buildings which were,
one could only speculate, the scenes of secret
clandestine nocturnal activity going on in there.
People we knew made it to the bars, as I said, as
well as my own uh car, uh survived bottle throwing
and vegetables, vegetable throwing, and fast food
throwing, all sorts of things.
```

Much more than in the preceding examples, Zane's remarks invoked a specificity of place, starting with the explicit statement (line 1) that situates the 'discos and bars' within a context of racial and economic inequality. Yet the details of the 'real balancing act' (line 3) that Zane described did not involve the clubs so much as their patrons and the conditions forced upon them as they travel through the neighbourhood en route to the gay clubs. Zane's use of syntax throughout this passage – passive voice, nominalisation and cognate verb/object constructions – helped maintain this focus throughout the discussion of travel and transit. Importantly, this syntax did not appear while Zane was talking about patrons' experiences inside the clubs, a bit later during the interview; by his description, the clubs' interior space became sites for expressions of gay agency.

But the exterior terrain was another matter entirely. Zane's references to 'car vandalisation, people being robbed and brutalised for their money' (lines 4–5) and to 'pelting with beer bottles or rotten vegetables' (lines 8–9) suggest that the surrounding neighbourhood was a dangerous terrain. And he confirms those remarks with his references to 'secret nocturnal activity' (line 14) taking place in 'abandoned, vacant project buildings' (line 12), and the bottle-throwing and vegetable-throwing. Such references do not indicate who initiated those activities or who took part in them. However, as a long-time DC resident, Zane was familiar with the stereotypes about poverty, crime and urban decay that informed city-wide discussions of the Navy Yard area during the years leading up to the City Council's endorsement of the stadium construction project, and he knew that I was also familiar with this discourse. Describing the clubs' location in 'a poorer, black section of town' (line 2) brought those stereotypes into his description of the neighbourhood and obviated any need for additional remarks about local agency and responsibility.[7]

The subjects that Zane does name in this narrative are the 'people' who 'survived bottle throwing ... and fast food throwing' and ultimately 'made it to the bars'. These are the people who engaged in the 'real balancing act' identified in line 3. As remarks throughout the narrative suggests, their travel to these clubs made them targets of physical assault, but their arrival at these sites confirmed that their journey was not unduly interrupted by that experience. Certainly, the violence described in Zane's narrative is a real experience, but it is also a transitory experience and (compared with the descriptions of violence presented in the preceding examples) it is devoid of human connection, and a momentary inconvenience. Framed in that fashion, Zane's narrative is not about 'secret nocturnal clandestine activity' (line 14), but about 'people we knew mak[ing] it to the bars' (line 15), regardless of the trials and tribulations that happen on the way.

In Example 5, Robbie's remarks about 'the last time [he] went' (line 21) to the gay entertainment zone in the Navy Yard area continues this story, also speaking from the point of view of someone who has experienced forms of assault at first hand. Robbie, a gay-identified white man in his late twenties, visited the Navy Yard's gay clubs frequently in the 1980s, but did so less often in the 1990s as incidents of vandalism and street crime involving gay club-goers as the primary targets began to be reported throughout the neighbourhood.

***Example 5:* I don't go down to any of that area much, crime's just too bad**
Speaker: Robbie Gray
Interviewer: William Leap

```
Q: … Now, down here in this area, what- is there a name for this area?
A: Just southeast.
Q: OK. [reads caption on his map] 'Used to be L and F'.
A: I can't remember what it's called, I haven't been there. [next remark inaudible]
Q: And we have Tracks. And what does this say?
A: Dance club.
Q: Got it, and then we have:
A: La Cage, Ziegfeld's, and the naughty places.
Q: The naughty places, what are they?
A: Ahh, well there is a supposed health spa down there, like Glorious or something. And there's this 'adult arcade' place, and there is also some bathhouse or something, Washington Club or something.
Q: This is a not an area that you are familiar with.
A: I know La Cage pretty well, but I don't know the others.
Q: And Tracks, you know?
A: Not so much anymore. I don't go down to any of that area much, crime's just too bad. Last time I went there with my friend, every window was busted out of his car when we came out.
Q: Really!
A: Every car down the whole lot. The police station is right there, all the way around the block, so at
```

least about twenty cars, windows had been busted out. Nobody seemed to know anything or say anything.
Q: So that might cause you to think twice about going here or even going to Tracks?
A: Right.

Like Zane, Robbie does not identify the persons who initiated the vandalism in these comments, but here the details are not necessary given local discursive assumptions. Robbie is talking about the fact that the dance clubs and other gay venues are located within an area of the city where 'crime's just too bad' (line 21), and to visit these sites, club-goers have to 'go down to that area' and engage a terrain of risk and danger. Because the club-goers are not residents of the high crime area, and not the instigators of the acts of vandalism, these references to location and crime mark the club-goers as persons who are 'out of place'.

Being 'out of place' indexes the references to movement and disconnection that appear repeatedly in descriptions of gay city geography. But in these remarks, movement and disconnection coincide with a privileged form of risk-taking. Robbie reported that he 'do[es]n't go down to any of that area much' (lines 20–21) because of the reported increase in neighborhood crime, yet he visited this area often enough to be able to talk knowledgeably about the local terrain. Robbie's being 'out of place' does not prevent him from moving throughout an area of the city where 'crime's just too bad'. In fact, being 'out of place' may assist his efforts in that regard. If he is unfamiliar with specific sites, this lack of knowledge reflects a disinterest based on moral evaluation, not a response to the danger and violence that might be adjacent to the site. Note, for example, his reference to the gay entertainment venues that were located along O Street SE prior to stadium construction as 'naughty places' (line 10).

Perhaps these statements of disinterest are another form of disconnection, and another way for Robbie to indicate that he has made no investment in this neighbourhood, and has no obligation to continue going there. So even if this is an area of the city where violence was directed against same-sex identified women and men, Robbie's perspective of outsider/privilege ensure that violence is not something that adversely affects his ability to make use of the gay terrain. He can easily relocate his club-going to a different area of the city, if crime continues to become problematic. And his comments in subsequent segments of the interview indicate that is exactly what he did, shifting focus to Dupont Circle and ultimately to an area in northern Virginia.

Discussion

The comments in the previous section show how the stories in Examples 1–5 provide a site for the construction of connections between sexual sameness and verbal/physical assault; for reasons explained in the beginning of this chapter, and in the introduction to this special issue, I will refer to these stories as *homophobic narratives*. Viewed in ideological terms, however, homophobic violence is not the only 'condition of existence' that is represented to speakers and audiences in these stories (paraphrasing Althusser 1971:164.) Out of these narrative representations also comes a set of claims about 'how speakers fit in and that they fit in' to the urban landscape, as same-sex identified DC-area residents. In this case, the effects may allow the moral geography indicated in the narrative to assume a distinctively neoliberal framing; that is, not only is the object of homophobic violence repositioned into a stance of agency, but agency is connected to 'logics of individualism and entrepreneurialism', self-interested choice-making, responsibility for personal well-being, and a citizenship based on consumer-ship and clienthood (after Leitner et al. 2007: 2).

The remainder of this chapter shows how stories that represent verbal and physical assault in homophobic terms 'become' stories that impose a neoliberal moral geography on the urban landscape.

Homophobic narratives and trauma

To begin with, stories representing homophobic assault in this fashion are not unique linguistic products. They are part of a large category of personal stories termed *narratives of trauma* (Hesford 1999; Harvey et al. 2000; Larrabee et al. 2003) or, more directly, *survivor stories* (Alcoff and Gray 1993). Stories about the experience of rape, sexual abuse and partner violence (Bonomi et al. 2006; Gilgun 1995; Hollander 2001; Wood 2001; Zarkov 2007), narratives of displacement (Agger 1994; Bek-Pedersen and Montgomery 2006; Gifford et al. 2007; Malkii 1996), Holocaust survival narratives (Laub 1992; Nutkiewicz 2003; Reiter 2000), as well as stories about political torture and genocide (Ramanathapillai 2006) are also included in this category.

These stories are always told after the conclusion of the indicated event; they are retrospective, in Kleinman's sense of the term, cited above. They are also a form of life story narrative. Besides having 'extended reportability', they consistently 'have as their primary evaluation a point about the speaker, not a general point about the way the world is' (Linde 1993:21).[8] In this case, the 'point about the speaker' has to do with the experience of severe forms of physical or emotional disruption as well as the social and emotional consequences that occurred in its aftermath. Moreover, while the details of traumatic experience are displayed through narration, these stories also make clear that the experience of trauma created emotional distress that is, in some sense, 'always beyond speech' (Frank 1995:10). As Agger explains, traumatic experience may be acknowledged in these stories, yet it's never fully described: the 'wordless nothing' is another characteristic of stories in this category (Agger 1994:126).

The issue here is not merely the failure of language to capture the affective dimension of traumatic experience. Elements of a traumatic event may be foreclosed from the narrative because speakers choose to withhold what they consider 'private' information from the 'public' record of the traumatic experience (Nutkiewicz 2003). Similarly, elements may be foreclosed when speakers organise (or are forced to organise) their stories of traumatic experience around a particular subject position – victim, helpless/vulnerable figure, self-sacrifice/martyr, survivor, hero – the selection of which then makes broader demands on the details of narrative form. Such a process unfolds within therapeutic contexts where speakers are literally trained to tell trauma stories that conform with clinically privileged narrative formats, with some form of post-traumatic stress disorder (PTSD) being an especially favoured option in that regard (Alcoff and Gray 1993; Larrabee et al. 2003).

A similar process unfolds in a courtroom, where judge and jury find a woman's description of her experience of sexual assault to be convincing only when the woman's testimony satisfies a legal standard of 'utmost resistance' (Ehrlich 2001).[9] To meet this standard, women have to demonstrate that they tried to fight back in the face of sexual aggression. Usually, however, strong emotions of 'fear, shock and confusion' become dominant motifs in these women's narrative self-representations, as they revisit the experience of rape in their written deposition and in the courtroom setting. In this way, women 'represent themselves as experiencers of cognitive or emotional states or as patients—entities that were acted upon' rather than as individuals who tried to resist in the face of sexual aggression (Ehrlich 2001:97). Such remarks support the defendant's claims that sexual activity simply 'got out of hand', without any participant assuming responsibility for its occurrence, a position that the defendant reinforces by narrating events from *his* position – unjustly accused assailant – by relying almost entirely on agentless passive verb constructions and other forms of depersonalised syntax.

To refer to Fred's description of his mugging in Rock Creek Park (Example 2) or Zane's description of his travels through 'a poorer, black section of town' (Example 4, line 2) to get to the (safety of the) Navy Yard's dance clubs (Example 4) as trauma narratives or survivor stories is to propose an incomplete description of the narrative product and the textual work that produced it. There are properties of trauma narratives foregrounded in both of those stories, but as I explained in the close readings of those texts above, neither Fred nor Zane limited their remarks to victimhood or survival. In Fred's case, he refused to end the story, lying on the ground, robbed and humiliated. He immediately reclaims agency and place, determines his mistake and what he can do to ensure that he avoids this condition in a future time. Zane used a complicated syntax to keep references to violence at distance from the references to the 'people we knew' who 'made it to the bars' (Example 4, line 15). In this way, what started as a discussion of detached violence quickly became and remained a depiction of a journey through conditions of adversity and into sites of safety.

Distinguishing between sovereignty and agency

There appears to be an inter-dependent relationship in these narratives between the responsible party that initiates violence and the party that becomes the target of violence but could under some narrative conditions become a heroic figure in spite of the violent conditions.

Judith Butler describes the narrative work that allows the separation of references to the responsible party from references to the remainder of the hurtful event as a 'loosening of the link between act and injury' which then 'opens up the possibility of a counter-speech, a kind of talking back that would be foreclosed by a tightening of that link' (Butler 1997:15). Example 1 contains no such 'loosening'. Examples 2–5 show how speakers can use this process to frame stories of verbal and physical assault that meet individual interests. Importantly, as these examples show, the resulting counter-speech never obscures the fact that verbal and physical assault occurred, but by pushing references to those who initiate the violent acts (the *sovereign subject*, in Butler's phrasing) into the textual margin, counter-speech broadens the narrative space within which other components of the experience of injury can be explored. Hence the explicit discussion of speaker reaction to the sovereign subject's acts of wounding combined with assertions of speaker-agency in Examples 2–5, textual material that was not present in Example 1 where the actions of the sovereign subject dominated the narrative detail.

When sovereignty wanes, heroic narratives emerge

Butler's argument leads her to suggest a '... notion of agency and, ultimately, responsibility' that

> more fully acknowledges the way in which the subject is constituted in language, how what it creates is also what it derives from elsewhere. While some critics mistake the critique of sovereignty for the demolition of agency, I propose that agency begins where sovereignty wanes. (Butler 1997:15–16)

Examples 1–5 speak to Butler's proposal in two ways. First, as the close reading of these examples has shown, sovereign subject and agency are not arbitrarily drawn distinctions, but are points of reference prompting the formation of fundamentally different narratives about verbal and physical assault. Secondly, the narrative formation emphasising the activities of the sovereign subject, as in Example 1, has little to say about the agency of the other subjects referenced in the event. In the remaining stories (Examples 2–5), the actions of the sovereign subjects are not constantly foregrounded. Sovereignty may be referenced in these stories, but here, adapting Butler's phrasing, 'sovereignty (also) wanes' and it is the speaker's agency that moves into the foreground of the storyline.

The foregrounding of agency need not occur at the same point in all of these stories, of course. References to speaker agency are suggested throughout Example 2, but they cluster toward the end of that narrative (Example 2, lines 25–32). Speaker agency is deferred until the final lines in Example 3 (lines 15–17), while it begins on line 5 in Example 4 and on line 5 in Example 5. Even so, references to agency in these stories share certain similarities, many of which resemble attributes associated with the heroic figures in mythological narrative (Campbell 1949:245–51).

Frequently, as Campbell suggests, narratives take the form of a journey, in which the narrator/hero travels out of the familiar setting, across a 'threshold of adventure' into a prolonged experience of darkness and danger, multiple challenges and tests, an interim period of safety, happiness, and/or personal transformation, followed by the ultimate work of return. Similarly, Examples 2–5 are structured in terms of journeys that take the subject away from familiar terrain and into an unfamiliar location: Fred left his workplace (Example 2, line 30) to go walking in Rock Creek Park; Chester heard about incidents of queer bashing happening in otherwise unidentified locations 'downtown' (Example 3, line 5); Zane introduced his remarks with the phrase: 'a poorer, black section of town' (Example 4, line 2); and Robbie speaks of locations that are 'down there' (Example 5, line 12).

An important part of Campbell's heroic journey is 'the return', the moment when the hero moves back across the 'threshold of adventure' and into the familiar terrain (often the homeland) where the 'call to adventure' was first sounded. Stories representing homophobic violence do not usually talk about 'the return'. Instead, and particularly when agency is foregrounded and 'sovereignty wanes', the end point of the story is usually the interim period of safety, happiness and/or personal transformation. This use of a mid-point ending may appear to rupture the continuity of the broader narrative: Example 2 does not indicate whether Fred got home safely, only that (as he now tells the story, after the fact) the moment of assault became an object-lesson in city-living, prompting him to think more responsibly about obligations, risks and dangers. Similarly, in Example 4, the 'people we knew' may have 'made it to the bars' (line 15), but what happened to Zane's friends during the remainder of the evening remains undisclosed. In this way, these stories offer a reminder that same-sex identified subjects will always have to contend with issues of struggle in the urban setting. The remainder of Campbell's heroic journey lies in front of them; additional heroic stories have yet to be told.

The framing of the heroic journey within homophobic representation also positions the city as an accessible terrain. Even if a site is located at distance from other, more popular gay venues, neither its isolated location nor its distance from other sites prevents gay subjects from travelling, across the city or into the suburbs, as their personal needs or interests require. Nor is there any citation of the concerns about safety and vulnerability that so frequently appear in women's narratives about urban experience (Bondi and Damaris 2003; Elwood 2000; Hollander 2001; Koskela 1999). Thus Chester claimed that he was aware of the queer-bashing taking place 'downtown', but he chose to look beyond those references to danger to find statements confirming that there were 'people somewhere in this town walking around' (Example 3, line 17). And similarly, while Zane was explicit about the 'bottle throwing and vegetables, vegetable throwing, and fast food throwing, all sorts of things' (Example 4, lines 17–18) that he and his friends had to endure in order to reach the gay venues in the Navy Yard, he did not describe those conditions as deterrents to travel. In fact, he used them to strengthen the claims to agency – the gay club-goer as 'survivor' and heroic figure – that his narrative was placing on display.

Robbie was even more explicit in his depiction of the accessibility of the urban terrain. While he reported that he visited the Navy Yard area frequently up until the time that 'crime [became] just too bad', he only visited certain sites: 'I know La Cage pretty well', he told me, 'but I don't know the others]' (Example 5, lines

17–18). Now, given the crime problem, he no longer 'go[es] down to any of that area much' and prefers to visit gay venues elsewhere in the DC area.

The Dupont Circle area was another popular gay entertainment district in Washington DC during the 1980s and 1990s, and I asked Robbie whether this part of the city provided him with alternative venues, the way it did for other men interviewed for the gay city project. He told me that he visited venues in this part of the city, but that he no longer did so very often or with much enthusiasm:

> like, downtown Dupont seems, it is real, very much a city, you have homeless people everywhere and all sorts of weird people and everything, you have a real big mix there and that's nice to visit but I don't necessarily want to live there.

He continued:

> The only reason I go down there is to go into a club. Or maybe going to Dupont Italian Kitchen, or to a restaurant. I don't feel any connection at all with Dupont. So I just go there to use the services, just like I would in Bethesda or some other place.

The accessibility of the urban gay terrain is still being foregrounded in these comments. Robbie reports travelling without hindrance from his home in Northern Virginia to sites in the Navy Yard area, and now to Dupont Circle, to Bethesda (one of the Maryland suburban communities on the northwest side of the District), and 'elsewhere'. The work of sovereign subjects has disappeared entirely from these remarks. And while conditions of verbal and physical assault are still present in the real-world setting, those conditions are no longer referenced in the narrative. Instead, Robbie's assertions of agency are being framed through references to disconnection; that is, he is willing to visit these sites, but is disinterested in making an enduring emotional investment in any of the venues that he frequents.

The gay narrative hero as a neoliberal citizen

Other narratives reviewed here have also referenced similar acts of self-serving independence. At the conclusion of Example 2, Fred recasts the experience of homophobic assault into an 'I got what I deserved' critique for leaving the office during the workday. The same stance underlies Chester's reshaping the queer-bashing stories into moments of gay self-socialisation, and also Zane's insistence that 'bottle throwing [and] ... fast food throwing' can become emblems of heroic triumph.

Even though the heroic figure plays a significant role in the storyline in these examples, the heroic figure is not a narrative stance that is unique to gay city narratives – or to gay narratives in any form, for that matter. Besides the connection to mythological texts worldwide, as Campbell (1949) explains, there are parallels between attributes of 'the hero' and at least two of the 'cultural discourses of masculinity' in terms of which heterosexual men reportedly negotiate and mediate homosocial desire: discourses of *dominance* (to be strong, authoritative and in control) and discourses of *male solidarity* (wanting and needing to do things with groups of men, excluding women; Kiesling 2005:695–6). All four of these men are expressing dominance, each in their own way, and each expression giving a personal imprint to the details of their narrative. Their expression of male solidarity is more variable, and perhaps it is better examined in each case as a site of yearning/desire than as actual practice. The point is, when read in these terms, the statement of moral geography that is sensitive to same-sex identified speaker's interests is still masculine, but no longer gay-specific.

But there are also parallels outside of the context of the masculine terrain, for example, the attributes that characterise the female subjects in recent Walt Disney productions, including *Mulan*, *The Little Mermaid* and *Pocahontas* (Davis 2006). These female subjects are very different from Snow White, Cinderella and Sleeping Beauty, whose demure, helpless behaviour shaped the storyline of Disney media productions in earlier times. For example, instead of being dominated by powerful forces which they cannot control, today's Disney heroines courageously engage the world's dangers and are often successful at subduing sources of evil without any need for Prince Charming to intervene. Frequently, in fact, in a rewrite of the older Disney scenario, it is now the Disney heroine who rescues Prince Charming from *his* moment of peril.

Davis summarises the female subject position represented in these recent Disney productions as one in which the female subject exhibits 'independence, strength of will, a determination to engineer her own fate, and insistence on being true to [herself]' (Davis 2006:176) regardless of the surrounding conditions. This position bears striking similarity to the 'logistics of individualism and entrepreneurialism' outlined in notions of neoliberal subjectivity discussed above. Importantly, in addition to being attested in the narratives representing homophobic violence explored here and in the depictions of female subjects in recent Disney media productions, similar assertions of subjectivity can be found in women's testimonials when they call into the programmes on the Shopping Channel (Bucholtz 1999), in the 'stylisation of elites' depicted in the print advertising of frequent flier programmes (Thurlow and Jaworski 2006), in the restructuring of personal communication prompted by cell phones and instant messaging (Cupples and Thompson 2010; Donner 2008; Joinson 2001; Katz 2006) and in the highly stylised deference that customers expect to receive in today's globalised service economy (Cameron 2000).

That these similarities in claims to subjectivity extend across a broad range of gendered, sexualised, class, geographic and other social inflections is not accidental or artificial. At issue here is an emergent subject position, similar to the flexible citizenship associated with privileged displacement of elites within the current transnational moment (Ong 1999:110–38). But in this case, it is a subject position forged in response to major shifts in political economy that have made private sector venues and public/private sector partnerships the primary terrain for the development and management of social policy and, thereby, the focus for mediating 'rights and responsibilities' that formerly united citizens within the public sector (Low 2003:16–22; Ong 2006:1–27). Hence the point in Leitner et al.'s (2007:2) comment about citizens being redefined as consumers and clients.

In all of the narratives of homophobic violence reviewed in this chapter, the narrators position themselves as citizen/consumer/clients. In the sense of this definition, their heroic journeys are tied in some fashion to practices of consumption.[10] As is true for the foregrounding of agency in these narratives once sovereignty wanes, this theme is represented variably in these stories, depending in each case on how much emphasis the narrative gives to the sovereign agency or to the speaker's claims to subject position.

In Example 2, Fred was walking in the park when he should have been at his workplace and at his desk. In the final lines of the story (lines 29–32), he justifies becoming the target of violent attack as just retribution for his failure to be a responsible employee. These remarks do not alter his status as object of violent attack; that part of the narrative, like Dan's in Example 1, remains consistent with the context-free narrative framework. But Fred moves away from that framework in the code (Example 2, lines 25–32) and measuring the experiences in the park against the obligations of neoliberal citizenship allows him to claim proactive ownership over the aftermath of the event. There are lessons to be learned, their outcome could have been worse, there still could be danger. To assume this more subject-centred stance Fred must sharpen his sense of self-governance, the first step toward which is to agree to become a more responsible citizen/consumer/ client (e.g. not to leave work at midday to go walking in the park).

In Example 3, Chester reports learning that there were 'people somewhere in this town walking around' (lines 16–17) at his work-site. But he also learned from the college athlete's story that there were economic consequences associated with a male-centred sexual sameness, practised without caution and discretion. A chance encounter with the wrong stranger could turn into robbery, in the sense of the athletes' examples. It was unlikely that the police or insurance company would assist the victim in restoration of lost valuables. Further, any public attention associated with an incident of queer bashing in the 1960s placed the subject at risk of loss of employment, since there were no policies offering protections to sexual minorities in the workplace at the time. Public attention introduced the additional risks of police harassment and public humiliation, and in some instances made those targeted by queer-bashing subjects for blackmail. In other words, Chester did more than suspend references to violence, so that details of place can serve as an object-lesson to strengthen the narrative recovery of gay geography. Chester's decision to go downtown and locate the 'people somewhere ... walking around' becomes an act of self-interested choice-making that was mindful of, and was made in spite of, these sinister economic consequences.

The connections between agency, commercial practices and consumption are indicated more explicitly in Examples 4 and 5, since both stories are situated within the Navy Yard's gay entertainment area and concern the speaker's efforts to visit the area sites without obstacle. Importantly, both stories describe subjects engaged in acts of 'self-interested choice-making' and assuming 'responsib[ility] for their own well-being' in the Navy Yard setting. In Zane's case, these choices and acts of responsibility centre around 'making it to the bars' and, in a fashion similar to Chester's rewriting of queer bashing, the 'sovereignty' of the verbal and physical assault associated with the neighbourhood context is subordinated to the commercial-centred, heroic quest. In Robbie's story, choice-making and responsibility are about external options, and lead him to shift his club-going to the Dupont Circle area, but ultimately to describe that area and the city as a whole, a terrain in which he has no personal investment, but merely an accumulation of sites available for personal appropriation: 'I just go there to use the services, just like I would in Bethesda or some other place.'

The neoliberal gay hero is not 'about sex' anymore

Curiously, while the characteristics of neo-liberal subject position being endorsed in these narratives are closely tied to commercial practices and consumption, none of those characteristic necessarily speak uniquely to notions of sexual sameness or to any notion of sexuality. Indeed, the particulars of desire, object choice, and erotic activity begin to lose potency within the narrative, when agency, related to homophobic representations of verbal and physical assault, is freed from sovereignty and begins to be framed in neoliberal terms.

For example, there is nothing uniquely sexual (or same-sex-based) about the remorse over a failed work ethic that Fred embraces in the outcome of Example 2. Similarly, the gay venues identified in Zane's narrative are given important positioning in the storyline because of their safety/citadel functions; the eroticised entertainment (dancing, drag shows, gay strippers) that the sites provide may have been incentives for travel, but offered no protection from 'bottle throwing' that threatened to interrupt the subject passage through the neighbourhood. And there is nothing sexual in Robbie's dissatisfaction with Dupont Circle – 'homeless people everywhere and all sorts of weird people and everything ... a real big mix there' – although a neoliberal disdain for the visible by-products of urban restructuring is certainly attested in his remarks.

Why does neoliberalism become a dominant theme in these stories of sexually-related verbal and physical assault? Certainly, differences in research design are at issue here. For example, Myslik (1996) was interested in conditions at a single DC location (the Dupont Circle area), whereas the locations of interest to the gay city project were not pre-determined, but identified through comments made during the respondents' interviews. In this sense, the gay city project favoured individualised story-telling, creating a space for other forms of personalised narrative to emerge, including narratives affirming claims to neoliberal citizenship.

But the incentive for the neoliberal framing of the personal narrative requires further explanation. As suggested in the opening section of this chapter, I see the major influence in this regard as timeframe.[11] Myslik conducted his research project in the early 1990s. During this time, the neoliberal-based restructuring of DC metropolitan terrain was just beginning. The gay city research project began in the mid-1990s and continued into the first years of the new millennium (and beyond); this timeframe corresponds to the years when neoliberal restructuring agendas were having their effects on the city centre and its adjacent neighbourhoods. Under these agendas, low income city residents were displaced and gay venues were being shut down to make room for new construction projects: office buildings, condominium projects, retail centres and entertainment facilities. These projects served an affluent clientele. They imposed images of upscale value, progress and renewal onto the DC landscape – and onto public discussions of that landscape. These discussions renewed efforts to 'clean up the city' – that is, to curtail services to the homeless and other urban poor, limit the public visibility of those on the racial and sexual margins, convert abandoned housing units into upscale urban residences, and the like.

Ironically, same-sex identified men who were not displaced by restructuring agendas found that these changes in DC geography could offer multiple benefits. Gay life was no longer restricted to certain sections of the urban terrain. Now any area of the city could be considered gay space, if gay men found reasons to make use of the services and resources in those areas (remember Robbie's remarks on this point) *and* if they could afford to do so. Sexually related verbal and physical assault always remained an issue for these men, of course. But it was not a barrier to urban experience, as they described it – even when they represented these incidents in terms that suggested homophobic undercurrent. Their sense of the urban gay terrain and opportunities always seems much larger than that defined by the homophobic moment.

While these self-serving messages about DC area sexual geography, deeply embedded in the assumptions of neoliberal restructuring, did not appear in stories like Example 1, these messages were articulated repeatedly in the depictions of that of DC geography collected during the gay city research project. And those messages were articulated explicitly as respondents pushed references to sovereignty into the textual margins, and represented incidents of verbal and physical assault by emphasising their own claims to agency. Through this narrative work, these men showed 'how [they] fit in and that [they] fit in to the given terrain' and, by doing so, 'confirm that [they] and given landscape are well matched' (Modan 2007: 91). The surprising point, perhaps, is that being 'well-matched' in this case has moved male-centred sexual sameness deep into a normative terrain that, in Lisa Duggan's words, 'does not contest dominant heteronormative assumptions and institutions, but upholds and sustains them while promising the possibility of a demobilized gay constituency and a privatized, depoliticized gay culture anchored in domesticity and consumption' (Duggan 2003:50). Duggan refers to this political stance as 'the new homonormativity' (Duggan 2003:50). Judging by the ways that this position is expressed in the representations of sexually based verbal and physical assault reviewed here, there is nothing explicitly *homo-* about the normative moral terrain to which these normative practices inscribe.

Notes

1 Joining me on the research team were graduate students in American University's Department of Anthropology as well as several DC-area residents interested in the issues that the project was exploring. Women's sexual geographies have been addressed in this project (Carnes 2009; Michels 2003) and transgender geographies

are now being explored (Edelman 2009). The respondents for the inquiry discussed in this chapter included men from Caucasian, Hispanic, Latino and Afro-Caribbean backgrounds. They were selected through several methods of snowball/convenience sampling. Respondent selection was also stratified to ensure that the representation of voices extended across divisions of age, race, ethnicity, years of local residence, neighbourhood of residence, federal vs. non-federal employment, and the like. Interview formats included one-on-one conversations and focus group sessions. Where possible, African American and Hispanic/Latino respondents were interviewed by men of similar racial/ethnic and linguistic background.

2 Washington DC is located within a federally administered 'district', which was created at the end of the eighteenth century when the state of Maryland and the Commonwealth of Virginia ceded land to the federal government to provide a site for the new nation's capital city. Since the 1970s, Washington DC residents have elected a mayor and members of a DC city council. However, any action taken by the council can be invalidated by vote of the US Congress, whose members also control the allocation of federal funds for the DC city budget and the DC city government has limited opportunity to raise tax revenue under its own authority. Because DC is not a state, DC residents have no representation with vote in the US Congress and thereby no representation in the Congressional decision-making process. In effect, while Washington DC is the nation's capital city, it is also a site of internal colonial rule.

3 Althusser writes: 'It is not their real conditions of existence, their real world, that "men" [*sic*] "represent to themselves" in ideology, but above all it is their relation to these conditions of existence which is represented to them there. It is this relation that is at the centre of every ideological, i.e. imaginary, representation of the real world. It is this relation that contains the "cause" which has to explain the imaginary distortion of the ideological representation of the real world. ... [I]t is the *imaginary nature of this relation* which underlies all the imaginary distortion that we can observe (if we do not live in its truth) in ideology' (Althusser 1971: 164). Statements of moral geography, as Modan (2007) defines them, and as the same-sex identified men's stories about verbal and physical assault display them, function in this fashion. A moral geography defines an imaginary relationship to real world conditions – an interpretation rather than a literal depiction of the real-life conditions within which the subjects are located. I see a similar, imaginary relationship between narrator and real-world condition in formation when narrators tell stories about sexually related verbal and physical assault.

4 Respondents did not refer to their sense of gay geography having a centre point in the gay city interviews, but these interviews were conducted several years after the time-period of Myslick's research. By then, the effects of urban restructuring were noticeable on the gay geography throughout the city (Leap 2009:211–13.) The gay terrain in Dupont Circle was reorganising, and so were local understandings of its detail, on the part of the area's 'straight' as well as gay residents (Hersker 2002:165–249).

5 Chester refers here to a form of homophobic violence widely reported in the years before Stonewall and immediately thereafter. The assailant locates a man who is looking for a sex-partner in a public location and feigns an interest in liaison. They depart to a secluded location. Upon reaching the site, the assailant uses verbal threats (and sometimes physical assault, as well) to extort money, jewellery and other personal resources from the now intimidated and terrified victim.

6 Leap (2009) examines the spatial and sexual politics underlying the decision to locate the baseball stadium in the area previously occupied by the gay entertainment zone.

As Williams (2001) explains, the neighbourhood has been a site for urban renewal projects and similar eco-political tensions since the end of the Second World War.

7 Zane's references are part of a 'language' that DC residents (including some residents of the Navy Yard area themselves) regularly used when speaking about the Navy Yard area prior to stadium construction. The devaluing of the neighbourhood helped encourage the neighbourhood's selection as the site for the baseball stadium; stadium projects, like all anchoring initiatives in the urban restructuring agenda, always promise to bring economic uplift and thereby an end to 'poverty crime and urban decay' once they are initiated.

8 Indirect narration is possible under this genre, with one speaker recounting the experiences of another party. Such narratives become problematic, as Zarkov's (2007) examples from conflict period in post-socialist Yugoslavia indicate. International journalists and human rights workers repeatedly referred to Bosnian and Croatian Muslim women as 'rape victim, powerless and ashamed' at the same time as many of these women, who saw themselves as survivors of sexual assault, 'not only spoke out and demanded justice but worked for it in the midst of the war' (Zarkov 2007:147). Indirect retelling is also central to the research process, and the fact that the academically constructed narrative is part of the category that its construction intends to explore is another problematic feature in this discussion.

9 For example, Schmitt and Martin (1999:377) reference a case that could not be prosecuted because the victim was 'too frightened to "resist" her assailant' even though rape was defined in the given jurisdiction as non-consensual intercourse where the victim either 'resists and her resistance is overcome by force or violence' or the victim is 'prevented from resisting by the threat of great bodily harm'.

10 Without using the same terminology, Davis (2006), Do Rozario (2004) and Stone (2008) suggest that similar notions of citizen/consumer are implicit in the subject position claimed by Pocahontas and other female subjects in the new Disney Media productions. Certainly the reinforcement of the image of that subject position, through mass marketing of action figures, decorative jewellery, costuming and other commodities, helps underscore the authority of the subject position, albeit outside of the text.

11 See also the historical discussion in Arrington et al. (2008).

References

Agger, Inger (1994) *The Blue Room*. London: Zed Books. https://doi.org/10.1086/494793

Alcoff, Linda and Gray, Laura (2003) Survivor discourse: transgression or recuperation? *Signs* 18(2): 260–90.

Althusser, Louis (1971) Ideology and ideological state apparatuses (notes toward an investigation). In *Lenin and Philosophy and Other Essays* 127–86. New York: Monthly Review Press.

Arrington, Monsello with Berkeley, Skytrinia, Gonzalez, Luz Clara, Hickey, Darby, Kirby, J., Langston, Barrett, Saunders, Penelope, Smith, Erika and Turner, Zee (2008) *Move Along: Policing Sex Work in Washington, DC*. Washington DC: Different Avenues.

Bek-Pedersen, Katherine and Montgomery, Edith (2006) Narratives of the past and present: young refugees' construction of a family identity in exile. *Journal of Refugee Studies* 19(1): 94–112. https://doi.org/10.1093/jrs/fej003

Bondi, Liz and Damaris, Rose (2003) Constructing gender, constructing the urban: a review of Anglo-American feminist urban geography. *Gender, Place and Culture* 10(3): 229–45. https://doi.org/10.1080/0966369032000114000

Bonomi, Amy E., Allen, David G. and Holt, Victoria L. (2006) Conversational silence, coercion, equality: the role of language in influencing who gets identified as abused. *Social Science and Medicine* 62: 2258–66. https://doi.org/10.1016/j.socscimed.2005.10.022

Bryant, Karl and Vidal-Ortiz, Salvador (2008) Introduction to retheorizing homophobias. *Sexualities* 11: 387–512. https://doi.org/10.1177/1363460708091740

Bucholtz, Mary (1999) Purchasing power. In Mary Bucholtz, A. C. Liang and Laurel A. Sutton (eds) *Reinventing Identities: The Gendered Self in Discourse* 348–68. New York: Oxford University Press.

Butler, Judith (1997) Introduction: on linguistic vulnerability. In *Excitable Speech: A Politics of the Performative* 1–42. New York: Routledge.

Cameron, Deborah (2000) Styling the worker: gender and the commodification of language in the globalized service economy. *Journal of Sociolinguistics* 4(3): 323–47. https://doi.org/10.1111/1467-9481.00119

Campbell, Joseph (1949) *The Hero of a Thousand Faces.* Princeton, NJ: Princeton University Press.

Carnes, Michelle (2009) Do it for your sistas: black same-sex desiring women's erotic performance parties in Washington DC. Doctoral dissertation, Department of Anthropology, American University, Washington DC.

Cramer, Elizabeth P. (ed.) (2002) *Addressing Homophobia and Heterosexism on College Campuses.* Binghamton, NY: Harrington Park Press.

Cupples, Julie and Thompson, Lee (2010) Heterotextuality and digital foreplay. *Feminist Media Studies* 10: 1–17. https://doi.org/10.1080/14680770903457063

Davis, Amy M. (2006) *Good Girls and Wicked Witches: Women in Disney's Feature Animation.* Bloomington, IN: Indiana University Press.

Di Leonardo, Micaela (2008) Introduction: new global and American landscapes of inequality. In Jane L. Collins, Micaela di Leonardo, and Brett Williams (eds) *New Landscapes of Inequality: Neoliberalism and the Erosion of Democracy in America* 3–20. Santa Fe, NM: School for Advanced Research.

Do Rozario, Rebecca-Anne C. (2004) 'The princess and the magic kingdom': beyond nostalgia, the function of the Disney Princess. *Women's Studies in Communication* 27: 34–59. https://doi.org/10.1080/07491409.2004.10162465

Donner, Jonathan (2008) The rules of beeping: Exchanging messages via 'missed calls' on mobile phones. *Journal of Computer-Mediated Communication* 13: 1–22. https://doi.org/10.1111/j.1083-6101.2007.00383.x

Duggan, Lisa (2003) Equality, Inc. In her *The Twilight of Equality: Neoliberalism, Cultural Politics and the Attack on Democracy* 43–66. Boston, MA: Beacon.

Edelman, Elijah Adiv (2009) The power of stealth: (in)visible sites of female-to-male transsexual resistance. In Ellen Lewin and William L. Leap (eds.) *Out in Public: Reinventing Lesbian/Gay Anthropology in a Globalizing World* 164–79. Malden, MA: Wiley-Blackwell. https://doi.org/10.1002/9781444310689.ch9

Ehrlich, Susan (2001) *Representing Rape: Language and Sexual Consent.* London: Routledge. https://doi.org/10.4324/9780203459034

Elwood, Sarah A. (2000) Lesbian living spaces: multiple meanings of home. In Gill Valentine (ed.) *From Nowhere to Everywhere: Lesbian Geographies* 11–28. Binghamton, NY: Harrington Park Press. https://doi.org/10.1300/J155v04n01_02

Franck, Kevin C. (2002) Rethinking homophobia: interrogating heteronormativity in an urban school. *Theory and Research in Social Education* 30(2): 274–86. https://doi.org/10.1080/00933104.2002.10473195

Frank, Arthur W. (1995) *The Wounded Storyteller: Body, Illness and Ethics.* Chicago, IL: University of Chicago Press. https://doi.org/10.7208/chicago/9780226260037.001.0001

Gifford, Sandra M., Bakopanos, Christine, Kaplan, Ida and Correa-Velez, Ignacio (2007) Meaning or measurement? Researching the social contexts of health and settlement among newly-arrived refugee youth in Melbourne, Australia. *Journal of Refugee Studies* 29(3): 414–40. https://doi.org/10.1093/jrs/fem004

Gilgun, Jane F. (1995) We shared something special: the moral discourse of incest perpetrators. *Journal of Marriage and the Family* 57(2): 265–81. https://doi.org/10.2307/353682

Harvey, David (1989) *The Condition of Postmodernity.* Oxford: Blackwell.

Harvey, David (2005) *A Brief History of Neoliberalism.* Oxford: Oxford University Press.

Harvey, Mary R., Mischler, Elliot G., Koenen, Karestan and Harney, Patricia A. (2000) The aftermath of sexual abuse: making and remaking meaning in narratives of trauma and recovery. *Narrative Inquiry* 19(2): 291–311. https://doi.org/10.1075/ni.10.2.02har

Herek, Gregory M. (2004) 'Beyond homophobia': thinking about sexual prejudice and stigma in the twenty-first century. *Sexuality Research and Social Policy: Journal of NRSC* 1(2): 6–24.

Hersker, Alan (2002) The landscape from within: locale and the construction of place in Dupont Circle. Doctoral dissertation, Department of Anthropology, American University, Washington DC.

Hersker, Alan and Leap, William L. (1996) Representation, subjectivity and ethics in urban gay ethnography. *City and Society* 8: 142–7. https://doi.org/10.1525/ciso.1996.8.1.142

Hesford, Wendy (1999) Reading rape stories: material rhetoric and the trauma of representation. *College English* 62(2): 192–221. https://doi.org/10.2307/379018

Hollander, Jocelyn A. (2001) Vulnerability and dangerousness: the construction of gender through conversation about violence. *Gender and Society* 15(1): 83–109. https://doi.org/10.1177/089124301015001005

Irvine, Judith and Gal, Susan (2000) Language ideology and linguistic differentiation. In Paul V. Kroskrity (ed.) *Regimes of Language: Ideologies, Politics, and Identities* 35–84. Santa Fe, NM: School of American Research Press.

James, Daniel (2000) The town with no plaza: memory and monuments in Berisso's centro civico. In *Doña María's Story: Life History, Memory, and Political Identity* 1–28. Durham, NC: Duke University Press.

Joinson, Adam N. (2001) Self-disclosure in computer-mediated communication: the role of self-awareness and visual anonymity. *European Journal of Social Psychology* 31: 177–92. https://doi.org/10.1002/ejsp.36

Katz, James E. (2006) Mobile communication and the transformation of daily life: the next phase of research on mobiles. *Knowledge, Technology and Policy* 19: 62–71. https://doi.org/10.1007/s12130-006-1016-4

Kiesling, Scott Fabius (2005) Homosocial desire in men's talk: balancing and re-creating cultural discourses of masculinity. *Language and Society* 34: 695–726. https://doi.org/10.1017/S0047404505050268

Kleinman, Arthur (1988) The personal and social meanings of illness. In *The Illness Narratives: Suffering, Healing and the Human Condition* 31–55. New York: Basic Books.

Koskela, Hille (1999) Gendered exclusions: women's fear of violence and changing relations to space. *Geografiska Annaler* 81: B(2): 111–24. https://doi.org/10.1111/1468-0467.00067

Larrabee, Mary Jeanne, Weine, Stevan and Woollcott, Phillip (2003) 'The wordless nothing': narratives of trauma and extremity. *Human Studies* 26: 353–82. https://doi.org/10.1023/A:1025706628725

Laub, Dori (1992) Bearing witness: or the vicissitudes of testimony. In Shoshana Feldman and Dori Laub (eds) *Testimony: Crises of Witnessing in Literature, Psychoanalysis and History* 7–92. New York: Routledge.

Leap, William L. (1999) Sex in private places: gender, erotics and detachment in two urban locales. In William L. Leap (ed.) *Public Sex, / Gay Space* 115–40. New York: Columbia University Press.

Leap, William L. (2002) Not entirely in support of a queer linguistics. In Kathryn Campbell-Kibler, R. J. Podesva, Sarah J. Roberts and Andrew Wong (eds) *Language and Sexuality: Contesting Meaning in Theory and Practice* 45–64. Stanford, CA: Center for the Study of Language and Information.

Leap, William L. (2009) Professional baseball, urban restructuring, and (changing) gay geographies in Washington, DC. In Ellen Lewin and William L. Leap (eds) *Out in Public: Reinventing Lesbian/Gay Anthropology in a Globalizing World* 202–21. New York: Blackwell. https://doi.org/10.1002/9781444310689.ch11

Leitner, Helga, Sheppard, Eric S., Sziarto, Kristin and Maringanti, Anant (2007) Contesting urban futures: decentering neoliberalism. In Helga Leitner, Jamie Peck and Eric S. Sheppard (eds) *Contesting Neoliberalism: Urban Frontiers* 1–26. New York: Guilford Press.

Linde, Charlotte (1993) *Life Stories: The Creation of Coherence*. New York: Oxford University Press.

Low, Setha (2003) Unlocking the gated community. In *Behind the Gates: Life, Security and the Pursuit of Happiness in Fortress America* 7–26. New York: Routledge.

Malkii, Lisa (1996) Speechless emissaries: refugees, humanitarianism and dehistoricization. *Cultural Anthropology* 11(3): 377–404. https://doi.org/10.1525/can.1996.11.3.02a00050

Michels, Melinda Relayne (2003) Where the girls were: the geographies of lesbian experience in Washington DC during the late 1960s and 1970s. Doctoral dissertation, Department of Anthropology, American University, Washington DC.

Modan, Gabriella Gahlia (2007) *Turf Wars: Discourse, Diversity and the Politics of Place*. Malden, MA: Blackwell. https://doi.org/10.1002/9780470773970

Myslik, Wayne (1996) Renegotiating the social/sexual identities of places: gay communities as safe haven or sites of resistance? In Nancy Duncan (ed.) *Body Space* 156–69. London: Routledge.

Nutkiewicz, Michael (2003) Shame, guilt and anguish in Holocaust survivor testimony. *The Oral History Review* 30(1): 1–22. https://doi.org/10.1525/ohr.2003.30.1.1

Ong, Aihwa (1999) The pacific shuttle: family, citizenship and capital circuits. In Aihwa Ong *Flexible Citizenship: The Cultural Logics of Transnationality* 110–38. Durham, NC: Duke University Press.

Ong, Aihwa (2006) Neoliberalism as exception, exception to neoliberalism. In Aihwa Ong *Neoliberalism as Exception: Mutations in Citizenship and Sovereignty* 1–29. Durham, NC: Duke University Press.

Pascoe, C. J. (2007) *Dude, You're a Fag: Masculinity and Sexuality in High School.* Berkeley, CA: University of California Press.

Pharr, Suzanne (1998). *Homophobia: A Weapon of Sexism*. Inverness: Chardon Press.

Portelli, Alessandro (1991) *The Death of Luigi Trastulli and Other Stories: Form and Meaning in Oral Narrative.* Albany, NY: State University of New York Press.

Ramanathapillai, Rajmothan (2006) The politicizing of trauma: a case study of Sri Lanka. *Journal of Peace Psychology* 12(1): 1–18. https://doi.org/10.1207/s15327949pac1201_1
Reiter, Andrea (2000) *Narrating the Holocaust* (trans. Patrick Camiller). London: Continuum.
Schmitt, Frederika E. and Martin, Patricia Y. (1999) Unobtrusive mobilization by an institutionalized rape crisis center: 'all we do comes from victims'. *Gender and Society* 13(3): 364–84. https://doi.org/10.1177/089124399013003006
Stone, Kay (2008) *Some Day Your Witch Will Come*. Detroit, MI: Wayne State University Press.
Thurlow, Crispin and Jaworski, Aaron (2006) The alchemy of the upwardly mobile: symbolic capital and the stylization of elites in frequent flyer programs. *Discourse in Society* 17: 99–135. https://doi.org/10.1177/0957926506058066
Viteri, Maria Amelia (2008a) Out of place: translation of 'race', ethnicity, sexuality and citizenship in Washington DC and San Salvador, El Salvador. In Adi Kuntsman and Esperanza Miyake (eds) *Out of Place: Interrogating Silences in Queerness/Raciality* 241–64. York: Raw Nerve Books.
Viteri, Maria Amelia (2008b) Seeking a relevant queerness: sexual, racial and nationalist negotiations of identity amongst the Latino immigrant community in Washington DC. Doctoral dissertation, Department of Anthropology, American University, Washington DC.
Wood, Julia (2001) The normalization of violence in heterosexual romantic relationships: women's narratives of love and violence. *Journal of Social and Personal Relationships* 18(2): 239–61. https://doi.org/10.1177/0265407501182005
Williams, Brett (2001) A river runs through us. *American Anthropologist* 103(2): 409–31. https://doi.org/10.1525/aa.2001.103.2.409
Zarkov, Dubravka (2007) *The Body of War.* Durham, NC: Duke University Press. https://doi.org/10.1215/9780822390183

Index

Note: italic page numbers indicate tables and figures; numbers in brackets preceded by *n* are chapter endnote numbers.